JOHN A.

John A. Macdonald (*c. 1863*) *by William Sawyer, based on an earlier photograph. Here this Kingston artist projects a sensual quality unmatched in any other portrait of Macdonald.*

RICHARD GWYN

THE MAN WHO MADE US

The Life and Times of John A. Macdonald
VOLUME ONE: 1815–1867

VINTAGE CANADA

VINTAGE CANADA EDITION, 2008

Published in Canada by Vintage Canada, a division of Random House of Canada Limited, Toronto, in 2008. Originally published in hardcover in Canada by Random House Canada, a division of Random House of Canada Limited, Toronto, in 2007. Distributed by Random House of Canada Limited, Toronto.

Vintage Canada and colophon are registered trademarks of Random House of Canada Limited.

www.randomhouse.ca

LIBRARY AND ARCHIVES CANADA CATALOGUING IN PUBLICATION

Gwyn, Richard, 1934–
John A. : the man who made us : the life and times of John A. Macdonald / Richard Gwyn.

Includes bibliographical references and index.
Contents: v. 1. 1815–1867.

ISBN 978-0-679-31476-9 (v. 1)

1. Macdonald, John A. (John Alexander), 1815–1891. 2. Canada—History—19th century. 3. Canada—Politics and government—19th century. 4. Prime ministers—Canada—Biography.
I. Title.

FC516.M29G89 2008   971.05'1092   C2008-900315-2

Printed and bound in the United States of America

4 6 8 9 7 5 3

To Carol
My wife, and my love

Contents

Introduction

～

The spirit of past ages never dies—
It lives and walks abroad and cries aloud.
Susanna Moodie, *Victoria Magazine*, 1847

If an international competition were ever to be staged to identify the world's most complex and contradictory country, Canada would be a serious contender. The winner, surely, would be India, with its sixteen official languages and more than two hundred local languages, its sacred cows and cutting-edge computer software, its combination of being both the world's largest democracy and the only nation-state with a caste system. Canada might well come in second. It's become a commonplace to describe the country as "the world's first postmodern country," given its unparalleled ethnic diversity, its decentralization (exceeded, if at all, only by Switzerland and Belgium), the in-rush of immigrants (the largest proportionately among developed nations), the expanding population of Aboriginal peoples (second only to New Zealand), and the ever-increasing number of "nations" within the nation-state—Quebec as the latest to join the list.

In quite a few ways, we were postmodern before we ever became modern. That was the way we were in John A. Macdonald's time. In 1884, Goldwin Smith, the leading political commentator of his day, summarized Macdonald's lifelong mission as "to hold together a set of elements, national, religious, sectional and personal, as motley as the component patches of any 'crazy quilt,' and actuated each of them by paramount regard for its own interest." Here, Smith identified exactly Macdonald's supreme talent—that he knew how to herd cats.

No one else in Canada came close to Macdonald; after him, perhaps only Mackenzie King did, his paramount art being that of doing as little as possible for as long as possible. At the time, few others anywhere could match him. Even without the spur of chauvinism, any reasonable ranking of nineteenth-century democratic leaders would be Abraham Lincoln, Benjamin Disraeli, William Gladstone, John A. Macdonald. (Otto von Bismarck, no democrat, would otherwise rank near to the top.) Macdonald happened to perform on a stage that was small and threadbare. But in the primordial political tasks—the managing of men (then, only them) and the winning of their hearts and minds, and so their votes—contemporary equals are not easy to identify. Nor were there many nation-builders like him in his day: Bismarck, Giuseppe Garibaldi and Simón Bolívar. His achievement may have been the more demanding because none of the others had to create a country out of a crazy quilt.

Within the range of Macdonald's accomplishments, there are sizable gaps. The largest, surely, is that, unlike Lincoln, he never appealed to people's "better angels." He was a doer, not a thinker, although highly intelligent and omnivorously well read. He lacked the certitudes of a moralist, instead taking human nature as he found it and turning it to his purposes. He was, that is, a very Scottish Scot. He of course drank too much. And although he was in no way the first to use patronage and election funds for partisan purposes—a cherished and well-embedded Canadian tradition (which still thrives)—Macdonald gave the practice credibility and durability by his masterful exercise of it. That's a shoddy legacy for the father of a country to leave behind.

Yet his accomplishments were staggering: Confederation above all, but almost as important, if not more so, extending the country across the continent by a railway that was, objectively, a financial and economic insanity. Also, the National Policy of tariff protection, which endured in one form or other into the 1980s. And the RCMP or, more exactly, its precursor, the North-West Mounted Police. The first immigration from outside the British Isles, and Canada's first labour legislation. On the ledger's other side, he was responsible for the CPR scandal, for the execution of Louis Riel and for the head tax on Chinese workers.

He's thus not easy to scan. His private life was largely barren. Yet few other Canadian leaders—Pierre Trudeau, John Diefenbaker for a time, Wilfrid Laurier—had the same capacity to inspire love. One MP—a Liberal—wrote in a magazine article of Macdonald's hold on his supporters: "They would go through fire and water to serve him, and got, some of them, little or no reward. But they served him because they loved him, and because with all his great powers they saw in him their own frailties." The novelist Hugh MacLennan, in his *Scotchman's Return*, caught many of the layers within him: "This frail-looking man with the immense and rueful patience of a Celt. . . . This utterly masculine man with so much woman in him . . . this lonely man flashing gay out of his inner solitude . . . this statesman who understood that without chicanery statesmanship is powerless." Macdonald was as complex and contradictory as his own country.

Add a last, lesser, legacy of Macdonald's to the list. In writing this book, I have made a host of spelling "mistakes," but have paid them no heed. Each has been signalled clearly by a red line that my computer's U.S. text system inserts beneath the offending word. The mistakes aren't really mine, though; they are

Macdonald's. He had an order-in-council passed directing that all the government's papers be written in the British style, as with "labour" rather than "labor."

Discoveries of this kind have been for me one of the chief delights of writing this book, and even more so of researching it. All historians, professional or freelance like myself, are keenly aware that these small epiphanies are the joy that more than compensates for the later pain of trying to transfer from mind to computer screen whatever it is one wants to say. The discovery, for instance, that, at least in parts of nineteenth-century rural Canada, unmarried mothers were often regarded far less as sinners than as a "species of heiress"; as one observer noted, their condition both confirmed their fecundity and, as dowry, they brought children who would soon be able to work on the farm. The discovery, one of slightly grander moment, that the principal reason the Confederation Fathers spent almost no time discussing the respective powers of the national and provincial governments— the obsession of our politicians ever since—was that most Canadians then were self-sufficient farmers (even making their own clothes and soap and candles) and didn't want governments to do much for them or to them. The discovery, most substantial of all, that the single most important decision Canadians made in the nineteenth century was not to become a confederation, but, rather, not to become Americans. And the discovery that the National Policy, a phrase always applied only to Macdonald's policy of tariff protection for Canadian manufacturers, began instead with Confederation itself, with tariff protection as a later sub-policy, together with other highlights such as his building a transcontinental railway.

Macdonald made us by making a confederation out of a disconnected, mutually suspicious collection of colonies, and by later magnifying this union into a continental-sized nation. He could not have brought off Confederation without the others of the "Big Four"—George-Étienne Cartier, George Brown and Alexander Tilloch Galt. Among them, though, the irreplaceable man was Macdonald. He understood as well something more fundamental. The United States had emerged from its Civil War as a putative superpower. Britain, the global superpower, wanted to pull back from North America in order to attend to its empire. For Canada to survive on its own, it had to demonstrate that it possessed the will and nerve it took for a nation to survive. Confederation was the essential means to that end. What Macdonald understood as no other, excepting perhaps Galt, was that Confederation was only a means, not an end.

I began work knowing precious little about Macdonald and his times. What I knew was negative—that while Macdonald was the most important of all our prime ministers, the last full-scale, critical, biography of him had been written more than half a century ago. It is the greatest biography in Canadian historiography—Donald Creighton's two volumes *The Young Chieftain* and *The Old Politician*, published in 1952 and 1955. They are magisterial and encyclopedic, composed with narrative flair. But times move on, new evidence emerges, attitudes and assumptions change and open doors—maybe trap doors—to new interpretations of old givens. Anyway, why should the United States, where history was once dismissed as "bunk," each year publish up to a half-dozen biographies of historical figures or major studies of past doings that attempt to extract contemporary lessons from long-ago events, while Canada settles for so few—precariously close to none at all? Our history, as we know perfectly well, lacks the drama of revolutions and civil wars, of kings and queens losing their heads. But it is our history. It is us. It's where we came from and, in far larger part than often is recognized, it is why we are the way we are now, no matter all the transformational changes since—demographic, economic, technological, lifestyle. Moreover, as was always Macdonald's core conviction, human nature itself changes little.

I came to this biography sideways. This book started out to be a slim one, then threatened to grow obese, then was sliced into two more or less manageable halves. This is to say that I began boning up on Macdonald for a Brief Life series on historical figures for another publisher. Out of this cramming came one, to me, unarguable conclusion: Macdonald deserves a new full-scale biography, and Canadians deserve the chance to rediscover him. With quite considerable daring—in Canada, history really is often now treated as "bunk"—Random House of Canada accepted the challenge, eventually taking the double dare that an originally planned single volume should be divided into two. This book is the result of that dare.

A last note on my work habits. Early on, Carol, my wife, found a large poster of Macdonald created originally to promote Macdonald's cause in CBC-TV's *The Greatest Canadian* contest. She installed it in my attic office. Throughout my labours, he's looked down, quizzically and mischievously.

ONE

Lairds Ourselves

~

Mark my words, John will make more than an ordinary man.
Helen Macdonald's judgment on her eldest son

Where John A. Macdonald was born and when he was born are unknown. Or, rather, are not known exactly. About the essentials of his beginnings, there are no doubts whatever. He was born in the Scottish industrial city of Glasgow in 1815.

There were historical dimensions to both place and date. Glasgow was the lustiest child of Britain's Industrial Revolution: a sleepy town of only twenty thousand in 1791, its shipyards along the Clyde, its engineering works and factories and its "dark Satanic mills" had sent the town's population soaring above one hundred thousand by the time of Macdonald's birth, less than a quarter-century later. As well, 1815 was the year of the Battle of Waterloo. That cataclysmic military clash didn't so much ensure Napoleon's defeat (which was inevitable eventually, anyway) as ensure that Britain, its strength multiplied by its long industrial lead over all its rivals, would become the global powerhouse of the nineteenth century. By pure happenstance, Britain's global reach created a possibility that its leftover colonies in North America, strung across the top half of the continent like widely spaced and oddly sized beads, and having little in common other than their mutual Britishness (for the most part), might yet—just—remain independent from their overwhelming neighbour, the coming hegemon of the twentieth century. For that to actually happen, however, required the arrival of a leader who could cajole and bluff and bully these colonies into becoming a whole larger than the sum of their parts. In 1815, little of this was of the slightest interest to anyone in the British Isles. Yet it was in Glasgow in that year that Canada's future began to take shape.

The minutiae of Macdonald's birth need to be cleared up. Throughout his life and for the near century and a quarter that has followed his death, his birthdate has been commemorated as January 11, 1815—as in the joyous celebratory dinner staged each year in Kingston, Ontario, for example, and in the inscriptions on all the plaques and statues that honour him. But this particular day may be a mistake. The January 11 date is taken from the entry for his birth made by his father, Hugh Macdonald, in his memorandum book. The entry recorded in the General Register Office in Edinburgh, though, is January 10.* Similarly, precision about where specifically Macdonald was born, while a matter of lesser consequence, is as difficult to determine. The delivery may have taken place at 29 Ingram Street in Glasgow or, not far away, at 18 Brunswick Street, both on the south side of the Clyde River, because the family moved between these locations around the time of his birth. To pick at a last

---

*Hugh Macdonald recorded the birthdates of all his children in the 1820 edition of his memorandum book.

unknowable nit, Macdonald's father recorded the moment of birth as 4:15, without specifying afternoon or early morning.

The other defining attributes of Macdonald's birth are known beyond argument. His parents were middle class, if precariously so. They were Scots, and so of course was he. And soon after his birth, they chose to immigrate to Canada rather than take the advice of Samuel Johnson about the most attractive prospect that any Scotsman could ever come upon and follow the usual road to London.

~

Immigration always happens for one of two reasons or for both simultaneously: either individuals or families are pushed out from their homeland by poverty, oppression, failure or plain bad luck, or they are pulled towards a new country by the tantalizing promise it holds for new beginnings and new opportunities. Both factors applied to the Macdonalds, but in distinctive ways, when they set out across the Atlantic in 1820. John A. himself was then five years old. An early biographer described him as having "a bright eye, a lively manner and a head of curly brown hair which darkened into black as he grew up." At least supposedly, he showed early promise of having the gift of the gab, once giving a speech to a gathering of relatives by mounting a table, from which, as his gestures became ever more dramatic, he projected himself to the ground.

As soon as the Napoleonic wars ended, England was gripped by a depression that cut most deeply into its farming counties; the same outwards push existed in Scotland, given force there by the clearances of people from the land to make way for sheep—as often, despite later myth, by Scottish landowners as by English ones. The great migration from the British Isles to both Canada and the United States dates from this period, although it

remained relatively small until the 1830s, later multiplying expo-
nentially through the 1840s as the Irish fled from the horrors of
their Great Famine. To magnify the force of the outwards push,
the British governments of the day accepted the thesis of
Thomas Malthus that population growth would always outpace
the growth in food production. To avoid social unrest, perhaps
even the ultimate horror of a revolution of the kind from which
Napoleon had sprung, successive governments encouraged the
"idle poor" to move elsewhere.

The Macdonalds, though, were not a family of farmers. And
although hard up, they weren't poor, not in the sense of their
being malnourished and in rags. The force that pushed them out
was failure—quite unnecessary failure, and the product almost
entirely of the fecklessness of Macdonald's father, Hugh.

Before Hugh Macdonald is introduced, it's necessary to go
backwards one further genealogical step to Hugh's own father, John
Macdonald. Although he never left Scotland, John Macdonald set
the family on its transatlantic journey. When he came down from
the Highlands—pushed out by the clearances implemented by his
laird, the Duke of Sutherland—he went first to a little village in
the Strathfleet Valley and then on to the Sutherlandshire town of
Dornoch, where he set up as a shopkeeper. John Macdonald was
widely liked—a contemporary described him as having "a tender
nature, full of humour, a quick and winning manner, with a bow
and smile for everyone he met." Many of those qualities would pass
to his grandson, as did his longevity, for he died at the age of
eighty-six. John Macdonald's most distinctive legacy to his grandson was his head of abundant but curiously crinkly hair. His most
important legacy to his heirs, though, was to get them out of the
beautiful but bleak Highlands into a settled community, and to
raise them there to at least the lower rungs of the middle class.

Hugh Macdonald squandered the greater part of what had been

handed down to him. Born in Dornoch,* he moved in early adult-hood to the growing city of Glasgow and there owned and operated a succession of small enterprises—one, for instance, making bandanas. Their common characteristic was that they all failed. Hugh was known as a decent, amiable man, good in conversation and impossible to dislike. This quality served him well: after one bankruptcy, when he was at serious risk of being sent to a debtors' prison, he was allowed not only to remain free but to keep his library and household effects, later selling them to pay for the tickets for his transatlantic passage. Two attributes that Hugh passed on to his son were that he had a hot, Celtic temper, and that he drank a lot.

Hugh Macdonald's most considerable accomplishment during his relatively short life was to marry Helen Shaw. It happened in 1811, when she was at the relatively advanced age of thirty-four and he at the comparatively tender one of twenty-eight. Helen was an exceptional woman, the rock upon which the small tribe took its stand facing outwards to the world, arms linked. She kept the family going through thin and thick. A surviving por-trait of her, done in at least middle age, depicts accurately her rock-like qualities of strength and determination. "She was a little above the medium height, large limbed, and capable of much endurance," commented the contemporary biographer E.B. Biggar.† "Her features were large, and as some considered coarse; but there beamed through her dark eyes a depth of apprehension mingled with such graciousness and good will." She

---

*A small town, then and now, Dornoch has one claim to fame as the site of the last judicial execution for witchcraft in Britain: in 1727, a court ruled that a Janet Horne had turned her daughter into a pony.

†E.B. Biggar's *Anecdotal Life of Sir John Macdonald*, hurried into print in 1891, the year of his death, is the source of most of the best-known anecdotes about him. The first biography of Macdonald, *The Life and Times of the Right Honourable Sir John A. Macdonald*, published as early as 1883, was written by J.E. Collins, an

Helen Macdonald. She was determined that her son would make his mark in life.

read widely, and as Biggar wrote, "had she possessed the advantages of a high education, and the opportunities some get in life, she would have been a noted woman."

While the portrait of Helen Macdonald suggests the depth and liveliness of her eyes, it betrays little hint of the most attractive of her qualities—her capacity for gaiety. She and John A. loved to trade stories and jokes, his being the racier. Biggar commented, "She appreciated a droll saying or a droll situation." Once, when Macdonald ascended to the social height of being elected president of Kingston's St. Andrew's Society, he led a gathering preceded by a piper to her house; when she heard the wail of the bagpipe, Helen came downstairs and danced a jig in the street.

She was wholly Scots, and above all a Highlander. Her preferred language was Gaelic. Her father fought for Bonnie Prince Charlie at Culloden, and afterwards, as did many Scots, joined the British Army. She could be stonily stubborn, a quality that repeatedly taxed Macdonald's talents once he became the de facto head of the family. She possessed an exceptional memory—a gift she passed on to her son—and functioned as the family historian and the teller of Highland tales.

---

expatriate Newfoundlander. By a curious coincidence, Collins also wrote the first biography of Louis Riel as well as a bodice-ripper of a novel, *Annette, the Metis Spy: A Heroine of the N.W. Rebellion.* He died in New York, of drink, in 1892.

Of her children—two boys and two girls at the time of leaving Glasgow—there was never any doubt that her favourite was her elder son, John Alexander. "Mark my words, John will make more than an ordinary man," she said on many occasions.

~

Besides the push of failure at home, there were more positive attractions pulling the Macdonald family to Canada. Of these, the most apparent was that Hugh Macdonald, unlike the great majority of immigrants,* possessed the priceless asset of connections. In and around Kingston, the town where they were headed, there was a cluster of Macdonald relatives and cousins. That most were distant relatives mattered not the least; they all belonged to the same clan. The most important person by far was Colonel Donald Macpherson, who was married to Helen Macdonald's stepsister. The colonel, who twice fought for King and Country against the Americans (during the War of Independence and the War of 1812), retired afterwards to the garrison town of Kingston, built a large stone house called Cluny (meaning "meadow") and settled down as one of the community's principal citizens. Before leaving Glasgow, Hugh Macdonald knew that Colonel Macpherson would find space in his house for him and his family for at least a transition time, and that afterwards Macpherson would help with advice and contacts as Hugh set up his first business.

How much Hugh Macdonald knew about Canada before he left is unknowable. Information was available, however, in book-

---

* Immigrants were then commonly referred to as "emigrants," because the significant point was that they were leaving Britain rather than that they were coming to Canada.

lets such as *The Emigrant's Guide to the British Settlements in Upper Canada and the United States of America*, published the same year that the Macdonalds left. In some ways, Canada was distinctly unappealing. Its total population was only a little more than half a million, the great majority being French-speaking Canadiens. The particular part of Canada where they were headed—Upper Canada (now Ontario)—had fewer than two hundred thousand people; mostly, the land was untouched, primeval forest broken here and there by the crude log shacks of pioneer settlers. All of Canada was incomparably poorer and less developed than any of the thirteen American colonies.

Yet Canada possessed two considerable attractions. Land itself was free to most settlers. To the Macdonalds, this bounty was irrelevant, since they were headed for a town and not for a clearing in the wilderness. The country's second general attraction, that there were no class divisions, was a derivative from the first and exactly fitted the ambitions, however muddled, of Hugh Macdonald. As the Scottish settler George Forbes wrote to his brother back in Aberdeenshire: "We in Canada have this glorious privilege that the ground we tred is our own and our children's after us." And he went on to describe the fundamental difference between Canada and any part of Britain, or indeed anywhere in Europe. "Here, we are lairds ourselves."

Had John A.'s parents moved from Glasgow to somewhere else in the British Isles, the upwards drive that Macdonald eventually undertook would have butted sooner or later against the steel ceiling of the British class system. In Canada, by contrast, there was no aristocracy at all other than a few fragments within the Family Compact—the small clique who, as politicians, public officials and judges, ran the country on behalf of the governor general. (Lower Canada, or Quebec, was markedly more hierarchical.) Instead, the vast majority of Canadians were either middle class or believed that they could become middle class, or, since the term "middle class" wasn't yet used, they were "respectable" citizens—law-abiding, churchgoing, debt-free, or attempting diligently to be all three.

The idea of classlessness was lodged deep in the Canadian consciousness from its very beginnings. In *Roughing It in the Bush*, Susanna Moodie noted crossly of her servants, "They no sooner set foot upon the Canadian shores than . . . all respect for their employers, all subordination is at end." She went on to record, though, that "with all their insolent airs of independence, I must confess that I prefer the Canadian to the European servant."

In fact, a respectable claim can be made that in one vital respect, the country Macdonald's parents were taking him to was more democratic even than the United States, that great experiment in egalitarianism. In the South and in parts of New England, there was an aristocracy, and, in the North, a class of self-made millionaires who cascaded their wealth upon their heirs. Above the border there was virtually no over-class, but no under-class either. There were no slaves in Canada, they having been liberated by Governor John Graves Simcoe's decree of 1793, and there was no equivalent of the proletariat now developing rapidly in the great northern cities of the United States. Almost all Canadians were indeed "lairds," in possibility and in self-perception, if not in actual fact. They could rise as high as their talent, ambition and luck might take them.

It's unknowable whether Hugh and Helen Macdonald had any idea of the benefit they were conferring on their elder son by bring-

---

* While Simcoe's legislation ended the slave system, it did not immediately end slavery: owners of existing slaves were allowed to hang on to their "property," although almost all were released within a few years. By gaining legal equality, blacks in Canada did not in any way gain social and economic equality.

ing him to a society where, compared with almost any other society in the world, there were fewer barriers to whatever upwards rise he might attempt. But that's what they did by not taking the well-travelled road down to London and, instead, taking a ship to a far-away country in which there were just about no roads at all.

TWO

A Boy's Town

Remember, oh remember, the fascination of the turkey.
John A. Macdonald, to a girl he owed a dance

When the Macdonalds came up the St. Lawrence River from the Gulf in 1820, they would have seen the same strangely foreign prospect, at first impressive but after a while depressing, that Catharine Parr Traill described in *The Backwoods of Canada* a few years later: "I begin to grow weary of its immensity . . . we see nothing more than long lines of pine-clad hills with here and there white specks that they tell me are settlements." At long last there was a real town—Quebec City. There, their ship, the small, 600-ton *Earl of Buckingham*, discharged its six hundred passengers, the Macdonalds included. Behind them, at last, were six weeks of the appalling food,* overcrowding, incessant lice and rats and complete lack of privacy that everyone in steerage

---

* To minimize the cost of feeding their passengers, some captains were known to supply them on the first day with large helpings of porridge and molasses, making them so sick that, thereafter, they seldom demanded their full rations.

Quebec City. A thriving port, a British garrison town and the oldest city, by far, in Canada. This view is a steel engraving from a painting by William Bartlett prepared for his book Canadian Scenery Illustrated *(1842).*

experienced, along with the constant damp and seasickness that even those in cabin class endured. They must have been delighted to see the end of this decaying vessel—indeed, two years later it drifted into Galway Bay and broke up in pieces.

Left on the dock at Quebec City was the small tribe of Macdonalds, as well as their orphaned cousin Maria Clark, who had accompanied them on the voyage. It numbered Hugh and Helen Macdonald, both now in their forties, and their four children: Margaret, the oldest at seven, nicknamed Moll; then John A. and James, one year younger; and lastly two-year-old Louisa, known as Lou. (A fifth child, the first-born William, had died back in Glasgow.) Scots, unlike the English and even the Irish, to a lesser extent, almost never sent a single family member ahead to scout the terrain but moved any distance as a complete family.

They would have been amazed by the scene that greeted them once they entered the port: endless lines of log rafts with a crude shack at their centre, stretching out for miles along the river and waiting to load the pontoons of huge, squared timbers they had brought all the way from the Ottawa Valley onto one of the same sailing ships that had just transported the immigrants. Their stop at Quebec City would have been exciting—lots of familiar redcoats and Royal Navy tars, but also the unfamiliar language of most of the local inhabitants. And they would have taken a little time to look over the sights—the massive hulk of the Citadel, the steep bank soaring upwards from the St. Lawrence over which Wolfe's Highlanders had scrambled, the imposing churches and nunneries and the low stone houses packed together along narrow streets as in some Breton town.

By now, the Macdonalds had completed barely half their journey. Beyond Quebec City there were no roads, or none that anyone would risk trying by stagecoach. Canada's entire highway system was made up then of its rivers and lakes. (The one great cross-country trip, undertaken just for show, was Governor General Lord Sydenham's amazing 1840 journey from Toronto to Montreal in a sleigh with a bed in it, completed in just thirty-six hours, a record that stood until the railways came along.)*

Their second voyage lasted some four weeks, first from Quebec City to Montreal, then on to Kingston. It would have been as uncomfortable as their ocean crossing. They made their way first in a bateau and then in a Durham boat, each open to the elements, moving slowly up the St. Lawrence, sometimes pushed by sail-power, sometimes pulled by oxen and by oars, but often both pulled and pushed by the male passengers as they jumped into the chill water to squeeze the boat past shallows and between rocks.

---

* The real hero of this feat wasn't so much Sydenham as a stagecoach operator in Toronto (York), William Weller, who organized the relays of horses needed to maintain an average speed of fifteen miles an hour. For his contributions, Weller received four hundred dollars and a gold watch.

On August 13, 1820, the family made it to Kingston. In Colonel Macpherson's house, packed in with his own family, they could at last rest, eat properly, clean their clothes and, most important, begin to learn about their new country.

~

Of all the towns in early Upper Canada where Hugh Macdonald might have gone, Kingston was perhaps the best possible place for an imaginative boy to grow up. With a population of around four thousand people, it was the biggest centre in the colony, even larger than York (to be renamed Toronto in 1834). Above all, it encompassed within its boundaries an uncommonly wide range of human experience.

It had a military garrison of red-coated British soldiers, who regularly emerged from Fort Henry to march through the streets to the beat of drums and the peep of pipes. It was a port. Tied up alongside its finger piers jutting out from the shore, throughout the summer and into the fall, were thirty to forty sailing ships, from three-masters to fore-and-aft schooners, and, later, steamships belching columns of smoke as they prepared to chug off to York and Montreal, Oswego and Niagara. To the north, the dense, forbidding forest came close to the town's limits; inside it, almost always hiding out of sight, were Indians. From spring to fall, waves of immigrants arrived in Kingston; after a few weeks' rest and burdened down by provisions, the newcomers would head on, either westwards to the softer, richer country beyond the town of York or, by turning right at some point along Lake Ontario, plunge northwards into the forests to try their luck at some isolated spot as pioneers—in the manner of Susanna Moodie and Catharine Parr Traill and their unhardy husbands. Kingston itself lacked a rural hinterland because the Precambrian

Shield came right to the town, but farmers did well in the good soil of Prince Edward County some forty miles to the west and supplied the growing town with food.

The Kingston of those days was rude and rowdy and raunchy rather than scrubbed and neat and dignified as today. It was also exceedingly dangerous. Immigrants often arrived riddled with disease, touching off a typhoid epidemic in 1828, a cholera epidemic in 1832, a truly terrible typhus epidemic in 1847 (during which 1,200 immigrants and townsfolk had to be buried in a mass grave) and yet another cholera outbreak in 1849. Soldiers and sailors brawled with each other and with the locals in incomparably rougher versions of the occasional town-gown confrontations of today.

Kingston's one constant has always been its history. Whoever occupied it commanded the entry point to the chain of Great Lakes as well as the exit point from the interior, on down the

Kingston. When the Macdonalds arrived in 1820, it was Upper Canada's largest town, with some four thousand people. It was also an important transshipment point for goods going up or down the St. Lawrence. Again, a view by William Bartlett.

St. Lawrence River to the Atlantic. The French built Fort Frontenac as far back as 1673. The Loyalists arrived in 1784, laid out a plan of streets and housing plots, and drew lots for the best of them. The town's importance as a transfer point for cargo and people would soon be enhanced by the construction, eastwards, of the Lachine Canal to Montreal and, northwards, of the Rideau Canal, snaking its way up to Bytown (later Ottawa). The starting point was the mouth of the Cataraqui River, which formed Kingston's harbour.

Later, a major share of Kingston's historical aura would derive from its association with Macdonald. No other Canadian leader has ever been as intimately connected to any place as he was to Kingston. A boy when he arrived, he was educated and established himself in business there; he represented the town for the greater part of his political career, winning thirteen elections there; and he is buried in its Cataraqui Cemetery. Kingston still commemorates him on two occasions each year—the anniversaries of his birth and his death. Above all, Kingston provided Macdonald with the raw material for the greatest of his political gifts—his matchless understanding of life as it is actually lived and of people as they actually live it, with all their faults and follies, interspersed with occasional spasms of altruism and even idealism. Charles Dickens, who came through in 1842, dismissed Kingston as "a very poor town"; had he stopped for a while, Dickens would have found it a microcosm of the human condition.

Cows and sheep, pigs and chickens ran freely through Kingston's streets, which, when it rained, were deep in mud, dirty and pungent from the leavings of animals—and sometimes of humans too. The only means by which a pedestrian could make it from one planked sidewalk to the opposite side of the road without sinking into the gummy, stinking mass was by using the occasional narrow crosswalk of flagstones or cobbles. The Precambrian Shield lay just below the surface, so the sewer system was primitive, with shallow and odiferous "privy pits." In winter, workers carried the night soil onto the ice in the harbour, to slide to the bottom once spring arrived. Of course, all these things were standard in British North American towns in the early nineteenth century, their one aesthetic advance over today being the absence of any overhead tangle of telephone and hydro wires.

Rural Canadians, who made up more than four in five of all Canadians, lived lives that for a great many were nasty, brutish, short and bitterly cold. Alexander Tilloch Galt, who would work alongside Macdonald in the battle for Confederation, provided a first-rate summary of country life in a report to his London bosses in a British land-settlement company: "A settlement in the backwoods of Canada, however romantic and pleasing may be the accounts generally published of it, has nothing but stern reality and hardship connected with it," he wrote. "Alone in the woods in his log cabin with his family, tired from his day's work and knowing that the morrow brings but the same toil, the migrant will find but few of his fancies realized . . . for the first years, the emigrant to succeed must work as hard and suffer perhaps greater privations than had he remained in Great Britain."

Unlike today, though, conditions in the towns were, if anything, worse than those in the countryside—except, perhaps, for women, who suffered terribly from the loneliness of pioneer life. In towns and villages, women at least had companionship and some kind of support networks. But townies were much more likely than their country kin to succumb to diseases caused by everything from epidemics to poor or non-existent sanitation. Unlike pioneer settlers, they were self-sufficient neither in food nor in wood for winter fuel. In the towns, a great many jobs ended in early November; the ports closed because of ice, and all public works and construction were halted. At the same time that the price of food and firewood soared, the wages of those still at work in small manufacturing plants, stores and offices were often cut by a third or even half. As the winter wore on, workers spent as much as a fifth of their miserable wages on wood to keep themselves warm. The cost of bread typically went up by as much as 50 per cent. Commonly, those who had jobs went straight to bed when they returned to their barely heated lodgings. Some practical types even committed crimes so they would be sent to a partially heated jail. The late spring, when food and fuel prices were at their highest, was known as "the pinching season."

Yet, as historian Judith Fingard has noted, there was a conspicuous "absence of mass demonstrations and violent crime amongst the poor during the winters of greatest suffering."* The poor were kept quiescent by exhaustion, by the bitter cold and, far from least, by a deep and seldom-questioned respect for the law. Macdonald learned all about this real, unromantic, urban Canada while he grew up in Kingston, and from his boyhood stays with his roving family in nearby Prince Edward County he gained an understanding of rural Canada as well.

Kingston was actually better off than other towns in Upper Canada. An 1837 guide for emigrants called it "perhaps the finest-built town in the Province," while T.R. Preston, an English visitor at around the same time, said it "resembled an English village but somewhat stragglingly built, though it possessed in its substantial parts some very substantial homes." Kingston possessed

---

* The source is Fingard's study "The Winter's Tale: The Seasonal Contours of Pre-Industrial Poverty in British North America, 1815–1860."

one invaluable urban asset: lots of limestone. When the Macdonalds arrived, most houses were constructed of logs or hewn lumber—a motley array of dwellings often destroyed by fire. With the completion of the Rideau Canal, though, a lot of Scottish stonemasons were suddenly looking for work, and by the 1840s Kingston had begun to acquire more substantial buildings made of the local stone.*

A few of the leading citizens commissioned remarkable houses in the delicate Adamesque style and began to install beautiful mouldings and chimney pieces in their mansions. Some major public buildings, far grander than the small town itself, were constructed during these years—a hospital, a penitentiary, a lunatic asylum, a courthouse and, later, a superb town hall. Kingston even became important enough for a stagecoach to make a twice-weekly trip between it and Montreal—a bone-shattering experience, for sure, but with the benefit that, unlike in England, highwaymen were rare.

The Kingston of Macdonald's day even encompassed some of the finer things of life. It had a lending library and two newspapers. Occasionally, travelling theatre groups performed for a night or two, and in the churches there were organ recitals and, on Sundays, sonorous, scary sermons. Band concerts were particularly popular, and for the active, so were cricket matches, fox hunts and horse races—all made possible by the military garrison stationed in the town. The military, moreover, made one major cultural breakthrough: on the frozen lake, members of the Royal Canadian Rifles developed, by hit and miss and bump and grind, a new game using skates, field hockey sticks and a lacrosse ball.

The most intense competition in Kingston revolved around

---

* In the absence of any zoning regulations, grand houses, shacks, stores and grog shops all jostled against one another.

the sexes, as Dickens would have noted had he lingered. The highest ambition of the wives of successful merchants and farmers was to marry off a daughter to a bachelor English officer. Few fulfilled this aspiration, because, in the cruel comment of one witness, they all "still smelt of bread and butter." Nevertheless, the young officers praised the way Kingston chaperones were less watchful than those back in England.

The underside of life flourished here too. One visitor described the streets as "swarming with drunkards and prostitutes"—the inevitable consequence of so many soldiers and sailors and immigrants passing through. Kingston's Common Council, or town council, reported in 1841 that there was a drink shop for every seven or eight men, ranging from taverns or pubs to "low dram shops" or shebeens. In counterpoint, a local temperance society was started up; it suggested, among other things, the installation of a treadmill as the best way to deal with drunkenness and better "the morals of the lower classes."

If Kingston was in many ways a brutal society, so at the time was all of British North America and, indeed, just about the entire world. Drunken soldiers and sailors were easy marks for muggers. Soldiers often deserted across the nearby American border; those caught were flogged at a triangular wooden frame, to the beat of a drum. Punishments everywhere were brutal: inmates in the penitentiary in Kingston included a child of eight who began his three-year sentence with a flogging by the cat; another inmate, ten years old, received 102 strokes of rawhide. Hangings were a public attraction—one steamer brought in two hundred "tourists," including children, to watch an execution. A man was hanged for stealing a cow.

After three months of living jammed up in the Macpherson home, Hugh Macdonald moved his family out on its own. He opened a store in the centre of town, and the six of them lived in the rooms above. Besides a mix of foodstuffs and hardware, he offered customers "groceries, wines, brandy, shrub [a cordial], vinegar, powder and shot, English window-glass and putty, etc." The enterprise failed quickly. Hugh opened another general store in another location. It soon failed too.

NEW GOODS

THE Subscriber begs leave to inform his friends and the public, that, in addition to his former Stock of dry goods, he has received an assortment of **FANCY GOODS**, suitable for the season.

The Subscriber has also, always on hand, a supply of Groceries, Wines, Jamaica Spirits, Brandy, Gin, Shrub and Vinegar, Powder and Shot, English Window Glass and Putty &c. &c. all of which he is now selling on the most reasonable terms.
HUGH MACDONALD.
Kingston, 3d July 1821.

Hugh Macdonald's ad in the Kingston Chronicle *of July 3, 1821, showed, for him, a rare business sense as the only one in the paper to carry an illustration of his wares.*

Amid these setbacks, the family had to come to terms with an almost unimaginable trauma: the second son, James, was killed at the age of five and a half by a family servant named Kennedy. It's impossible to be certain what happened. One day, Hugh and Helen went out, leaving John A. and James at home in Kennedy's care. The servant was a secret drinker. In one account, Kennedy got angry with James for crying for his parents and lashed out at him with a stick. In another, he lunged drunkenly at him and James slipped, hitting his head on an andiron. Whatever the cause, the young boy died while seven-year-old John A. witnessed his murder or manslaughter. The May 3 issue of the Kingston *Chronicle* in 1822 carried this sad obituary: "On Monday the 22 ult., James, second son of Mr. Hugh Macdonald, Merchant of this town, aged five years and six months."

That newspaper notice was the family's entire recorded response. No charge was ever brought against Kennedy. Hugh entered no record of the death in his memorandum book of family events, though John A. later added it to the chronology. No burial place for the boy has ever been identified; he is not listed among those interred in the family plot at Cataraqui Cemetery.* Nor is there any reference to the tragedy in any of the family letters that have been preserved. At the time, the most common reference likely to be mentioned in family correspondence would have been to a locket or brooch containing a circle of the lost child's hair, commonly worn for years afterwards by a bereaved mother. Yet no surviving letter contains any mention of such a commemorative object.

This silent reaction can be attributed far more readily to acceptance than to callousness. Then, death was part of life, and as any stroll through any old cemetery will confirm, to be young then was to be close to death. A survey done in Montreal in 1867 found that two out of every five children never reached the age of five. As well, grief may have been generally subdued because it amounted to an expression of doubt about the existence of an afterlife. Religion provided healing; a loved one who had died was often referred to as one who "went before"—to a place where the others would later join the departed.

The single certain consequence of this tragedy was that, henceforth, the Macdonald family's entire hopes rested on the shoulders of John Alexander—the last surviving male heir among the original three.

After his second enterprise in Kingston had failed, Hugh decided to change his location entirely. In 1824, four years after their

---

* This plot was purchased by John A. Macdonald in 1850. The remains of Hugh Macdonald, who had been buried in the old "Lower" Burial Ground, were brought there, but not, apparently, the remains of James Macdonald.

arrival, he moved the family out to Hay Bay, on the lakeshore to the west of Kingston, where he opened yet another store. Young John, by now nine years old, continued with his schooling in the nearby village of Adolphustown.

Each day he walked three miles to school and, in the late afternoon, three miles back. This commute was entirely ordinary. His sisters, Margaret and Louisa, made the same walk with him. The three of them played well together, often as soldiers in a game where he was always the officer, and they got into the usual scrapes. As the only boy now, and anyway his mother's favourite, John was spoiled rotten. Margaret, small and delicate, possessed an aptitude for seeming vulnerable. Louisa, by contrast, was tall, with a stern face and a long, thick nose. At best she could be called plain; in later years she protested that someone had compared her to her brother, "the ugliest man in Canada." Independent and stubborn like her mother, she was John A.'s pal.

~

One of the most surprising comments Macdonald ever made was to his confidential secretary and biographer, Joseph Pope: "I never had a boyhood. From fifteen I began to earn my living." It is Macdonald's rare lapse into unguarded bitterness that makes this admission so surprising. More astounding still, his complaint was quite untrue. Macdonald did indeed have to quit school at the age of fifteen, when he began his legal career, but this pattern was almost universal then. The phenomenon of adolescence had yet to be discovered (or invented); a survey done in 1871 found that one in four boys aged eleven to fifteen were working in some kind of a job. Typically for the times, Egerton Ryerson, the great Canadian educator, espoused the proposition that children were small men in need of greater instruction than older siblings. In any case, Macdonald's boyhood was more agreeable than that of most boys. At home, he experienced no shortage of love, and he benefited from the kindliness of an extended family. While the family was pinched for money, that was not in the least unusual, and of little concern to a boy.

The explanation for Macdonald's bitterness may reside in another comment he made to Pope. "If I had had a university education," he reflected, "I should probably have entered the path of literature and acquired distinction therein." Looking back from a time near the end of his life, Macdonald may have been expressing an uneasy sense that politics hadn't stretched his intellect enough and that he had missed out on opportunities to express the creative and imaginative side of his character.* Perhaps he was thinking enviously of British prime minister Benjamin Disraeli, his ideological and physical look-alike, who, amid the grinding pressures of politics, had found time to write no fewer than twenty novels, *Tancred* and *Endymion* the best received among them.†

While at school—the length of his tenure there being entirely average—Macdonald received an education that was well above the norm. The schools he attended, first in Kingston and then in Adolphustown, were the typical one-room schools where children of all ages sat at a raised board that ran around three sides of the room and served as their desk. They faced the fourth, open side, where the teacher had a smaller desk. The only other

---

* In 1830 there were only two universities in British North America—Dalhousie and McGill. Sending Macdonald to either of them would have been quite beyond the family's financial capacity.

† Macdonald, who closely followed news from Britain, would also have been aware that Disraeli eventually commanded advances of an amazing £10,000, more even than Dickens or Trollope—a reflection, naturally, more of his appeal as a celebrity than of his skill as a novelist.

pieces of furniture were a pail of water and a stove. Most teachers in the region were Scots, each known as a "dominie"—an apt phrase because of the strap they always carried. Books and paper were rare. For most children, this schooling was their entire education. In Ontario, school was not compulsory until 1874—and then for a minimum of only four months a year—a rule that was regularly ignored by farmers' sons.

Macdonald mostly had a grand time at school. Boys liked him because he could tell stories and knew tricks, and because he wasn't afraid of the masters. They also had a wary respect for his Scottish temper. Girls liked him, even though they teased him as "Ugly John"—as he most certainly was, with his absurdly crinkly hair and outsized nose. But they would have noted with approval, certainly with interest, that he was a bit of a dandy, with a taste in gaudy waistcoats. Wit more than compensated for his lack of looks. At one dance, Macdonald forgot he was due to partner a particular girl in a quadrille. She rejected his abject apologies until he flung himself at her feet, proclaiming manically, "Remember, oh remember, the fascination of the turkey." With her uncontrollable laughter came forgiveness. He did all the customary boyish things, getting into scrapes and, at the age of thirteen, writing florid poetry to a pretty cousin. Although he seldom took part in sports, he was good at running barefoot, at skating and at dancing. Early on, he showed some skill at mathematics, an unusual accuracy in spelling and an insatiable appetite for reading.

Two factors pushed Macdonald onto a life's arc different from that of most of his fellow students: he was a Scot, and he had a mother who was determined that he would be more than an ordinary man.

After a couple of years of making the long daily walk to the school in Adolphustown, John was sent by his parents to Kingston to attend the Midland District Grammar School. It was run by a graduate of Oxford University, the Reverend John Wilson. Annual tuition fees were seventy pounds, representing a steep sacrifice for the family. Here, Macdonald learned Latin and French as well as English and mathematics. (His French grammar book, dated May 28, 1825, still survives.) He stayed with the Macphersons, where he was thoroughly petted and spoiled. Years later, his nephew, John Pennington Macpherson, recalled in a slight biography of his famous relative how Macdonald would read compulsively, quite untroubled by the noisy antics and quarrels of the large family around him. In the summers he went back to the Bay of Quinte area—to Glenora, where his father had moved to run a grist mill. It, again, soon failed.*

In 1829, the fourteen-year-old Macdonald moved to a new establishment for "general and classical education" run by a recent newcomer, the Reverend John Cruickshank. There were some twenty pupils, from six to sixteen years old; among them was Oliver Mowat, later a Father of Confederation along with Macdonald and later still premier of Ontario. The school's standards were high, the local Scots having decided that the Midland District School was inadequate to give their children a quick start in life. What really set this grammar school apart was that it was coeducational, one of the first in Upper Canada. At the risk of reading too much into it, Macdonald's coeducational experience, reinforced by the female-centred household he grew up in, may explain one of the qualities that set him apart from most men of his day—and of a good many still. In the company of women, Macdonald was always wholly at his ease. He was never awkward or shy or predatory with them. He could flirt and play the gallant, but he never patronized women.

---

* The stone mill, little changed, still stands in Glenora, Prince Edward County.

As is common enough, Macdonald was his own principal teacher. He read omnivorously—history, biographies, politics, poetry, geography. His most remarked-upon scholastic skill was his handwriting—clear, large, even and fluid. (His letters would be a delight to later scholars.) Cruickshank was always proud to show Macdonald's compositions to new students, and he kept them for years afterwards as models of penmanship.

Macdonald's preparation for life ended in his fifteenth year. From then on, he began to live it. But he'd already learned a great deal about life's essence—the ways and the whys of how people behave.

THREE

The Right Time to Be a Scot

A man's a man for a' that.
Robert Burns

John A. Macdonald placed his first foot on life's ladder by apprenticing to an established Kingston lawyer. To qualify for this post, he had first to go to Toronto, to the offices of the Law Society of Upper Canada, and, before a panel of benchers, sit an exam that involved some Latin and some mathematics. He passed, paid the fee of fifteen pounds, and returned to Kingston as he had come, by steamboat. There was then no formal training for lawyers or any law degree. Now just short of sixteen, he worked long days as a law clerk, running errands and putting newly written letters through a letter press to squeeze out copies on onion-skin paper before the ink was dry; at night he crammed through textbooks.

To become a clerk to an established lawyer constituted a substantial step forward. The one taken by Macdonald was more like a leap. No matter how junior his post, he had gained entry to what was probably the most sought-after legal premises in Kingston—the office of George Mackenzie. Although only thirty-five, Mackenzie was already one of the town's most successful and highly regarded lawyers.

The crucial introduction to Mackenzie had come to Macdonald as a gift from the family's patron, Colonel Macpherson. Mackenzie would also have been well aware of the quality of the education his clerk had received at Reverend Cruickshank's school. A couple of years later, Macdonald's budding legal career benefited from his being asked by another relative, Lowther Macpherson, to fill in temporarily, with Mackenzie's permission, in his Prince Edward County law office while he himself was away trying to recover from an illness; Macdonald thereby gained management experience at the earliest age. While in Kingston, he made his first adult friendships, most particularly with a bright and attractive young man called Charles Stuart. The preceptor of St. Andrew's Church there took a liking to Macdonald and, while teasing him as "a free thinker of the worst kind," engaged him in biblical discussions that gave the young law clerk valuable practice in how best to organize his arguments. Moreover, around this time, Hugh Macdonald was rescued from his uninterrupted business failures by a relative, Francis Harper, who slipped him into a secure if lowly sinecure post as a clerk in Kingston's newly established Commercial Bank of the Midland District.

To all these individuals who enabled Macdonald to make his first career steps a good deal more quickly than he would have otherwise, and to others like them who later provided similar assistance as his trot quickened into a canter, there was one obvious and defining characteristic. Each of them was a Scot. Had Macdonald not been a Scot himself, he wouldn't have moved up nearly as fast. His own talents mattered a great deal, of course. But it mattered critically that other Scots were prepared to help him because he was one of their own; it mattered as much that they themselves were doing well enough to be able to provide real help. Before Macdonald's ascent is tracked, it's necessary first to place him in the context within which he operated. As he moved upwards, he did so as a member of a distinct and uncommonly successful ethnic group.

~

Macdonald came by his Scottishness through his parents, of course. The benefits of this gift to him were multiplied many times over by another happenstance—one of timing. Macdonald was a Scot when it was the best time in history to be a Scot.

Early in the nineteenth century, the Scots exploded outwards from a small, poor, backward society to become, collectively, one of the most admired and respected of all societies of the day; more remarkable yet, a great many of them had gone on to become the first "citizens of the world." Through the greater part of the century, Scots accomplished more in more places around the globe than did any other people. Nowhere was this more true than in British North America, the country to which Macdonald's parents had just brought him.

Until about the middle of the eighteenth century, Scots were regarded generally as rude and crude at best, and at worst as outright savages. They were brave, of course, with the special allure of a fiercely proud, freedom-loving people, but backward, self-enclosed, impossible to comprehend. (Indeed, they were not dissimilar to the Métis of the prairies, with whom Macdonald would later so tragically find it difficult to come to terms.) The Scots all knew how to eat porridge properly (standing up, with salt) and how to position exactly the *skein dhu* dagger (in the stocking, just below a kilt-clad knee). Suddenly, before the eighteenth century ended, all this parochialism was replaced by intellectualism and internationalism. Of the transformation, Voltaire would declare,

"It is to Scotland that we look for our idea of civilization."

In a transformation that has few national equivalents, a poor, quasi-feudal society turned almost overnight into a society of ideas and creative energy. The catalyst of change was the Scottish Enlightenment, which, during the period from 1740 to 1790, made the small capital of Edinburgh into an intellectual and cultural rival of any other city of the time, only London and Paris excepted. The two superstars of the Scottish Enlightenment were David Hume, the first modern philosopher, and Adam Smith, the first modern economist. At the time, a cluster of others were as well regarded as these two, among them Lord Kames, Francis Hutcheson, Adam Ferguson, William Reid and William Robertson.

This extraordinary story has been told lovingly and adroitly by Arthur Herman in his book *How the Scots Invented the World*, subtitled, with only a slight exaggeration, *The True Story of How Western Europe's Poorest Country Created Our World and Everything in It*. Herman's thesis is that Edinburgh attained "a self-consciously modern view" that is now "so deeply rooted in the assumptions and institutions that govern our lives that we often miss its significance, not to mention its origins." In fact, Herman never resolves satisfactorily why this achievement should have happened in the particular society of Scotland, so small and backward. The nearest he comes is to argue that, after union with England in 1707, Scottish intellectuals had to cope with the challenge, today common, of "deal[ing] with a dominant culture that one admired but that threatened to overwhelm one's own heritage and oneself with it."

Those Scots were grappling with some of the most intractable of challenges of our own time, such as how to exploit the benefits of capitalism without destroying society's ethical framework, and how to balance the aspirations of the individual against the needs of the collectivity. Hutcheson decreed that society's ultimate purpose was "the greatest good of the greatest number." In *The Wealth of Nations*, Smith unveiled one of the most liberating of modern ideas—that the interests of the community could be advanced better by the self-interest than by the "benevolence" of the butcher, the baker and all the other upwardly clambering capitalists.* Hume decreed that "Liberty is the perfection of society," but believed equally that "authority must be acknowledged as essential to its [freedom's] very existence." Two observations by Ferguson could have been minted as mantras for Macdonald: "Man is born in society and there he remains" and, even more so, "No government is copied from a plan: the secrets of government are locked up in human nature."

These Scots were all progressive conservatives. They believed in natural democracy and in meritocracy, and because they were intensely practical men they believed in education. A 1694 law decreed that each parish in Scotland had to have its own school; England wouldn't catch up until the end of the nineteenth century. Scots' churches (except for the Catholic ones) elected their own pastors. Yet the people were skeptical about the fashionable new doctrine of political democracy—and they were outright hostile to revolution. More than a fifth of the Loyalists, for example, were Scots, among them Flora Macdonald, the Scottish heroine who hid Prince Charles from the English soldiers after his defeat at Culloden, and who eventually made her way back to the Isle of Skye by way of Nova Scotia. A cause for this skepticism was their

---

* One observation by Smith in *The Wealth of Nations* of more direct interest to Canadians was that Britain should let go its North American colonies, both to escape from the cost of "supporting any part of their civil or military establishments" and, more urgently, from a cause as sure to be lost, in his view, as had the thirteen American colonies.

disbelief in the perfectibility of human nature. Ferguson warned, "The individual considers his community only so far as it can be rendered subservient to his personal advancement and profit." Common sense was their golden rule, not least in the Philosophy of Common Sense, which would play such a part in the development of higher education in Canada.

These enlightened Scots most certainly believed in progress, including technological progress. James Watt developed the steam engine, for example, and John McAdam, hard-surfaced roads. They also believed in the ability of a society to improve itself; otherwise, all that education and that unleashing of enlightened self-interest would be in vain. Yet they were very conservative. As Lord Kames put it, "Without property, labour and industry were in vain."

The Scottish Enlightenment had run its course before Macdonald was born, and as a young child he moved thousands of miles away from Scotland. Yet in Kingston most of his teachers were Scots. His mother's love of reading, which he inherited and which was so rare among his peers in those early years in Canada, came directly from the respect for knowledge that the Enlightenment implanted in all Scots. All kinds of echoes of the ideas initiated in Edinburgh can be found in Macdonald's own thinking—his disbelief in the possibility of human progress, his belief in the possibility of causing a society to progress (why else throw a railway across a wilderness?), his indifference to political democracy and yet his inherently democratic nature, as you'd expect for someone coming from a society whose national poet laureate had proclaimed "A man's a man for a' that." No less so, Macdonald would have accepted Robbie Burns's skepticism, so quintessentially Scottish: "The best-laid schemes o' mice an' men / Gang aft a-gley, / An' lea'e us nought but grief an' pain, / For promised joy." Macdonald wasn't a product of the Scottish Enlightenment, but he was, because of it, an enlightened man.

Macdonald's most direct debt to the Scottish Enlightenment was cultural. The Scots who produced all those ideas weren't solitary geniuses sharpening quill pens in attics. They thought collectively, amid company, and over dinners that ended with lots of broken crockery, or in pubs and taverns amid arguing and shouting and brawling. Even the brainiest among them put on no airs, nor suffered any in others. Their interest in ideas was how to get things done, not to talk about what should and might be done. As them, so Macdonald.

Benjamin Disraeli once remarked that although he had been in many countries, "I have never been in one without finding a Scotchman, and I never found a Scotchman who was not at the head of the poll"—that's to say, on top. This outwardness was one of the most remarkable after-effects of the Scottish Enlightenment. Commonly, minorities react to defeat and occupation by turning in on themselves; the Scots, a century after Culloden, burst out all over the world. The men from the Orkneys joined the Hudson's Bay Company—the joke went—to get warm. Their sheer hardiness as northerners, their conversion to modernity ahead of everyone else, and the excellence of their education (out of a population of 1.4 million at home, twenty thousand people earned their living through writing and publishing) gave them a confidence, a resilience and a distinctive sense of self. So did two other factors. The Enlightenment had changed everyone's image of the Scots. Any society that could produce a David Hume and an Adam Smith could not be a society of barbarians. Their reputation now went before them and opened doors to them.

In their own separate ways, a monarch and a novelist presented a second gift to the Scots. Early in the nineteenth century, Queen Victoria and Sir Walter Scott rediscovered the romance of the Highlands, or, more accurately, invented it. In truth, the Highlands were a brutal place; the standard of living there was lower than that of the Plains Indians of North America. But just as the film *Braveheart* was irresistible, so were Scott's novels and the tartans that Victoria made everyone wear at Balmoral. One of Macdonald's distinguishing characteristics among nineteenth-century Canadians was that, whenever he went to London and moved among "the greats" (whether by office or by birth), he held his own dignity. He never exhibited the least sign of "colonial cringe" or felt any need to apologize for being a colonial.

The Scots of the nineteenth century were by no means perfect: they were clannish, hot-tempered, parsimonious and they drank an incredible amount—"the most drunken nation on the face of the earth," according to *The Scots Magazine*. As the century progressed, Scottish culture turned increasingly inwards, judgmental and holier-than-thou. Macdonald, influenced by earlier attitudes, was a product of Scottish culture at its best.

⌒

For the Macdonalds, when they moved to Canada, the immediate benefit of being Scots was that they weren't alone in this strange, hard land but were enveloped by a clan. Besides the many Macphersons, the Macdonalds could claim ties of kinship to Shaws, Grants, Clarks and Greenes. In Kingston itself there were institutions like the St. Andrew's Society and the Celtic Society to provide the young Macdonald with contacts, social connections, insider gossip and information about upcoming business deals. Clannishness could hurt as well as help. As Pope wrote in his biography, Macdonald could never bring himself to trust fully a Campbell, even though one member of that clan, Alexander Campbell, was his later law partner and political organizer, simply because the Campbells had massacred the Macdonalds in the Pass of Glencoe in 1692.

As Macdonald moved upwards, the circles of Scots ready to let him through their doors kept widening. Among the first directors of the Bank of Montreal—*the* bank, by a wide margin—eight were Scots; Canada's entire banking system was modelled on Scotland's. Almost every member of the original Canadian Pacific Railway syndicate was a Scot, including the founder-president, George Stephen. So was the country's greatest railway engineer, Sandford Fleming, the inventor of standard time. By 1880, even though numbering just one in seven European Canadians, half of Canada's industrial leaders would be Scots or the sons of Scottish immigrants. In Montreal, the country's financial and industrial capital, the city's business leaders included a McGill, a MacTavish, a Redpath. At the country's largest corporate enterprise in the nineteenth century, the Hudson's Bay Company, four in five employees were Scots. The country's biggest and best newspaper, the Toronto *Globe*, was owned and edited by a Scot, George Brown. All three of Canada's first universities—McGill, Dalhousie, Toronto—were founded by Scots; in *The Scot in America*, published in 1896, Peter Ross reckoned that "the entire educational system of the country, from the primary school to the university, is more indebted to the Scottish section of the community than to any other."

As for politics, once Macdonald got there, he would be crowded around by fellow countrymen. Both he and Canada's second prime minister, Alexander Mackenzie, were Scots; so were the first two premiers of Ontario, John Sandfield Macdonald and Oliver Mowat. Of the "Big Four" among the Fathers of Confederation, all but George-Étienne Cartier would be Scots—Macdonald, Brown and Alexander Tilloch Galt.

Macdonald naturally played the advantage of Scottishness for all it was worth. When he met his first governor general, he did so wearing the "fine Macdonald Soft Tartan Kilt with Green Riband Rosette . . . [and] a silk Velvet Highland Jacket" that he'd bought in Edinburgh as part of his trip around Britain in 1842. He would drop Scottish sayings into speeches, such as "He'll cool in the same boots he got warm in."

Yet he didn't sound much like a Scot. His burr was far less pronounced than that of at least two other Scottish-born political personalities of his time, George Brown and Alexander Mackenzie. Alexander Campbell, who knew him well and was himself from Kingston, wrote in an undated memoir that Macdonald was "in tone of voice & manner as thoroughly a Bay of Quinte boy as if he had been born there."* A complicating factor here is that, as is often the case with good storytellers, Macdonald was an excellent mimic. Yet Campbell was on to something. In speech, as well as in many other ways, Macdonald was far more a Canadian than he was a Scot. One journalist wrote of Macdonald, "It was long a moot question where he was born." In a couple of substantial ways, he wasn't that much of a Scot: during all his many visits to England, he went only once to Scotland—on his first trip; also, he never had himself photographed looking like a Scot by wearing his tartan.

As a politician, Macdonald benefited in one last critical way from his Scottishness. For the most part, the four principal European ethnic groups in nineteenth-century Canada—English,

---

* An excellent article on Macdonald's speech patterns, from which some of this material is drawn, is Ged Martin's piece of splendid title in the *British Journal of Canadian Studies* (2004), "Sir John Eh? Macdonald."

French, Irish and Scot—thoroughly disliked each other, while the Irish (Protestant and Catholic) disliked their own countrymen, if anything, even more. Within these discontents, though, there was one striking exception: the French and the Scots got on exceedingly well. It made a great difference that the man who made us, and who did so primarily by connecting together, politically, Canada's two great ethnic solitudes, should have been a Scot.

⌒

In the light of what he would achieve as a man, one aspect of Macdonald's youth is surprising. No one who knew him then recalled his having ever displayed any vaulting ambition or recounted any anecdote about Macdonald describing some hero he planned to emulate or to exceed. True, his mother predicted great things for him, but many mothers say that about their children. Several of his boyhood contemporaries, as well as some of his teachers, expected him to do well. No one, though, forecast that he would do better, by far, than anyone in the country had ever done. They hadn't misjudged his talents; they had failed to take account of his capacity for growth and, no less, his inexhaustible competitiveness.

FOUR

Horse Dealing, Tavern Keeping and the Law

⌐

Say nothing on business without receiving a fee in advance.
Fellow lawyer's advice to John A. Macdonald

The suggestion that Macdonald should aim for a career in law had actually come first from his father. Hugh Macdonald pointed out that "the province was yet only in its infancy, was rapidly growing, and would soon need a horde of professional men." For Hugh, such acuity in financial matters was rare, but this time he was absolutely right. Although clearly unusually intelligent, Macdonald had no money, so the attraction of a legal career was obvious: law required no start-up capital and no training at a university. Once the apprenticeship was served, the profession guaranteed at least modest prosperity to all but the indolent or the inebriated. As John Langton, Canada's first auditor general, remarked, "I know of no money-making business in Canada except the law, store-keeping, tavern-keeping and perhaps I might add, horse-trading."

Practising law came as easily to Macdonald as breathing. He soon showed himself deft at mastering briefs, remembering and using detail to good effect and, most effective of all, having a talent for reading judges and juries. By the age of twenty-three he was already defending men on trial for their lives against some of the best-known counsels in the province. A few years later he was well on the way to establishing himself as a leading commercial lawyer. Had he stayed with the law, Macdonald would surely have made a great deal of money and, as did others, eventually used it to buy himself a knighthood and retire to leisurely comfort in England.

When George Mackenzie took Macdonald as an apprentice in 1830, Mackenzie specialized in corporate law, handling the accounts of local farmers, businessmen and merchants. Intelligent and amiable, he was one of Kingston's leading lawyers and would soon be nominated as the Conservative candidate for Frontenac. As a mark of his special regard for his clerk, Mackenzie invited Macdonald to board at his own house in Kingston. There the young man began to learn something about the graces in life, such as the joys of a fine dining room and an ample library.

From Mackenzie, Macdonald picked up two of the most valuable of all legal lessons. The first was to "say nothing on business without receiving a fee in advance." The other amounted to an admonition to remember that, in law, personality counts for a good deal more than knowing the statutes. Mackenzie, after hearing that his junior was acting in a standoffish manner with clients, warned him, "I do not think you are so free and lively with people as a young man eager for their good should be. A dead-and-alive way with them never goes." Later, in a third gift to his junior, Mackenzie sent Macdonald to the countryside to open a branch office for him in the town of Napanee, thereby providing independent responsibility and experience.

Hallowell (later Picton) is the Prince Edward County town where Macdonald filled in at the law practice of an ailing relative.

To a remarkable extent, good luck quickened the pace of Macdonald's advance as a lawyer, one of the comparatively few occasions in his career when he didn't have to create most of his own good fortune. Its source was the bad luck of several other lawyers. Macdonald's first stint on his own occurred when he temporarily replaced his sick relative, Lowther Macpherson, returning to Mackenzie's office when Macpherson died at sea after receiving treatment in England. In 1834 his own employer, Mackenzie, was struck down by the cholera epidemic of that year. Once he had set up his own shingle, Macdonald took over some of Mackenzie's accounts. Lastly, the sudden death in 1839 of another prominent Kingston lawyer, Henry Cassady, would enable Macdonald both to take over much of his business and to succeed him to the prime post of solicitor of the Commercial Bank of the Midland District.

Mostly, he advanced in his own way. From Mackenzie he had acquired the ambition to become a corporate lawyer. To do that, Macdonald opened his own office in Kingston in 1835. He posted a notice in the Kingston *Chronicle* that "John A. Macdonald, attorney, has opened his office . . . where he will attend to all the duties of the profession. Kingston, 24 August, 1835." At the time, he was only twenty years old, still a year short of being entitled to claim to be an attorney. He achieved that rank the next year when, after passing the necessary examination in Toronto, he was called to the bar. Soon afterwards, Macdonald himself took on two students of law. They were a remarkable pair. One was Alexander Campbell, later a cabinet minister under Macdonald and eventually lieutenant-governor of Ontario. The other was his one-time schoolmate Oliver Mowat, later a member of the legislature and, several years on, Macdonald's most relentless and effective political opponent as premier of Ontario. Macdonald came to loathe Mowat, remarking, in a reference to their schooldays together, "The one thing I have always admired about Mowat is his handwriting."

Macdonald set up his first office in rented quarters in Kingston's Quarry Street. A year later, early in 1836, both he and his entire family moved into a substantial house, two and a half storeys high and of roughcut limestone, on Rideau Street.* Within this residence, he had both his bedroom and his study in the attic, confirming that he was already a success as a lawyer and was now effectively the head of the family, in place of the diminished and scarcely more than tolerated Hugh Macdonald.

Three years later, Macdonald moved both his office and the family home to the more fashionable Queen Street. In this office, helped by his clerks Campbell and Mowat, he busied himself with lucrative

---

* This house, at 110 Rideau Street, still stands and has been converted into an exquisite small museum about Macdonald by its present owners, Donna Ivey and Norma Kelly. On a wallboard in the attic, the initials "L.M." have been carved, perhaps standing for Macdonald's sister Louisa, but more probably for his cousin Lowther Macpherson.

but tedious work, such as chasing down unpaid bills and searching titles. And then, abruptly, he gave it all up—not the law itself, but the kind of law he was engaged in. For two years, from 1837, Macdonald devoted himself entirely to the practice of criminal law.

His reasons for the switch can only be guessed at, because no record of his motive remains. However, a plausible explanation is easy to construct. As a criminal lawyer who took on dramatic cases, Macdonald got himself noticed well beyond the narrow confines of the Kingston business community. He was operating now in the arena where he would spend by far the greatest part of

A youthful Oliver Mowat, later Macdonald's implacable opponent as premier of Ontario, but at this time a clerk in his law office.

his life—the court of public opinion. And while there he was learning the arts of argument and of persuasion that would serve him all his political life. For a lawyer new in practice and still aged only twenty-two, he was taking a short-term gamble on a long-term goal, particularly given that he lost almost as many cases as he won.

Macdonald's first case involved William Brass, the son of a respected Loyalist accused of the horrendous crime of rape of an eight-year-old girl.* The sentence for such a crime was death.

* A prime source for the material in this section has been the excellent master's thesis "A Dead and Alive Way Never Does," by William Teatero for Queen's University in 1978.

Working with an experienced courtroom lawyer, Macdonald offered a triple defence: Brass was not guilty; he was the victim of a conspiracy; or he had been insane at the time the crime was committed. His legal opponent was William Draper, then solicitor general and later premier of the United Province of Canada. While Macdonald lost the case, the Kingston *British Whig* reported that "Mr. John A. Mcdonald [sic] . . . made a very able defence in favour of the unhappy prisoner." At Brass's execution, the rope proved to be too long and the wretched man fell to the ground from the gibbet, landing in his own coffin. He screamed out, "You see. I am innocent; this gallows was not meant for me." The sentence was nevertheless carried out, the second time with a rope of the proper length.

Macdonald won his next case. Peter Anderson was charged with the murder of a friend, James Cummings, whom he had followed into the woods with a rifle after a quarrel between them. Later, Cummings was found dead from a rifle wound. Macdonald handled this case alone. After extensive cross-examination of Crown and defence witnesses, he was able to argue that Anderson had been seen two miles from the scene of the crime at the time it was committed. To the surprise of the local newspapers, the jury rendered a not-guilty verdict. The *British Whig* praised Macdonald for "an excellent address." Campbell, who was then Macdonald's student at law, later observed in his memoir that Macdonald had won the jury over by his "humour and strong liking for anecdote more than for his professional knowledge."*

---

* There was always an edge to Campbell's comments about Macdonald. "He never became in my judgment a good lawyer," he said, "but was always a dangerous man in the courts." One cause, despite their long relationship, was very likely Campbell's resentment that Macdonald dropped him from the plum portfolio of minister of justice in 1885.

His third case attracted much wider attention. In 1837 William Lyon Mackenzie rose up against the colonial administration and staged a brief tragicomic uprising in the capital of York. In Kingston, eight of his supporters assembled with a few weapons, but when they realized that no one else was going to join them they returned home. Still, they had taken up arms against the Queen. Macdonald took the bold course of appealing directly to the judge for an acquittal of the rebels on the grounds that the self-incriminating affidavits the defendants had signed after their arrest had been executed illegally by a police magistrate. The judge agreed and directed the jury to acquit the eight accused.

Less dramatic in its legal consequence but of considerable political consequence was Macdonald's next case involving a prison warden, John Ashley, who had been arrested without a warrant and held for eight hours by Colonel Dundas, the commander of Fort Henry, on suspicion that he had provided the tools that had enabled fifteen rebel prisoners to escape by burrowing through the jail's four-foot-thick stone walls. On being released, Ashley brought a thousand-pound suit for damages. Macdonald argued that nothing justified Ashley's being arrested in this way and, in any case, that he was innocent. There was some evidence to show that other people had provided the tools. The judge instructed the jury to take account of the fact that the colonel had, at the time, acted in good faith. The jury disagreed and awarded Ashley damages of two hundred pounds. This time the Kingston *Chronicle* judged that Macdonald had displayed "much ingenuity and legal knowledge."

The case that in retrospect reveals the most about Macdonald's attitudes to the law occurred early in 1839, when he took up a cause that directly threatened any future political interests he might have. The 1837 rebellion had stirred up support in the United States, particularly along the northern border of New York State after Mackenzie fled there for safety. American citizens eager to liberate Canadians from political oppression set up a number of so-called Hunters' Lodges to work for the cause. In November 1838 a contingent of Hunters boarded the steamship *United States*, with two schooners in tow behind it, and set off for Prescott on the Canadian side. Some 180 of them landed at Windmill Point not far from Prescott. After assuring his men that a much larger force was right behind them, the expedition's leader got into a small boat and sped away across the lake. Those remaining took possession of a stone windmill and, led by Nils Gustaf von Schoultz, dug in there and waited for developments.

Schoultz was a mysterious figure. By origin a Swede, he'd fought with the Poles defending Warsaw against the Russians, was captured and then escaped (some said in exchange for becoming a Russian spy). He made it to Italy, where he married the daughter of a British general, then abandoned her and fled to the United States, entering into relationships with at least two other women who didn't know he was already married. After reading about Canadians' need to be liberated from British oppression, Schoultz joined the Hunters. He was attractive and brave, but befuddled. The local militia and British regulars soon surrounded the windmill. For two days the invaders remained untouched behind the stones walls of their redoubt. Then heavy cannon were brought up, forcing them to surrender. The death of a Canadian lieutenant in an early attack on the windmill, and the rumour that his body had been deliberately mutilated, made it difficult for the soldiers to protect their prisoners as they marched them to jail through Kingston.

Legally, the prisoners were without hope. Their trial was to be a military court-martial on the grounds they had made an invasion into Canada, and as a consequence no civilian defence

lawyer could argue on their behalf. Worse, because of the roused
public opinion, no local lawyer wanted even to advise the prisoners on how best to defend themselves. In a display of personal
courage and out of a conviction that everyone deserved a defence,
Macdonald stepped forward to help the first two men to be tried,
Schoultz and Daniel George, the expedition's paymaster.
Macdonald suggested a series of arguments to George, one being
that there was no proof he had ever fired a gun. George was nevertheless found guilty. Schoultz, for his part, declared himself
guilty. Standing stiff and proud before his fellow officers, he
explained that the lieutenant's body had been mutilated by pigs,
not by his men; that wounded Canadian soldiers had been cared
for; and that he now realized Canadians were not oppressed. The
one thing Macdonald could do for Schoultz was help him compose
his will; when Schoultz said he wanted to include in it a payment
for the service, Macdonald refused the offer. The two prisoners
died bravely.

One aspect of the case had lasting relevance. Schoultz and the
others were tried under a 1352 statute of Edward III that defined
as treason an act committed by a non-citizen who "most
wickedly, maliciously and traitorously, did levy and make war
against our Said Sovereign." Macdonald tried to defend his
clients against the application of that law. Almost exactly fifty
years after the Hunters' case, this archaic statute would be
deployed once again in Canada. On that occasion, the allegedly
treasonable act was committed by a Canadian who had become an
American citizen. The person responsible for the decision to
prosecute the offence under the old statute was the prime minister. He was Macdonald, by then Sir John A. The defendant was
Louis Riel.

Macdonald's last appearance as a defence lawyer occurred late
in 1839, when he represented a Mohawk Indian, Brandt Brandt,

charged with murdering a fellow Mohawk. Macdonald defended him with the aid of an interpreter. He cross-examined the Crown's principal witness, showing that the deed had been done in a house in the dark, when everyone there was drunk, making it impossible to be certain who had wielded the knife. The judge directed the jury that the facts could not sustain a verdict of manslaughter, so a conviction for murder was the only option. The jury nevertheless decided on manslaughter, and the judge sentenced Brandt to just six months in jail. Again, the *Chronicle* judged Macdonald's defence as "ingenious."

Macdonald never again appeared in the courts, except in civil actions. The immediate reason was the sudden death, on September 10, 1839, of the prominent lawyer Henry Cassady, who was also mayor of Kingston and solicitor to the Commercial Bank of the Midland District. At the age of just twenty-four, Macdonald took over many of Cassady's accounts and was chosen to succeed him in the prime post of solicitor for the bank. It's also easy to guess that, by now, Macdonald judged he had gained all the attention and publicity he needed for his legal career—or for another one.

Henceforth, Macdonald concentrated entirely on corporate matters. Though a major part of his legal work derived from the Commercial Bank accounts, he began to extend his reach to nearby towns such as Belleville and, eventually, to the financial centre of Montreal. Initially, most of his work involved debt collection and the foreclosure of mortgages, but he began to develop new lines of business. As early as 1842, he went into real estate, buying and selling lots and parcels of land in Kingston; he did well at first, but later all his gains were wiped out by a real estate crash. He eventually became a director of no less than a dozen Kingston companies, involved in everything from insurance to canals. In 1842 he used the opportunity of a trip to Britain to make legal and commercial contacts there; they eventually paid off in his becoming solicitor for the London-based Trust and Loan Company of Upper Canada.

In 1841 his father died, at the comparatively young age of fifty-nine. He was now officially head of the family and responsible for the financial security of his mother and two sisters, both unmarried. The strain took its toll. Beginning in 1840, and off and on through 1841, Macdonald was stricken by some ailment that, while never really identified, as was common then, left him weak and listless. His doctor thought that a long holiday, beginning with a sea trip, might do wonders for his health. That could mean only Britain; much more probably by coincidence rather than calculation, the prescription worked.

Macdonald sailed from Boston in January 1842 in the company of two friends, Thomas Wilson and Edward Wanklyn. Before leaving Kingston, he got into a high-stakes card game known as loo with some business associates and, over three nights, won the astounding sum of two thousand dollars. Afterwards, he vowed never again to gamble—and he never did, except once, when he made a throwaway bet at a horse-race and won.

Macdonald's stay in Britain, which eventually extended to six months, proved to be the most important holiday he ever took in his life. During it, he fell in love with the woman who would become his first wife. He also fell in love with England. More exactly, he came to understand the reasons for the love he already possessed for British culture, style and accomplishments. And radiant and compelling they were: a glowing young woman now sat on the throne; the glory of the defeat of Napoleon still reverberated in the recent past; the Royal Navy policed the seven seas;

London, with its incredible population of more than two million, was easily the largest and richest city in the world; British parliamentary and legal systems were regarded as models just about everywhere—except in France, and, as didn't really count, in the United States. Macdonald's anglophilia did not begin on this trip, but what he saw and experienced during his months there at the still-impressionable age of twenty-seven deepened his lifelong conviction that whatever was British was best—both in itself and also for Canada.

Of all the letters Macdonald wrote over the years to members of his family (of which, sadly, comparatively few have survived),* the letter he sent to his mother from London on March 3, 1842, stands apart from the rest by its sheer, uninhibited joy. He's excited and dazzled by the city, by its gargantuan buildings and affluence, and by himself. He's like the clever boy not quite certain of his gifts and aching for the approval of the one person whose applause, or censure, he really cares about. So he tells her everything.

"You would be surprised at the breakfasts I eat," he wrote. "Wilson laughs as he sees roll after roll disappear and eggs and bacon after roll. My dinners are equally satisfactory to myself. . . . Now only fancy, my commencing my dinner with a sole fried, with shrimp sauce, demolishing a large steak, and polishing off with bread and cheese and a quart of London Stout." He told her he was getting on well with the girls. Through a Lord De La Warr he had obtained "an order to see the Queen's private apartments" at Windsor Castle. He didn't go alone: "I had a very pretty girl, Margaret Wanklyn [a relative of his other companion from

---

* All these surviving letters, together with an excellent introduction, are contained in Keith Johnson's *Affectionately Tours: The Letters of Sir John A. Macdonald and His Family*.

Canada], on my arm, to whom the scene was also new," he enthused, "so we were agreeably engaged in comparing our impressions. Our ideas *sympathized wonderfully*." He also described his networking successes. "I have formed acquaintances and dined with two or three lawyers here by whose assistance I have seen all the great guns of the law." Among them, as he looked down from the gallery in the House of Lords, were "the great Law Lords, Lyndhurst, Brougham, Campbell and Cottenham. At the Guildhall, I saw Lord Denman and Sir Nicholas Tindal." Later, he went to the House of Commons, where he spotted "Peel, Goudham, Lord John Russell, Lord Stanley, O'Connell, Duncombe, Walkley." He had plans to go on to the Tower and dine with two members of Parliament. Still, he hadn't forgotten his domestic commitments: he would buy, as requested, damask, and "paper hangings and some chimney ornaments."

Macdonald gave to and received from his mother, Helen, pure unconditional love, right up to her death and then beyond; he was buried beside her in Kingston's Cataraqui Cemetery. In different ways, their lives were hard, and they both deserved this pure intercourse between them.

Yet, as so often with Macdonald, nothing was ever simple. He worshipped his mother, but he didn't copy her. She was deeply pious; he most certainly was not. She came from a long line of military men; he, as was most unusual among public figures of the day, never held an officer's commission in the militia and always regarded the military with a distinct skepticism. In the end, Macdonald did his own thing in his own way.

During his long stay in Britain, Macdonald travelled widely: to Manchester (where he bought wallpaper and the damask, and also a kitchen stove and iron railings); over to Chester to see a son of the family's now-deceased patron, Colonel Macpherson; on up to Scotland; and then a side trip to the Isle of Man to see yet more relatives. It was fully summer by the time he returned home.

Macdonald went back to the grind of law. His Kingston properties did exceptionally well for a time, until the real estate crash. Confident of his business skills nevertheless, Macdonald eventually bought and sold land all over the province, in Guelph and Toronto and Peterborough and as far away as Sarnia. At one time, he and Campbell jointly owned a steamship, though it promptly sank. Macdonald did better with a steam yacht that he managed to resell at a profit. Surprisingly, in view of his future history, Macdonald almost never invested in railways.*

Even as he was trying to become a tycoon, though, friends noticed a distinct change in the line of his interests. He asked one of them what he should do to prepare himself for political office should he ever seek it. Back came the reply, "Join the Orange Lodge and become an alderman." He asked Tom Wilson, his companion on the trip to Britain, about the financial side of political life. Back came the sound advice: "Secure a handsome independence first and then give as much attention as you please to the public weal."

---

* The authority on Macdonald's business affairs is the historian Keith Johnson, most particularly in his "John A. Macdonald, the Young Non-Politician," Canadian Historical Association, *Historical Papers*, 1971.

FIVE

A Conservative in a Conservative Country

~

In a young country like Canada, I am of the opinion that it is of more consequence to endeavour to develop its resources and improve its physical advantages than to waste the time of the legislature and the money of the people on abstract and theoretical questions of government.

John A. Macdonald

Macdonald took the advice and joined the Orange Lodge; to cover all bases, he later joined the Masonic Lodge and the Oddfellows. In February 1843 he announced that he would contest a vacant seat for alderman in Kingston's Fourth Ward. Helped by the *Chronicle*'s praise for his "well-known talents and high character," he won easily. As word of his new diligence in civic duties spread, he was elected president of Kingston's influential St. Andrew's Society. He was also an active supporter of the campaign to establish a university, Queen's, at Kingston.

He applied the same diligence to the task of sorting out his business affairs. For several years, Alexander Campbell had served him exceptionally well as a law clerk. Macdonald now promoted him to junior partner. Their agreement gave Campbell a third of the profits of the general business, excluding those generated by Macdonald from his own work as solicitor of the Commercial Bank. The deal was well structured: the practice would continue to provide him with a salary, but Macdonald no longer needed to be there all the time.

He closed the contract with Campbell on September 1, 1843. That same day he entered into another contract, a lifelong one. Macdonald married the woman with whom he'd fallen in love.

It had happened during his holiday in Britain the year before. It's just possible that the "very pretty" Margaret Wanklyn who had toured Windsor Castle on his arm had set him to thinking about the pleasures of the permanent company of a woman with whom he "sympathized wonderfully." On the Isle of Man, he had gone to call on his cousin, Margaret Greene, who was living in a farmhouse near the small capital of Douglas. Born a Clark in

Isabella Macdonald (née Clark), probably close to the time of her marriage. Her wan, girlish vulnerability helped get her in under Macdonald's radar screen.

the same Highland site of Dalnavert where Macdonald's mother had been born, Margaret had crossed the Atlantic to live with an uncle in Georgia. There she had married a John Ward Greene, the descendant of a hero of the Revolutionary War, but had been widowed a few years later and retreated back across the Atlantic to the Isle of Man to stretch out her finances. She was living comfortably but carefully with her two unmarried sisters, Jane and Isabella.

Macdonald and Isabella clicked almost immediately. By the time he left, Macdonald had secured from Isabella a commitment to come to

Kingston the following year, ostensibly to visit yet another of her sisters, Maria, now the wife of John Alexander Macpherson, a son of Colonel Macpherson. Isabella made the journey. As was by now inevitable, a proposal was made and was accepted. And so on that September morning, they exchanged vows and matching gold wedding rings in St. Andrew's Church in Kingston. Right after the wedding, Macdonald hurried over to his law office to sign his agreement with Campbell. By marriage, and thereby the acquisition of respectability, Macdonald had cleared the last hurdle to his political candidacy.

No election date had yet been announced, but it was now only a year away.

Because Macdonald would go on to become so successful a politician, it has often been taken for granted that his motive for getting into the game was to get to the top as soon as possible and, once there, to remain at the top for as long as possible. In fact, it's wholly possible that Macdonald's principal motive for entering public life was to make money.

The professions of law and politics are joined at the hip. They always have been: in particular, lawyers are practised in the arts of debating and oratory, two political skills of immense esteem in the nineteenth century. Of the eleven prime ministers back to Louis St. Laurent just over a half-century ago, all but three (Lester Pearson, Joe Clark, and Stephen Harper) have been lawyers. Lawyers are good at spotting loopholes in legislation and regulations, and at attitudinizing—projecting shock and disbelief—at the arguments of their opponents. Lawyers who leave politics can return more easily to their practices than can members of almost any other profession; there are more, and better, post-politics prospects for lawyers, from the bench to boards of public enterprises to commissions of inquiry.

Two pieces of evidence suggest that short-term practical considerations were indeed Macdonald's purpose. When asked why he had stood as a candidate, Macdonald answered, "To fill a gap. There seemed no one else available, so I was pitched on." Many years later, his minister of justice of that time, Sir John Thompson, asked Macdonald if it was proper for a friend to run for Parliament for only a single term. Macdonald replied bluntly, "Those are the terms on which I came into public life." In this strictly private conversation, he had no reason to dissemble.

As further evidence that Macdonald's motivation for entering public life was more to make money than to make a name for himself, not a single companion or friend, nor any member of the family, ever claimed to have heard him say during his early years that he planned to become a great man. By contrast, his closest contemporary British prime minister, Benjamin Disraeli, proclaimed uninhibitedly, "I love fame. I love reputation," while Pierre Elliott Trudeau, who comes closest to Macdonald in his hold on the Canadian imagination, wrote in a journal he kept as a youth, "I must become a great man . . . a future head of state or a well-known diplomat or an eminent lawyer."

John A. Macdonald as a young man— alert, active and, as so often, very clearly amused.

It's thus entirely possible that Macdonald initially saw politics as an opportunity to gain a quick understanding of government and to accumulate contacts that he could then deploy on behalf of old and new clients. Only later, as he realized how good he was at it, would politics become his life, fame his spur, and power his addiction.

As always with Macdonald, little is certain. He prepared himself with the focused rigour of someone girding for a marathon, not a sprint. Once elected, he set out systematically to turn Kingston into a political citadel from which he could sally out knowing he had a secure base to retreat to. And, of course, once in, Macdonald stayed on, and on and on.

The call came in the spring of 1844. A group of leading Kingston citizens asked him to run in the election that was coming due. They asked him to stand as a Conservative—he being conservative by nature, Kingston being Loyalist, and all those worthy types looking for someone sound and sensible to represent them. Macdonald agreed to their request and then told them exactly what they wanted to hear: that all politics is local—today it's a cliché, but at the time it came to Macdonald instinctually.* He promised he would address "the settlement of the back township district, hitherto so utterly neglected, and to press for the construction of the long projected plank road to Perth and Ottawa." He also said that he intended to get things done in the way they themselves would do it—by being practical: "In a young country like Canada," he declared, "I am of the opinion that it is of more consequence to endeavour to develop its resources and improve its physical advantages than to waste the time of the legislature

---

* The "all politics is local" aphorism is generally attributed to "Tip" O'Neill, the powerful Democratic House leader in the United States from 1977 to 1987.

and the money of the people on abstract and theoretical questions of government."

Macdonald and his supporters (all men of property, they being the only ones with the right to vote) were as one. That curious but occasionally insightful book *The Canadian Commercial Revolution, 1845–1851* contains a good description of the typical Canadian voter of the time: "They were energetic, progressive and materialistic . . . they were strong and shrewd men, disdainful of theories, and interested chiefly in the material realities of life."* In one respect, these unsentimental types might have wondered just what they were getting into. Part of Macdonald's reply to his petitioners had a decidedly teasing, over-the-top quality to it: "With feelings of greater pride and gratitude than I can express . . . [t]he mode in which I can best evince my high sense of the honour you have done me is, *at once*, to lay aside all personal considerations and accede to your request."

For the actual election, in the fall of 1844, Macdonald issued his own proclamation in the Kingston *Chronicle*. It repeated his local ambitions and dealt with a topic that concerned most voters in the staunchly Loyalist town, no less so than Macdonald himself: "I, therefore, scarcely need state my firm belief that the prosperity of Canada depends upon its permanent connection with the Mother Country and that I shall resist to the utmost any attempt which may tend to weaken that union."

The balloting—each elector casting his vote not by marking an X on paper but in the "manly" manner of shouting his choice out loud—took place on Monday, October 14, and throughout the next day. Macdonald won easily, by 275 shouts against just 42 for his opponent, Anthony Manahan. As was far from always the case,

---

* *The Canadian Commercial Revolution* was published in 1936 by the historian Gilbert Norman Tucker. It was his doctoral thesis.

the casting of the votes and their counting were conducted "in a most peaceful and orderly manner," according to the *Chronicle*.

But one thing had gone wrong for Macdonald. He had always assumed he would be serving as a member in a legislature that met in his home town of Kingston. Lord Sydenham, the first governor general of the new United Province of Canada, which had just replaced the separate provinces of Upper and Lower Canada, had announced in February 1841 that Kingston would be the capital of his domain. This town of some five thousand souls had gone into an instant and ecstatic boom—as had Macdonald's law practice. Civil servants streamed in, along with the governor general and his mini-court. Construction was soon under way for at least four hundred new houses. Town officials took delighted note of the fact that a grand new town hall was being constructed which just happened to have, in its second storey, two high-ceilinged chambers ideal for the Legislative Assembly and the

Kingston, c. 1863. Some fine three-storey buildings by now, and horses and carriages, but still a street of deep, foul-smelling mud.

Legislative Council, or upper chamber. Until this building was completed, the Assembly met in a newly built but empty hospital, with eighty-four overstuffed armchairs equipped with an attached writing tablet hurried in for the eighty-four legislators.

If Kingstonians were pleased, few others shared their enthusiasm. French-Canadian members complained loudly that, compared with Montreal or Quebec City, this new capital was dull and, worse, homogeneously English; one of the French members referred to "cet enfer de Kingston." The demands of the French, headed by the emerging leader Louis-Hippolyte LaFontaine, could not be denied. In September 1843 a new governor general, Sir Charles Metcalfe, announced that Kingston's brief hour of glory was over and, perhaps initiating the tradition of resolving national problems by displeasing everyone more or less equally, that the seat of government would henceforth rotate every three years from Montreal to Quebec City to Toronto.* Macdonald's inaugural appearance in the legislature thus was in its new temporary quarters in St. Anne's Market in Montreal. There, he would begin to learn for the first time about the "other" Canada.

In nineteenth-century Canada, the observation that all politics is local would have been treated not as an insight but as a banality. With occasional exceptions, such as the campaign to achieve Responsible Government or, later, Representation by Population, almost all politics was about local issues. Debates that engaged the general public were almost always those inspired by sectarianism—

---

* A few years after Kingston's fall from grace, an English visitor noted that the town had "a rather dreary appearance" and that many streets were "over-run with grass."

French versus English, Catholic versus Protestant, and sometimes Protestant versus Protestant, as between Anglicans and Methodists. Just about the only non-religious exception to the rule of the dominance of localism was the issue of anti-Americanism; it was both widespread and, as was truly rare, a political conviction that promoted national unity because it was held as strongly by the French as by the English.

Almost all politics was local for the simple reason that almost everyone in Canada was a local: at least 80 per cent of Canadians were farmers or independent fishermen. Moreover, they were self-sufficient farmers. They built their own houses. They carved out most of their implements and equipment. They grew almost all their own food (tea and sugar excepted) or raised it on the hoof. They made most of their own clothes. They made their own candles and soft soap. Among the few products they sold into commercial markets were grain and potash. Few sent their children to school. They were unprotected by policemen (even in the towns in Upper Canada, police forces dated only from the 1840s). For lack of ministers or priests, marriages were often performed by the people themselves. Even the term "local" conveys a false impression of community: roads were so bad and farms spaced so far apart that social contact was limited principally to "bees"—barn and house raising, stump clearing and later, more fancily, quilting.

Government's reach in Canada was markedly more stunted than in England. While there had been a Poor Law there from 1597, the first statute of the Legislature of Upper Canada provided specifically that "Nothing in this Act . . . shall introduce any of the laws of England concerning the maintenance of the poor."* The churches were responsible for charity, and in some

---

* The Maritimes, then quite separate colonies, had both Poor Laws and Poor Houses.

areas for education.* It was the same for that other form of social activism, the Temperance Societies, commonly brought into being by the Methodist, Presbyterian and Baptist churches. The unemployed were "the idle poor," and no government had any notion that it should be responsible for their succour. Governments collected taxes (almost exclusively customs and excise duties) and were responsible for law and order, maintaining the militia, and running the jails, where the idea of rehabilitation as opposed to punishment was unknown. But without any income tax, there was comparatively little the government could do even if it wished. Consequently, the total spending on public charities, social programs and education amounted to just 9 per cent of any government's revenues. To most Canadians in the middle of the nineteenth century, government was as irrelevant to their day-to-day lives as it is today to the Mennonites, Hutterites and Amish.

Because Macdonald was an avowed conservative, he was little different from almost everyone else; the other major party, the Reform Party (which changed its name over time to the Liberal Party), was at least as conservative as the Conservatives. Later, the populist Clear Grits arose in Upper Canada to advocate such disturbing American notions as the secret ballot and direct democracy. In mid- to late-nineteenth-century Canada, though, conservatism was as widely held a political attitude as liberalism would become a century later. It took a long while for things to change. In one post-Confederation debate, in 1876, held during an economic depression, a Liberal MP argued that the government should assist the poor. Another MP rounded on him to declare, "The moment a Government is asked to take charge and feed the

---

* The first legislation in British North America to establish free education was in Prince Edward Island in 1852. Nova Scotia followed in 1864, and Ontario only after Confederation.

poor you strike a blow at their self-respect and independence that is fatal to our existence as a people." The shocked second intervenor was also a Liberal, as was the government of the day.

Amid this emphasis on the local, there was, nevertheless, one broad national dimension. Governments were remarkably ready to go into debt—proportionately more deeply than today—to build up the nation itself. Here, Conservatives were actually greater risk-takers than the Reformers. Bishop John Strachan, a leading member of the arch-conservative Family Compact, held that "the existence of a national debt may be perfectly consistent with the interests and prosperity of the Country." In the early and middle part of the century, mostly Conservative governments bankrolled major public projects—first canals, such as the Welland, the Lachine and the Rideau—and then a spiderweb of railways, nearly all of them money-losing. These Conservatives were, of course, undertaking projects that benefited their supporters, but they were also building the country.

Politicians performed one social program of vital importance—patronage. When Macdonald first entered the legislature, though, relatively little patronage was available for politicians to distribute. Purity wasn't the cause: impotence was. In the early 1840s, patronage was allocated almost entirely by the governor general. The fight through the decade for Responsible Government, or for the transfer from London to Canadians of responsibility over almost all internal or domestic matters, would really be a contest between the governor general and Canadian politicians over who should get to dish out patronage.

Although they did a good deal less than today's politicians do, nineteenth-century legislators performed with a good deal more flourish. Speeches, delivered in the long, declamatory cadences of high rhetoric, could last two, three, even five hours. Among epithets used commonly in the province's Parliament

were "poltroon," "blackguard," "traitor," "infamous traitor,"
"coward," "cur," "jackal." Here, as recorded by newspaper
reporters,* are the exchanges in a debate on May 8, 1846:

> Mr. Deblurey[†]: "Mr. Chairman, if you are absolutely unable to keep
> the hon. Member in order, I will cross the floor and make him observe
> the respect due to a member addressing this House."
>
> Mr. Aylwin, (clenching his fist and extending his arm over his
> desk): "Take care. Take care. Take care." (Great excitement). Later,
> Mr. Aylwin again (shaking his fist): "Come over here, if you dare,
> your scoundrel." (Mr. Deblurey attempted to go over but was pre-
> vented by two of the members).
>
> Mr. Hall: "Are we in a Canadian legislature to be bullied and
> browbeaten?" (The whole house was on its legs in a moment. Some
> cried, "Leave the chair," some, "Call the Speaker," others "Clear the
> gallery," and several gentlemen went to the gallery to tender assis-
> tance to the ladies, who were, of course, greatly alarmed).
>
> Macdonald then intervened, declaring: "He would pull Mr.
> Aylwin's nose."

The newspapers did a great deal to raise the political temperature.
The Toronto *Globe* once described one member, Dr. John Rolph, as "a
sleek-visaged man with cold grey eyes, treacherous mouth and lips
fashioned to deceive," and as "dark, designing, cruel, traitorous."

---

* No official Hansard record existed during these years. In an inspired project,
the Parliamentary Library has assembled a "virtual Hansard" by collating the
near-verbatim reports of debates as published in the newspapers of the time on
the basis of accounts sent in by shorthand reporters. The post-Confederation
series is all but complete; that for the pre-Confederation Legislative Assembly,
though, extends only up to 1856. One editorial challenge is that newspapers
often gave short shrift or no shrift at all to members of parties they opposed.

[†] His actual name was De Bleury.

The assaults went beyond the verbal to the physical, particularly during the evening sessions as the intake of liquor
increased. During an 1849 debate on an especially contentious
issue, Macdonald first denounced a speech by a Reform minister, William Blake, as "most shameful," then sent him a note
challenging him to a duel. Blake accepted, but the sergeant-at-
arms managed to head them off. George-Étienne Cartier and a
Lower Canada (Quebec) member followed up a comparable
shouting match by actually arriving at a duelling ground; nothing
happened, because their seconds had "forgotten" to bring any
ammunition.

Macdonald came into the legislature quietly. During his first session he made not a single speech, asked not a question, made not
a single interjection. He spent a great deal of time in the
Parliamentary Library, boning up on the rules and precedents,
reading speeches, figuring out the jousting techniques involved in
asking questions of ministers and responding to their replies. He
sat in the back row—and he still got himself noticed.

He did so by the classic device of being different. He was
clean-shaven at a time when the legislature and the courts were a
thicket of muttonchop whiskers, hedge-sized moustaches and full,
patriarchal beards. He wore his ties loose, in a carefree Byronic
manner; his clothes, colourful, almost foppish, shouted out the
message "Notice Me." A vivid description of Macdonald's appearance and demeanour at this time was provided by one of his early
biographers, E.B. Biggar, in his *Anecdotal Life of Sir John
Macdonald:* "His walk, then, as ever, was peculiar. His step was
short, and when he went to a seat, there was something in his
movement which suggested a bird alighting in a hesitating way

from flight. His quick and all-comprehending glance, and that peculiar jerking of the head, bore out the comparison in other respects." Shrewdly, another early biographer, J.E. Collins, compared Macdonald's posture and choice of clothes to those of "an actor." As a further advantage, Macdonald's frizzy hair and large, bulbous nose—"qui faisait toute sa gloire," in the wonderful phrase of François-Xavier Langelier, who for long sat across from him as an opposition MP—made him stand out from the crowd.

Much as is the case with Parliament today, the legislature was essentially a large club. Members hurled insults at each other but behind the curtains turned into convivial friends, because they were all in the same, adrenaline-charged, winner-take-all game. Few, if any, members of that assembly would have been as "clubbable," in the British phrase, as was Macdonald. People liked him because he liked them. It helped materially that he wasn't moralistic, whether about drink or anything else, but was a man of the world, unshockable and unjudgmental. Also, he was funny.

Macdonald found his voice during his second session, in 1845. He spoke, in these first efforts, not merely like a voice from the past but like one from an antediluvian past. In February he took part in a debate on a motion calling for reform of the law of primogeniture, which required that, when a property owner died intestate, all his holdings went to his eldest son. Macdonald was appalled that some share of such estates might instead be reserved for younger sons. "The law of primogeniture was the great bulwark between the people and the Crown and the Crown and the people," he declared. "It was the younger sons of England that had made it great in peace and war. What would have been the younger Pitt or Fox if, instead of being sent forth to seek their fortunes, the estate of their father had been divided: they would have been mere country squires." He cited the example of the Duke of Wellington, almost penniless, but "left with his sword in his hand." To pass a motion "merely because it would please the people" would be an "act of madmen," Macdonald concluded. The motion was defeated.

In May of the following year, Macdonald made an interjection on a bill, moved by Reform leader Robert Baldwin, to change on a trial basis the practice of electors shouting out their vote choices at the balloting stations in Montreal, where there had been violence in some places. Once again, Macdonald was appalled. He admitted that proposals for a secret ballot had been made in the British Parliament, but only to "prevent the landlord's influence over the tenant." In Canada, where so many citizens were landowners, there was "no one exercising an illegitimate influence over them." So, concluded Macdonald, "every man in Canada would, and did, make public his opinion." The public ballot was retained. That same session, Macdonald also showed that he had a temper. He provoked a member of the High Tory Boulton family to challenge him to a duel. Macdonald refused to back off, but other members intervened and heads, on both sides, cooled down.

Most of the time, Macdonald applied himself to strictly local matters. He introduced a bill to incorporate the Wolfe Island, Kingston and Toronto Railroad Company, and as well a petition for a Catholic college, Regiopolis, to be established at Kingston. He attracted the attention of journalists—one in the *Montreal Transcript* described him as "very popular . . . I should say he is 'a rising man' and not likely to disappoint the expectations of his friends." At the very least, he had by now made Kingston into a citadel for himself.

SIX

Going Headlong

The rod cannot always be smiting.
John A. Macdonald

In 1843 Margaret Greene, the sister of Macdonald's wife, Isabella, left the Isle of Man, where she had introduced the couple, and moved back to Georgia—to the ancestral estate of her late husband's family, which she had now inherited. She and Macdonald exchanged letters, he at times offering her advice on legal and real estate matters. On July 11, 1845, he wrote Margaret a letter utterly different in nature.

This letter, sent less than two years after John and Isabella had married, and one year after he became a member of the legislature, was the saddest and most fateful he would ever write. Although he did not yet know it, his life was about to change totally and irreversibly.

"My Dear Sister," Macdonald began, "Isabella has been ill—very ill—with one of her severest attacks. She is now just recovering and I hope has thrown off for the time her terrible disease. Still, this is not certain, and at all events it has left her in the usual state of prostration that follows every attack." Clearly this was not the first "attack" Isabella had suffered. He had planned for them to go to New York, as they had done the previous year—exactly why and for how long, Macdonald doesn't say—but that was now doubtful. "It may be days—nay weeks—before she has rallied sufficiently to attempt any journey. What to say or do, I know not."

Just one day later, Macdonald wrote again to his sister-in-law. His mood had deepened into despair. "Her pain has in a great measure left her, but her debility is in the greatest degree alarming. She is weaker than

Margaret Greene, Isabella's elder sister and Macdonald's confidante as he tried to cope with his wife's illness.

she has ever been, and there are symptoms, such as an apparent numbness of one limb, and an irregularity in the action of the heart, that made me send for Dr. Sampson, altho' against Isabella's wish. He saw her this morning and says he cannot relieve her, and I ought not, my beloved sister, to disguise from you, that he thinks her in the most precarious state." He praised Margaret Greene for her "strength of mind" and, his despair now bringing him close to the point of abandoning all hope, wrote that "unless God in his infinite mercy works an immediate change for the better, it is impossible for her to remain in her exhausted state for many days." Isabella in fact didn't die; neither, though, would she ever recover.

There were a great many bonds between Macdonald and Isa, as Isabella was often called. They were cousins. They both were Scots. She was thirty-three when they married and must have been well aware both of the ticking of her biological clock and of the sparseness of marital opportunities in the rural Isle of Man. For him, on the eve of entering politics, having a wife meant that voters need not worry that he might misbehave and embarrass them. That their ages were inverted—he a mere twenty-eight on their wedding day—wouldn't have struck Macdonald as unusual, because there was a similar gap between his own mother and father. He was a good catch, although by no means a great one—he was still building his law practice and his background was barely middle class. His looks, to the extent they mattered, were odd, but not alluringly ugly in the manner of, say, his contemporary Thomas D'Arcy McGee.

Isabella, for her part, possessed a certain pale prettiness, but in no way was she beautiful. The first known portrait of her was done around the time of her marriage. A second was done around 1852 by the same Kingston artist William Sawyer who painted the distinctive portrait of Macdonald that is the frontispiece of this book; a locket version of Isabella's image appears later in this chapter. As well, in 2006 another portrait, either of Isabella or much more likely her sister Margaret Greene, was purchased by the Agnes Etherington Art Centre in Kingston.* The Sawyer portrait shows Isabella with a high forehead, her mouth slim but determined, her hair dark and thick, her nose long and delicate, her eyes a bright, pale blue. Isabella seems not to be wholly there but withdrawn and passive, as though observing herself rather than being on display for the benefit of observers.

---

* This portrait is of the correct period—the 1840s—and comes from the Kingston area. The woman in it has dark eyes, though, rather than the light-blue eyes Isabella was known to have.

Isabella may have possessed some ineffable quality now impossible to pin down, or she may have been an enigma without a riddle. In the mysterious way of these things, she connected to some romantic core hidden deep within John A., composed in part no doubt of the traditional male urge to protect. Her means for achieving this bond was spontaneity. She was open, vulnerable, breathy: "*You* know how *headlong* I ever go," she wrote in a letter to Margaret. Macdonald was never cynical, but he most certainly was unsentimental and fully capable of being hard. With Isabella, he expanded his emotional range to that of love. The use of that word to describe his feelings for her can only be speculative. The fact is that when Isabella began to reveal the extent of her frailty, Macdonald demonstrated an exceptional tenderness towards her and, a good deal rarer among husbands, a durable tolerance for her weakness.

The full nature of their relationship can only be guessed at. Just two of Isabella's letters survive, both of them to her sister. We thus have no record of Macdonald's and Isabella's voices when they were talking to each other.* Her own voice comes across as, well, "headlong": people and subjects are all jumbled together. The first of these letters was written on June 11, 1845, a month before Macdonald's anguished letter. She is a bit cross, because Margaret had apparently delayed a planned visit to Kingston: "I have of course countermanded yr bonnet dearest sister. But it was to have been lovely. An exquisite lavender satin & blonde but you will do penance in yellow stockings for it as I thought we have been so becoming & sweet. Jane shall shall [sic] wear her *purple* if it *were at night*—for I wont let *her* off. Bye

---

* The paucity of surviving letters by Isabella is striking because, being frequently away from Macdonald for extended periods, she must have written often to him and to other family members.

the way, Mama has bought a London cap to send you. Mrs. Abbott had just received it when M. saw & pounced on it. But I'm so mad about that bonnet I won't tell you what it is like, & I don't think I'll be satisfied till I get a red petticoat for you to wear with the yellow stockings." The rest of the letter continues this girlish, gushing tone.

Isabella's second extant letter, of 1848, also written to Margaret, is even gushier. "Gush," though, is a misleading descriptor. What we are reading now is the cry of someone sensing that she is drowning. By this time indeed Isabella was struggling, growing ever weaker, against an illness that was reducing her to a hollow shell. This letter begins by referring to one of Margaret's friends, a Mrs. Biddle: "I sincerely sympathize in your leaving dear, dear Mrs. Biddle & most precious Husband. Full well I know your spirit *must* be born down by the hourly *yearning* for her society. . . . My dear, dear Mrs. Biddle. How I reverence her! How my weary, *weary*, spirit bows before her. May God's holiest, richest mercies *rest, now & ever, abidingly*, on her and hers." She names another of Margaret's friends: "I rejoice you are with Mrs. Field. Dear beautiful, *Porcelain* Mrs. Field, so different from the *gilt delf* of every day life. I really would dread seeing her often, my own darling precious sister, *you* know how *headlong* I ever go & I much fear I would love her but too fondly."

She was, surely, writing far less about Mrs. Biddle and Mrs. Field than about herself.

John and Isabella Macdonald were married for fourteen years. For the first two years or so, they were wholly happy. For another dozen she was a bedridden invalid, struck down by an illness no doctor could diagnose or cure, interspersed initially by occasional brief and unpredictable respites that, over time, became rarer and briefer. Her doctors could prescribe just one effective medicine. It was opium, in ever larger quantities.* It brought her relief, but it also took her ever further from her husband and from real life. During this long, empty period, Macdonald would hurry home from the legislature or his law office, often to dine alone because she was too weak even to accompany him by sitting up in bed. The house was silent most of the time because the noise of guests would give her a headache. Inevitably, they had less and less to talk about, and less and less in common. Also inevitably, he took to drink.

The first two years of his marriage to Isabella would be the single span of time in John A. Macdonald's entire adult life in which he experienced a normal marriage and family life. In place of the small daily epiphanies of any couple, whether they are in love or are merely companionable, Macdonald's entire life would be politics. This was one reason—the tragic one—why he became so good at it.

There was a particular cause for Macdonald, in his letters to Margaret Greene of July 11 and 12, 1845, to be so close to utter despair. In the previous few months his mother had suffered two strokes. As hardy Highlanders do, she recovered, but for the rest of her life she would need permanent care. As head of the family,

---

* Opium was widely available in the mid-nineteenth century and a common ingredient in patent medicines, such as Winslow's Soothing Syrup, Godfrey's Cordial and McMunn's Elixir of Opium, all of which could be bought without a prescription at drugstores. In its most common form, especially favoured by women, it was sold as laudanum.

Isabella's downstairs bedroom at Bellevue House in Kingston. It was from here, while bedridden, that she ran the household like "the Invisible Lady."

Macdonald was now responsible for ensuring that his mother was looked after, for making similar arrangements for his wife as she too became an invalid, and for the financial and other needs of his two unmarried sisters. While doing all this, Macdonald was at the same time trying to advance his career in politics and to maintain his law practice, now under the strain of his many absences on personal and political business.

Many would have buckled. Macdonald just got down to doing what he could. He conceived the idea—presumably on the advice of doctors—of taking Isabella to Savannah in the Deep South, where she might better regain her strength by escaping the long blast of a Canadian winter. Before leaving, he had to sort out a family dispute caused by his own sister Margaret (Moll) refusing to accompany Isabella partway southwards, as she'd undertaken to do, because she had to remain behind to watch over their mother. Eventually, Margaret agreed to go with them as far as

Oswego, New York, and Macdonald then set off. It was a nightmare journey. Transportation systems were rough and ready; accommodation for travellers was spartan. On July 18 he wrote to Margaret Greene from Oswego: "We arrived here this morning at about one o'clock my dearest sister. The exhaustion produced by carrying Isabella down to the boat was dreadful to witness. We thought she would die on the dock. . . . The weather was so stormy, that all our party were sick, Isabella dreadfully so, and yet strange to say her health and strength seemed to return to her." They went on to Syracuse, and then, by train, to Philadelphia, where "her fatigues were very great and she was obliged to subdue pain by opium, but still she kept up her spirits & at about four o'clock we arrived at this House. Only think what a journey she had. First to be carried down a narrow stair at Jersey & over to the cars; 2nd a journey in the cars for about 70 miles to Bristol; 3rd To be carried in a chair from the cars to a steamboat, 4th a voyage of 22 miles to this city, and lastly and worst of all a quarter of a mile's drive in a hack over rough streets. . . . She from fatigue and opium combined slept from 10 o'clock last night until the morning and is now easy and in good spirits. She never speaks of it, but I am perfectly conscious of how much she suffers."

A few days later, still in Philadelphia, in another letter to Margaret, Macdonald recounted, first, that Isabella "exerted herself too much, so that in the evening she was a good deal exhausted, and was threatened by tic, so that she had recourse to opium," and then reported, "She has had a good day today, has walked a good deal & eaten pretty well." In early November they reached Baltimore, where they had reserved rooms in a hotel near the railway station, but finding them wholly unsatisfactory they moved to another establishment. "The consequence of all this was great exhaustion and great suffering by Isabella. She was in great agony all night, and was obliged to have recourse to opium, externally and internally in great quantities." On a brighter note, Macdonald reported that "Isa . . . says she does not anticipate suffering from our today's journey, as the weather is calm."

At the small town of Petersburgh, he wrote, "The house we stayed in was dirty, the food badly dressed and the beds overrun by ants." They hurried on the 160 miles to Wilmington: "She bore it like a *Shero** as she is, but as you may well believe dreadfully exhausted by the exertion. She passed a miserable night and continues today to pay the penalty for her extra exertions." On a cheerier note, Macdonald reported they had passed their time reading a "strange mélange" of books, among them *The Bible in Spain*, Thomas Carlyle's *Life of Schiller*, Bishop Moore's *Sermons*, and were about to "take up Lord Mahon's *History of England*."

They pressed on, by steamer, reaching Savannah on November 20 after a calm journey—"There was scarcely a curl on the sea." There they rented two "quiet" rooms. Isabella, though, "has been very miserable since our arrival. The tic encouraged by her weakness from fatigue has made a furious attack upon her which she is *manfully* resisting with the assistance of the blister and the pill-box." Now that he was in the Deep South and it was late November, Macdonald appreciated the benefits of being there. "The weather here is so fine & warm that I cannot fancy it winter at all." He would have loved to stay, rather than going back "among the frosts & snows of Canada, sucking my paws like any other bear." Political duties compelled him to return, though. He made an adroit appeal to Margaret Greene to enable him to slip

---

* Macdonald's use of *Shero* poses a tantalizing mystery, perhaps an insolvable one. None of the standard etymology dictionaries consulted by the author cite any uses of the word in the nineteenth century; rather, "shero" is a modern neologism (s-hero) minted by the feminist movement. It seems that Macdonald either invented it as a tease or overheard it, perhaps from his strong-minded and highly intelligent mother.

away: "I need not say however that it would afford me great pleasure to reflect that you were near her, when I am far away."

Macdonald's manipulation achieved its purpose. In a letter sent from Kingston on February 27, 1846, he told Margaret, "I am sanguine in my hopes and belief, that in the fine climate she [Isa] now enjoys, and under your affectionate and judicious care she may yet be restored to me, in health, strength and spirits."

No such recovery occurred. Instead, a miracle did. After a reunion late in 1846, Isabella let Macdonald know that she was pregnant. He moved her to New York, where medical standards were higher (and a great deal more expensive). On April 5, 1847, he wrote to Margaret Greene from New York—"this American Babylon"—to report: "Doctor Washington still says she is in very critical condition arising from the continued attacks of uterine neuralgia. These attacks, he apprehends, may bring on a premature confinement. . . . Still he is not without hopes of being able to prevent an abortion. She is quite calm & resolute, and is much encouraged by Maria's presence." (Maria was yet another of Isabella's sisters, of whom there were four in all.)

That summer, Macdonald's mother suffered a third stroke. He wrote encouragingly to her that "such attacks are not uncommon in aged people." He then switched to some role-reversing nagging: "These illnesses should have the effect of inducing you to be more particular in keeping your system in order, and conquering your antipathy to medicine."

But soon it was time for an exultant letter. On August 2, 1847, Macdonald was able to write to his mother from New York that Isabella had gone into labour and a specialist, a Dr. Rodgers, had come to administer "the *Lethean* or somnific gas," although able to risk only a small dose because of her weakness. "She suffered dreadfully all night and about 8 this morning was so weak that the Doctors determined to use the forceps, as she was quite unable to deliver herself. They succeeded to a miracle, and I am delighted to tell you that she was delivered of a healthy & strong boy." The child instantly dominated their lives. Macdonald reported triumphantly to Margaret Greene that "his eyes are dark blue, *very large & nose* to match. When born his length was 1 foot 9 inches & very strong and healthy, though thin, but as Maria told Dr. Washington, that was not to be wondered at, seeing he had been living on pills for so long." Isabella, at the end of her "head-long" letter to Margaret Greene, for once found the words to express what she truly wanted to say: "My very soul is bound up in him. God pardon me if I sin in this. But did I not purchase him dearly?" They named their baby son John Alexander.

By September, Macdonald was back in Canada—and back in politics. "Our poor Isabella was a good deal agitated at my leaving her," he tells Margaret Greene in a letter written from Montreal. "The *Boy* is flourishing like a *Green bay Horse* so writes Margaret [his own sister Margaret, who'd gone down to New York], and that he is becoming strong & fat." Isabella remained in New York that winter, cared for by her sister Maria, while Macdonald's sister Margaret returned to Kingston to look after their mother. Macdonald himself was now alone, in Montreal, where the government had moved. He told Margaret Greene, "I feel quite solitary & miserable living in lodgings alone. I would spend a pleasant winter if Isabella were only here."

In the late spring of 1848, Isabella came back from New York to join Macdonald in Kingston. They moved to Bellevue, an airy Tuscan-style villa with large, well-landscaped grounds. Its usual nickname was the Pekoe Pagoda, but Macdonald called it the Eyetalian Willar. (It is now a National Historic Site of Canada.) A

particular attraction of the house for
Isabella was its distance from the
noise of the town, which always
upset her. A far greater attraction,
of course, as Macdonald wrote to
Margaret Greene, was "the society
of her boy. At first he was shy and
uncomfortable in her room, which is
to some degree darkened and as she
could not handle him, or toss him
about, which the young gentleman
insists upon from all who approach
him." But "he is now however great

*A miniature of an oil portrait of Isabella by
William Sawyer, dated 1852.*

friends with her, and sits most contentedly in the bed with her,
surrounded by his toys which he throws about, much to her
inconvenience I am sure, tho' she will allow it."

If the spirit was now willing, the flesh was soon assailed
again. On August 1, 1848, Macdonald informed Margaret that
Isabella was consistently coughing. "On her route & after her
arrival [home], there were occasional appearances of blood from
her lungs. . . . [Dr. Hayward] discerns no symptoms of ulceration
or permanent affection—but I fear, I fear." A few days later, he
confirmed the alarming new symptom. "The chief cause of
uneasiness is the occasional appearance of blood in her handker-
chief when she coughs." A fortnight later, Dr. Hayward told him
that "the cough & the blood of course indicate something wrong,
some cause of irritation. And yet she has none of the evidence on
which a medical man could state there was any ulceration." Still,
the baby John Alexander was there to lift her spirits: "He sits by
the hour now with his Mother as contentedly as possible, and
smiles & crows away from one end of day to the other."

Three weeks later, a nurse went to check on John Alexander in his room next door to Isabella's on the ground floor. He was still and cold in his cot. "Convulsions" was the explanation given; it may have been sudden infant death syndrome. He was buried in the Garrison Burial Ground near the grave of the grandfather he'd never seen, Hugh Macdonald.

In those days, the death of young children was common. This infant, though, had been brought into the world amid excruciating pain, and during his brief life he had given to his mother and father a joy they had never dared imagine they might possess. He was never forgotten.

In 1865, the remains of the infant John A., as well as those of Hugh Macdonald, originally interred in the old Garrison Burial Ground that was by now in a state of disrepair, were removed to the new Cataraqui Cemetery (of which Macdonald was a founding subscriber) and there placed in the family's burial plot. Many years later, Macdonald's second wife, Agnes, came upon a small dusty box while cleaning the attic of Earnscliffe, their house in Ottawa. Inside it were some odd wooden objects. When she showed them to her husband, Macdonald explained they were John Alexander's toys; through all the many moves he had made from city to city and from house to lodging house to bachelor quarters and back again to a house, Macdonald had kept with him these relics of his lost son.

Thereafter, Macdonald's marriage became "a grey, unrelieved tragedy," in the fine phrase of his principal biographer, Donald Creighton. From then on, and until his life was over, he applied all his passion to politics.

SEVEN

New Guys with New Ideas

The British people of the North American Colonies are a people on whom we may safely rely, and to whom we must not grudge power.
Lord Durham, in his report of 1839

By luck, Macdonald began his political career in 1844, at the best possible time for a newcomer to arrive at least in the wings of the political stage. Shortly before he got there, the Canadian political system had been decisively shaken up and had set off in an entirely new direction. Shortly afterwards, the system was galvanized by the introduction into it of a new, almost revolutionary, idea in governance. The decisive change was caused by a new constitution that joined the two previously separate colonies of Upper and Lower Canada (today, Ontario and Quebec) into the United Province of Canada; for the first time, the country's two European peoples, French and English, were brought into direct political contact. The almost revolutionary idea was that of Responsible Government: it called for the colony's government to be responsible to the elected legislature, not, as before, to the governor general. Under the old system, the governor general exercised unchallengable authority as the personal representative of the monarch; he selected and appointed all the ministers, who then functioned as his ministers rather than as those of the legislature and the voters. Transferring responsibility to elected ministers who commanded a majority in the legislature effectively ceded to the colony full self-government in domestic affairs. Only Confederation, still two decades away, would change the country as radically as these two measures.

For the politicians, whether Macdonald or anyone else, the effect was like that of a comprehensive spring cleaning. As Creighton observed in *The Young Politician*, almost all the leading political figures of the era before Responsible Government "failed, with astonishing uniformity, to survive very long in the new political atmosphere." Macdonald thus joined the system at the very moment when it was time for new guys with new ideas. Except that Macdonald did not—yet—have any new ideas. He survived, nevertheless, because he was street-smart and a quick learner. Still, he contributed nothing to the transformational changes themselves, and it took him time to figure out how to take advantage of the extra space at the top that had just been opened up for someone like him.

Macdonald also had to cope with practical constraints. During his first term, from 1844 to 1848, he was a backbencher, literally as well as figuratively, because he chose to sit in the very back row. His appearances on the actual stage itself were in the junior cabinet posts of receiver general and commissioner of Crown lands, in each instance briefly. During his second term, from 1848 to 1852, he sat in opposition, because the Conservative government had lost to the Reform Party. Mostly what he did during this time was to listen and learn, to make useful contacts and to acquire insider know-how, all of which would be highly useful, whether he chose to give politics up for the law or try clambering up the ladder.

As an even more practical constraint, Macdonald was having problems with his law practice. Campbell complained, justifiably, that he was being underpaid, particularly because Macdonald was often absent on political business. In 1846 they rewrote their original agreement, this time dividing the general profits equally between them, giving Campbell a third of the Commercial Bank business and allowing him a lump payment of £250 a year to compensate for Macdonald's absences. This arrangement tightened Macdonald's finances at the very time he had to look after a permanently invalided wife as well as his mother, who kept suffering strokes even while recovering from the latest, and provide for the financial needs of his unmarried sisters, Margaret and Louisa.

Before we carry on with the chronicle of Macdonald's career, it's necessary—anyway, it ought to be useful—to describe the new political environment within which Macdonald now found himself operating.

Here, all readers to whom this mid-nineteenth-century period of Canadian politics is a well-annotated book should jump ahead to the next chapter. However, their ranks may be relatively thin. A great many Canadians have come to assume that their country began on July 1, 1867, not least because we celebrate each year that anniversary of Confederation. But Confederation wasn't the starting point of all that we now have and are. It developed from its own past, and that past, even if now far distant from us, still materially affects our present and our future.

The most explicit description of the continuity of Canadian politics across the centuries is made by historian Gordon Stewart in his book *The Origins of Canadian Politics*. There he writes, "The key to understanding the main features of Canadian national political culture after 1867 lies in the political world of Upper and Lower Canada between the 1790s and the 1860s."* His argument, one shared fully by this author, is that all Canadian politics, even those in our own postmodern, high-tech, twenty-first-century present, have been influenced substantively by events and attitudes in the horse-and-buggy Canada of our dim past.

One key example would be the role of political patronage in Canadian politics. Except on rare occasions, our two mainstream parties have either no ideology at all or only fragments of it. Their distinguishing difference is not in their titles, Liberal and Conservative, but in the fact that, at any one time, one party is in and the other is out. Without patronage, it would be just about impossible for either organization to function as a national party. Other motives, of course, attract individuals to join one or other of the mainstream parties, which alternate, rather irregularly, in office: idealism, the attraction of public service and, no less, the adrenaline high that is generated by the fierce competitiveness of the political game. But the prospect of good, high-status jobs matters as critically—in effect, no patronage, no national political parties. (Regional parties have in their very regionalism a substitute for ideology, as do the rarer ideology-driven parties like the New Democrats and the Greens.) Two international comparisons may confirm the point: in Britain, from which we originally copied a great deal, there is relatively little patronage but a considerable difference in ideology between Labour and Conservative; in the United States, always our principal comparison, there is about as much patronage as there is north of the border, but Democrats and Republicans differ in their ideology or, perhaps more particularly these days, in their cultural

---

* Stewart, an expatriate Scot, teaches at Michigan State University.

assumptions. Patronage really is as Canadian as maple syrup.

Another example, this one unique to Canada, is the effect on our political system of the ongoing alliance of convenience between the French and the English, or now, more accurately, of francophones and English-speaking Canadians. No less so before Confederation than after it, whichever party has been able to forge a partnership with francophone Quebecers has almost automatically become the government and remained in power for a long time. Few of Macdonald's political insights were as perceptive as his recognition early on that a sta-

Lord Durham, known as "Radical Jack." He found "two nations warring in the bosom of a single state" and set out to assimilate the second one—les Canadiens.

ble national government would be impossible without abundant amounts of patronage and a close, mutually self-interested apportionment of the spoils (including that generated by government spending) between the French and the English.

Now to go back to our future, this of course being also Macdonald's present.

~

The catalyst of fundamental change in pre-Confederation politics were the rebellions in 1837–38 by the Patriotes in Lower Canada led by Louis-Joseph Papineau, which was a serious uprising, and by the rebels in Upper Canada led by William Lyon Mackenzie, which was more of a tragicomedy. Both uprisings provided a warning to London that, as had gone the American colonies a half-century earlier, so the colonies of British North America might also go. To deal with the crisis, the Imperial government sent out one of its best and brightest.

John George Lambton, Earl of Durham, arrived accompanied by an orchestra, several race horses, a full complement of silver and a cluster of brainy aides, one of whom had achieved celebrity status by running off with a teenage heiress and serving time briefly in jail. Still in his early forties, "Radical Jack" was cerebral, cold, acerbic and arrogant. After just five months in the colony, he left in a rage after a decision of his—to exile many of the Patriotes to Bermuda without the bother of a trial—was countermanded by the Colonial Office. Back home, he completed, in 1839, a report that was perhaps the single most important public document in all Canadian history.* Lord Durham himself died of tuberculosis a year later.

Parts of Durham's report were brilliant; parts were brutal. The effects of each were identical: they both had an extraordinarily creative effect on Canada and Canadians. The brutal parts of Durham's diagnosis are, as almost always happens, much the better known. He had found here, he declared, "two nations warring in the bosom of a single state . . . a struggle, not of principles, but of races."† The French Canadians, *les Canadiens*, had to lose—for

---

* The only serious competitor for the title of "most important" would be the Rowell-Sirois Report of 1940, from the commission established originally to equip the federal government with the tools to cure the Great Depression of the previous decade. When this mission was fulfilled anyway by the economic boom generated by the Second World War, the commission's report was used to justify transferring jurisdictional responsibilities and revenues to the federal government in order to transform Canada into a welfare state.

† Durham's use of the word "race" will strike contemporary ears as odd. It was used then to describe people now usually referred to as "ethnic groups."

their own sake. They were "a people destitute of all that could constitute a nationality . . . brood[ing] in sullen silence over the memory of their fallen countrymen, of their burnt villages, of their ruined property, of their extinguished ascendancy."

In fact, Durham was almost as harsh about the English in Canada. They were "hardly better off than the French for the means of education for their children." They were almost as indolent: "On the American side, all is activity and hustle. . . . On the British side of the line, except for a few favoured spots, all seems waste and desolate." He dismissed the powerful Family Compact as "these wretches." Still, he took it for granted that Anglo-Saxons would dominate the French majority in their own Lower Canada. "The entire wholesale and a large portion of the retail trade of the Province, with the most profitable and flourishing farms, are now in the hands of this dominant minority." All French Canadians could do was "look upon their rivals with alarm, with jealousy, and finally with hatred."

The only way to end this perpetual clash between the "races," Durham concluded, was for there to be just one race in Canada. The two separate, ethnically defined provinces of Upper Canada and Lower Canada should be combined into the United Province of Canada. As immigrants poured in from the British Isles, the French would inevitably become a minority. To quicken the pace of assimilation, the use of French should cease in the new, single legislature and government. To minimize the political weight of Lower Canada's 650,000 people, compared with Upper Canada's 450,000, each former province, now reduced to a "section," should have an equal number of members in the new legislature.*

---

* Officially, Upper Canada now became Canada West, and Lower Canada became Canada East. In fact, almost everyone continued to refer to the new sections by

Montreal. Place d'Armes, with a view of Notre Dame church, c. 1843. It was Canada's only real city, the first to install such technology as gas lights and the horse-drawn omnibus.

Durham's formula worked—but backwards. Quebec's commitment to *la survivance* dates less from Wolfe's victory over Montcalm (after which the Canadiens' religion and system of law were protected by British decree) than from 1839, when Durham told French Canadians they were finished. The consequence of this collective death sentence was an incredible flowering of a national will to remain alive.*

In the years immediately following 1839, a sociological miracle occurred in Lower Canada: a lost people found themselves.

---

their old titles, and for simplicity's sake this older terminology to describe today's Ontario and Quebec is used throughout this text. (In fact, the legislature relegalized the use of the old Upper and Lower Canada terms in 1849.)

* A parallel exists with the publication in 1965 of George Grant's *Lament for a Nation*, predicting Canada's inevitable absorption by America. In response, English-Canadian nationalists suddenly stood on guard for their country.

Historian François-Xavier Garneau, the poet Octave Crémazie, and Antoine Gérin-Lajoie, author of the patriotic lament *Un Canadien Errant*, created the beginnings of a national literature. Étienne Parent, a brilliant journalist, wrote a long series of articles calling for sweeping social, educational and religious reforms. The *Instituts canadiens* were founded as a means of generating intellectual inquiry and speculation and as a form of adult education. Montreal's Bishop Ignace Bourget, an ultramontane,* or right-wing Catholic, attracted major orders of priests—the Jesuits and the Oblates—and four orders of nuns to staff the new *collèges classiques*, from which a new and educated middle class would soon graduate. In 1840 there was just one priest for every two thousand parishioners; by 1880 there was one for every five hundred. As historian Susan Mann Trofimenkoff wrote in *The Dream of Nation*, "the clergy was as much a means of national unity as the railroad." The culmination of this new surge in national self-assertiveness, the Société St-Jean-Baptiste, was established in 1843.

Few in Upper Canada noticed. Their attention was focused on the other part of Durham's report, one calling for a totally different kind of Parliament. It was to be a responsible Parliament, with a cabinet composed of members of the majority party rather than chosen at the pleasure of the governor general. In a phrase of almost breathtaking boldness, Durham wrote, "The British people of the North American Colonies are a people on whom we may safely rely, and to whom we must not grudge power."

Durham almost went right to the constitutional finish line. He recognized the advantages of Confederation: "Such a union

---

* The term *ultramontanism* meant "over the mountains" to Rome. The movement began as a reaction, led by Pope Pius IX, to the ascendant liberalism sweeping across Europe; it was defensive but also reformist.

would . . . enable all the Provinces to cooperate for all common purposes," he said. "If we wish to prevent the extension of this [American] influence, it can only be done by raising up for the North American colonist some nationality of his own." At the last instant, Durham drew back from specifically recommending Confederation because he doubted that Canada possessed politicians of the calibre needed for so ambitious an undertaking.

At the time, Durham's report attracted little applause either in Canada or in Britain. A century passed before it came to be recognized by some as "the greatest state document in British imperial history." His recommendation for Responsible Government began a fundamental reordering of the Empire, and it set the political maturation of the British North American colonies in motion. Had that precedent—and its logical successor of Confederation—been applied to Ireland, as William Gladstone attempted in his Home Rule Bill in 1886, thousands of lives could have been saved.

Embedded in the proposal for Responsible Government was a fundamental illogicality. The colonial secretary, Lord John Russell, spotted it immediately: it would be "impossible," he wrote his cabinet colleagues, "for a Governor to be responsible to his Sovereign and a local legislature both at the same time." To stop Responsible Government, the British government sent out another of its best and brightest, Lord Sydenham, then in the cabinet as president of the Board of Trade. Still in his thirties, multilingual, highly professional and confident to the point of cockiness, Sydenham was one of the ablest of governors general— and one of the most dashing. Described as "worship[ping] equally at the Shrine of Venus and at the Shrine of Bacchus," he died following a fall from his horse after a visit to his mistress. He was also one of the more corrupt. The election of 1841, which he ran single-handedly, has few equals in Canadian history for chicanery, gerrymandering, vote-rigging, bribery and the systematic use of violence. Sydenham's candidates won handily.

To implement the part of Durham's program that the British government found wholly acceptable—the assimilation of the French—Sydenham moved the seat of government to Kingston, its attraction being that it was entirely English-speaking. All the legislative documents were unilingual; and the Throne Speech, read by Sydenham himself, was in English only.* Following his death later that year, his successor, Sir Charles Bagot, quickly recognized that Britain had positioned itself on the wrong side of history. "Whether the doctrine of responsible government is openly acknowledged or only tacitly acquiesced in, virtually it exists," Bagot wrote home in 1842.

In fact, Britain ceded Responsible Government with remarkable readiness. The quite separate colony of Nova Scotia actually gained it two months ahead of Canada, in 1848. But it had been allowed effectively in 1846, when Britain adopted free trade and abolished its protectionist Corn Laws and Navigation Laws. Thereafter, Canada and several other colonies were free to make their own trading arrangements, thereby exercising de facto self-government.

The fight for Responsible Government mattered, though. It entered Canadian political mythology as a sort of non-violent version of the Boston Tea Party. And the struggle brought together one of the most important and appealing of all Canadian

---

* The initiation of the new legislature of the United Province of Canada was accomplished through the swearing in of Sydenham as governor general in Montreal on February 10, 1841. Proclamations in both languages were posted on the main streets, but they were all ripped down overnight.

Robert Baldwin. He won Responsible Government, or self-government, for the colony of Canada. High-minded and single-minded, he was known as the "Man of the One Idea."

political partnerships, one that would provide Macdonald with a template of the way to fashion and sustain a political alliance between the country's two principal European races.

⌐

One of these partners was Robert Baldwin. The son of a successful lawyer, William Baldwin, who had originated the idea of Responsible Government, Robert came from the same social circles as the Family Compact. He was highly intelligent and of irreproachable integrity. Robert took over the cause from his father and, in January 1836, sent a letter to the Colonial Office. In it, he made a case for Responsible Government on the politically shrewd grounds that it was essential for "continuing the connection" with Britain. Durham's advocacy of the idea can be dated to this letter.

The other partner in the emerging alliance was Louis-Hippolyte LaFontaine. He was the prototype of the commanding *le chef* figure whom Quebecers have so often followed. Grave in manner and exuding gravitas, LaFontaine was blessed with a resemblance to Napoleon that he assiduously fostered. As a one-time Patriote, he had nationalist credentials that were unimpeachable.

Soon after the formal creation of the United Province of Canada, LaFontaine spotted an opening for himself and for his Canadiens. Skilfully used, the new configuration could lead not merely to *la survivance* in defiance of Durham's assimilation program but to substantive economic benefits for his people. He saw that an alliance between his bloc of French members and the Reform group led by Baldwin would form a majority in the legislature. Baldwin would get the Responsible Government he so desired (even if it was of small interest to LaFontaine, who, by inclination, was a conservative). In exchange, LaFontaine would get the keys to the patronage treasure chests that Responsible Government would transfer from the governor general to the Canadian politicians in

Louis-Hippolyte LaFontaine. With Baldwin, he forged a French-English political alliance that turned Durham's policy upside-down.

power. Though a partnership of convenience, the alliance was also one of principle and of personal trust. In the election of 1841, with LaFontaine badly in need of a winnable seat, Baldwin found one for him among the burghers of the riding of Fourth York in Upper Canada. A year later, LaFontaine returned the compliment by handing to Baldwin the equally unilingual riding of Rimouski. (And at the personal level, Baldwin sent all four of his children to French schools in Quebec City.)

To move the Imperial government over to the "right" side of history took a new governor general, Lord Elgin. Exceptionally able, he was Durham's son-in-law and, later, viceroy of India— the top position on the Imperial ladder.* The key year was 1848, when an election returned a majority for Baldwin and

---

* Lord Elgin was the son of the British ambassador in Athens who spirited away the Elgin Marbles to the British Museum.

Governor General Lord Elgin, with his wife, Mary Louisa, her sister and an aide. Unusually able and far-sighted, he ended Durham's assimilationist policy by reading the Throne Speech in English and then, for the first time ever, repeating it in French.

LaFontaine. Acting on the principle of the sovereignty of the people, Elgin accepted the result and invited the pair to form the first biracial ministry. (Technically, LaFontaine, the leader of the largest bloc of members, was the premier. In practice, Baldwin functioned as co-premier, a system followed throughout the life of the United Province of Canada.) At the opening of that year's session of the Legislative Assembly, Elgin read the Throne Speech in English, as all his predecessors had done, and then, after a fractional pause, read it again in French. Canadien members burst into wild applause and song; one so forgot himself that he rushed up and kissed the governor general on both cheeks.

The main immediate beneficiaries of the change were the graduates now pouring out of Lower Canada's *collèges classiques.* Historian Jacques Monet has memorably described what happened in his essay "The Political Ideas of Baldwin and Lafontaine": "With a kind of bacterial thoroughness it [Quebec's emerging middle class] began to invade every vital organ of government and divide up among its members hundreds of posts." Monet went on to remark that Canadiens "came to realize that parliamentary democracy could be more than a lovely ideal: it was also a profitable fact."

Elgin accepted this downgrading, for himself and for his successors. In a dispatch to the colonial secretary he remarked that, henceforth, governors general would have to depend on "moral influence," adding, surely without really believing it, that this could "go far to compensate for the loss of power consequent on the surrender of patronage." Even Baldwin, himself skittish about patronage, declared stoutly in a legislature speech that "if appointments were not to be used for party purposes, let those who thought differently occupy the treasury benches."*

～

As always in government, some of the consequences of Responsible Government were unanticipated. The transfer of power from the governor general to elected politicians meant that Canadians hereafter placed blame for the mistakes that all governments make no longer at the entrance to their governor general's residence but at the doors of their cabinet ministers and premiers. Certainly, the tone of Canadian politics worsened from this time on. Sectarianism, or the injection into politics of the rivalries, suspicions and hatreds between religious groups, now became the dominant issue in Canadian politics. No less significant, once the premiers occupied the shoes of the governors general, they began to acquire some of the quasi-dictatorial habits of those who had run the country before the change to Responsible Government in 1848. Cabinet ministers now became the premiers' ministers, just as they had once been ministers of the

---

* In the nineteenth century, the customary term for patronage was the much more descriptive one of "jobbery." It had, in fact, an honorable intellectual parentage. Adam Smith, in his great *Wealth of Nations*, argued that the loss of the American colonies might have been prevented had only some of their leaders been offered "the great prizes which sometimes come from the wheel of the great state-lottery of British politics." Perhaps what the Founding Fathers were really after was less liberty than patronage.

Crown's representative. The ascent to an imperial prime ministership—best described by Donald Savoie in his *Governing from the Centre*—began very early in this country's history; it happened, moreover, far earlier here than in the United States, occurring there largely because the United States acquired immense foreign responsibilities—always quasi-imperial in their nature—which was not at all the case here. An imperial prime minister is another political attribute that is as Canadian as maple syrup.

These were epochal changes to Canada's political makeup. Yet Macdonald's contribution to them was almost non-existent. He made a few somewhat critical but carefully noncommittal comments about Responsible Government as a potential threat to the connection with Britain. For the most part, though, he simply listened and learned. It wasn't long, now, before the era of Responsible Government would be replaced by the era of government by Macdonald.

EIGHT

A Short Time before the Long Game

My plan thro' life is never to give up; if I don't
carry a thing this year, I will next.
John A. Macdonald

Macdonald's appointment by Conservative premier William Draper to the junior cabinet post of receiver general on May 22, 1847—roughly equivalent to being minister of revenue today—constituted a respectably rapid promotion. By then he'd been in the legislature for just three years and was only thirty-two years old. The Toronto *Globe*, the champion of the Reformers, dismissively advised its readers that he was "a harmless man" who, during two sessions of the legislature, had "barely opened his mouth." The *Montreal Transcript* was more positive, describing Macdonald as "a rising man." Nevertheless, there was more to the *Globe*'s judgment than partisanship.

Macdonald's public record was certainly thin. In each legislature session he'd seldom delivered more than one speech, and his contributions had almost all been on secondary issues. He still seemed undecided whether to make politics or the law his primary career. Indeed, Macdonald had been offered his first cabinet position—as solicitor general—as early as the winter of 1846–47 but turned it down because "it would make me too dependent on Govt and I like to steer my own course." During his ten months in the two junior portfolios that he did accept (the second being the somewhat more substantial one of commissioner of Crown lands), he made no great impression. Late in 1847, Macdonald introduced a bill to amend the charter of King's College in Toronto in a manner that would square the interests of the founding Anglicans with those of other religions, notably Catholics, then excluded from the college. His attempt at conciliation failed, and he had to withdraw the bill.

A sharper observer would, nevertheless, have marked Macdonald as a legislator with potential. From the start, he was a popular member of the cosy club that all parliaments become. He sat through the interminable debates, cheering on fellow Conservatives and heckling opposition members—principally the loose group of Reformers—with teasing quips. He spent many hours studying in the library. He schmoozed and chaffed and drank with the best of them, and for as long as any of them. And while he seldom spoke, his speaking style was fresh and effective. Rather than the hours-long orations then the convention, Macdonald's speeches were short (seldom more than thirty minutes in duration) and conversational in tone, as though he were talking to each member across a dinner table.

As a politician, Macdonald suffered from one serious defect, especially in those days when oratory mattered and there were no microphones to add body and timbre to a speaker's voice. Even his highly laudatory biographer Joseph Pope admitted that Macdonald "could not be called a great speaker" and that his voice, "while pleasant, was not strong, nor remarkably distinct." Journalists covering the debates complained constantly that his low voice and manner of delivery—"careless utterance, irregular inflections of voice and general disregard for acoustic effect," in the phrase of one—caused them to miss parts of his speeches. The leading journalist Hector Fabre (later a senator and diplomat) noted that "he is languid at times at stating his case and rather gropes through his opening sentences."

Macdonald rarely prepared his speeches in advance but felt his way along, testing out arguments and lines that might get through to his audiences, and chopping and changing them until he was hitting the mark. Pope, with a tone of amused resignation, recalled that Macdonald often wrote down the topic headings for his speech on the back of an envelope, which he then "not infrequently contrived to mislay." As a consequence, despite some disorganization, he kept that vital ingredient of spontaneity. There may have been defects in his speeches in conventional terms, but Macdonald consistently held his audiences. Even in his earliest years he pulled members into the House because he put on such a good show. Fabre remarked on the "matchless tact" with which Macdonald crossed swords with opponents, scoring points but never drawing blood, because, as he put it, Macdonald was "too clever and too well-versed in the knowledge of mankind to be cruel: his executions are always amusing; they extort a smile even from the gloomiest victims." Above all, his listeners knew that at one point or other Macdonald would make them laugh—and that often he would make them laugh at themselves.

Macdonald possessed another invaluable asset that made him difficult to outpoint in extemporaneous debates: he had an exceptional memory. He possessed, as many successful politicians do, an uncanny ability to remember names and faces. The examples are endless. J.P. Reeves, once a resident of Kingston, met Macdonald after an absence of more than twenty years when he was a member of a guard of honour in Belleville. "Hello, Reeves. Stand at ease," said Macdonald, after which they talked about old times. A Mr. Munroe, whom Macdonald had met once at a convention in Kingston in 1849, he remembered by his correct name when they met again thirty-three years later in St. Thomas. Either in jousts in the legislature or in contests with hecklers on the stump, Macdonald repeatedly gained an advantage by tossing out extracts from documents he had read long before, including statements once made by his opponent of the moment. The combination of his memory and his constant reading left him never short of quotations from British authors such as Trollope and Dickens. His journalist friend T.C. Patteson once got into a literary argument with colleagues and, to settle it, wrote a letter to Macdonald asking what line followed "Ye gentlemen of England who sit at home at ease." Back instantly came the answer, written on the reverse of Patteson's note, "Ah, little do you think upon the dangers of the seas."

Perhaps the most striking example of Macdonald's memory concerns a newspaper article that he scanned quickly in 1840 and then, forty years later, referred to while giving a speech in the Commons. In the speech, Macdonald recalled that "an Indian once said to myself, 'We are the wild animals; you cannot make an ox of a deer.'" He then used this example to support his argument that "you cannot make an agriculturalist of the Indian." The original article, written by an Anglican missionary to a Mohawk community at Napanee, near Kingston, described how an Indian chief had told him that God had made all kinds of different animals, from the wily fox to the industrious beaver, and also all kinds of different men. "Now you cannot teach the fox to live like the beaver, nor can you make the Indian work and live like the white man," reasoned the chief. "I have a farm and could live by it, but when the season comes for game or fish . . . I am tempted to go and look for it, even to the neglect of sowing and gathering my crops." With such a memory bank to draw on, Macdonald was not an easy opponent to outwit.

Behind the scenes, Macdonald's aptitudes and talents were beginning to get recognized. William Draper, an able man but lacking in the political skills needed to be a successful premier, began to regard him as a protégé. In March 1847 he summoned Macdonald to Montreal to help him brief the new governor general, Lord Elgin—in particular to make sure that Elgin understood the party sufficiently well not to "mistake ultra Toryism for Conservatism (i.e., selfishness for patriotism)." Elgin later described Macdonald in a dispatch home as "a person of consideration," although, for reasons not entirely clear, relations between the two men were never cordial.

Yet Macdonald remained an on-again, off-again politician. He had ample personal reasons for his ambivalence. Home was now either a silent house in which the prostrate Isabella waited for him to return to inject life and energy into it, sometimes silently turning accusatory eyes towards him when he arrived late, or, ever more often, the bleak anonymity of a boarding house in whichever city—Montreal, Toronto, Quebec—the legislature had rotated to. He had to worry about his mother, who, as she suffered a succession of twelve strokes, was looked after by his sister Louisa. "Poor Mama

Helen Macdonald in the 1860s. Hardy and strong, she survived eleven of twelve strokes. Her preferred language was Gaelic.

has again been attacked with another apoplectic affliction, and only the most prompt and vigorous measures have restored her," he wrote to Margaret Greene on September 18, 1847. In that same letter he spelled out the range of his personal problems: "Isabella is struggling for strength enough to join me in Canada this winter. I doubt much whether she will be able to muster vigour enough to do so, and I fear that neither Margaret nor Louisa will be able to go to New York to look after matters." Isabella did come back the following spring; that summer their infant son, John Alexander, died in his crib.

All that was left to Isabella now was Macdonald himself. Yet the demands of his cabinet portfolio and, at the same time, of ever-mounting difficulties at his law practice kept pulling him away from her. The more he moved away, the more frantically she tried to hold on to him. "She is just putting the finishing stitch to a new waistcoat for me, which I am to sport as a winter vest." Late in 1848, Macdonald wrote to Margaret Greene to report: "I returned last week from Toronto, my dearest sister, where I had been for the fortnight previous, attending the sittings of the Court of Queen's Bench," to find that Isabella "had been practising sitting up for a few minutes daily in my absence in order to be able to surprise me by coming to dinner which she effected. We had our little table brought to her bed room, and there we dined in State." He would leave the house at nine each morning, returning around six, and he admitted that "her time passes very monotonously out here."

Isabella did have some duties to occupy herself. "She had as much to do as she is able for, in directing the household affairs, managing her servants etc., and I can assure you, such is her attention and method that confined to the room though she may be, she makes a capital housekeeper," he told Margaret Greene. Everything was kept neat and tidy, and "*my* dinner, the great event of each day, about which poor Isa takes the greatest pains, is served up as well as one could wish." Even when confined to bed day after day, as was increasingly the case, she still struggled to keep connected to him—just. "She is like the 'Invisible Lady' that used to exhibit, not 'show' herself some years ago," he told Margaret Greene. "The invisible Lady's voice orders & behests are heard and obeyed all over the house & are carried out as to cupboards which she never sees & pots & pans that have no acquaintance with her. Not a glass is broken or set of dishes diminished, but she knows of, and calls the criminal to account for."

Politics, though, kept demanding his attention. He had to go to Montreal, "but not for long," and yet, "the idea of my going distresses her so much that I would not go, were it not a matter of necessity."

In a letter Macdonald sent to Margaret Greene in January 1850, he sounds like someone feeling himself pulled apart by horses charging in different directions. "Since September last I have been alone and without a [law] partner," he wrote. "Isa says I work too hard, & in truth I begin to feel that I do, but like a thief on the treadmill, I *must* step on, or be dragged."

Macdonald's reference to his being without a partner derived from his difficulties with Alexander Campbell. Macdonald's constant absences, and the fact that he sometimes dipped into the firm's funds to cover his political expenses, had made Campbell

Alexander Campbell, Macdonald's first law partner, later his political Mr. Fix-It and then a cabinet minister. No one worked more closely with Macdonald for a longer period, but they were never real friends.

more and more dissatisfied with their partnership arrangement. Their bank account was overdrawn, and the firm was eighteen hundred pounds in debt. Campbell wrote him crossly, "Your absence from home and your necessities have been I think the *main* although not by any means the only cause of the annoyances that have arisen." In reply, Macdonald assured him, "I think I have hit on the *only* mode by which we can prevent inextricable confusion." He offered a new arrangement of a fifty-fifty split of all revenues, including those from the Commercial Bank, and the assurance that, "when in Kingston, Macdonald to attend to business." Campbell initially accepted the arrangement. He wrote reassuringly to Macdonald that he was "anxious that your political career should not be cut short at this point." Later, Campbell changed his mind. Their partnership was dissolved in September 1849, with Macdonald buying back Campbell's share for £1,250. Macdonald engaged other partners, but never again one as competent as Campbell. Yet despite their business breakup, Macdonald and Campbell maintained their close political partnership.

In the meantime, Macdonald found himself increasingly pinched for money. "I am more than usually *tight* now," he wrote to a friend, reminding him of a debt of "five pounds for books, besides some interest." In a later letter to another friend he used the expressive phrase "I haven't got a shilling to jingle on a tombstone."

Given all the costs Macdonald was covering—Isabella and her servants, his mother, his unmarried sisters, his own expenses—it was no surprise that he should be financially strapped. But he ought not to have been as short of revenues as he in fact was. As a member of the legislature, he'd made useful new business contacts in addition to the networks he'd already developed in Kingston and Montreal, and extended across the Atlantic to

England. His political responsibilities were a major distraction, but the root cause of his money problems was that he simply wasn't a very good businessman. A friend and fellow Conservative, the Hamilton businessman Isaac Buchanan, once wrote in affectionate censoriousness, "I would not have supposed it possible that a man of so much intellect and general versatility could on this one matter [finance] be such a child." No doubt he was exasperated as well as amused by Macdonald's overconfidence in his financial capabilities, as when he wrote to Buchanan, who was himself highly successful, "I thoroughly understand that business and can invest without chance or risk of loss." In truth, Macdonald never applied himself consistently to the task. There was something of his father in him: he was much the smarter and the more purposeful, but in financial matters he too was dreamy and, in the end, not at all as interested in making money as in spending it.

By this time, Macdonald had undergone one other major change in his circumstances. In the election held early in 1848, he won easily in Kingston, but the Conservatives were voted out of office and lost half their members.[*] A new Reform government took office, run jointly by Baldwin and LaFontaine. Macdonald and his colleagues were beached on the Opposition benches.

<hr/>

For a time, there was a real possibility that Macdonald would never get back to the government side of the chamber, or even to the chamber itself. In August 1849 the Kingston *Chronicle* ran a story

<hr/>

[*] Macdonald's patron, Draper, had managed to avoid the firing line ahead of this debacle by getting himself appointed to the bench.

that he had made up his mind to resign, and it went on to speculate about possible successors. Two days later the anonymous author of a letter to the newspaper called on fellow Conservatives to persuade Macdonald to stay. Throughout his long career, Macdonald regularly mused out loud about resigning, and sometimes specifically threatened to do so. Most times he did this to discipline his supporters or to vent his own frustrations. On this occasion, he may well have meant it. Campbell, in a letter written to him several years later, referred to these times: "You will remember that throughout your long and apparently hopeless opposition [1848 to 1854] I always deprecated your retiring from parliament, as you often threatened to do." A threat made to someone as close to him as Campbell was almost certainly a serious one; it's entirely possible that Campbell leaked the information to the *Chronicle* to head him off—as it turned out, successfully.

Macdonald's political letters during this period provide indirect evidence that he was serious about quitting. Almost always, they brim with mischievousness, energy and guile, such as when he recommends arguments that candidates could use on the stump and then dismisses his own concoctions as "bunkum arguments." But most of the political observations he made to correspondents through the late forties and early fifties are bland and routine. Their tone was that of someone disengaged from what he was doing.

In the end, despite the vacillations, Macdonald decided to remain a full-time politician. Somehow, along with his work, he would juggle both his family responsibilities and his financial obligations. He described his political strategy as playing "the long game." He was resilient, tenacious, indefatigable. As he said in one speech, "If I don't carry a thing this year, I will next." His favourite phrase for minimizing setbacks and miscalculations was the old saying "There's no use crying over spilt milk."

So he continued to play the long game. Macdonald remained an active local member, lobbying for legislation to benefit hometown institutions such as Queen's University, Regiopolis College and the Kingston Hospital. His reward was a repeat victory in the 1851 election, his third in a row, not only for himself but this time also for three other Conservative candidates in the surrounding Midland District. He had earned, now, not just a local but a regional base. That the Reformers continued their hold on power, and the Conservatives did poorly elsewhere, only increased his stature.

~

At this same time, he began gathering around him one of the most useful of all political assets—a stable of close friends who would be reliable, long-term allies. Campbell functioned as Macdonald's local campaign manager and as a general "fixer" throughout Upper Canada, recruiting candidates, handling election funds, distributing patronage to pro-Conservative newspapers. Another member of Macdonald's Kingston mafia was Henry Smith, a fellow lawyer who had helped him found Kingston's Cataraqui Club "for the discussion (under proper restrictions) of the various subjects which ought to interest society." They were so close that Macdonald asked Smith to intervene for him in an "affair of honour" arising from a nasty exchange in the House with an opposing member—an episode that could have led to a duel between them.

The most important member of the network that Macdonald was building systematically was a fellow Scot, John Rose. After earning a degree at the University of Edinburgh, he had immigrated to Montreal in 1836. There, Rose quickly became one of city's leading corporate lawyers; later he moved to London,

John Rose, a highly successful Montreal lawyer who became a substantial financial and social figure in London. He and Macdonald were exceptionally close, intellectually as well as personally.

England, where he became an insider in financial and political circles, serving on two royal commissions, and, as a friend of the Prince of Wales, a society leader. Although fascinated by the political game, Rose was only twice, briefly, an active politician in Canada, as a junior minister in 1857 and, for two years, as Macdonald's first post-Confederation finance minister. They respected each other's intelligence and enjoyed flouting convention; once, while young, they crossed the border and pretended to be strolling entertainers, Rose as a bear and Macdonald playing some instrument. Macdonald's secretary, Joseph Pope, reckoned that of all his intimates, "personally, he was most attracted to Rose."

Ogle Gowan was another important member of the network, though in a very different way: with him came votes. Gowan was the grand master of the Orange Lodge. In hindsight, those Orangemen are seen today as anti-Catholic and anti-French fanatics. Many were. Many, though, joined only for the business and social contacts the lodge provided. Gowan himself was a moderate. He forged an alliance with Irish Catholics in Upper Canada and lost his position when hard-liners decided he had "sold out to the Pope." It was only after Gowan's defeat as grand master that the organization took on its full anti-French colour. He and Macdonald became friends in the mid-1840s when they were working together to replace Family Compact Tories with moderate Conservatives, largely because the old Tories looked down on

Orangemen as not respectable. Nevertheless, Macdonald always held Gowan at a certain distance and never gave him the high-level government posts he sought. Their friendship ended in 1862 when Gowan was charged with the rape of a serving girl: although he was acquitted, his political career was ended. Macdonald's last contact with Gowan was to appoint him to the minor post of inspector of money orders in the post office.

Quite different was another Gowan, James Gowan, a cousin, who, when appointed to the bench in 1843, was the youngest judge in the British Empire. Sophisticated, intelligent and an outstanding judge, although refusing all promotions

Ogle Gowan. As grand master of the Orange Lodge—a moderate later pushed out by hardliners—he brought to Macdonald the greatest of all political assets: votes.

(during his long career on the bench only two of his judgments were overruled), Gowan exchanged letters with Macdonald over the decades on everything from politics to literature. Near the end of his life, Macdonald appointed Gowan to the Senate, where, although nominally a Conservative, he functioned as an independent.

Macdonald gave at least one strong signal that he still wasn't really committed to politics. At the close of the 1840s, Canadian politics were dominated by a crisis that touched directly on the subject that most commanded Macdonald's heart—Canada's connection to Britain. Yet he had almost nothing to say about this defining issue.

In the mid-1840s, the British prime minister, Robert Peel, adopted free trade. One objective was to reduce the cost of importing food, so as to help the starving Irish through the potato famine. The main reason was that Manchester free-traders such as Richard Cobden and John Bright had won the argument that Britain, as the world's leading economy, would gain by opening wide its doors to raw materials while exporting its cornucopia of manufactured goods.* No nation was more affected by the abandonment of Imperial Preference than Canada. Within a few years, all the protective tariffs that subsidized its exports to Britain—principally of lumber and flour—vanished. A few years later the Navigation Laws, which gave an advantage to colonial shipping, were repealed. Wheat exports dropped by more than 50 per cent, and flour exports by 40 per cent. Cheaper and better wood began to be shipped to Britain from the Baltic. In 1849 Governor General Elgin estimated that "property in most Canadians towns, and most especially in the capital [Montreal], has fallen 50 percent in value . . . three-fourths of the commercial men are bankrupt."

Across Canada there was widespread anger and a sense of abandonment. To magnify this discontent, the Imperial government had refused the demands of Tory Conservatives to disallow

---

* The most approving comment about Britain's adoption of free trade came from across the Atlantic, from Andrew Carnegie, the Scot expatriate now well on his way to fame and fortune in the United States. Trade didn't follow the flag, declared Carnegie; rather, "trade follows the lowest price current. If a dealer in any colony wished to buy Union Jacks he would order them from Britain's worst foe if he could save sixpence."

a Rebellion Losses Bill introduced by the co-premier, LaFontaine. The bill provided compensation for property damaged during the Rebellion of 1837–38, and many of the beneficiaries would be those Lower Canadians who had actually rebelled against the Crown. On April 25, 1849, riots instigated by local Conservatives broke out in Montreal. That night, the rioters (all of them English-speaking) broke into the Parliament Buildings and put them to the torch; the buildings were burned to the ground, and almost all the books and collections in the parliamentary library were destroyed.

In response, Montreal businessmen and financiers organized a petition condemning British policy. Eventually, the document carried more than one thousand signatures, among them two Redpaths, three Workmans, two Molsons, a future prime minister (John Joseph Abbott) and three future cabinet ministers of Canada. In October, a mass meeting in Montreal approved a manifesto calling for "a friendly and peaceful separation from the British connection and a union upon equitable terms with the great North American Confederacy of Sovereign States"—in other words, for annexation.

Macdonald kept almost completely silent about this direct challenge to the British connection, though he helped to organize a meeting in Kingston of a new British America League. After roundly rejecting annexation, the league argued instead for some form of reciprocity pact or cross-border free-trade deal with the United States to replace the lost British market. The Kingston meeting attracted few other leading politicians, excepting Macdonald, a home-towner. He did not make a speech or play any role in drafting the communiqué. By the time the league ceased to function, towards the end of 1850, Macdonald had already cut his association with it.

In fact, with the ending of a worldwide depression in 1850,

most of the lost prosperity quickly returned. Montreal business-men and financiers abandoned their temporary interest in protest and transferred their allegiance to the cause of reciprocity with the United States. Elgin exercised some brilliant diplomacy to arrange a pact between the two countries in 1854. The real political significance of what had happened was that during the turmoil Macdonald had scarcely stirred.

Two factors may have caused Macdonald to make up his mind sometime in the early 1850s that politics, and not the law, would be his life's work. The first was that, late in 1849, Isabella told him a second miracle was about to occur in their married life: although now forty years old, she was pregnant again. On December 9, 1849, Macdonald informed Margaret Greene, with mixed hope and fear, that "Isa views her coming trials with great fortitude & from her courage & patience I have every hope of a happy issue. Still she prepares for the worst." A month later, he reported that "all arrangements have long been made, and she now awaits for the issue with patience and fortitude. She has given me many directions about herself and her offspring, which any evil happen, & having done all that she can do, is now content." But Macdonald was not able to focus only on his wife and unborn child. A fortnight earlier, he told his

Hugh John as a baby, c. 1852. He was the only child of Macdonald and Isabella to survive. His mother was too ill to care for him, and he and Macdonald later became estranged. The artist is Sawyer.

sister-in-law in another letter that his mother, following yet another couple of attacks, was "perfectly resigned to her probable fate and sudden exit."

By early February 1850, Macdonald was writing that Isabella's "immediate confinement is much to be desired, this continuance of suffering wears down her strength." A few days later he reported again that "the struggle has exhausted her very much, but she has kept up her spirits." Finally, on March 13, 1850, Macdonald declared in triumph, "We have got Johnnie back again, almost his image." The baby was less "delicate" than the brother he would never meet, but "born fat & coarse." He was called Hugh John, names that connected him to both his father and his grandfather.

The second explanation for Macdonald's decision about his career was that, sometime early in the decade, he realized that he could get right to the top. He was, still, a relatively new guy, and he had at last begun to frame in his mind a genuinely new idea. As well, his mother, still watching over him despite her repeated strokes, had always told him that he was destined one day to be "more than an ordinary man."

NINE

Enlarging the Bounds

If a Lower Canada Britisher desires to conquer, he must "stoop to conquer." He must make friends with the French; without sacrificing the status of his race or lineage, he must respect their nationality.

John A. Macdonald

Almost without exception, almost every party that has formed the government in Canada has embodied two defining characteristics: it has been a centrist coalition, and it has been a French-English alliance. These ruling principles of Canadian politics were invented by Macdonald. In this sense, he can lay claim to a second "Father of" title—as the architect and builder of Canada's political Big Tent.

In February 1854, while still in opposition, Macdonald wrote a long letter to James McGill Strachan, a Toronto lawyer, alderman and Conservative supporter, in response to his criticism that their party was habitually ineffectual. Macdonald began by admitting that Strachan was quite correct, saying, "We are a good deal hampered with 'old blood.'" He reassured Strachan that the party's leader, Sir Allan MacNab, whom Macdonald always referred to with mixed exasperation and affection as "the Gallant Knight," will "not be in our way." MacNab, he continued, was "very reasonable and requires only that we should not in his 'sere and yellow leaf' offer him the indignity of casting him aside." In case the doubts he had expressed about his leader should ever get back to MacNab, Macdonald added that he himself "would never assent to" MacNab's being dumped, "for I cannot forget his services in days gone by."

The preliminaries done, Macdonald got down to the point he wanted to make to Strachan: the Conservative Party could be, and had to be, radically reorganized and re-energized. "My belief is there must be a material change in the character of the new House. I believe also there must be a change of Ministry after the election, and from my friendly relations with the French, I am inclined to believe my assistance would be sought." As for other changes after the election, "There would be a new House & new people to choose from, and our aim should be to enlarge the bounds of our party so as to embrace every person desirous of being counted as a 'progressive conservative.'"

In those few sentences, Macdonald sketched out a formula to create a different kind of Conservative Party—an entity quite unlike any other party then functioning in Canada. He was proposing that the Conservatives stretch themselves in two directions they had never gone before or had seldom ever thought about: first, to reach out to French members to try to form an alliance with a group among them.* And, simultaneously, to open themselves—"to embrace," as Macdonald put it—all voters who were prepared to be progressive about some issues, even while being conservative about others. There would be a cost to this dual expansion: certain ridings would have to be reserved for candidates who were not themselves Conservatives, and, by

---

* William Draper, Conservative leader and premier when Macdonald entered politics, made some attempts to reach out to Canadien members, but he lacked the skills to make it happen.

extension, some cabinet posts also. Patronage would likewise have to be divvied up to accommodate more than party members. Another complication, potentially even greater, was that quite a few Conservatives, above all those who were members of the Loyal Orange Lodge, were decidedly hostile to French Canadians. They would have to be persuaded that finding space among themselves for a bloc of Canadien members was a worthwhile price to pay to achieve power—principally on the grounds that this was the only way for the Conservatives to ever do so.

Macdonald had come to his Conservatism without having given it much thought, if any at all. Being a Conservative was of course a virtual precondition for getting elected in Loyalist Kingston. All his friends and business partners were Conservatives. They favoured what he favoured—loyalty to the Crown, hostility to the universal franchise, deep suspicion of anything American, a great respect for law and order and an abiding skepticism about change as a virtue in its own right. In the middle of the nineteenth century, little in this litany of attitudes and assumptions made the Conservative Party in the least unusual. The Reformers, now in government, were about as conservative in their views, and even more timid than the Conservative Party about spending money on nation-building projects such as railways and canals. The pro-clerical *bleus* in Lower Canada were more conservative still. The only exceptions were, in Upper Canada, the populist Grits and, in Lower Canada, the liberal *rouges*, who opposed the right-wing conservatism of Montreal's ultramontane Bishop Ignace Bourget.

In fact, this kind of taxonomy of parties and groupings in mid-nineteenth century Canada is far too neat and tidy. In the contemporary sense of the term, parties scarcely existed then. Many members, no matter on what label they gained election, performed thereafter as "loose fish," as the term went. They voted, this is to say, not with their party but as they judged best, in their own and their constituents' interest; nor were they penalized for their lack of discipline. Indeed, party discipline of the contemporary kind was widely condemned as "partyism"; the ideal, if seldom achieved, was that the legislature should function as a debating chamber somewhat like a Greek *agora* or a New England town hall. As a consequence, and as one of the most striking differences between politics then and now, premiers (or co-premiers, as a further complication) functioned roughly as leaders of a permanent minority government, always at risk of defeat and having forever to bargain with groups of members or with individuals for their temporary support. This challenge applied no less to the Reformers, who were more often in office, than to the Conservatives. Thus, after Baldwin and LaFontaine retired, a leading Reformer, Francis Hincks, became premier. An able man but forever dogged by scandal, Hincks led a fragile government that depended on the support of a small group of Canadiens led by a fellow Reformer, Augustin-Norbert Morin.

Just one party had about it some of the attributes of modernity (in an ideological sense rather than an organizational one): those intriguing newcomers to the Canadian political scene, the populist Grits. Early in 1850, a number of high-minded types gathered at the Toronto offices of a young lawyer turned journalist, William McDougall, to form an association of what one of them called "only men who are Clear Grit." The name stuck, and the new movement spread rapidly in Toronto and through the rich farmlands to the west and south. The old rebel, William Lyon Mackenzie, returned from exile to join it. In many ways, the Grits prefigured by more than a century the populist Reform Party of the 1980s and 1990s. They advocated direct democracy (including the election of many office holders), the secret ballot, fixed parliamentary terms and Representation by Population (although not the universal franchise). They produced a lively newspaper, the *North American*, edited by McDougall. The movement's most important qualities were energy and purposefulness. In the short term, its principal political effect was to split the non-Conservative vote in Upper Canada.

In many ways the political system was often downright amateurish, certainly by contemporary standards, if in some respects engagingly so, because nineteenth-century politicians often said what they meant rather than what they thought their party wanted them to say. And the "partyism" we now take for granted as the way parties should function is indeed thoroughly bureaucratic. But then it was all quite chaotic and intensely local, with petty and immediate issues repeatedly trumping national ones.

Macdonald now began to plot a way through this congenial chaos towards some political order. In no way was he seeking order for the sake of implementing particular policies, national or otherwise. He was seeking it for the sake of power, because he had come to realize, by some combination of instinct and experience, that the precondition for power, for gaining it and even more for holding it, was order and organization. Feeling his way along, and without any precedents to guide him (none existed in Britain at this time),* Macdonald was working his way towards turning the Conservative Party, with all the "loose fish" swimming inside it or every now and then darting towards and then away from it, into an entity that roughly constituted a precursor to Canada's national political parties of today.

He was out to reorganize the Conservatives in three radical respects. First, he wished to make it a centrist party, so that its

---

* The first, modern-style, organized political party in Britain can be dated to Gladstone's Liberals of the 1880s.

members wouldn't repeatedly charge off on their own pet cru-
sades. To do this, he wanted it to be filled with "progressive
Conservatives" rather than the old bewhiskered crowd of
Family Compact Tories. They, he wrote cuttingly, had "little
ability, no political principles and no strength in numbers,"
adding, in case anyone doubted his feelings, that they had "contrived . . . to make us and our whole party stink in the nostrils of
all liberal-minded people." In one particularly graphic phrase,
Macdonald denounced those he called "pre-Adamite Tories"—
those who hadn't evolved much beyond the dinosaurs. He would
quit, he wrote to a Conservative friend, "rather than have anything to do with such a reactionary party." Second, Macdonald
wanted to make it a true national party. This required forging an
alliance between the Conservatives and a bloc of Canadien members. LaFontaine and Baldwin had already followed this route,
but their alliance had lasted only a few years, with both leaders
retiring soon after they had achieved their goal of Responsible
Government. By contrast, Macdonald wanted to create a
French-English union that would be the foundation of a permanent governing party. Lastly, he aimed to use patronage not just
to reward supporters but to attract newcomers into the party,
and to keep supporters loyal when particular actions by their
party might otherwise have caused them to waver.

The consequence of all this work would be power, for the
Conservatives and for Macdonald. This power, though, would be
in the hands of moderate men, both French and English—"moderate" being one of his favourite words. This new, organized
coalition would be made up of three groups: his own Conservatives, with the "pre-Adamite Tories" among them kept firmly
in check; a bloc of Canadiens, the obvious ones to target being
the *bleus;* and, finally, a number of "loose-fish" Reformers who
would hop abroad the bandwagon as it rolled towards power.

From this mélange emerged as oddly named a party as any that ever made it to the Canadian political stage: the Liberal-Conservative Party. (The name had to have been Macdonald's, but no specific evidence of its authorship exists.) To a substantial extent, the new nomenclature was pure illusion. The party's so-called Liberal wing comprised just a few Reformers whom Macdonald seduced into joining him by promising them cabinet posts. Their presence, though, discomforted his Reform opponents and, no less usefully, diminished the influence of the new party's outright Tories. At the same time, Macdonald's concoction had substance. Combined with the bloc of *bleu* members, the coalition would have a quasi-permanent majority in the legislature and, thereby, a firm hold upon power. The result would be Canada's first stable government—giving it at least the possibility of administrative professionalism. Moreover, because this government would be composed of both French and English Canadians, the two sides would learn about each other—and about accommodation and compromise.

In trying to get all these factions heading in the same direction, Macdonald faced one distinctively Canadian problem. If a Liberal-Conservative alliance was imaginable, so too was its mirror image of a Conservative-Liberal alliance—or an alliance between the Reformers and "progressive Conservatives." The leading Reformer was George Brown, owner and publisher of the Toronto *Globe*. The same idea had, in fact, occurred to him. "Between the great mass of the Reformers of Upper Canada and this largest or liberal section of the Conservatives, there is little difference of opinion," he said in a statement reported in his newspaper on February 27, 1854. "Not one great principle divides them. Nothing but old recollections of antagonism."

In the contest between them, Macdonald had one decisive asset. As he had written to Strachan, he enjoyed "friendly relations with the French." By contrast, Brown had far too often denounced "French domination," either personally or through the pages of his *Globe*, and the Grits were even more virulent in their criticism of the French. Macdonald saw this door of opportunity opening before him, and through it he slipped.

⌐~

Where Baldwin and LaFontaine had left off, Macdonald now took over. In part, his plan was of course pure opportunism. It was also, though, the product of an idea about Canada's very nature that was uncommonly imaginative and generous. Indeed, it's not easy to identify any leading English-Canadian politician, all the way down to the 1960s (when the rise of separatism in Quebec caused everyone's mind to focus wonderfully), who came close to matching the vision of the country that Macdonald expressed at this time.

Macdonald didn't go in for grand ideas or for the "vision thing." He expressed his understanding of Canada's nature in colloquial language in a private letter, one written to a correspondent who disagreed with almost everything he was saying. There was no benefit to Macdonald in this exercise, therefore. He wrote it in order to think out what it was that he actually believed.

This remarkable statement, often quoted but most times only in summary form, is contained in the letter Macdonald wrote in January 1856 to Brown Chamberlain, the editor of the Montreal *Gazette*. Typically, he began with a joke. He had been lax, he admitted, in replying to Chamberlain's earlier letters, so "I have hunted up your old letters, so that you see I *cherish* them, if I do not reply." Next came some gossip. Then, without any peal of oratorical trumpets, Macdonald set out some of the most insightful passages in all Canadian political prose.

The truth is you British L[ower] Canadians never can forget that you were once supreme, that Jean Baptiste was your hewer of wood and drawer of water. You struggle like the protestant Irish in Ireland, like the Norman invaders in England, not for equality but *ascendancy*. The difference between you and those interesting and amiable people is that you have not the honesty to admit it. You can't and won't admit the principle that the majority must govern. The Gallicans may fairly be reckoned as two-thirds ag-st one third of all the other races who are lumped together as *Anglo-Saxon*. Heaven save the mark! Now you have nearly one-third if not quite of the representat-n of Lower Canada, & why is it the misfortune of your position that you are in a minority & therefore can't command the majority of votes. The only remedies are immigration and copulation and these will work wonders.

... No man in his senses can suppose that this country can for a century to come be governed by a totally unfrenchified Gov-t. If a Lower Canada Britisher desires to conquer, he must "stoop to conquer." He must make friends with the French; without sacrificing the status of his race or lineage, he must respect their nationality. Treat them as a nation and they will act as a free people usually do—generously. Call them a faction and they become factious.

Supposing the numerical preponderance of British in Canada becomes greater than it now is. I think the French would give more trouble than they are now said to do. At present, they divide, as we do, they are split up in several sections, & are governed more or less by defined principles of action. As they become smaller and feebler, so they will be more united, from a sense of self-preservation they

will act as one man & hold the balance of power. . . . So long as the
French have 20 votes, they will be a power & must be conciliated.

Then came some political gossip, followed by his customary
jaunty ending. "I scarcely think you can read this scrawl. It is
written by the light of one dip & my eyes are rapidly becoming
irascible. Good night to you."

Even all these decades later, after such an overflowing abundance of books, of learned articles and speeches and conferences
and colloquia, all explaining what it is that Quebecers really
want, it is hard to identify an analysis that comes nearer to understanding the way Canada is defined by the political dynamic
between a threatened minority and a casually confident majority
than this exposition, written late at night by a guttering candle
and tossed into the mail without a single word or sentence
altered. Much that is in it—the invocation to "respect their
nationality" as an obvious example—is as relevant today as it was
then. Such a capacity for understanding and generosity would be
uncommon under any circumstances, but especially in an unsentimental and pragmatic power-seeking politician. A comment
about Macdonald by Pope is relevant here, namely that there was
"an entire absence of prejudice in his large and liberal mind." He
took people as they were, with all their faults and frailties, and
almost never judged them or moralized about their failings.

Macdonald also exploited people for his own partisan purposes when their religion or culture or language might be of use
to him. His goal wasn't to preserve the French fact in Canada for
its own sake, but rather to achieve national harmony so the government could get on with its business—and, as doesn't need to
be added, to gain and retain power. In mid-nineteenth-century
Canada, though, it took an unusually large and liberal mind to
conceive that government itself had to function so as to accommo-

date, year in, year out, the inescapably conflicting interests of the
two European peoples—or nations—who made up the national
political community.

There was another, seldom-appreciated reason why Macdonald
understood French Canadians so readily. He wasn't an English
Canadian himself. He was a Scottish Canadian.

~

Macdonald himself was a member of a small, threatened people.
Between Scots and French there had been the Auld Alliance of
the two of them against the English; but that was now history.
Current, though, was the fact that the Scots, like French
Canadïans, had their own religion, their own educational and
legal systems, and even, if growing weak, their own language. So
they were at ease in each other's company. French-Scottish marriages were common, in contrast to their scarcity among the
English and the Irish. André Siegfried, who came over from
France to survey Canada much as de Tocqueville did in America,
wrote in his 1907 work, *The Race Question in Canada*, "They [Scots]
manifested a real goodwill towards the French, and the latter
were the first to recognize it." And Wilfrid Laurier once said,
"Were I not French I would be honoured to be a Scot."* It's hard
to doubt that when Macdonald looked at Lower Canada, he sometimes saw Scotland.

About Macdonald's personal command of the French language itself there is uncertainty. The evidence is mixed. George-
Étienne Cartier's assistant, Benjamin Sulte, wrote in his memoir

---

* Laurier actually spoke English with a slight Scots accent, having learned the
language in the Lower Canada settlement of New Glasgow—an area originally
settled by Scots.

that "Macdonald was fond of reading French novels—he always kept them close at hand." No supporting evidence for this claim exists, and Sulte may have chanced upon a French novel on Macdonald's desk that actually belonged to his second wife, the creditably bilingual Agnes. The historian Ged Martin has reported that a unilingual Canadien member, François Bourassa, claimed to have had a number of conversations in French with Macdonald while the two whiled away the time in the legislature.* Yet the Montreal lawyer and journalist François-Xavier-Anselme Trudel commented in an article published in 1887 that Macdonald knew not a word of French. The probability is that Macdonald in fact spoke very little French (the Bourassa story may just have been family myth) but could read it comparatively well—not to the level of being able to enjoy French novels but sufficiently to comprehend the letters that, for instance, Étienne-Paschal Taché, twice his co-premier, regularly sent him in French.

The Big Tent that Macdonald was out to erect was thus to be held up by four supports: Conservatives willing and able to be reasonably progressive; Reformers looking for a sanctuary; a dependable bloc of Canadiens; and Macdonald himself, as master builder and circus barker. Once set up and shown to be durable, this became the political edifice that almost every one of Macdonald's successors down to today would attempt to emulate.

---

* Ged Martin unearthed the François Bourassa story in Roger Le Moine's 1974 book, *Napoléon Bourassa l'homme et l'artiste*. The French novel Macdonald supposedly was reading was *Le Diable boiteux* [The Devil on Two Sticks] by Alain-René Lesage. It's about romantic misadventures involving greybeards marrying young girls, and bankrupt heiresses marrying fortune hunters. It's hard to believe it would be to Macdonald's taste.

In the fall of 1853, the Hincks-Morin government entered its death throes. Hincks became the subject of press stories that he and the mayor of Toronto had refinanced the city's debt by a private manoeuvre that earned them each ten thousand pounds. The press hounds kept on sniffing and came up with reports about railway stock that Hincks had picked up for a song and some bargain-priced government land he had profited from.

The inevitable election finally came in June 1854, after Hincks had lost two successive confidence votes in the legislature. In the election, Macdonald, for the first and only time in his career, made the corruption of his opponents his central theme, coining the phrase that Hincks and his ministers were "steeped to the lips in corruption"—an exercise in verbal cleverness he would come to regret because it would be quoted back at him. He won handsomely in Kingston. Across Upper Canada, though, the Conservatives did comparatively poorly, in part because Macdonald was known to be friendly towards the French—the Orange Order, had, by this time, turned against his key Orange ally, Ogle Gowan. As an additional handicap, the Conservative leader for whom people were actually being asked to vote was not Macdonald but Sir Allan MacNab—a decent old duffer and military hero of the 1838 Rebellion, but indiscreet enough to say "all my politics are railroads" at the same time that he was president of the Great Western Railway and leader of the opposition. MacNab was a figure out of the past. "The party is nowhere, damned everlastingly," Macdonald wrote despondently to Alexander Campbell after the election. At that very point, Hincks lost yet another confidence vote and suddenly resigned.*

---

* Apologists claimed that Hincks had clung to office only to prevent Brown from replacing him with a ministry from which all French Canadians would be excluded. This effort may account for his being rewarded in 1856 with an appointment by the British government as governor of Barbados and the

MacNab was now called in by the governor general to form a new government. A lot of baling wire went into its assembly. All the Canadien ministers who had served under Hincks were kept in their posts. There were six newcomers—three Conservatives, with MacNab at their head, and three Reformers, to give some credence to the Liberal-Conservative label. Macdonald, as the new attorney general for Upper Canada, held the cabinet's most important portfolio. And of these two principal figures, MacNab was for show and Macdonald was for real.

As attorney general, Macdonald now had a quite comfortable income of £1,250 a year. He was able to sort out without strain many of the responsibilities that fell to him as head of the family. In 1852 a most unexpected family event had occurred: his sister Margaret, aged thirty-nine, married James Williamson, a professor of science at Queen's University.* It was a successful marriage, and Macdonald developed a high regard for Williamson, who, although bookish and humourless, was well liked by colleagues and students. Macdonald's nickname for Williamson, an ordained Presbyterian minister, was the affectionately teasing term "the Parson."

Margaret's marriage left Louisa isolated as the remaining unmarried sister. Macdonald arranged for her to move into the

---

Windward Islands. He later returned to Canada as Macdonald's post-Confederation minister of finance.

* Macdonald actually missed the wedding because he was detained in Quebec City on legislature business. He got Louisa to buy his present for the couple: "I wish that Moll should have a good kit, & I wish you to spend £25 for her on such things as you like. Don't say anything to her about it."

Margaret Macdonald. To everyone's surprise (not least to Macdonald, who missed her wedding), she suddenly married a Queen's University professor, James Williamson. They became the de facto parents of Hugh John.

James Williamson, dour and humourless, yet well liked by his students, other professors and Macdonald. (This photo, as well as the photos of Margaret and Louisa, is from Lady Macdonald's personal album.)

Williamson household with their mother, Helen, for whom she had been caring. Showing the Macdonald streak of stubborn independence, Louisa insisted that she not go there as a dependant. Macdonald's solution was inventive and perhaps unique. He rented the house—Heathfield—that the Williamsons owned, naming Louisa as his representative. This arrangement ensured that, technically, the Williamsons were now boarding with Louisa in their own house. Louisa was entitled to sit at the head of the table, except when Macdonald visited and she moved to one side. As the "tenant," Louisa had the right to invite friends to visit, rather than merely joining gatherings arranged by the Williamsons. She also rented (again with Macdonald's financial aid) a portion of the garden, where she grew her own flowers and vegetables; Professor Williamson had his own vegetable plot and charged the general household for any produce consumed by the group. The real hero of this arrangement was Margaret: she understood, as few chatelaines would do, Louisa's fierce determination not to become a kind of paying guest in her sister's house.

Nothing, though, could change the state of Macdonald's own marriage. There was one small ray of hope. In 1855, when the government moved from Quebec City to Toronto, the national capital for the next four years, Isabella decided to join him, and she made the journey from

Louisa Macdonald. Difficult, fiercely independent, a lifelong spinster, but also Macdonald's favourite sister.

Kingston by train that October. They rented an apartment in a boarding house on Wellington Street, near the city's western outskirts. Hugh John, now five years old and living more often with his surrogate parents, Margaret and James Williamson, than with the invalid Isabella, was brought up to Toronto to join his father and mother.

By this time, Toronto had suddenly taken off as a community. New immigrants poured into the city, swelling its population to forty thousand. (Kingston's population, meanwhile, remained unchanged at five thousand.) Toronto's own manufacturing plants and the success of the farmers to the southwest brought it prosperity. Substantial buildings such as the St. Lawrence Hall, the Mechanics' Institute and St. James' Cathedral had been completed, while the University of Toronto was starting to grow. The city itself stretched in long blocks from the Don River to Bathurst Street and north all the way to Gerrard Street.

Yet, sadly, the three Macdonalds could not turn themselves into a real family. Most of the time, Isabella remained secluded in her darkened sickroom, constantly complaining about the light and the noise. Macdonald's reports to family members about her condition continued through the depressing cycle of "Isabella has been very, very ill," then, hopefully, that "she is evidently on the mend," then, mournfully, that she was "desperately ill all last week." Only rarely could Isabella even leave her bed to play with her son. Hugh John was regularly sent off to stay at the homes of friends and relatives in the new city. The ever-optimistic Macdonald reported to his mother that in these houses "there are young people, well brought up, so that he has the advantage of a good companionship." When back home again, Hugh John would play with his father. "He and I play Beggar My Neighbour," Macdonald wrote, "and you can't fancy how delighted I am when he beats me." In another letter to his mother, Macdonald made, perhaps intentionally, perhaps by accident, a most revealing comment about his son's reaction to the stress being imposed on him: when he asked Hugh John where he would prefer to live, in Toronto or in Kingston, the child replied, "I like Kingston best because my Grandmother lives there." Effectively, the boy had told his father that he would be happier living away from his permanently sick mother.

That same stress, a compound of guilt, repressed anger and bleak hopelessness, applied no less to Macdonald. As attorney general, he often had to work late or go on trips, duties that gave him an excuse to absent himself from the gloomy apartment. One letter to his mother in January 1856 captures the magnitude of the strain between him and Isabella: "I get lots of invitations here. I was asked out for every day last week, but declined of course on account of Isa's illness. Next week, or rather this week, is the same thing. But I am obliged to refuse."

In all his letters to his relatives, Macdonald seldom strayed beyond family matters into politics. The letter he wrote to his mother on March 17, 1856, contains a striking exception. After news about Isabella and Hugh John, Macdonald suddenly exploded into rage: "I am carrying on a war against that scoundrel George Brown and I will teach him a lesson that he never learnt before. I will prove him a most dishonest, dishonourable fellow."

⌒

In all of Canada's political history there has never been a personal contest like that between Macdonald and Brown. No other two rivals were so clearly above the ordinary. They were at odds about the fundamentals of the country itself and about the nature and purposes of politics. Their personalities and styles were near opposites, except that each was combative, competitive and quick to anger. On one occasion they came close to blows in public, and for eight years they said not a word to each other, even though they crossed paths regularly in the legislature building. Yet it would be their joint partnership during the critical years of 1864 to 1866, teeth gritted and tempers tamped down, that would bring about Confederation.

Brown is the great might-have-been of nineteenth-century Canadian politics. He possessed the intellect, charisma and strength of character to match Macdonald's more subtle talents. The difference between them was, in the strictly political realm and in the famous formulation of the philosopher Isaiah Berlin, that one of them was a hedgehog and the other a fox. Brown was Berlin's hedgehog: he was seized of one great idea—Representation by Population, the basic democratic principle that each person's vote should be equal. Macdonald, the fox, was at ease with a multiplicity of ideas, some contradictory, as he constantly changed course and doubled back (including on himself), never accepting defeat as permanent or regarding victory as anything but temporary. Above all, Macdonald was almost infinitely adaptable: "The great reason I have always been able to beat Brown," he wrote, "is that I have been able to look a little ahead while he could on no occasion forgo the temptation of a temporary triumph."

Despite Brown's exceptional talents, Macdonald would forever dance ahead out of his reach. "A campaign," *Globe* editor Sir John Willison remarked astutely in his *Reminiscences*, "is George Brown in the pulpit and John A. making merry with the unrepentant on the outskirts of the congregation." (By an uncanny coincidence, almost exactly the same kind of contest between two out-of-the-ordinary political leaders was in progress in Britain at the time, where the rivals were William Gladstone and Benjamin Disraeli. Again, moralist contended with worldly-wise realist, professor of ethics with student of human nature, hedgehog with fox, and, least consequential of all, Liberal with Conservative. The transatlantic difference was that, in Canada, it would be Macdonald who trounced Brown, while in Britain the outcome in terms of longevity in office—the only measure that counts in politics—would be Gladstone over Disraeli.)

Brown was a formidable and attractive figure. His most obvious attribute was sheer physicality. Six foot two, large and immensely strong, he had flaming red hair and radiated energy: he ate fast, rode fast, took steps two at a time—and sometimes four. He was intellectually capacious and fearless. He immigrated to New York with his father to help him run a newspaper. In 1843 he came north to edit a Free Kirk paper. Soon after settling in Toronto, Brown leaped into publishing on his own. The first edition of the *Globe* appeared in 1844, the same year Macdonald was elected to the legislature. Its editorials were forceful and trench-

ant, its news up to the minute, and
its pages were printed on the new,
highly efficient Hoe rotary press.
Brown published the paper first as a
semi-weekly, then a tri-weekly, and,
in 1853, a daily. Its circulation soon
topped an amazing twenty thousand,
as the new railways extended its
reach. It was easily the largest, most
influential and most profitable newspaper in the country.

Intellectually and morally, his
most attractive cause was the abolition of slavery. One of his speeches
on the subject attracted praise from
the great philosopher John Stuart
Mill.* As well, and far ahead of his
time, he called for reforms in penitentiaries, urging that convicts be

George Brown, founder/publisher of the
Globe, *easily Canada's most influential*
newspaper, and a Reform leader. The rivalry
between him and Macdonald has no equal in
Canadian politics. He had a fine mind, but
was narrow and bigoted.

treated as human beings who might be capable of change.
Although not a textbook democrat—no different from
Macdonald, Brown opposed universal suffrage, fearing it would
lead to American-style demagoguery—he staged Canada's first
mass political convention.

Yet there were flaws in Brown of narrowness, intolerance and
intellectual and moral arrogance. One of the ablest journalists of
the time, Edward Farrer, wrote of him, "He was a good, and in his
way a great man, but Scotland never sent forth a more bigoted son
of the manse." Another exceptional journalist, George Sheppard,

---

* Brown condemned the slavers with the vivid phrase "men-stealers," describing
them as "a disgrace not only to Americans but to the whole world."

an editorial writer with the *Globe*, similarly judged, "Take him on the ground of abuses . . . and he is the strongest public man in Canada. . . . But off this ground he is an ordinary man." Brown personally, and the *Globe* on his behalf, railed regularly against "French domination" and "Priestcraft." He could never understand that his campaign for Representation by Population (Rep by Pop) was at one and the same time self-justifying and destructive: it would fulfill the individual rights of English Canadians by matching their representation to their ever-increasing numbers, but it would do so at the cost of threatening the collective rights of French Canadians. Brown could not understand that, while for one people the issue was justice, for the other it was survival.

Brown contested the 1851 election in two constituencies, as was then permissible, losing one to William Lyon Mackenzie but winning the other. He soon emerged as the effective leader of the Reformers. The battle between him and Macdonald was quickly joined. In his first speech, in September 1852, Brown argued for the separation of church and state on the basis of the "voluntary principle," which decreed that separate schools should be supported by their own faithful rather than by the state. Macdonald responded with the kind of wilful exaggeration he knew would drive Brown to sputtering fury: if the rule was to be that "every man should support his own religious teacher by his own means," he declared, then this surely had to mean that "the Indians and heathen ought to support their own missionaries." It was a glib, if temporarily effective, response to Brown's essential argument that "the law shall know no man's religion."

The angriest confrontation between them was not about principle. It was a squalid affair, revealing on Macdonald's side a capacity for narrowness and vengefulness, magnified in this instance by sheer hot-headedness. Back in 1849, Baldwin, as premier, had set up a commission to inquire into allegations of mistreatment by

Henry Smith, the warden of Kingston Penitentiary. He had chosen Brown as secretary of the inquiry, and the resulting report
was largely Brown's work. Its findings were devastating. As many
as forty men and women were being flogged each morning; one
had received 168 lashes in twenty-eight days; boys as young as ten
had been lashed for laughing and whistling; and the convicts were
perpetually half-starved. The commission, on Brown's urging, recommended a series of reforms. In the event, other than Smith's
dismissal, few recommendations were implemented—principally
because Macdonald repeatedly denounced the report. He took
this position because Warden Smith was the father of his friend
and fellow Conservative Henry Smith; mostly, though, because
Brown was the principal author of the report.

Over the next half-dozen years, Macdonald four times raised
the commission report in the legislature, twice moving a resolution for it to be made the subject of a legislature inquiry—
unsuccessfully, both times—and repeatedly accusing Brown of
personal bias. On the last occasion, in 1855, Macdonald flatly
accused Brown of having fabricated evidence, shouting out
"Liar" when Brown rejected the charge. For a time it seemed that
the two men would come to blows on the House floor. Brown
called for a legislature committee to investigate Macdonald's allegations. While the evidence was overwhelmingly against
Macdonald, the committee's Conservative majority found words
to exonerate him. The affair petered out, leaving a residue of
unrestrained hatred between the two men.

Their most substantial confrontation was over Rep by Pop.
Year after year, Brown moved resolutions calling for an amendment to the constitution of the United Province of Canada so
that Upper Canada's ever-growing population could be matched
by a corresponding number of seats. Macdonald's reply, in March
1853, was succinct: "If there is one thing to be avoided, it is

meddling with the constitution of the country . . . [it] should not be altered till it is evident that the people are suffering from the effects of the constitution as it actually exists."

The statistics were on Brown's side. Once published, the census for 1851 showed that Upper Canada's population had edged ahead of Lower Canada's for the first time—952,000 to 890,000. Immigration was certain to widen this gap rapidly. Nor was politics on Macdonald's side: a number of his own Conservatives now agreed with Brown.*

Brown had another advantage. If his tone was angry, the answering voice from Lower Canada was no less furious but incomparably less effective. The ascendant new order in Lower Canada was ultramontanism, or right-wing Catholicism, narrow, defensive, authoritarian, all amplified by the personality of its leader, Montreal bishop Ignace Bourget. Opposition to him did exist, from the anti-clerical *rouges* and the intellectually progressive *Instituts canadiens*. But Bourget dominated the scene. His political power would grow to the point where he could inform the faithful, "It is the duty of electors to give their votes only to those who will comply entirely with the teachings of the Church"—the *bleus*, or the Conservatives' allies. That kind of voice grated harshly on the ears of other Canadians. There was thus a ready public echo for Brown when he thundered that Rep by Pop was "the question of all questions—it lies at the foundation of all reforms."

Sectarianism, once contained by the Baldwin-LaFontaine concord, was now unconstrained. Brown's equivalent to Macdonald's

---

* "Rep by Pop" was a most persuasive slogan, although what Brown really had in mind was rep by section—namely, that Upper and Lower Canada should have seats in proportion to their respective total populations. As was most curious, throughout the long Rep by Pop debate, little notice was ever taken of the fact that Upper Canada's own constituencies were even more unbalanced, varying as widely as from 4,100 for Brockville to 80,000 for Huron-Bruce.

Toronto, c. 1856. The stately Osgoode Hall stands in the background, showing that Toronto is becoming a city. Note the width of the streets, the lack of trees and the many wooden buildings.

"Treat them as a nation" letter was one he sent late in 1852 to selected Reform supporters: "What has French-Canadianism been denied? Nothing. It bars all it dislikes—it extorts all its demands—and it grows insolent over its victories." Brown admitted that his insistence on Rep by Pop might help the Conservatives by compelling the *bleus* to persist in supporting them. Here, the moralist turned into a dogmatist: "And what if they did?" Brown asked rhetorically. "It is our duty to act uprightly and leave consequences in higher hands. Should we do evil that 'good' may come? And such 'good'—a base vassalage to French-Canadian Priestcraft." The *Globe* said it all again in public: "We lie helpless at the feet of the Catholic priests of Lower Canada" and "Let the Pope put plaster on his mouth once and for all."

Viewed in the hindsight of the secularized, post-Christian Canada of today, the strength of sectarianism in the mid-nineteenth century isn't easy to comprehend. In fact, the cause was the most obvious of all: religion mattered a great deal to almost everyone then. At the University of Toronto, for example, all students were required to study metaphysics and ethics during each of the four years it took to earn their degree.* Not only did people care deeply about their particular faith, but it defined what they supported and whom they opposed. The resulting religious tensions were then magnified by race: Protestant English versus French Catholic in Lower Canada; Orange Ulster Irish versus Green southern Irish in Upper Canada. And because there was no explicit separation between religion and the state, as there was in the United States, there were no barriers to sectarianism. The shrewdest comment on the relationship between the state and the churches in Canada at this time was made by W.L. Morton in *The Shield of Achilles:* "Church and state could not really be separated, because religion dominated the state."

In the end, the greatest surprise about sectarianism in nineteenth-century Canada is not that it existed and was divisive, but that it was so seldom violent. Ireland's civil war never crossed the Atlantic.

These problems were now Macdonald's. After the muddle that followed the drawn election of 1854, the so-called Liberal-Conservative Party had backed into office. MacNab was the premier; the man with the power was Macdonald. Power came to him because he was remaking the party in his own image. And also because, as attorney general for Upper Canada, he held the single most important portfolio. After a decade in politics, Macdonald was now just one rung—a very short one—from the top. He also, for the first time, had a real job.

---

* One of the might-have-beens in the development of Canadian intellectual life is Thomas Huxley, the great champion and popularizer of Darwin's theory of evolution, who applied for and almost secured in the mid-1850s the post of professor of natural history at the University of Toronto. The slot was filled, instead, by the brother of Premier Sir Francis Hincks.

TEN

Forms Are Things

‾◟

It is of the very last importance that the administration of the
affairs of the country should be according to the law.
John A. Macdonald

T
o single out the two defining characteristics of
Macdonald's term as attorney general is easy: he
loved the job, and he held on to it for as long as he
could. He snapped up the portfolio when he was
first offered the position in 1854. He kept it during all the years
he was premier of the United Province of Canada (whether as
premier in actual title or, initially, as de facto leader behind
MacNab). Post-Confederation, by then holding the title of prime
minister, Macdonald continued to reserve for himself the successor portfolio of minister of justice for another full decade.*

---

* Before Confederation and after it for several decades, premiers and prime ministers functioned at the same time as a regular cabinet minister. The practice
eventually died out, although John Diefenbaker was both prime minister and
minister of external affairs for a time in the years 1957 to 1959. A rough contemporary equivalent would be that deputy prime ministers, largely a symbolic
title, always hold a departmental portfolio.

Any attempt to describe Macdonald's performance as the Crown's principal law officer has to adopt an unfamiliar perspective: rather than the usual one of him as political leader and schemer, it has to be of him as an administrator, or of someone doing a particular job. As an administrator, Macdonald performed in a way almost unknown today: he worked entirely by himself. Just about all leading politicians did that then; Macdonald, though, worked harder at more things than almost anybody else. For a start, he wrote, or more often delivered extemporaneously, all his own speeches, only occasionally asking a supporter or aide to help him with some preliminary research. He wrote all his own letters, in longhand, from lengthy policy memorandums to the governor general to governmental minutiae: "You will see by the enclosed that Hopkirk highly commends acting landing waiter Kidd for an increase say to 6/sh a day," he scrawled. "If you see no objection I would be glad to see Kidd get the increase." As campaign organizer of the Conservative Party, he sent a stream of letters containing comments such as, "I shall have all the Crown prosecutors appointed this week, if possible. We must as *perhaps* we are on the eve of an election, take political considerations only into our minds," or, "I am told there are a dozen [Conservative] candidates in the field for West Middlesex & that the consequence will be a Grit triumph. Now my dear fellow, set your wits to work, & choke off as many of them as possible."

After becoming premier in title in 1856, Macdonald effectively performed in three jobs—as premier, as attorney general and as Conservative Party organizer and manager. It wasn't until 1864, though, that he took on Charles Drinkwater as his first full-time secretary, or "stenographer clerk," a post he then made permanent in his office.* At the time he engaged Drinkwater, Macdonald had

---

* Before Drinkwater, R.A. Harrison, later chief justice of Upper Canada, and

taken on a fourth job: he appointed himself minister of militia.

These multiple duties encompassed only his political and governmental affairs. He needed at the same time to make enough money from his law practice to meet the expenses of an invalid wife, a growing son, an ailing mother, an unmarried sister and himself. He kept on trying to earn extra money by land speculations, acquiring extensive property in Guelph and Toronto and holding on to undeveloped "wild land" that might tempt some optimistic immigrant, but he seldom made money on any of these ventures. His burden lightened a little once Margaret married Professor James Williamson and they willingly took care of Hugh John as their surrogate son. As

By the mid-1850s, Macdonald had become attorney general and, effectively, Conservative leader. He'd also emerged as a political strategist, turning the old Tory Party into a centrist party for, in his words, "progressive conservatives."

another relief, in 1854 he took on a bright young attorney, Archibald Macdonnell, to replace Campbell as his law partner.

Macdonald was able to do so much because he worked hard in furious bursts, made decisions easily and confidently and absorbed files at remarkable speed; also, far from least, he approached life with a cheerful and hopeful disposition. He never doubted that he could overcome every challenge, even if some time had to pass before he figured out a solution.

Hewitt Bernard, later his brother-in-law, functioned as Macdonald's private secretary while also performing other departmental duties.

Generally, historians have given Macdonald low marks as an administrator. A major cause for this judgment was the outcome of his most closely scrutinized performance—the land and other claims of the Métis, first in Manitoba, then in Saskatchewan, both of which ended in the twin disasters of the Riel uprisings. Another reason was that, every now and then, Macdonald got things thoroughly botched up because he had drunk too much.

Other more recent historians, as well as some well-qualified contemporaries, gave Macdonald at least a passing grade as an administrator. The only study dedicated specifically to this subject—a thesis written by Joyce Katharine Sowby, "Macdonald the Administrator: Department of the Interior and Indian Affairs, 1878–1887"*—reached the opposite conclusion: "Contrary to the claims of the Liberal politicians and press of the time and of many historians since, [Macdonald] was actively involved in the administration and policy-making of his two departments. He gave close attention to the day-to-day work of the departments: evolving policy; dispensing patronage and consulting about personnel matters; reorganizing duties and providing additional staff and space for his burgeoning departments." The historian Keith Johnson reaches a similar conclusion in his long essay on Macdonald in *Pre-Confederation Premiers: Ontario Government Leaders, 1841–1867*: "He took these duties seriously and performed them conscientiously and well. He worked hard, though not always to a regular schedule, and he expected industry and efficiency from

---

* Sowby's master's thesis, an exceptional one, was written in 1984 for Queen's University.

his staff." Auditor General John Langton, a highly capable, politically neutral colleague, said of Macdonald in 1855, "He can get through more work in a given time than anybody I ever saw, and do it well." *

Macdonald shared this laudatory view of his own administrative capabilities. He wrote to one correspondent, "I have infinitely more to do in my own legitimate sphere than any one man ought to have to do, and if it were not that I am a quick worker I should have been hopelessly in arrears." He would also brag— with some justification—that he could lay his hands on every letter of consequence he'd ever received and on copies of his replies.† Indeed, this orderliness is the reason why the archival record of Macdonald's correspondence is so voluminous.‡ Joseph Pope wrote of his own experiences with Macdonald, "He attached great importance to his correspondence, and made a point of answering all letters addressed to him as promptly as circumstances would permit." He recalled also that Macdonald "was exacting in his demands. He required all a man's time. The thought of holidays never entered his mind."

Later doubts about Macdonald's administrative competence may have been caused by the difficulty commentators had in accepting that anyone so jaunty and theatrical and consumed

---

* Langton developed a system of reporting the budget accounts in the 1850s that remained Ottawa's standard system down to the 1970s.

† He did not keep *all* copies of his own letters or of incoming ones. At the end of an 1856 letter to Brown Chamberlain of the Montreal *Gazette* in which he had made some frank political observations, Macdonald advised, "I hope you burn my letters. I do yours." In fact, Chamberlain kept the letter.

‡ Even his bitter opponent, Sir Richard Cartwright, admitted that Macdonald could "generally lay his hand on any document he wanted, even after a long lapse of years."

with partisan politics, besides being occasionally inebriated, could keep his desk clean and his paper moving. Yet that is what Macdonald did, particularly when he was new to the government grind. He actually improved the bureaucracy a bit: soon after becoming receiver general in 1848, he revised the hours of work in government offices and forbade absences on personal business. When he became attorney general in 1854, he reorganized the department so that legal and penitentiary matters were dealt with separately. Among his acts as premier was the appointment of Langton as the first auditor general and, in 1857, the enactment of the Civil Service Act, patterned on the one in Britain, which introduced competitive examinations for positions, although in practice it didn't have much effect on patronage appointments.

Over the years, Macdonald's interest in administration dwindled. He remarked that when new to office he had been "the devil of a departmental reformer"—implying that, in hindsight, he had concluded that all his worthy attempts to improve the bureaucracy had accomplished little.

About some administrative niceties, Macdonald was a good deal less than fastidious. On one occasion, when his personal affairs required him, as the Canadian president of a British company, to secure a charter for it from the legislature, he properly recused himself from involvement because he was then the attorney general. Instead, he gave his long-term deputy minister, close friend and sometime apartment-mate, Hewitt Bernard, a commission to secure the franchise.

~

While Macdonald was attorney general for Upper Canada, with another member carrying the title of attorney general for Lower

Canada,* no one doubted that he was the senior law officer of the Crown; for most Canadians he was *the* attorney general. The zest and enthusiasm that Macdonald brought to his job comes ringingly through in a letter he wrote to the provincial secretary on April 17, 1856:

"The Justices of the Peace had no power to arrest Lanton† for a crime [horse-stealing] committed in the United States, unless under the Statute 12 Vic., Cap. 19, & then only on a specific application for the extradition of the prisoner. . . . In this case it appears that the man Lanton was illegally arrested & improperly put into the hands of the pursuing parties. There is too much reason to fear that Lanton, a man of colour, fugitive from the United States, was the victim of a scheme to kidnap him. The conduct of the Magistrates, even if it was caused by their ignorance, is highly reprehensible . . . & I respectfully recommend that they be discharged."

This particular letter confirms a cardinal characteristic about Macdonald's approach to the law. The fact that it shows a Canadian politician acting to protect an escaped American slave was, while gratifying to contemporary readers, not the point. Rather, the point was that, to Macdonald, it was the law itself which had to be protected. As went the law, in his view and in that of most Canadians, so went society itself.

When Macdonald insisted, as he did repeatedly, that Canada had to remain British, he really meant that it had to remain in and under the British system of law, written and understood, from the presumption of innocence to the acceptance that a

---

* Officially, their titles were those of attorneys general for Canada West and Canada East, or for each of the new "sections" within the United Province of Canada, but the old Upper and Lower Canada titles were widely used.

† Archy Lanton was an escaped American slave who had made it across the border.

man's house was his castle, to immunity from arbitrary arrest, to trial by a jury of peers, to the equality of all before the law (and thereby equality for an escaped slave who wasn't even a Canadian), to judicial impartiality, to the gradual evolution of the law by the technique of precedent. The core reason Macdonald was loyal to Britain throughout his life was that he was fiercely loyal to British law, never having the least doubt it was far superior to that of any other nation, not least that of the United States, with (in his mind) its ill-considered innovations such as elected judges.

Macdonald liked the law for the uncomplicated reason that he was good at it. During his brief stint as a trial lawyer, he had won several cases by identifying or inventing loopholes through which his client could escape. It was because he had spent years studying parliamentary rules and procedures, as few members bother to do, that he would be able to pull off one of his most brilliant (also one of his least scrupulous) political tricks—the famous "double shuffle" of 1857, by which he tumbled a Reform government out of power just two days after it had gained office.

Most directly, Macdonald loved the law for its own sake. One of his most self-revelatory comments was "Forms are things"; that is to say, the way something is done matters as much as what is done. He never questioned that unless the law remains majestic, it can look like an ass.

He loved the law almost as much as he loved politics. An early post-Confederation deputy minister, Edmund Meredith, recorded in his diary that his minister had suggested to Macdonald that he might consider taking the post of chief justice of the planned new Supreme Court of Canada. Macdonald replied, "I'd as soon go to Hell."

Macdonald's duties as attorney general covered a great swath of territory. Besides his general responsibilities for the nation's laws and their improvement, he had to make recommendations to the governor general about the resolution of death sentences and possible revisions of lesser sentences. He appointed all the judges. He had charge of the penitentiaries. A whole range of other matters came within his purview, from the incorporation of companies and municipalities, to labour disputes, to the choice of county towns, to a host of militia matters such as determining eligibility for pensions in compensation for service in the conflicts of 1812 and of 1837–38.

The most significant example of the range of Macdonald's duties as attorney general occurred in 1857.* The year before, a royal commission had been established to recommend "the best mode of so managing Indian property as to secure its full benefit to the Indians without impeding the settlement of the country." The objective was to avoid the succession of murderous— literally—Indian wars that erupted continually in the United States. The commission recommended measures to protect the Indians from "contamination by the white settlers" and to enable them to "assimilate the habits" of the white men. Macdonald translated these recommendations into the Gradual Civilization Bill of 1857 and steered it through the legislature. Essentially, it confirmed the policies followed for the preceding hundred years by British authorities. Any adult Indian male judged to be of good character, educated and free of debt could apply and, after a

---

* Much of the material for this section is drawn from the research done by historian Donald Smith of the University of Calgary and reported in his long article "John A. Macdonald and Aboriginal Canada," published in *Historic Kingston*, 2002.

three-year trial period, achieve outright ownership of fifty acres of reserve land. Such Indians would gain the franchise and become full citizens of Canada, while at the same time ceasing to be Indians in the official sense of that term. The policy combined paternalist protection with explicit assimilation; it accepted that Aboriginal people were "wards" of the government, but to gain the benefits of the white man's "civilization" they had to cease being Indians.

The new act was approved by the legislature without amendment, with little debate and by a margin of 72 to 1, the single naysayer being the old William Lyon Mackenzie who asked querulously, "Why should we wish to civilize them?" One member, Benjamin Robinson, who had negotiated several Indian treaties, protested that Indian chiefs had not been consulted. He told the legislature members, "At their Council meetings, the Indian chiefs deliberated quite as sensibly as honorable members did in this house, and sometimes even more so." The Gradual Civilization Act set the stage for the complete handover of responsibility for Indians from Britain to Canada in 1860.

Macdonald's own views about Indians were the same as those of most Canadians at this time: they should be protected from whites but assimilated into white society. In two respects he differed from the general opinion. The letter of the law itself and the treaties negotiated with the Indians were of cardinal concern to him. Macdonald consistently rejected requests by individuals, including Conservative supporters, for permission to buy reserve lands that they had persuaded bands to sell them.

As well, Macdonald had personal knowledge of Indians that was unusual among politicians and officials of the time. While running a law office in Napanee in 1832–33, he had got to know some members of the nearby Mohawk Band in Tyendinaga Township by singing in the choir of the Anglican missionary

there. He also knew some members of
a band of Mississauga in the Bay of
Quinte area. He became friends with
the remarkable Reverend Peter Jones
(his real name was Kahkewaquonaby,
meaning "Sacred Feathers"), who
had converted to Christianity and
had married an Englishwoman, Eliza
Field, a marriage the Kingston
Chronicle denounced as "improper and
revolting." By contrast, Macdonald
approved of marriages between
Indians and non-Indians as a way to
speed the process of assimilation.[*]

*The Reverend Peter Jones (Kahkewaquonaby).
He was one of a number of Indians whom
Macdonald, as was unusual for the times,
knew personally. Highly intelligent, Jones
shocked some contemporaries by marrying a
white woman.*

Two other aspects of his work as
attorney general reveal his particular
attitude to the law: sentencing and
judicial appointments.

About sentencing, Macdonald was stern but scrupulous; every
now and then, though, he could be remarkably progressive. In
nineteenth-century Canada, the criminal law was not only about
crime and punishment but also about morality, or at least many
people thought it should be. Indictable offences included
"sabbath-breaking," "blasphemy" and the "seduction" of an
unmarried female. Upper Canada's leading criminologist, Israel
Lewis, proclaimed that "all Criminal Law should be considered a

---

[*] Macdonald was friendly also with John Cuthbertson, the son of a Scottish fur
trader who had married a Mohawk woman.

transcript of the Divine Law." Macdonald didn't agree with that view—his opponent, George Brown, probably did—but the notion that the law ought to serve some higher purpose exercised wide appeal.

At the same time as the law was, at least sometimes, moral, it was often brutal. Executions were public and frequently treated as occasions for a family outing. Children as young as ten years of age were sent to penitentiaries and could be flogged there. Debtors' prisons and duels continued in Canada long after they'd been proscribed in Britain, and the list of crimes punishable by execution was far more extensive.

Macdonald's ambivalence about all these aspects of the law shows in his attitude towards sentencing, that part of the legal system where he had the greatest operational influence. Just a month after becoming attorney general, he wrote to the provincial secretary to declare that a five-year sentence for rape, notwithstanding a plea for mitigation by a member of the legislature, "was altogether an inadequate punishment for the offence." Not long after, he took the same view about a five-year sentence for horse stealing. He accepted the point that public opinion could be a part of the sentencing process: a six-month term imposed on two soldiers who had attempted to commit sodomy while drunk was too lenient and "would have, in my opinion, a bad effect to have it known among the soldiery and by the public generally that so heinous and demoralizing a crime" should have received only "a punishment often inflicted for mere assault."

Still, youth and gender did bring out his kindlier side. When a girl of thirteen was sentenced to three years in a reformatory (her crime is not recorded), Macdonald said this punishment would "only be a means of further contamination," and he urged that her sentence be reduced. He argued to the provincial secretary that while imprisonment for life was the legally correct

sentence to be imposed on a Samuel Ross for the offence of stealing from the mails, yet "this sentence may with propriety be
commuted" to three years, because of "the youth of the prisoner
. . . and especially to relieve the anxiety which has injured the
health and threatens the life of his mother." However, in another
instance, "the ground of poverty of the petitioner alleged as a
reason for the remission of the sentence of her husband [seven
years, for manslaughter] is in my opinion insufficient."

Macdonald believed in at least the possibility of rehabilitation. Of a convicted arsonist he wrote, "As he is a young man, six
years of compulsory labour may wean him from his degrading
habit and make him a useful member of society." But fundamentally he was skeptical that criminals could be rehabilitated. He
warned the Kingston Penitentiary warden, John Creighton,
"Your natural kindness of disposition may lead you to forget that
the primary object of the Penitentiary is punishment, and the
incidental one, reformation," adding, "there is such a thing as
making prisons too comfortable and prisoners too happy." Always
insightful about human nature, Macdonald understood that
reformers could be deceived by the behaviour of certain prisoners: "The most brutalized man is commonly the most insensible,
or rather insensitive and therefore the most docile," he once
observed to the chief justice, while "the man of quick and sensi-
tive feeling is fully alive to the shame of his position and frets
against the prison restraints." A striking difference remains
between Macdonald's consistent skepticism about reform and
rehabilitation and George Brown's idealistic call that prisons not
remain "the moral tomb of those who enter them." Macdonald
may have been a product of his times; Brown was ahead of them.

If indeed at times stern, he seldom deviated in his scrupulous-
ness. The law itself, in its exactitude, equality and clarity, was
Macdonald's abiding concern. When G.C. Reiffenstein, a confiden-

tial clerk in the receiver general's department, was arrested for for-
gery, convicted and sentenced to four years in the penitentiary, a
great many respectable people lobbied on his behalf for clemency.*
Macdonald yielded not an inch. "The first duty of a Government is
to administer even-handed justice; the second, is to satisfy the
public that it has been so administered. Now there are many poor
and ignorant men in the Penitentiary who committed no greater
crime than Reiffenstein, and should therefore receive no greater
punishment." Reiffenstien served three years of his sentence, was
paroled, and to the horror of fellow civil servants went right back
to Ottawa. Macdonald's response, as recorded by Deputy Minister
Edmund Meredith, was succinct: "Cut him dead like any other
felon." (In fact, Reiffenstein managed to restore his reputation and
made a new and successful career as an insurance agent.)

Macdonald so revered the law that in one respect he gave it precedence over politics—not always, but with reasonably respectable
frequency. Less than a year after becoming attorney general, he
had to fill an impending vacancy in the post of chief justice of
the Court of Common Pleas. He wrote to an attractive candidate,
"We are satisfied that these requirements are to be found in yourself and that no more worthy successor to Mr. Macaulay could be
found." The candidate was Robert Baldwin, the former premier
and leader of the Reform Party, which was now in opposition. In
the event, Baldwin turned down the offer.

"My only object in making Judicial appointments, is in the
efficiency of the Bench," Macdonald informed one cabinet minister.

---

* Reiffenstein's actual arrest, in 1869, was the talk of Ottawa, primarily because
the police came to his house and arrested him at his own dinner table.

He later told a Nova Scotia supporter that his test was "to consider fitness as the first requirement for judicial appointments . . .
political considerations should have little or no influence." He was
protesting too much, but not entirely. Richard Cartwright, who
loathed Macdonald, conceded in his *Reminiscences*, "Sir John was
always anxious, as far as political exigencies would permit, to
maintain the dignity of the Bench." Pope, more predictably, wrote
of his "solicitude for the high character of the Bench."

A good example of Macdonald's practising what he preached
was his appointment of Samuel Hume Blake to the prime judicial
post of vice-chancellor of Ontario. He was the brother of Edward
Blake, then the most prominent and effective of his Liberal opponents. To a colleague, Macdonald admitted that "Blake's politics
make his appointment difficult," but he alone was "of heavy
enough metal to preside in the court." As striking was his pro-
moting William Johnston Ritchie as chief justice of the Supreme
Court, a man who not only had been a Liberal but, in
Macdonald's own words, "an anti-confederate and a strong one."
As he had done with Blake, Macdonald justified his choice on the
grounds that "the Supreme Court is weak, and we can only feed it
from above."

Inevitably, Macdonald did not always practise what he
preached about judicial appointments. As he explained to one
supporter, the fact that Judge Ross of Toronto was a well-known
Liberal made him highly desirable: "He is a Grit and it would be
a good answer to the allegations of our opponents that only
Tories are appointed."

Macdonald could also be concerned about the dignity of the
bench. Post-Confederation, after appointing Lewis Wallbridge, a
Liberal, to be chief justice of Manitoba, he commented, "He will
be a good judge. . . . It is so seldom one can indulge one's personal
feeling with due consideration for public interest." Macdonald

remained concerned, however, that the new appointee's blackened and stumpy teeth would impair his gravitas, and he asked a colleague to prevail on Wallbridge to get himself a new set of teeth.

Macdonald's interest in the law never slackened, and it extended to just about every aspect of it. He was particular about the details of the law. "Certainty of punishment, and more especially certainty that the sentence imposed by the Judge will be carried out, is of more consequence in the prevention of crime than the severity of the sentence," he advised his friend, Warden John Creighton. He was as particular about the generality of the law. During the 1865–66 invasions of Canada by Fenians, or Irish Americans, public pressure developed for individuals to be arrested on mere suspicion of supporting the Fenians. Macdonald rejected the demands: "This is a country of law and order," he said, "and we cannot go beyond the law."

Without question, Macdonald loved the law. Politics, though, he worshipped. And that is where his thoughts and talents now turned.

ELEVEN

The Double Shuffle

Ah John A., how I love you. How I wish I could trust you.
Reform-Liberal member during conversation with John A. Macdonald

To clamber the political ladder's last, short rung, Macdonald needed to ease his own leader, Sir Allan MacNab, from the top spot. His challenge, though, was a good deal more complicated than that. Given the rule that whoever commits regicide almost never succeeds to the throne, Macdonald needed to dispatch MacNab while leaving no impression of his own footprints on his departing leader's back.

MacNab, "the Gallant Knight," had the round, red face and white whiskers of Charles Dickens' Mr. Pickwick. He was also a proud man, certain to react strongly against any suggestion of betrayal. Macdonald's solution was to get others to do the deed for him. In the spring of 1856, all three Reform ministers in the Liberal-Conservative cabinet resigned, claiming that the government no longer commanded their confidence. Shortly afterwards, Macdonald and the single other remaining Conservative minister resigned, ostensibly to maintain solidarity with their former

Premier Allan MacNab, the Conservative leader whom Macdonald eased out so he could get to the top. He was famous for declaring, unapologetically, "all my politics are railroads."

colleagues. MacNab was left with no choice but to resign himself. Racked by gout and in acute pain, he had himself carried into the chamber on a stretcher to cast his vote against his own demise. Immediately afterwards, a new Liberal-Conservative ministry was formed. Nominally, its premier was a Canadien, Étienne-Paschal Taché. Beside him, still in the attorney general portfolio he had held since 1854, was Macdonald. No one had any doubt that Auditor General John Langton had it right when he described Macdonald as "the recognized leader."

Macdonald protested his innocence. "Heap as many epithets and reproaches on me as you like," he told the House, "but this I contend, that having performed my portion of the contract, having stuck to my leader, having tried every means of keeping the cabinet together, I had a right as a gentleman and a man of honour to go into a new government with a Speaker of the Legislative Council, or anyone else."* Taché, by creating the illusion that a new government had been created, had allowed Macdonald to switch leaders with a certain, minimal, decency. In a letter to Henry Smith, though, Macdonald dropped the pretence: "I might, as you know, have been Premier, & insisted on Taché's claims lest it be said that in putting McNab [sic] out I was exalting myself."

---

* The Legislative Council, of which Taché was a member, was the pre-Confederation equivalent of the Senate.

However he had got there, Macdonald was now at the ladder's top.

~

The heights suited Macdonald. He performed there with a political skill never seen before on the Canadian political stage. It was from this time on that he set out systematically to develop the kind of organized centrist party that he had sketched out in his letter to John Strachan two years earlier about the need for a "material change" in the party to bring in "'progressive' Conservatives" and Canadien members. By today's standards, the Liberal-Conservative Party was neither organized nor disciplined, and the tripod on which it rested—of Conservatives, *bleus* and fair-weather Reformers—was decidedly wobbly. Yet it was a genuinely centrist party and, by its interweaving of French and English, a genuine national party, the first since Baldwin and LaFontaine.

This Big Tent party would soon demonstrate that it possessed a quality then exceedingly rare in Canadian politics—durability. The Liberal-Conservative Party had this attribute because it was a distinctively Canadian political party. It was, that is to say, a party of compromise, of endless accommodation between its constituent groups, of wheeling and dealing, horse-trading, temporary alliances and pacts, disagreements and splits, and broken deals—most of which unravelled at some time or other and then had to be reassembled laboriously.

In this sense, what was most remarkable about Macdonald's achievement was not that he should have become Canada's first prime minister, on July 1, 1867. It was, rather, that long before then he should have become the country's first truly *Canadian* prime minister (or premier, as he was called then). Macdonald fashioned a mould into which almost all successful Canadian political leaders have fitted themselves and their parties.

At the time, very few people appreciated the magnitude of Macdonald's achievement in keeping together, and maintaining on a more or less even keel, a party that encompassed such disparate elements as Conservatives and Tories, French and English, Orange Irish and Green Irish, Catholics and Protestants (and among the latter, the Anglicans who believed they were, and certainly should be, the established church, as well as grittier denominations like the Methodists). Most who followed politics in those days loathed "partyism," or the notion of an organized, impersonal and bureaucratic political machine. Few appreciated then that in so inchoate and dispersed a country a national political party was one of the few instruments available to give it a spine. The journalist Goldwin Smith understood what was going on: while he abhorred what he saw as Macdonald's corruption of Canadian politics, he could not hide his admiration for Macdonald's irreplaceable skill in keeping together what Smith called a "crazy-quilt" of a country. (Wilfrid Laurier also understood, which was why, when his time came, he governed like a francophone Macdonald.)

Patronage; abundant and endlessly inventive political deviousness and guile; an exceptional understanding of human nature; a natural tolerance for the inescapable intolerances of groups and individuals—these were Macdonald's essential operating tools. Add to them another quality as critical as any of the rest: likeability. Some opponents—Brown, Cartwright, later Edward Blake—hated Macdonald with a ferocious intensity. But a vast number of people of all kinds—supporters and opponents, legislature members and rank-and-file Conservatives, voters and non-voters—liked him and gave him the benefit of the doubt even when he didn't deserve it. Other politicians were admired and looked up to: Robert Baldwin, George Brown and the Patriote leader Louis-Joseph Papineau. But Macdonald alone was widely liked, and by quite a few was loved.

A great many people never called him "Macdonald." Rather, it was "John A."—even to his face—a signal of ease, familiarity, trust. Maybe he was a rogue, but he was *their* rogue. Among other Canadian leaders, only Diefenbaker gained the same familiarity, as "Dief," and in his case the diminutive came almost as often from anger as from affection.

Macdonald worked hard at being liked, most especially by his own supporters. "I dare say you are very busy from night until morning, and again from noon 'til night," Alexander Campbell, his ex-partner and now political crony, wrote to him. "That drinking with the refractory members is in your department, I take for granted. Another glass of champagne and a *story of doubtful moral tendency* with a little of the Hon. John Macdonald's peculiar 'sawder' are elements in the political strength of a Canadian ministry not to be despised." Macdonald distributed his "sawder" to all points of the compass. The best anecdote involves a passerby noticing Macdonald and a Reform-Liberal sitting together outside the chamber, with the opposition member's head resting on Macdonald's shoulder, as he remarked mournfully, "Ah John A., how I love you. How I wish I could trust you." The best description of Macdonald's seductive allure was made—later— by a Liberal MP, W.F. Maclean, who, in a magazine article, wrote that Macdonald "had a wonderful influence over many men. They would go through fire and water to serve him, and got, some of them, little or no reward. But they served him because they loved him, and because with all his great powers they saw in him their own frailties."

The importance of all the other assets that Macdonald deployed to keep together his coalition should not be underestimated. He was above all a politician who enjoyed politics immensely and who went at it with a zest and dedication matched by no other Canadian leader of his time.

Unique to Macdonald also was the fact that he loved the political game, absolutely revelled in it, for its own sake. He just had fun. The failing of one Conservative member, he complained to another, was impatience: "He destroyed one or two marvellous good plots of ours by premature disclosure." And he counselled a supporter he was trying to recruit as a candidate (in the end, successfully) that conversations with the governor general, Sir Edmund Head, "will do you good, as you have a great game to play before long."

From this time on, Macdonald sent out a stream of political letters—an absolute torrent of them. He gave advice to the editor of the pro-Conservative *Hamilton Spectator* on how to execute a reversal in policy: "It's a damned sharp curve, but I think we can make it." He showered upon members and supporters what he called "good bunkum arguments" on how to deal with such dangerously popular issues as Rep by Pop. He kept in close touch with Conservative newspaper editors, often accompanying his comments with references to likely advertising and printing contracts. "Splits," or more than one Conservative candidate running in the same riding and so dividing the vote, kept him in a state of constant agitation. In one letter to a supporter, Macdonald raged, "We are losing everywhere from our friends splitting the party. If this continues it is all up with us." As well, he scouted for candidates, gave them advice and sometimes provided campaign funds (at times from his own pocket), although men standing for office were expected then to cover their own electoral costs. He kept in touch with important non-Conservatives such as the education reformer Egerton Ryerson, who might be able to influence Wesleyan Methodists to vote

Conservative (he did), and the leading Reformer Sidney Smith, whom he hoped to persuade to join the Liberal-Conservative cabinet (he did). And when elections approached, his advice to candidates was candid: "Canvass steadily and vigorously, yet quietly—get your own returning office, a true man selected."

The fairy dust that Macdonald sprinkled over everything was, of course, patronage. There was nothing new in this. Patronage has fuelled Canadian politics from its earliest days. Macdonald's oldest preserved letter, dated November 22, 1836, was about patronage. "I am infinitely obliged to you for the hint respecting the clerkship of the peace," the young lawyer wrote gratefully to a Macpherson cousin. He would remain silent, Macdonald wrote, until the incumbent had committed himself to leaving, "in which case I shall call upon you to exert your kind endeavours on my behalf." As Macdonald's letter suggests, patronage flourished because, as is the case in all underdeveloped countries, secure, white-collar jobs were scarce, and because no criteria existed to determine who merited them, other than political favouritism. The political scientist S.J.R. Noel has used the term "clientelism" to describe the condition of mutual dependency that patronage involved—the client needing anything from a land grant to a railway charter to a soft job, and the patron needing votes, or perhaps just deference.* Moreover, as Noel observed, clientelism was "long assumed to be a normal part of the political process because it was a normal part of practically everything else." Patronage was a major issue in the Rebellions of 1837–38; it was also the prime issue in the fight for Responsible Government. The railway boom, which began shortly before Macdonald's political career, attracted extensive offers of patronage

---

* In Noel, *Patrons, Clients, Brokers: Ontario Society and Politics, 1791–1896.*

simply because of the huge sums of capital involved. The promoter of the Great Western Railway, Samuel Zimmerman, claimed that at any time more members could be found in his apartment than in any room in the legislature.

While Macdonald was doing nothing in the least new by distributing patronage, he used it in a radically new way. He employed it systematically as a tool to build and nurture the Conservative Party as an effective and ongoing institution. Unlike amateurish predecessors in all parties, he aimed not simply to please supporters by dishing out jobs, contracts, appointments and emoluments, but to make more Conservatives, both by solidifying the gratitude of those who were already members of the party and by attracting newcomers. He distributed patronage in sophisticated ways that derived from his understanding of human nature. He urged one candidate to "keep the Whitby Post Office [position] open until after the election" because "it may be valuable to have the office to give away." He urged another to make the same kind of appointments before the election to make gratitude certain, but with no public announcements and the winners being told "they will be appointed immediately after the elections" so as to encourage them to "work harder for your return." Over time, he became progressively more adept. Local members had to give their approval to patronage choices; those favoured had to have proof of having worked for the party; and no one could get a post by displacing an incumbent.

Perhaps what was most original about Macdonald's system was that he was entirely open, and entirely unapologetic, about what he was doing. He made little attempt to pretend that his purpose was good government rather than the good of the party. And he made certain that his own supporters understood his rules. When party members in Toronto complained they weren't getting their share of goodies, Macdonald retorted, "As soon as

Toronto returns Conservative members, it will get Conservative appointments."

It wasn't all crass. If patronage was not about good government, in the sense of getting the best people in the right posts, Macdonald did care about the well-being of individuals. Some of his choices really amounted to charity. He wrote to one official, "De L'Armitage is dying of congestion of the liver or some such devilry and is obliged to give up his Rifle Company. He wants much to retain his rank. Pray do this for him & break his fall." And, to a cabinet minister, "I have a letter from Noel wanting the Notaryship of the Bank. Can you give it to him[?] Poor fellow, he wants it badly enough."

In truth, Macdonald didn't so much systematize patronage as personalize it. For his system to work, he always had to be there at its centre, with his winning personality, his remarkable range of contacts, his exceptional memory for names and deeds, his incomparable knowledge of politics and the governmental apparatus, and, far from least, his uncommon ability to work extremely hard at high speed. At the same time that he was creating a national, centrist party, he was creating a Macdonald party.

Besides doing all this, Macdonald had yet one more substantial job: he had to run the country. For all practical purposes he had being doing that since mid-1854, when he functioned behind the facade of MacNab, just as he now functioned behind the facade of Taché. Within a few years of reaching the top, Macdonald had concocted solutions to two deeply divisive sectarian disputes that had bedevilled Canadian politics for more than a decade—the Clergy Reserves and separate schools. He then went right on to dispose of a third, entirely new issue that was almost as polarizing as the first two—the location of a permanent capital. All three involved an exercise in accommodation and compromise for the sake of national harmony.

The first of the conflicts to develop concerned the Clergy Reserves. By virtue of the Constitutional Act of 1791, one-seventh of all the land in Upper Canada had been reserved for "the clergy," with the revenues allocated to the established Anglican Church and, later, to the Church of Scotland (by coincidence, Macdonald's own church). All other churches, the Roman Catholic and the newly expanding Protestant denominations, were exceedingly unhappy to be excluded from this support. Brown in particular was outraged, because this system violated his cherished "voluntary principle"—that each church should be supported entirely by its own believers. Proposals for reform had always splintered on the rock of opposition from Tory Conservatives, the great majority of whom were Anglicans.

Macdonald's solution gave something to everybody. The Clergy Reserves would be secularized, and the funds allocated to municipalities for the support of public schools. The incumbent clergy of the Anglican Church and the Church of Scotland, though, would continue to receive payments until they died. When Macdonald first introduced legislation to deal with the Clergy Reserves, in October 1854, his strongest critics were his own Conservatives. But Brown, in a speech of exceptional generosity, agreed that a genuine advance had been made, even if it was still insufficient. The Tories who protested were now isolated.

Macdonald's two speeches in support of this legislation are among his most expressive. In a rare departure from the practical and the immediate, he used them to speak directly about the public interest and how it should be advanced. He was shrewd enough to say little about the details of how he proposed to dispose of the Clergy Reserves fund, talking instead about how the political process itself ought to work. Macdonald talked, that is to say, about the art of compromise.

He made his first comments on October 27, 1854, during a debate about a private member's bill to regulate religious holidays. After Brown delivered a strong speech criticizing what he saw as special treatment for Roman Catholics, Macdonald addressed the wider issue of religious tolerance. "It was of the very greatest importance for the mutual comfort of the inhabitants of Canada to agree as much as possible," he declared, "and the only way they could agree was by respecting each other's principles, and as much as possible even each other's prejudices. Unless they were governed by a spirit of compromise and kindly feeling towards each other, they could never get on harmoniously together."*

Ten days later, Macdonald spoke directly on the Clergy Reserves legislation. His bill had been attacked, he remarked, both by those who opposed any changes to the existing system and by those who opposed continuing payments to incumbent clergy. The effect, he said, would be "that the agitation will still be kept up. On the one hand, the 'drum ecclesiastic' will be beaten at every election, the worst feelings would be excited . . . whilst others would be constantly attacking the charge of paying the salaries of these 'drones' as these people would be called."

Compromise was the only solution. "There is no maxim which experience teaches more clearly than this, that you must yield to the times. Resistance may be protracted until it produces rebellion." Macdonald continued, "I believe it is a great mistake

---

* As is the case with most early newspaper reports of parliamentary debates, the language of this quotation is curiously stilted, with Macdonald appearing to have spoken in the past tense. No Hansards were published before Confederation.

in politics and in private life to resist when resistance is hopeless. I believe there may be an affected heroism and bravado in sinking with the ship, but no man can be charged with cowardice if, when he finds the ship sinking, he betakes himself to the boat." He then returned to his theme: "I call on the hon. gentleman [Brown] and upon the Church whose interests he advocates, to yield. I call on them to cease this agitation. They may smart under a sense of wrong and may feel they are deprived of rights, but . . . one thing is clear that the blow must fall, that seculariza-tion must take place. Why then resist against all hope? Why con-tinue to agitate the public mind? Why not yield to inevitable necessity?" Macdonald won this battle against sectarianism by a comfortable margin of 62 to 39 votes. With the Clergy Reserves of Upper Canada settled, Macdonald moved on to deal with Lower Canada's issue of its quasi-feudal seigneurial system, which gave the seigneurs ownership of the land and left their *cen-sitaires* as landless tenants. Other legislation in 1854 abolished the seigneurial system.*

Another year, another battle. The issue this time was sepa-rate schools. Pressure for them to be supported by public funds came from the Irish Catholics, whose leader was the newly appointed bishop of Toronto, Armand-François Charbonnel, a hard-line ultramontane. Macdonald crafted legislation that met the bishop roughly halfway. The largest bloc of Upper Canada members were now the populist Grits, deeply mistrustful of any-thing Catholic and ardent believers in what was known as the "double majority" parliamentary convention—that no legisla-tion affecting Upper Canada should be passed unless it was

---

* That Lower Canada's agricultural productivity was at most one-fifth of that of Upper Canada was widely attributed to its antiquated seigneurial system.

approved by a majority of Upper Canadian members. (Likewise for Lower Canada, in reverse.)

Securing legislative approval would be difficult. To manoeuvre himself into position, Macdonald concocted a clever and partially plausible argument. "He should be sorry," he told the House, if a legislature, "the majority of whose members were Protestants professing to recognize the great Protestant principle of the right of private judgment, should yet seek to deprive Roman Catholics of their power to educate their children according to their own principles."

Nevertheless, the legislature's majority of Reform and Grit Protestants had every intention of doing just that. Macdonald, though, had spotted a loophole in the "double majority" rule that gave these members their de facto veto. This was that while Upper Canada members had to approve legislation affecting their own territory, no one had ever said that this opinion needed to be expressed by the majority of all elected Upper Canada members rather than just the majority of those in the House when the vote was called. Macdonald waited until the final days of the 1855 session, and as soon as many of the Reformers and Grits had left for home he introduced a bill to extend the privileges of separate schools, much as Bishop Charbonnel had demanded. To the belated fury of the now shrunken opposition, the measure was brought quickly to a vote. It passed by a clear majority of the members present, many of them being Canadien members in alliance with Macdonald.

Macdonald subsequently justified his tactic on the grounds that the alternative was to withdraw all public funds from an established institution, the separate schools. Such a draconian solution could work only "if they [the opposition] could make the world all of one way of thinking . . . yet he doubted very much if things would go on one bit better on that account." This was gamesmanship: Macdonald had won, but the cost of his victory was to further inflame sectarian rage.

~

Macdonald experienced more success with another issue that was potentially sectarian rather than explicitly so—the choice of a single permanent capital.* One point was certain: whichever city or hamlet was chosen, either the English Protestants of Upper Canada or the French Catholics of Lower Canada would be furious. Indeed, feelings on the issue were so strong that more than two hundred votes on it were taken in the Legislative Assembly.

There are two particularly good stories about how Ottawa got picked: that Queen Victoria threw a dart at a map, or that Lady Head, the governor general's wife, made a sketch of the view from what is now Parliament Hill and showed it to an impressed Queen. Common to both stories is the point that the Queen made the choice—and she, of course, could do no wrong. In fact, Macdonald concocted the Queen's intervention in conjunction with Sir Edmund Head. He and Head had become close, in part because their Toronto houses were near each other, but more because Head, an academic, found in Macdonald an intellectual kin rare in the colony. Head, who favoured Ottawa on the grounds that it was "the least objectionable" of all the contenders, first sent a message to the Colonial Office that "it would not be expedient that any answer be given for 8 or 10 months." Only after a delay that cooled everyone's tempers did the Palace send its reply:

---

* The capital by this time rotated between Toronto and Quebec City, Montreal having lost the honour as a result of the burning of its parliament buildings in 1849 by a Conservative-organized mob.

Ottawa was indeed Her Majesty's choice. Macdonald got the deed done while appearing to have had no part in it.

He wasn't yet finished with it, though. On July 28, 1858, while the House was debating an address to the Queen on the subject, a Canadien member moved a cleverly worded motion that opposed not the choice of Her Majesty—an unimaginable act—but the objective suitability of Ottawa. Most of the customarily tame bloc of *bleus* broke away from their alliance with Macdonald, and the errant motion was passed 64 to 50. This defeat put the life of the Taché-Macdonald government in peril. Brown, overexcited, moved a motion of adjournment to give everyone time to think. The *bleus* realizing now how they could make up for their disloyalty, streamed into the House to vote en masse against Brown's routine motion. Macdonald's hold on power was thus restored. One day later, however, on what he chose to call "an insult offered to the Queen," Macdonald and his ministers resigned.

Governor General Head now invited Brown to form a government. He agreed and did so. Just two days later, though, Brown was out and Macdonald was back again in power. These events were so unprecedented, and so surreal, that a legend grew that Macdonald had planned all along to lure Brown into a trap and there to crush him. Brown indeed was crushed, but he trapped himself; Macdonald had merely closed the gate over Brown's prone body.

Brown's miscalculation was that once he'd agreed to replace Macdonald's government, the parliamentary rules of the day required all the incoming ministers to resign and regain their seats in by-elections. While his ministers were temporarily absent, Brown would lose his majority in the House. To survive, he had to have an election, which, under the circumstances, he was virtually certain to win. However, as Head had warned

One of the earliest Canadian newspaper cartoons (c. 1858) mocking Macdonald's political trickery in the "double shuffle." Signed "H.R. in Toronto," it may have been drawn by the English cartoonist John Doyle—whose grandson, Arthur Conan Doyle, created Sherlock Holmes.

Brown when he first called on him, the preceding election had taken place only seven months earlier; to avoid back-to-back elections, Head advised Brown that he had to reserve the right to invite the just-resigned Macdonald to try to form an alternative new government. On Monday, August 2, Brown lost a vote in the House. He asked Head for a dissolution so an election could be called. Head refused. Brown resigned immediately, a bare two days after having taken office.

All observers now assumed that the same cycle would drag down Macdonald as soon as he attempted to form a cabinet. Macdonald, though, had already found his loophole. He had all his old ministers re-sworn again, but each in a new portfolio. (Macdonald's new post was postmaster general.) A day later, he switched his ministers back to their original portfolios, thereby avoiding the need for any of them to resign. No Reform lawyer was able to find any specific illegality in this double shuffle.

As Macdonald later said teasingly about Brown, "Some fish require to be toyed with. A prudent fish will play around with the bait some time before he takes it, but in this instance the fish scarcely waited till the bait was let down." The consequences of this political *commedia dell'arte* were that Macdonald got Canadians a capital that began its life behind the protection provided by the Queen, Brown got humiliated and Macdonald came away with a reputation for political knavery.* While absurd in itself, the incident marked the start of Macdonald's ascent to the status of a political legend. At this instant he gained another political asset at least as valuable: he secured the most important ally he would ever have: George-Étienne Cartier.

⁓

When the paths of Macdonald and Cartier first crossed, Macdonald paid him little attention. In a letter to a friend on January 27, 1855, he mentioned, in a review of his Canadien members, that "[Joseph-Édouard] Cauchon will prove a valuable man from his energy & talent" and that "[François-Xavier] Lemieux brings the whole strength of the Quebec district with him." Of Cartier, he said only, "He will represent the Montreal section . . . which was wholly without a representative." In his next reference, in February, Macdonald was somewhat more positive: he reckoned that Cartier was well suited to his portfolio of provincial

---

* Many years later, when Macdonald was sent a copy of Collins's 1883 biography of him—the first—he didn't bother to read it but "turned," as he put it in a letter to a friend, to just two sections: one, understandably enough, was the Canadian Pacific Scandal; the other was the "double shuffle."

George-Étienne Cartier. Macdonald praised him as "bold as a lion." Their French-English alliance revived that of Baldwin and LaFontaine. It was the foundation on which Confederation was built.

secretary, "which only requires industry and method, both of which he has to a remarkable degree." He still described Cauchon as "the ablest French-Canadian in the House"; a few days later, his skepticism returning, Macdonald described Cartier as "active—too much so."* A guess at why they didn't click immediately would be that Cartier, who could be full of himself, may have failed to give Macdonald due deference in their earlier encounters.

Cartier was exactly what Macdonald needed as French lieutenant: he commanded a disciplined bloc of French-Canadian members and was a national figure in his own right. As important, he quickly became Macdonald's principal link with Montreal's powerful community—overwhelmingly anglophone—of businessmen and financiers.

Cartier has slipped to the margins of Quebec historical consciousness: the one-hundredth anniversary of his death, on May 21, 1973, passed almost without notice.† It didn't help that Cartier once described himself as "an Englishman who speaks French." He bought all his clothes in London; he subscribed to

---

* Cauchon eventually crossed the floor to join the Liberals, becoming a minister in Alexander Mackenzie's government.

† There is a bust of him (in a Roman toga) in the Quebec City legislative building, and in Montreal, besides parks and schools, he is commemorated with an eighty-seven-foot-high statue inscribed with his cry, "Avant tous, je suis Canadien."

ten English magazines, but none from France. He was a passionate monarchist, declaring that the Conquest "saved us from the misery and shame of the French Revolution" and naming one of his daughters Reine-Victoria. Anglophilia aside, it is a fact of life that Quebecers generally lose their hearts to wounded heroes, such as Henri Bourassa or René Lévesque, rather than to winners—Cartier, Laurier, Trudeau. Yet Cartier was wholly and completely a Canadien. He was never happier than when belting out voyageur songs at his regular and raucous *conversations;* when introduced to the Prince of Wales, he broke into a French-Canadian chanson. In 1834 he was the first secretary of the new Société St-Jean-Baptiste, of which the slogan was "Nos institutions, notre langue, nos droits." He was one of the Patriotes during the 1837–38 uprising.

Cartier's near disappearance from the memory of his own people isn't justified by the legacy he left them. Montreal in the mid-nineteenth century was Canada's most important city—really its only one. Nevertheless, Toronto posed a substantive threat to Montreal's dominance. It had an incomparably richer hinterland in the dark soil of southwestern Ontario, attracted many more immigrants and was close to booming American cities such as Buffalo, Rochester and Syracuse. Yet Montreal would keep ahead of Toronto as Canada's metropolis for a full century after Cartier's death—until the 1970s, when the respective population counts of the two cities at last switched around. This lead was based on a political-industrial alliance, for which Cartier largely created the template. In his fine biography *George-Étienne Cartier: Montreal Bourgeois,* Brian Young writes that "his career demonstrates the power of railways in 19th century Montreal," and he goes on to describe Cartier as playing a leading role "in the transformation of Montreal civil society and in the imposition of fundamental social, economic and legal institutions."

Intuitively—he was in no way an intellectual—Cartier understood that the Empire of the St. Lawrence no longer depended on
the great river and chain of inland lakes but on the newfangled railways, those slim, arrow-straight, year-round transportation systems. "The prosperity of Montreal depends upon its position as
the entrepôt of the commerce of the West," he said. "We can only
maintain that position if we assure ourselves of the best means of
transport from the West to the Atlantic." The Grand Trunk, then
the world's longest railway line, had its headquarters in Montreal.
The company was there, bringing with it Canada's first wave of
industrialization, because Cartier was the Grand Trunk's solicitor
for eighteen years. During most of that time, he was also a senior
cabinet minister. Cartier piloted the Grand Trunk's charter
through the legislature in 1854; later, he functioned as the company's lobbyist, protecting it from what were called "the evils
of competition." As a result, Montreal became the country's
industrial and financial centre, with the Bank of Montreal as its
fiscal fulcrum. Above all, it had Ottawa as its patron. It would take
separatism to turn Montreal into a second-tier city.*

Born in 1814, a year ahead of Macdonald, Cartier came from a
family, for three generations, of merchants. He himself became a
lawyer. He had excellent connections (including in the Catholic
Church) and considerable charm. He drank enough to be convivial
but with none of Macdonald's escapist intensity. He could also be
intimidating: he was known to bully servants and he issued several challenges to duels. On one occasion, he and his opponent
actually fired shots, both missing—almost certainly deliberately.

---

* Over succeeding years, a succession of transportation and communications
enterprises, all either government agencies or dependent on government support, would locate in Montreal—Canadian National Railways, the National Film
Board, Telefilm Canada, Telesat Canada.

Cartier was a force of nature. He was short (five foot six inches), stocky, immensely strong, indefatigable (he often put in fifteen-hour days, and one of his speeches lasted seven hours in English, after which he repeated it in French). His self-confidence was boundless. When a Conservative member criticized him for not consulting widely, he answered, "That is quite correct, I do not consult anybody in making up my mind." When another member observed that Cartier "never sees a difficulty in anything," he answered, "And I have been generally pretty correct." He was fastidious about his dress, usually wearing a long black Prince Albert coat and a silk hat. He flirted a lot. "Feo" Monck, the sister of the governor general, recorded in her diary that when she asked Cartier his favourite occupation, he answered, "The activity of the heart." His mistress, Luce Cuvillier, a smoker of cheroots and, even more daringly, a wearer of trousers, was a great admirer of Byron and George Sand. She and Cartier lived openly together and travelled together, most often to London. In his will, he praised Luce's "sagesse et prudence" and left her six hundred dollars—a sizable sum—in his will.*

First elected in 1848, he joined the cabinet in 1855. After Taché retired, the government became the Macdonald-Cartier administration, with Cartier as attorney general for Lower Canada. As part of the contortions that ended the 1858 "double shuffle," the supposed new government was titled the Cartier-Macdonald ministry. Macdonald described the bloc of Canadien members who kept him in power as his "sheet anchor."

---

* His wife, Hortense, was deeply pious. A family friend remarked that she would have been happiest as a nun—provided she was the Mother Superior. After Cartier's death she moved to Cannes with her two daughters, dying there in 1898. One daughter, Hortense, lived on in Cannes until 1940, when she left hurriedly as the Germans approached. She died in London in 1941 at the age of ninety-three.

Character drew Macdonald and Cartier together. Both were bold—"as bold as a lion" was Macdonald's own description of Cartier. Neither was daunted by difficulties or defeats. Both loved Britain: Cartier's retirement plan was "to settle myself in London." Both feared the United States. About patronage and election funding, their views were identical, with Cartier being the less restrained of the two by a wide margin. He was well known for paying ten dollars for a vote, although for Irish votes he offered "a barrel of flour apiece and some salt fish thrown in for the leaders."

If Macdonald and Brown were a pair of rivals for whom few, if any, equivalents exist in Canadian history, Macdonald and Cartier were a pair of allies with few peers. They fought together for just under twenty years, 1854 to 1873; had they not stood side by side, there could have been no Confederation.

Politics, though, had not, yet, become Macdonald's whole life. His other life, his personal one, was dipping down now to one of its lowest points.

TWELVE

Isabella, Hugh John and Daisy

Tell Hugh that I am extremely pleased at the
report of Mr. May [his teacher].
John A. Macdonald's rare praise for his son

The "grey, unrelieved tragedy"—in Creighton's phrase—Macdonald had been living through for twelve years came to its final, inevitable end in the very last days of 1857. He'd long given up any hope, or pretence, that Isabella might recover. He no longer sent out letters that said, as they once had, "Isabella is not worse than she was yesterday." He no longer composed elaborate explanations to family members or to the increasingly comatose Isabella about why he had to stay late at the office or leave for some trip on political business.

In the summer of 1857 Macdonald went to England as part of a delegation seeking to raise capital for a new railway to the Maritimes. (The mission failed.) There, in his spare time he ordered a Highland dress outfit for Hugh John, to enable him to "bare his bottom with due Celtic dignity." Once back, Macdonald went first to Kingston, where Isabella was being looked after by his sister Louisa, and then on to Toronto, the seat of the government. Late in December (which meant he'd skipped spending Christmas with Isabella), Macdonald hurried back to Kingston, either because he had been warned or because he had a premonition that the ultimate crisis had arrived. For three days he sat beside Isabella's sickbed. On December 28 she died. No cause was given, but she was by then so weak that almost any ailment would have been enough.

On December 29 a notice in the Kingston *Daily News* invited "friends and acquaintances" to attend a funeral at the house his mother now lived in with Louisa. Isabella was buried in the family plot in Cataraqui Cemetery alongside her father-in-law, Hugh, and her infant son, John Alexander.

~

The exact nature of Isabella's prolonged ailments cannot be identified with any certainty. An argument can be made that many of them were located in her head.

The most extensive examination was that made by Dr. James McSherry, reported in two articles in *The Canadian Bulletin of Medical History* and the magazine *Historic Kingston*. His basic diagnosis was that "the probabilities are Isabella had pulmonary tuberculosis, a hysterical personality, complicated migraine and opiate dependence." He wrote that everything that is known about her "does not fit any recognizable medical pattern." And he added, "One can only wonder at John A. Macdonald's patience and kindness."

The "tic" to which Macdonald often referred was not a facial tic, as the term would be understood today, but, McSherry believed, "a generalized pain in the head." Much of her weakness may have derived, as might not have been fully appreciated at the time, from atrophy caused by prolonged bed rest. In one letter,

Macdonald described how, following an attack, "her bed had not been made for ten days, but this evening I managed to have her shifted to the sofa & she has now got back, much fatigued by the change, but is now, of course much more comfortable."

As is inevitable when the evidence is so old and so fragmentary, some of the medical puzzles do not yield to easy explanations. Isabella was weak, obviously; yet she remained strong enough to give birth twice and suffered no reported miscarriages. In frank puzzlement, McSherry writes, "It is difficult to imagine any medical condition which would produce such gross deterioration in physical well-being while preserving menstrual function and fertility."

The diagnosis of tuberculosis—then known as "consumption"—seems highly persuasive. Tuberculosis, though, can be transmitted by intimate contact, and she and Macdonald engaged in conjugal relations; as well, neither of her sons suffered from the disease. A medical friend of the author, Dr. Bryon Hyde of Ottawa, agrees with McSherry's primary diagnosis of pulmonary tuberculosis but reckons that the more likely cause was either of two comparable diseases, bovine tuberculosis or brucellosis; these, while similar to tuberculosis, are much less readily transmittable between humans and were prevalent in Georgia, the state where Isabella lived for several years. Hyde makes another interesting point. From today's perspective, the quantity of opium prescribed to Isabella is shocking, but, in fact, it made substantial sense because it significantly reduced her coughing and so minimized her loss of blood.

McSherry opens up an important non-medical aspect of Isabella's tribulations. He writes of "the frankly manipulative appearance of much of [her] behaviour. Any time Macdonald was about to leave, her condition worsened; as soon as he returned, it improved. Her calmness and courage while he was around would certainly have encouraged him to linger." McSherry speculates that Isabella may have capitalized on a genuine illness as a way of putting distance between herself and the intimidating, female-dominated Macdonald household—his two sisters and most particularly his formidable mother. Separated from her own relatives and in a strange land, Isabella may have been suffering a form of "culture shock." It's easy to guess that these hardy, practical Scots women would have regarded her as soft and gushy, not at all the right chatelaine for their John A.

It's impossible to know whether Macdonald actually loved Isabella. Most likely he did, at least in the earliest years of their marriage, and it may have been her flightiness and fragility that initially attracted this unsentimental, worldly man to her. The emotional cost to Macdonald of seeing his gay, girlish wife turn into a pain-racked, stupefied wreck of a human being, and then linger in that condition for a dozen years, can only be guessed at.

All that can be said with reasonable confidence is that if Macdonald did once lose his heart to Isabella, he never lost it again—or never again in the same way. Many years later, his son, Hugh John, fathered a daughter who was always known in the family by her nickname Daisy. These Macdonalds lived in Winnipeg, but as a young girl Daisy stayed with her grandfather in Ottawa while she went to school there, and she spent several summer vacations with him. They adored each other. Daisy's real name was Isabella.

~

Isabella's great gift to Macdonald was to give him a son and heir, Hugh John. Yet Macdonald all but "lost" him. When Hugh John was born, Macdonald's cry had been, "We have got Johnnie back again, almost his image." Hugh John would never know this, of

course, but as he grew up he must have sensed that he was com-
peting with an opponent he could never beat—his own, long-
dead, infant brother. The relationship between father and son was
never relaxed or close, and quite often it was strained.

There was the practical fact that the demands of politics on
Macdonald made him a virtually absent father. He did try: he sent
Hugh John that Highland dress, arranged for a tutor to come to the
house when the child was ill and bought him a Shetland pony and a
"waterproof" to wear while he was out riding; later, Macdonald
sorted out the complications when Professor James Williamson's
servant balked at having to look after the pony and its sleigh and
harness. And once, early in 1861, Macdonald sent to Hugh John, by
way of Louisa, the kind of message any son would ache to hear
from his father: "In the first place, tell Hugh that I am extremely
pleased at the report of Mr. May [his
teacher]." Macdonald then added,
"Tell him that I am quite proud of it
and that I have shown it to all my
friends." No doubt Hugh John would
have far preferred to have heard those
words directly from his father.

By then, Hugh John had become, all but formally, the son of
Macdonald's sister Margaret and
her husband. They had brought him
up at their home in Kingston from
his earliest years, with occasional
exceptions, such as when he joined
his family in Toronto. It's not quite
true, though, that Hugh John was a
surrogate son to a comparatively
elderly couple who could not have a

*Hugh John. By now a young lad, he regarded
Macdonald's sister Margaret and her husband, James Williamson, as his surrogate
parents. (This photo is also from Lady
Macdonald's album.)*

child themselves. True for Margaret, who had married on the cusp of forty, but not for Williamson. Before coming to Canada, he had been a minister in Scotland with a wife and son. When his wife died, soon after giving birth, Williamson decided to immigrate to Canada. He left behind the boy, James, to be brought up by his sister-in-law. In *Private Demons: The Tragic Personal Life of John A. Macdonald*, Patricia Phenix describes how young James tried frantically to maintain contact with his father, writing him pleading letters to be allowed at least to visit, but almost never getting a reply. The dereliction may have been more Margaret's than Williamson's. She, having come to regard Hugh John as her own son (he was after all her nephew), may well have feared that James, once in Kingston, would have competed with Hugh John for the attention of the man who was in fact his biological father. It's also possible that Macdonald himself was secretly glad to have so easy an out from the responsibilities of single fatherhood.

Isabella's death made Macdonald a middle-aged widower—and therefore once again a bachelor. From now on, he lived in board-ing houses or in apartments. Often he roomed with other legisla-ture members and with his principal civil servant, Hewitt Bernard. Inevitably, he drank a great deal more than before, spending longer hours in the Smoking Room of the Legislative Assembly. From this point on it becomes more difficult to know what Macdonald actually meant when he reported to his sister Margaret, as in a March 1858 letter, "I was very unwell last week so as to be confined to bed for three days and was hardly able to crawl to the House." Most likely he was afflicted with some com-bination of both illness and inebriation.

In some ways, Macdonald's personal life improved. He could go places when he wanted to, and no longer needed to feel guilty for having invented some excuse to avoid hurrying back to Isabella's side. His mother, Helen, continued to suffer strokes, yet she remained indomitable. She now lived with the Williamsons, but in her stubborn way she insisted on paying Macdonald rent, including a small sum for the use of the garden and yard and a share of the cost of the male servant. At the same time, Macdonald's law practice seemed to be in exceptionally good shape under his energetic young partner, Archibald Macdonnell.

Macdonald even managed to survive unscathed a near-death experience. In July 1859 he boarded the steamer *Ploughboy* for an excursion to Sault Ste. Marie. The ship's engine failed and the vessel began drifting towards the rocky coastline amid ever-rising wind and waves. Only when it was near shore did the anchors finally catch, after having dragged for close to twelve miles. "None of the party will be nearer to their graves until they are placed in them," Macdonald wrote to Louisa, adding, "The people behaved well, the women heroically."

Without Isabella and without Hugh John, Macdonald no longer had anything to distract him from "the long game." From now on, his personal life provided him with so few emotional demands or outlets for affection that he was free to apply all his abundant energy and passion exclusively to politics.

THIRTEEN

Double Majority

～

Is it a decree of destiny that Mr. Macdonald shall be the everlasting
Prime Minister? We must face issues.
The Colonist, June 19, 1858

As the decade of the 1850s drew to its end, Macdonald
was approaching a political peak. He had outma-
noeuvred Brown over the "double shuffle" with all
the ease of a feral cat toying with a mouse. The bloc
of *bleu* members who followed faithfully behind Cartier assured
him of a semi-permanent majority in the legislature. His
Liberal-Conservative Party, while shaky in several places,
hugged the vital centre of the political spectrum, with the
Tories in its ranks lapsing into sullen silence. As the de facto premier since 1854 and as co-premier in title since 1856, he'd held
that post longer than had anyone in the life of the United
Province of Canada. He'd deployed his tactics of compromise
and accommodation to dispose successfully of long-standing
issues such as the Clergy Reserves, the seigneurial system and
separate schools, and had managed to select a single capital for
the nation. Encomiums about Macdonald that floated across the
Atlantic from the upper reaches of the Colonial Office described

him as "a distinguished statesman" and "the principal man" in
Canada. It's always easier, though, to stumble when standing on
a peak than on flat ground.

The warning to Macdonald came from an inconsequential
source. On June 29, 1858, a small newspaper, the *Colonist*, ran a
startling editorial titled, "Whither Are We Drifting?" After cit-
ing examples of national drift, it asked, "Is it a decree of destiny
that Mr. Macdonald shall be the everlasting Prime Minister? We
must face issues. Worse can happen than a ministerial defeat."
What was truly startling was the fact that the *Colonist* was a pro-
Conservative newspaper—and that it was on to something.
A disconnection had opened up between the governed and the
governing; a disconnection, that is, between reality and politics.

Early in 1858, a letter proposing an extravagant idea crossed
Macdonald's desk. In it, Walter R. Jones of Kingston suggested
that the government should encourage the formation of a company to build a railway "through British American territory to
the Pacific." The next step should be "a line of steamers from
Vancouver Island to China, India, and Australia." Although the
historical record contains nothing more about Jones, his letter
catches perfectly the spirit of the times.

The years from the late 1850s to the mid-1860s were either the
best that Canadians experienced throughout the entire nineteenth century or a close second-best.* Everything was booming.
The economy was benefiting triply: from the Reciprocity Treaty

---

* The rival time span occurred near to the century's close and continued into the
next, prompting a new prime minister, Wilfrid Laurier, to predict that the twentieth century would belong to Canada.

(a free trade deal) with the United States, a general upturn in world trade, and the special demands created in Britain by the Crimean War and the closing of the rival lumber trade from the Baltic. Immigration was booming, at the same time as outmigration to the United States had slowed substantially. Towns such as Toronto and Quebec were acquiring some of the characteristics of cities, while Montreal, with close to one hundred thousand inhabitants, was not that far behind Boston. Promising new manufacturing towns were taking shape, including Hamilton and Brantford; London, in just the last half decade of the fifties, tripled its population to fifteen thousand.

The word "progress" was on almost everyone's lips. In *The Shield of Achilles,* edited by W.L. Morton, the historian Laurence S. Fallis notes that there was "an almost total absence of a literature of pessimism in the Province of Canada." Optimism was generated by the abundance of jobs and by rising wages. By no coincidence, a great many of the country's finest and boldest buildings, most spectacularly the Parliament Buildings in Ottawa, but also churches, cathedrals and public halls such as Toronto's St. Lawrence Hall, date from this period. One other agent of change affecting Canada more decisively than any other country in the world was the steam engine, and the parallel lines of steel that stretched out beyond the horizon.

Initially, Canadians went timidly into the Age of Railways. In 1844, a decade and a half after George Stephenson's famous Rocket made its first run in England, there were just fifty miles of track in the entire country. Then Canadians embraced the new age of transportation totally and extravagantly: by 1854 there were eight hundred miles of track; by 1864 there would be more than three thousand, including the Grand Trunk, reputedly the longest line in the world, stretching all the way from Quebec City to Sarnia. Soon, there were lines all over the place, built by the

Great Western, the Northern Railway, and the St. Lawrence and Atlantic. In fact, almost all these companies lost money and had to be subsidized by government. Often the railways disappointed; their underpowered locomotives repeatedly broke down and could be halted by even minor snowdrifts.

Railways were by no means the only catalyst of change. Canada's Pioneer Age was beginning to pass. The last parcel of "wild land" in the Bruce Peninsula was sold in 1854; the first "macadamized" roads were being built; and a few towns even boasted street lights. In some homes, parlour organs broadened the means of entertainment beyond fiddles and squeeze boxes. People had begun to realize that each new mechanical advance was not a fluke but the product of a system that would forever produce more and more marvels, from the mechanical harvester and the sewing machine to the telegraph. Many of these inventions brought

Poster for the Grand Trunk Railway, the longest railway in the world. The illustration shows the tubular iron Victoria Bridge, which spanned the St. Lawrence River. It was completed in 1859 and, the next year, was opened officially by the visiting Prince of Wales. Both railway and bridge reflected the emerging expansionist and confident Canada.

further radical changes, such as the division of labour and the elimination of distance. During this period, no change would be more transformational than the publication in 1859 of a massive, near-unreadable tome—Charles Darwin's *On the Origin of Species by Means of Natural Selection*. Decades would pass before the

One Canadian sage compared the transformational effect of the railways to that of the invention of printing. They made a huge difference, although the small-engined locomotives had a hard time pushing through the snow on the Grand Trunk rails.

"melancholy, long withdrawing roar"* of the loss of faith would reach Canada, but a defensive response came early when the curriculum of the required courses at the University of Toronto was altered to incorporate natural theology and "evidences" of the validity of Christianity.

Nothing, though, changed Canada more than did the railways. In 1849 the Montreal engineer Thomas Coltrin Keefer, a kind of nineteenth-century Marshall McLuhan, published a pamphlet, *Philosophy of Railroads*, in which he proclaimed, "Steam has exerted an influence over matter which can only be compared with that which the discovery of Printing has exercised upon the mind." A century later, the historian Michael Bliss revisited this idea in his book *Northern Enterprise:* "Steam conquered space and time. It

---

* From Matthew Arnold's "Dover Beach," published in 1867.

seemed to liberate communities from the tyrannies of geography and climate. . . . Steam changed the land itself, for wherever the rails went, they gave the land value." From now on, Canadians were less and less immured in their villages and small towns. They could reach out to each other to exchange everything from goods to ideas. Newspapers—the Toronto *Globe* most particularly—ceased to be purely local; business, from nail-makers to insurance companies, began to operate on a province-wide basis. Goods became more diverse and more competitive, and food became fresher and more varied. Mrs. Beeton's monumental cookery book became available in 1860. Time became standardized—by Sandford Fleming. In short, Canadians began to become a single community.

This was the environment, optimistic and expansive and ever more agreeable, in which a great many Canadians lived during the last years of the 1850s and the first of the 1860s. Keefer proclaimed, "Ignorance and prejudice will flee before advancing prosperity." The magazine *Canadian Gem and Family Visitor* told its readers: "Canada is destined to become one the finest countries on the face of the globe." The geologist and surveyor of the west, Henry Youle Hind, in his book *Eighty Years Progress of British North America* predicted "a magnificent future . . . which shall place the province, with the days of many now living, on a level with Great Britain herself, in population, in wealth, and in power." That the nineteenth century would belong to Canada seemed obvious; the politicians, though, were talking quite differently.

The changing circumstances did effect political change. Railways gave politicians a whole new range of power: they could decide who would win a charter to build and operate a company, and where its line should go. It could also give them personal profits—Premier MacNab as president of the Great Western; Cartier as solicitor for the Grand Trunk; and Hincks, the ex-premier, as a major shareholder in the same company. A British lobbyist for the Grand Trunk remarked, "Upon my word, I do not think that there is much to be said for Canadians over Turks when contracts, places, free tickets on railways or even cash was in question." Put simply, there was now incomparably more money than ever before rattling around inside the Canadian political system. Keefer described the period as "the saturnalia of nearly all classes connected with railways." Surprisingly, Macdonald himself never seems to have benefited personally from this first railway boom, and the only shares he appears to have bought were a modest number in the Great Southern Railway. But Canadian politics had undergone a sea change from its glory days of fighting for Responsible Government.

Macdonald ought to have been thoroughly enjoying himself. The boom made people happy, and happy voters are grateful voters. Yet time and again, Macdonald's naturally sunny nature seemed clouded by an undertone of dissatisfaction—as if he himself was wondering, "Is that all there is?" The frustration came through in comments he wrote to friends: "I find the work and annoyance too-much for me," and, "*Entre nous,* I think it not improbable that I will retire from the Govt." He even let down his guard enough to allow some of his pessimism to creep into letters to his family. To his sister Margaret, he wrote, "We are having a hard fight in the House & will beat them in the votes, but it will, I think, end in my retiring as soon as I can with honour"; and to his mother, "We are getting on very slowly in the House, and it is very tiresome." In 1859 the rumour spread that Macdonald intended to retire. Joseph Pope wrote of Macdonald, "I believe, [he] had fully made up his mind to get out." The entreaties of Conservatives eventually kept Macdonald at his post, but, as Pope wrote, "sorely against his wishes."

Macdonald expressed much the same sentiments in public. At a formal dinner given for him in Kingston in November 1860, he lapsed into quite-out-of-character self-pity. "When I have looked back upon my public life," he said, "I have often felt bitterly and keenly what a foolish man I was to enter into it at all (Cries of 'No, no'). . . . In this country, it is unfortunately true, that all men who enter the public service act foolishly in doing so. If a man desires peace and domestic happiness, he will find neither in performing the thankless task of a public officer."

One factor exacerbating Macdonald's pessimism was sheer loneliness. He lived in boarding houses, as, for example, jointly with a Mr. Salt on Toronto's Bay Street. In 1861 he wrote to his sister Margaret about his new apartment-mate, an Allan McLean: "He is a very good fellow but rather ennuyant and I will be glad when he goes. I am now so much accustomed to live alone, that it frets me to have a person always in the same house with me."

His natural optimism was rubbed down further by the progressive weakening of his beloved mother, Helen. She died on October 24, 1862. Alerted by Louisa, Macdonald was at her side through her last days. She too was buried in the family plot at Cataraqui Cemetery. Of his own family, only Margaret and Louisa remained; also Hugh John, but by now he had become a detached son. From this time on, Macdonald had less and less reason to go to Kingston, and, inevitably, he became increasingly distanced from his own childhood and youth.

While Macdonald was subject to occasional depressions, this general mood of listlessness and pessimism was alien to him. His usual philosophy of life is set out in a reply he wrote to a friend who had complained about financial problems. "Why man do you expect to go thro' this world with trials or worries. You have been deceived it seems. As for present debts, treat them as Fakredden [sic] in Tancred treated his—He played with his debts, caressed them, toyed with them—What would I have done without those darling debts said he." Macdonald then described his creed: "Take things pleasantly and when fortune empties her chamberpot on your head—Smile and say 'We are going to have a summer shower.'"

Not until later did Macdonald—by now without any real confidante—reveal a major cause of his sense of alienation and purposelessness. The occasion—to cite it here requires slipping out of the straitjacket of chronology—was a dinner in Halifax in September 1864, right after the close of the first Confederation conference in Charlottetown. During his speech, Macdonald turned confessional in a way that was most unusual for him. "For twenty long years I have been dragging myself through the dreary wastes of Colonial politics," he told his audience. "I thought there was no end, nothing worthy of ambition, but now I see something which is worthy of all I have suffered in the cause of my little country." By that vivid phrase—"twenty long years . . . through the dreary wastes"—Macdonald was coming very close to saying that his entire career had been an exercise in pointlessness.

Macdonald loved power for its own sake, and he loved the political game for itself, so it would be far too sweeping to conclude that he meant literally what he was saying. But there is hard truth in that analysis. Macdonald had not come into politics with any grand goal or vision, and after two decades in politics, a good half-dozen of them at the top of the ladder, he had yet to accomplish much that would linger after he left. During this time he had missed out on several chances to make real money or to have a normal family life. Most particularly, Macdonald was failing in politics itself. Rather than the national harmony that should have resulted from his turning the Conservative Party into a centrist group, by forging a French-English alliance and by settling long-standing disputes, what had grown stronger over these same years was disharmony, division and sectarianism.

———

Religion was the "other" of these times. Almost every topic of public debate was dominated by and deformed by sectarianism. It was Canada's equivalent to the division then rapidly taking hold in the United States between the slave-owning South and the anti-slavery North. The Orange Order, its membership constantly augmented by new Irish Protestant immigrants, was becoming ever more explicitly anti-Catholic, and the moderate Ogle Gowan was steadily losing ground to the hard-liner John Hillyard Cameron. At the same time, the Catholics in Lower Canada were becoming ever more ultramontane, or authoritarian. In Toronto, Bishop Armand-François Charbonnel declared that any Catholic who possessed the vote but failed to use it to elect candidates committed to expanding separate schools was guilty of a mortal sin. Differences in religion multiplied those of race, and the reverse equally.

In particular in Upper Canada, there was an ever-rising anger at the political power exercised in the national legislature by Lower Canada's Canadiens, this in important part because of the very alliance that Macdonald had forged with Cartier and his bloc of *bleus*. As was rare, Macdonald's political antennae failed to function. He dismissed Representation by Population as "too abstract a question [for the public] to be enthusiastic about." Rather, and as always in politics, appearance mattered far more than fact, and the appearance here was that the minority—a defeated one, moreover—was now in charge.

The responses went far beyond mutterings in the various Orange Lodges. The *Globe* laid it out explicitly: "Our French rulers are not over particular, we are sorry to say, and we are powerless. Upper Canadian sentiment matters nothing even in purely Upper Canadian matters. We are slaves. . . . J.A. Macdonald may allow his friend to buy an office, he may even take a thousand pounds of plunder, if he likes; so long as he please Lower Canada, he may rule over us." George Brown was even more intemperate: he railed in the *Globe* against "a deep scheme of Romish Priestcraft to colonize Upper Canada with Papists . . . a new scheme of the Roman hierarchy to unite the Irish Roman Catholics of the continent to a great league for the overthrow of our common [public] school system."

Macdonald was by no means without sin himself. While he deplored sectarian strife with a vigour few other English-Canadian politicians matched, he also exploited it. In a letter to education reformer Egerton Ryerson, after mentioning a grant to the university that Ryerson favoured, Macdonald urged, "The Elections will come off in June, so no time to be lost in rousing the Wesleyan feeling in our favour." He wrote to Sidney Smith, a Reformer he was trying to lure into his cabinet, "We must soothe the Orangemen by degrees but we cannot afford now to lose the Catholics." It was in this letter to Smith that Macdonald laid down his often-quoted maxim of how to rule: "Politics is a game requiring great coolness and an utter abnegation of prejudice and personal feeling."

Two solutions existed. One was Macdonald's policy of compromise, endlessly and exhaustingly pursued by guile, skill, outright deviousness and a sizable portion of self-interest. He still had Gowan on his side, and he had bought off the *bleus*, a great many them right-wing ultramontanes, by patronage. Despite its patches and outright holes, the Liberal-Conservative Big Tent still stood.

A second solution existed. Known as the "double majority," it amounted to a mechanical device for keeping Upper Canadians and Lower Canadians apart from each other politically. Up to a point, this system could work for regional matters, but national or province-wide measures became virtually impossible to put into effect. The solution merely papered over the problem, at the cost of making government paralysis all but inevitable and permanent.

Macdonald began by refusing to accept the double-majority rule. Gradually, he came to apply the rule he himself had spelled out in his legislature speech of 1854, of "yielding to the times" rather than engaging in "affected heroism or bravado"—and, also, of saving his political skin. He now proclaimed, "In matters affecting Upper Canada solely, members from that section claimed the generally exercised right of exclusive legislation, while members from Lower Canada legislated in matters affecting only their own section." This compromise ceded the double majority in fact, if not officially. It worked, but at the cost of making the legislature largely unworkable.

Paralysis was never absolute, of course. Work began in Ottawa in 1860 on the construction of a complex of Parliament Buildings of exceptional grandeur—and cost. In 1859 Macdonald's finance minister, Alexander Tilloch Galt, enacted higher tariffs on British imports to preserve Canada's vital Reciprocity Treaty with the United States. British manufacturers protested furiously, but the Colonial Office endorsed Galt's schedule. Effectively, London thereby added full economic self-government to the political self-government already ceded to Canada. And the term "world class" began to be applicable to Canada. Besides the Grand Trunk as the world's longest railway, the Victoria Bridge, spanning the St. Lawrence at Montreal and a marvel of tubular iron, was the

The Parliament Buildings under construction, c. 1862. They were huge, dramatic and extraordinarily ambitious for so small a colony. They were also the one thing in Ottawa that everyone liked.

world's longest; completed in 1857, it was opened officially in 1860 by a visiting royal prince.

But the dominant, all-consuming issue in Canadian public life remained sectarianism. To increase the tension, Brown's call for Representation by Population had become unanswerable. The census for 1861 showed that Upper Canada now had 285,000 more inhabitants than Lower Canada. More and more Conservatives were coming to accept that Upper Canada had to be given more seats in the legislature, in proportion to its population. Cartier—naturally—was adamantly opposed to any change in the balance of seats between Upper and Lower Canada, and Macdonald had to stand in solidarity with him or lose his *bleu* supporters. Yet rejecting Rep by Pop only magnified the fury in Upper Canada.

A yet-more-radical solution now began to be proposed—to disassemble the Province of Canada and recreate its two original provinces. Each province could then have whatever number of constituencies it wanted, because the two legislatures would be quite separate. But Canada itself would be no more.

Brown, who had begun to assert his authority over both the moderate Reformers and the radical Grits, took up this notion of sundering the nation. An editorial in the *Globe* threw down the gauntlet: "The disruption of the existing union" was needed to remove Canadien influence over Upper Canada. This would satisfy Lower Canada by giving it "a position of comparative independence." The alternative would be to "sweep away French power altogether."*

Macdonald's response was defiant. "I am a sincere unionist," he declared. "I nail my colours to the mast on that great principle." There had to be both union with Britain and "union of the two Canadas," he said. "God and nature have joined the two Canadas and no faction should be allowed to sever them." He had an obvious self-interest in keeping a Canadien bloc onside to compensate for the paucity of Conservative members in Upper Canada. His problem was that a call for compromise and accommodation had none of the mobilizing power of Brown's war cry for Rep by Pop.

There was only so much that Macdonald—or anyone—could do about sectarianism itself. Any real solution would have to wait for the time when Canadians cared less deeply about their religion, and about the religion of others. On a personal level,

---

* This near declaration of race war was written not by Brown but by his able and extremist chief editorial writer, George Sheppard.

though, there was something that Macdonald could do about his sense of malaise, of being unfulfilled, of feeling he was making no mark that he would leave behind: to find a woman to marry who could fulfill him.

In no way did Macdonald take advantage of his widowerhood to gain a reputation similar to that which would later earn his cabinet colleague Charles Tupper the nickname "the Ram of Cumberland." In the engagingly eccentric book *Kingston: The King's Town* (1952), Queen's University professor James Roy declared flatly that Macdonald "was known to have an amorous disposition," but provided not a scintilla of proof. As for sex specifically, Macdonald's prevailing attitude appeared to be that of worldly amusement. Apprised of one minister's marital misdemeanours, Macdonald responded by quoting the maxim, "There is no wisdom below the belt." As could be expected, the evidence of Macdonald's amorous activities as a widower is scanty. Most accounts pass over it in silence. Enough evidence exists, though, to suggest that during this period Macdonald may have had some kind of a relationship with at least five women, and in one instance to have come very close to an offer of marriage.

There's no question whatever that Macdonald liked women and, as is considerably less common, that he was entirely at ease in their company. In the very practical and rather prosaic Canadian society of the mid-nineteenth century, this alone would have made him a considerable catch. About that society, the visiting Englishwoman Anna Jameson observed, astutely and tartly, "I have never met with so many repining and discontented women as in Canada. . . . They seem to me perishing of ennui, or from the want of sympathy which they cannot obtain."

To any woman of spirit, Macdonald, by contrast, would have been catnip. There was his Windsor Castle companion of 1842, Miss Wanklyn, with whom he "*sympathized* wonderfully." Later on that same trip, he spent the considerable sum of seven pounds fifteen shillings on a riding whip as a present for an unnamed lady, very likely the same Miss Wanklyn. In 1845, while taking Isabella to Georgia, he sent one letter to Margaret Greene that captures his delight in female company: "I forgot to tell you that Mrs. Robinson, a sweet pretty woman, called on Saturday & I went to find her out today, but the directory was vague & I was stupid and & so did not see her again, much to Isabella's delight, who says she does not like me taking so much to your lady friends." That confidence committed to paper, Macdonald became bolder. "I always considered you a *Charming Woman*, but I did not calculate for all your friends being so. From those I have seen, I have only to say that you will confer a great favor* on me by sitting down & writing me letters of cre-dence to *every one* of your Yankee friends, and it will go hard but I [will] deliver most of them." It would appear that Isabella had good reason to be glad that Macdonald had failed to say "Hey" to Mrs. Robinson.

That Macdonald understood how to charm women is con-firmed by the extraordinary St. Valentine's Day ball that he organized for February 14, 1860, while living in Quebec City. It was held in the Music Hall of the St. Louis Hotel, the city's grandest. The chamber was packed with large garlands of roses and graced by busts of Queen Victoria and the Prince of Wales (who was booked to visit the colony later in the year). The walls

---

* Macdonald's spelling of "favour" in the American style of "favor" was unusual; he may have picked it up osmotically because he was writing from south of the border.

St. Louis Hotel, Quebec City. It was here, in 1860, that Macdonald staged the splendid, if extravagant, St. Valentine's Day ball that featured a huge pie from which twenty-four blackbirds emerged.

were adorned with new mirrors everywhere and thirty small wreaths of artificial flowers stitched by the Sisters of Charity. A fountain splashed out eau de cologne. The bill for food and drink came to an incredible $1,600, and the list included sparkling Moselle, sherry, port, ale, porter, and both red and white wine. Close to one thousand guests were invited, and on arrival each lady was presented with a valentine on which Macdonald had penned "very, pretty remarks." There was music throughout the evening, and dancing far into the night. As a highlight, when an exceptionally large pie was carried into the centre of the room, four and twenty blackbirds flew out from it once it was opened. Macdonald never organized another gala like it again. He was premier, after all, and he had no need to stage an extravaganza to impress local society. In this instance, given the day he chose for the party, it's entirely possible that he was trying to impress a particular woman.

In fact, after Isabella's death, Macdonald wouldn't have had to work hard to impress. His looks remained odd, but he was growing into them. He was self-assured, clever, funny, a delight for any woman to find seated beside her at a dinner table. He also possessed the aphrodisiacal allure of power. His one glaring defect was that he drank far too much—and this may have deterred the woman he came closest to proposing to during this period. She was Susan Agnes Bernard, the daughter of a wealthy Jamaican sugar planter and the sister of Hewitt Bernard, Macdonald's own top civil servant. They met once by accident in Toronto, then by Bernard's design in Quebec City, where Susan Agnes was living with her mother. They met there several other times, and it was reported that Macdonald asked her to marry him. Nothing came of it in the end, but Susan Agnes will make another appearance in these pages.

The most intriguing case of a might-have-been involves Elizabeth Hall, herself a widow. Macdonald and her late husband, Judge George B. Hall, had become friends when both of them were freshmen legislature members after the 1844 election. Hall died in 1858, and as a favour Macdonald wound up his estate and set up a trust fund for his children. Macdonald described Hall as "a warm, personal friend," and Hall, just before he died, wrote to Macdonald to say, "Have had a hard tussle with grim death. . . . If I don't see you again may we meet in Heaven." While settling his friend's legal affairs, Macdonald saw Elizabeth Hall often. Their relationship continued, and on December 21, 1860, she wrote him a letter that, between some bits of business information, positively aches with her longing for him.

"My loved John," she began, and then discussed the sale of some of her effects, the progress of the railway being built to Peterborough and the condition of the mails. She used this point to reach right out to Macdonald: "No hope now till I return from the backwoods where I only intend to stay a week & you will have no letter for that time—if that is a privation to *you* what must *I* feel if a fortnight without hearing from you. I cannot bear to think of it." Next came a description of a visit to neighbours, with her added comment: "A lady who was there made a set at me to find out if I was to be married in [the] Spring & I told her it was rumour, & my mother advised me when setting out in life to believe 'nothing I heard & only half of what I *saw*.'" Finally, she noted that the horses were being readied to take her for a drive, followed by a confident—or perhaps an overconfident—"Goodbye my own darling—love from loving Lizzie."

Unquestionably, something was going on between Macdonald and Elizabeth Hall. Most commentators have assumed that it was principally in Elizabeth's mind and that she made the mistake of pressing Macdonald too hard and lost him. Perhaps not, though; perhaps the opposite happened. What is truly fascinating about Elizabeth's letter is that it should exist at all. Macdonald kept very few personal letters, and none at all from either of his wives or from his mother. That he should have kept this one, hanging on to it for more than a quarter-century, suggests some recognition of a lost chance. Perhaps nothing happened because, with several children to bring up, Elizabeth Hall had too many dependants for him to cope with. She would, though, have already been well aware of his drinking "vice," and she possessed the invaluable asset of experience as the wife of a public man. So perhaps Macdonald let happiness slip through his fingers out of ineptitude or timidity.

Two of the other women are only wraithlike figures. There were rumours that the sister of a Prince Edward Island politician might marry him, but nothing came of the affair. And, at the close of a routine October 29, 1861, letter to one Richard William Scott, Macdonald added the tantalizing postscript: "P.S. You can make love to Polly." Here, Macdonald appears to have been telling

Scott that whatever may once have passed between him and the semi-anonymous Polly, the way was now open for Scott to press his own suit.

Then there is Eliza Grimason. Two writers, Patricia Phenix, the author of *Private Demons*, and more tentatively Lena Newman, the author of the excellent 1974 coffee-table book *The John A. Macdonald Album*, have suggested that a physical relationship may have existed between Macdonald and the lady. Eliza Grimason was a remarkable woman, and there's no question she adored Macdonald. No beauty by even the most generous estimate, but strong and confident, she owned and man-

Eliza Grimason, owner of the tavern in Kingston that Macdonald frequented. Rumours of a relationship between them were almost certainly untrue, but, even though they were from totally different social backgrounds, they were lifelong close friends.

aged Grimason House, Kingston's leading tavern.* She performed this role with such aplomb that, having started as an illiterate Irish immigrant, she went on to own properties with the handsome value of fifty thousand dollars. When they first met, she was just sixteen and he had turned thirty. Her husband, Henry, bought the property that became the tavern from Macdonald; when Henry died eleven years later, Macdonald did not press her for the balance of the payments, knowing she had three children to bring up.

Under her management, Grimason House became the most popular place in the town. It also became Macdonald's unofficial

---

* The tavern, now called the Royal Tavern, still exists, at 344 Princess Street in Kingston.

campaign headquarters. In one description, admittedly from the suspect source of James Roy, it was "the shrine of John A.'s worshippers with Mrs. Grimason as high priestess." The place was crowded, raucous, rowdy and raunchy. Macdonald went there regularly, bantering with the customers (mostly Conservatives), watching the cockfights (though not himself betting on them) and drinking a great deal. Election nights were his night. Eliza Grimason reportedly controlled one hundred votes, and she made her van available to take Conservatives to the polls, held "open house" for workers and voters and contributed to his campaign funds. According to Macdonald's early biographer Biggar, "when the returns were brought in, she would appear at Sir John's committee room, and walk up among the men to the head of the tables, and, giving Sir John a kiss, retire without saying a word." On the one occasion he lost, she was devastated. "There's not a man like him in the livin' earth," she said.

Many years later, Eliza Grimason came to Ottawa as Macdonald's guest at the opening of Parliament. He toured her round the buildings. Then she went to Earnscliffe to have tea with Lady Macdonald, whom Eliza judged "a very plain woman" but doing the job that needed to be done, because "she takes very good care of him." It's just not credible that Macdonald would have taken a former mistress around Parliament and then handed her on to have tea with his wife. The kiss she gave him in his committee rooms after he won each election must have been innocent, or the half-tipsy Conservative ward-heelers would have been shocked and, incomparably worse, they would have talked.

Macdonald's character, though, gave his friendship with Eliza Grimason a dimension that was far less common and far more interesting than any illicit relationship between them would have been. Their friendship was an extraordinarily democratic one. Macdonald, the nation's most powerful man, and a highly intelligent and well-read one to boot, was the true friend of a rough countrywoman who earned her living running a grungy tavern. Their friendship was so close, and so unaffected, that Macdonald in later years kept a framed photograph of Mrs. Grimason on his desk, beside one of his mother. It was because Macdonald knew people like Mrs. Grimason and her customers that he knew Canada better than any succeeding premier or prime minister ever did.

Maybe, post-Isabella, Macdonald could not allow himself to be close to another woman. One chronicler, the historian Keith Johnson, has written that Macdonald seemed to have a "central, emotional dead spot." That's too strong an assessment; all his life he could be extraordinarily tender with children and wholly at ease with them. But except for Isabella during their first few years together, he never again really let down his guard with a woman.

Here, as always with Macdonald, there is a glaring contradiction—although perhaps only an apparent one. Women adored him. That was the judgment of that sophisticated observer Sir John Willison, the editor of the *Globe*, who wrote in his *Reminiscences* that "because women know men better than they know themselves and better than men ever suspect, there was among women a passionate devotion to Sir John A. Macdonald such as no other political leader in Canada has inspired." (Since Willison was a confidante of Laurier, this was high praise indeed.) Willison ends, with the gallant flourish, "No man of ignoble quality ever commands the devotion of women."

One other aspect of Macdonald's relations with women deserves some attention, if cautiously so. In an essay on Macdonald in the 1967–68 edition of the *Dalhousie Review*, the historian Peter Waite first remarks that "his liking for human beings was genuine" and then goes on to make the intriguing comment,

"It is not too much to say that he often liked men as much for their bad qualities as for their good." A readiness to like people for their faults, or at least an acceptance that such failings are an integral part of the human condition, is more a female trait than a male one. In his own person, Macdonald was thoroughly masculine: he drank a lot, told bawdy stories, had a nasty temper and was highly competitive. But there was also a female side to his nature—an aspect of him caught by the novelist Hugh MacLennan's comment quoted in the introduction, "This utterly masculine man with so much woman in him." Whatever his own nature, he took people as they came and worked with their faults and shortcomings, rather than trying to reform them or to improve them. As well, the failings of human beings provided him with invaluable raw material for the endless anecdotes by which he gently tugged self-doubting opponents into his web.

Whatever his qualities, Macdonald, during the years on either side of 1860, succeeded neither with women nor with sectarianism. Perhaps he did win one signal victory over the latter challenge, though proof is impossible. A fascinating document exists that captures the essence of the policy of compromise and accommodation that Macdonald deployed to try to resolve the deeply divisive issue of sectarianism that so disfigured Canadian politics through the 1850s and early 1860s.

In a long dispatch to the colonial secretary in June 1857, the governor general, Sir Edmund Head, wrote, "If it is difficult for any statesman to stem their [sic] way amid the mingled interests and conflicting opinions of Catholic and Protestant, Upper and Lower Canadian, French and English, Scotch and Irish, constantly crossing and thwarting one another, it is probably to the action of these very cross interests and these conflicting opinions that the whole united province will, under providence, in the end owe its liberal policy and its final success." Head added, "In such circumstances, constitutional and parliamentary government cannot be carried on except by a vigilant and careful attention to the reasonable demands of all races and all religious interests."

To that analysis of Canada's essential nature, there was not a word Macdonald would have wanted to add. He may indeed have helped to compose many of them. He and Head had several long, private conversations when the government was located in Toronto. Pope wrote in his biography that Macdonald was "never so intimate with any Governor-General as with Sir Edmund." Moreover, the governor general needed to learn from Macdonald; when he first arrived in 1855, Head caused an uproar among Canadiens by commenting to an Upper Canadian audience on "the superiority of the race from which most of you have sprung."

If Head learned from Macdonald, the reverse was not true. In another dispatch home in 1858, Head suggested a federation of all the British American colonies. To Macdonald, such an idea was but an intellectual abstraction—perhaps nice, but irrelevant because undoable.

By this time Macdonald was well aware that something was fundamentally amiss in Canadian politics and governance. But he still had no idea what to do to cure the malaise. Around him, though, the times had begun to change.

FOURTEEN

The Shield of Achilles

~

I see within the round of that shield, the peaks of the Western
mountains and the crests of the Eastern waves.

Thomas D'Arcy McGee

The change in Canada that most affected Macdonald at the beginning of the 1860s was the size of the country. Not literally, of course. The United Province of Canada remained just as it had always been—an elongated oblong extending from the mouth of the Gulf of St. Lawrence to just beyond the western edge of Lake Superior, and encompassing only about half of today's Ontario and Quebec; an oblong, moreover, blocked from the sea except during the near half of the year that the St. Lawrence River was free of ice. Even though it took up an impressive amount of space on any map of the North American continent, it was a strangulated community.

The change in Canada's size was psychic. In the years immediately before 1860 a consciousness began to stir among Canadians that they were occupying the antechamber of a vast empire. They began to realize that their own United Province was only a part of the territory that existed above the forty-ninth parallel. Elsewhere in the immense, intimidating expanse of land there were no fewer than five other British colonies—to the east,

Nova Scotia, New Brunswick, Prince Edward Island and Newfoundland, and almost an unimaginable distance away to the west, the tiny colony of Vancouver Island, clinging to the edge of a second vast ocean. As well, roughly in the continent's middle, there was a small settlement out on the prairies in a place called Red River, which was administered—sort of—by the Hudson's Bay Company. Almost all this land was entirely empty except for Indians. All of it, though, was British.

Macdonald's interest in this additional territory varied from negligible to non-existent. Between sectarianism and the tensions dividing English and French in the United Province and, most immediately challenging of all, the gradual shift of opinion among his own Conservatives in favour of Rep by Pop, he had more than enough to cope with. About the West, as he later described his sentiments, he was "quite willing personally to leave that country a wilderness for the next fifty years." As for the Maritimes, although there were occasional proposals for a railway to connect quasi-inland Canada to tidewater at the ice-free port of Halifax, the costs would be horrendous, and no bank or financier in London showed the least interest in advancing the capital needed for such a project.

Yet change was happening in people's minds. It was very tentative and not at all well informed. But a shift in self-awareness about Canada's possibilities had begun that would, before many years, cause Macdonald to undertake the single most radical political project of his life.

One catalyst of change can be traced back to Montreal and to the middle of 1857. A new tri-weekly literary journal, the *New Era*, appeared there. As its opening attraction, it published a series of editorials on the topic "The Future of Canada." The ideas expressed in these essays were lively and novel. One declared that although Canada possessed the central spine of the St. Lawrence, it lacked the essential "one-ness of political life." After asking, "Who reads a Canadian book?" and noting that almost no one did, the journal threw out a challenge: "Come, let us construct a national literature for Canada, neither British nor French nor Yankeeish . . . borrowing from all lands, but asserting its own title." The journal questioned whether Canadian trade policy should be "unconditionally and absolutely in the hands of the Colonial Secretary" and urged the appointment of a Canadian "representative" in Washington. The solution to the country's general political problems, it declared, had to be "a Federal compact" within which each province would have its own Parliament while "conceding to the federal authority such powers as are necessary for the general progress and safety." A new federal constitution, though, was not enough: "The federation of feeling must precede the federation of fact."

What was happening here, as happened so rarely in the pragmatic, provincial world of mid-nineteenth-century Canadian politics, was original thought and unleashed imagination. The author was a newly arrived immigrant, Thomas D'Arcy McGee. He possessed, as was even rarer in Canada, the voice of a poet or, since the florid verse he scribbled out was scarcely poetry, then at least the voice of a romantic.

Irish, of course, born in 1825 in County Louth and the son of a coast guard, McGee got involved with the revolutionary Young Ireland movement, fled the island disguised as a priest, and made his way to Boston and later New York, earning his living as a journalist. He proclaimed, among a good many other bravura ideas, that the United States would eventually stretch "from Labrador to Panama" and that "either by purchase, conquest, or stipulation, Canada must be yielded by Great Britain to this Republic." Yet McGee grew restive in that country. Its practice of slavery disgusted him, as did, more personally, the anti-Irish bigotry of the anti-immigrant Know Nothing movement. McGee came north to Montreal in 1857 and to his astonishment found there, after all his years of fighting the English, "far more liberty and tolerance enjoyed by those in Canada than in the U.S." Besides his capacity for passion, McGee attracted attention by two qualities: he had great charm, and he was exceptionally ugly. He was short, swarthy, with a sort of squashed-up face. His wife, Mary, when asked whether she ever worried he might stray during his many trips away from home, responded, "Sure, I've got great faith in his ugliness."

Besides his editorials in the *New Era*, McGee developed a set speech that commanded ever-larger audiences. It was a hymn to a wider, bolder Canada: "I see in the not remote distance, one great nationality bound like the shield of Achilles, by the blue rim of the ocean . . . I see it quartered into many communities, each disposing of its internal affairs but all together by free institutions, free intercourse and free commerce. I see within the round of the shield, the peaks of the Western mountains and the crests of the Eastern waves . . . I see a generation of industrious, contented moral men, free in name and in fact." McGee was Canada's first nationalist.

D'Arcy McGee. Passionate, eloquent, hard-drinking, he was Canada's first nationalist, and, effectively, Confederation's poet laureate. His wife expressed her "great faith in his ugliness."

Nationalism was enough to put him at odds with Macdonald, so suspicious of any innovation that might weaken the British connection. Even more irritating was that McGee, when he got into politics, did so as a Reformer. In the *New Era*, he damned Macdonald's government as "one of expedients, a succession of make-shifts." McGee took a ministerial post in George Brown's two-day "double-shuffle" government, and afterwards enraged Macdonald by writing articles accusing Governor General Head of having colluded with Macdonald to oust Brown. Macdonald was annoyed enough to declare, "Never did a man throw away a fine career as he [McGee] has by his violence, falsehood & folly." From their first encounter, though, Macdonald and McGee saw something in each other. After McGee made his maiden speech in the legislature damning Macdonald's "timid, makeshift policy," Macdonald ambled over, extended his hand and congratulated him. McGee remarked afterwards how "ready and dextrous" the older man was, and how "good humour is his most apparent characteristic." No doubt that was just Macdonald's "soft sawder."

Over time, though, their early recognition of a connection between them would blossom into a partnership, both of political allies and of drinking buddies. Perhaps Macdonald saw in McGee, ten years younger, the kind of protege men in power often like to have around to mentor. Perhaps Macdonald responded to the romantic in McGee, aware in his inexhaustibly subtle way that a dreamer is as much a part of public affairs as is a doer. It is tempting to call Macdonald, Cartier and McGee the three musketeers of Confederation, but it would not be true: Cartier never liked McGee, perhaps because, with his quick wit and marvellous singing voice, he was more popular at parties.

With McGee, the idea of Canada as something larger than the sum of its parts entered the public discourse. It was an idea, moreover, that all those who crowded in to hear McGee's speeches applauded wildly, no matter whether they were Conservatives or Reformers or Grits, or entirely indifferent to all politics.

～

Another voice addressing itself to the possibility of a wider Canada also began to be expressed at about this same time—from Alexander Tilloch Galt. Its nature was quite different from McGee's, more precise, less flowery, more attuned to accounting than to poetry. But still, it was a voice able to inject credibility and solidity into the vague notion of a wider Canada.

One of Macdonald's most glaring political weaknesses was that, while he had many members in the legislature, the ranks of his ministers were conspicuously thin in the vital ingredient of talent. Galt was an obvious potential new recruit for the cabinet, except that he displayed great wariness about Macdonald. Luring Galt to his side now became Macdonald's principal project.

Born in 1817, just two years after Macdonald, and like him a Scot, Galt was the son of John Galt, a writer who once travelled with Byron through Asia Minor. He was well educated and exceptionally bright. He grew up tall, lean and hardy, once walking thirty-six miles in six hours. His father immigrated to Canada to manage a British-financed scheme for colonization in the area of Sherbrooke in Lower Canada. Galt joined his father, who soon returned to Britain. The young Galt rose quickly in the business: when he was just twenty-six he was sent back to London to become commissioner of the Canadian operations of the British American Land Company. He returned to Sherbrooke, did well and, as was common at the time, went into the legislature, as an Independent.

Once Macdonald had become premier, he was in a position to place an alluring bait in front of Galt. Cannily, he offered nothing at all; instead, he engaged in tantalizing teasing: "You call

Alexander Galt. The fourth of the four "Super-Fathers" of Confederation and its financial brain, he shared Macdonald's fear that Britain wanted to rid itself of Canada.

yourself a *Rouge*. There may have been at one time a reddish tinge about you, but I could observe it becoming by degrees fainter. In fact you are like Byron's Dying Dolphin, exhibiting a series of colours—'the last still loveliest'—and that last is 'true blue,' being the colour I affect," Macdonald wrote in a letter to Galt in 1857. "So pray do become true blue at once: it is a good standing colour and bears washing."

Galt preserved his virtue for another year and then joined the cabinet—but at a high price to Macdonald. By this time Galt had become convinced that the only solution to Canada's governmental inertia was to form a federation of all the British American colonies. He sketched out his idea in impressive detail, including a supreme court to settle jurisdictional disputes. In fact, neither Macdonald nor Cartier was in the least persuaded by Galt's ideas, but they both accepted fully the political credibility he could bring to the government. They offered him the finance portfolio, and he joined the cabinet in July 1858. Galt then exacted his price. In a long speech to the House, he set out on behalf of the government his idea for a federation of British North America. The response made right afterwards by Macdonald and Cartier was striking: after Galt had finished speaking, neither of them said a word.

As a further part of his price, Galt had secured from Macdonald approval for him to go with Cartier to London that October to try to sell his federation idea to the Colonial Office.

The response of the colonial secretary, Sir Edward Bulwer-Lytton,* was dismissive, principally because of London's skepticism that Canadian politicians were up to so ambitious a task, but also because the reaction to the idea in the Maritimes was negative.

Galt and Macdonald were never close. Macdonald once described him as "unstable as water, and can never be depended upon to be of the same mind for forty-eight hours together." This assessment wasn't off the mark; before advocating Confederation, Galt had advocated annexation with the United States. Nevertheless, he succeeded for the first time in actually discussing a possible federation with the Colonial Office and, however nominally, secured a commitment for that notion to be added to the grabbag of policies that belonged to the Liberal-Conservative Party. As important for the way the future would unfold, Galt, with his well-known competence for accounting on a grand scale, was now working alongside Macdonald.

A third voice could be heard musing out loud about the need for a wider Canada. It was that of the Toronto *Globe* owner and publisher, George Brown. A grand federation held few charms for him. Instead, the catalyst for Brown's interest was his realization that, with the new immigrants having settled on the last "wild" land in Upper Canada, this province—Brown's province—needed new worlds to conquer. The *Globe* expressed this expan-

---

* In his day, Bulwer-Lytton was far better known as a popular writer—as of the romantic novel *The Last Days of Pompeii*—than as a politician. Today, he's best known as the inspiration for the annual Bulwer-Lytton Fiction Contest for bad writing, which takes off from his famous opening line, "It was a dark and stormy night." This association is a bit unfair, given that Bulwer-Lytton also minted the aphorism that writers love to quote, "The pen is mightier than the sword."

sionist concept best in an epistle to its Toronto readers on December 26, 1856: "If their city is ever to be made great—if it is ever to rise above the rank of a fifth-rate American town—it must be by the development of the great British territory lying to the north and west."

The *Globe*'s reference was to the North-West Territories, stretching out all the way from Lake Superior to the Rockies. It was bald, empty prairie, except for the Indians and a small cluster of Métis and a few Canadian settlers at the bend in the Red River. The rest of the territory served as a gigantic trapping ground for the fur traders of the Hudson's Bay Company and as a killing ground of the buffalo. Commonly called the North-West, it was also known as Rupert's Land—after Prince Rupert of the Rhine, the dashing cavalry general and cousin of Charles II, who in 1670 had secured a monopoly charter over the territory for himself and a group of British financiers and businessmen.

By the late 1850s the members of the governing board of the Hudson's Bay Company had come to realize that their exercise of absolute rule over a land that was now desired by nearby British North Americans was anomalous and ultimately unsustainable. They continued to protest that the land of the North-West was arid and useless. At Red River, though, as the settlers there knew well, the soil was black and deep. One of Macdonald's ministers, Joseph-Édouard Cauchon, the commissioner of Crown lands, wrote a memorandum to cabinet arguing that the "Red River and Saskatchewan Country" could attract to Canada many of the immigrants now passing straight through to the United States.

Another possibility—a distinctly alarming one—was that the Americans might come into the North-West first. In fact, they were almost there already. By now a railway line had reached St. Paul, Minnesota. From there, by oxcart and by boat along the winding Red River, it was incomparably easier to send goods to and from the settlement of Red River than it was for Canadians to make the long, brutal slog westwards across the Pre-Cambrian Shield above Lake Superior. To heighten the threat, a scientist at the Smithsonian Institution, Lorin Blodgett, issued a report in 1857 describing the land beyond the forty-ninth parallel as "perfectly adapted to the fullest occupation by a civilized nation." In response, two surveying expeditions to the West were dispatched from Canada the following year, one headed by Captain John Palliser, a Britisher, and the other by Henry Youle Hind, a graduate of Cambridge who had settled in Toronto as the professor of chemistry and geology at Trinity College. To heighten the sense of cross-border rivalry and threat, Minnesota was elevated from a territory to a state in 1858.

Macdonald's response to all this expansionism was cautious to a degree. About a possible federation he said nothing at all. About territorial expansion he said as little as possible, influenced by the warning of his friend John Rose, a Montreal lawyer, that it would be expensive to protect "such an extent of territory, even if it is given up to us for nothing."

Britain, in the person of the colonial secretary, Henry Labouchere, nevertheless felt that something had to be done to regularize the situation in the North-West. At Westminster, a select committee of the Commons was set up to recommend on the future of the Hudson's Bay Company charter, including whether the territory should be offered to Canada and at what price. The company adroitly countered with an offer that it would accept a takeover in return for a payment of one million pounds. To present Canada's case to the Commons committee, Macdonald established a commission headed by his former leader William Draper, now a judge.

Very little came of any of this. Draper told the select committee that Canada "must assert her rights" in the North-West, but in the absence of clear instructions from Macdonald his presentation to the British MPs was vague and legalistic. The committee made only one innovative recommendation—for a second Crown colony to be established on the Pacific Coast, to be named British Columbia. By oversight (or perhaps by design), the Hudson's Bay Company charter was allowed to lapse of its own accord in 1859. A group of British businessmen bought up the company, calculating shrewdly they would make an easy profit once they were forced to resell it to Canada. The Hudson's Bay Company continued to rule over its land, but less and less to govern it. Among those who came increasingly to control their own lives were the Métis of Red River, a change in their sense of themselves that no one outside the settlement took any notice of.

For the first time, though, ordinary Canadians had become aware of the open territory to their west. Indeed, because of a gold rush at the Fraser River, they appreciated now that this immense territory stretched all the way to the Pacific. An eventual takeover seemed more or less inevitable, if in no way imminent. Canada's own version of Manifest Destiny beckoned.

That expansionary thought precipitated others. If Canada were to be extended to the Pacific, then logically it should be extended as well to the east, to the Atlantic. Yet if Canada proper were to be augmented by both the North-West and the Lower Provinces (as the Maritimes then were called), the population balance would tilt decisively against the Canadiens—everyone taking it for granted that the West would be colonized by settlers from Upper Canada and by new immigrants from the British Isles. The Canadiens, though, would oppose any such radical change in Canada's demographic character as a violation of the agreement between the two groups when the United Province had been formed; more to the point, they could forestall it by exercising the de facto veto they possessed through the double-majority convention. When Cartier and Galt went to Britain for their meetings in 1858, Cartier warned Colonial Secretary Sir Edward Bulwer-Lytton that, if forced to, he would exercise this veto. Nothing was resolved, but for the first time politicians were giving thought to the kind of problems that would emerge as soon as any serious attempt was made to add to Canada some or all of the other pieces of British North America.

Here, Macdonald allowed himself for the first time to express some views about a possible wider Canada. In the debate that followed the announcement that Draper would represent Canada's views on the North-West to the British Parliament, Macdonald made an intriguing comment quite different from his earlier cautious utterances on the topic of Canada's future. "The destiny of this continent," he told the House, could depend on the results of the parliamentary inquiry in London. "Upon that action may depend whether this country remains confined to its present boundaries or swells to the dimension of a nation; whether we are to be annexed to the neighbouring Republic or extend the boundaries of this country itself."

Macdonald was allowing the wheels of his mind to turn in public. Earlier he had dismissed the western territory as useless, and on one occasion expressed concern that Canada could be weakened by spreading out its settlers too thinly. Now he was declaring that adding the West to Canada could transform what was still only a province into something resembling a nation. While the word "federation" had not yet crossed his lips, Macdonald was here using the word that had always held talismanic importance to him—"annexation"—in the sense of stressing the need to make certain it never happened.

Proposals for a federation of the British North American colonies, or for a confederation of them—the terms were used interchangeably at this time—were not in themselves in any way new. The number of different proposals made for some form of federation or confederation before McGee and Galt took up the cause has been estimated at eighteen in all. The first person to advocate it—three-quarters of a century earlier—was Major Robert Morse, a British army engineer who, after surveying the Bay of Fundy in 1784 for possible settlements following the loss of the American colonies, suggested that all the colonies still remaining under the Crown should be banded together for their own protection. The same thought was expressed a few years later by two leading Loyalists, William Smith, later chief justice of Quebec, and Jonathan Sewell, who, in 1807, published a pamphlet about his idea: *Plan for a General Legislative Union of the British Provinces in North America.** In the late 1830s in Britain, a Canadian-educated British MP, James Roebuck, proposed it at Westminster; Lord Durham came very close to recommending it in his famous report; and the Colonial Office later drafted a report on how it might be constructed.

A major obstacle—one common to most transformational ideas—was that potential losers could count their losses before they experienced them, while gains for likely winners were futuristic. The Maritimes, all of which were separate colonies

---

* The most unorthodox version of confederation, submitted to the legislature of Upper Canada in 1825 and advocating a loose federation, was by Robert Gourlay, who turned out to have written it while in a lunatic asylum in England. Gourlay was an engaging eccentric and an agrarian radical. His most considerable accomplishment was, at the age of eighty, to contest a riding in Upper Canada and to marry his twenty-eight-year-old housekeeper. However, he lost both.

that had already won Responsible Government for themselves, had little interest in giving up London as their protector in favour of Ottawa. Upper Canada had little interest in offering the one lure Maritimers might respond to—a railway to Halifax—because it would be the principal payer of the scheme, while Montreal, where the headquarters of this intercolonial railway would be located, would be the chief beneficiary. As for the Canadiens, it was difficult to offer them any greater protection than the virtual veto over Canadian national affairs they already exercised.

This combination of indifference and skepticism among so many of the British North Americans had been more than enough to convince Bulwer-Lytton to give Galt and Cartier a dusty, evasive answer when they came looking for British support for Galt's federation concept. Further, the colonial secretary was sharp enough to guess that Macdonald's real motive for sending over the mission was "the convenience of the present Canadian administration"—in other words, to make certain that Galt joined his cabinet.

Yet again, inertia won the day. What was needed to make something actually happen was a crisis, one that would shake everyone from his own fixed position. Also needed at that moment of opportunity would be a political leader who knew how to herd cats.

⌒

Some commentators, the most influential among them Donald Creighton, have attempted to situate Macdonald among the early advocates of Confederation, as if to mingle his lustre with that of the cause of union itself. The weight of evidence is otherwise: even the inclusion of support for Confederation in the Liberal-

Conservative policy from 1858 onwards was strictly tactical. The most persuasive negative evidence comes from Macdonald himself—in his own words.

In advance of the impending next election—it actually happened in the summer of 1861—Macdonald published an *Address to the Electors of the City of Kingston* of some three thousand words in which he set out his policies on all the central issues of the day, including a bankruptcy law, university reform, the Grand Trunk Railway, law reform and Representation by Population. About this last, controversial, topic, Macdonald penned the evasive phrase "This is not a party question, and ought not to be made one."

About his thoughts on Confederation as he held them in mid-1861, Macdonald wrote, "The Government will not relax its exertions to effect a Confederation of the North American Provinces. We must however endeavour to take warning by the defects in the Constitution of the United States, which are now so painfully made manifest, and to form (if we succeed in a Federation) an efficient, central government." That was all he had to say. To have said less would have been difficult. His disinclination to commit himself to any "vision thing" came out of the policy of governance he was committed to. Back in 1844, in advance of his first election, Macdonald had promised Kingston's voters that he would not "waste the time of the legislature and the money of the people on abstract and theoretical questions of government."* After two decades of practical political experience, the abstract and the theoretical still left him cold.

About constitutions, Macdonald was at all times particularly

---

* Creighton's case for Macdonald as an early champion of Confederation rests primarily on a speech he gave in the House in April 1861 calling for "an immense confederation of free men, the greatest confederacy of civilized and intelligent men that has ever had an existence on the face of the globe." All those golden phrases, though, were simply Macdonald at his "buncombe" best.

wary. They should not be fiddled with, he believed, unless "the people are suffering from the effects of the constitution as it actually exists," as he had said in a legislature speech in 1854. Anyway, the substance of constitutions could be changed without an *i* or a *t* of them being amended. Canada had, after all, gained Responsible Government, although its constitution had been drafted specifically to exclude it; and the double-majority principle had entered into legislative life without any legal sanction. Britain, Macdonald's political ideal, had won and was now administering the world's second-greatest empire on the foundation of no written constitution at all. Put simply, Confederation at this time was, to Macdonald, an impractical irrelevancy.

But that left him with no governing principle at all—at the time when Brown's governing principle of Rep by Pop kept gaining ever more legitimacy and support. Even Antoine-Aimé Dorion, the leader of *rouges*, who were loosely allied to the Reformers, felt compelled to suggest in the legislature a possible trade of his agreement to Rep by Pop for disentangling the United Province of Canada into a loose federation of two provinces with some minimalist central government.

Macdonald was reduced to advising Conservative candidates who supported Rep by Pop how best to express their opinion without appearing to be splitting from the party. He wrote to a sitting member, George Benjamin, to "go for Rep by Pop as strongly as you like, but do *not* say that it must be granted if a majority of U.C. members say so. Say that the principle is so just & equitable that it must prevail and that you have no doubt it will eventually." He went on to urge Benjamin, "As you are situated, *do not put yourself in opposition to the French.* . . . The French are your sheet anchor."

Macdonald was being forced to perform like a gymnast edging his way along a high wire that someone else was jiggling. Of the six Upper Canada ministers in his government, all but one would eventually go public as supporters of Rep by Pop—the lone exception being Macdonald himself. At the same time, his French Canadians were becoming increasingly concerned that Macdonald could not forever forestall Rep by Pop. So, some *bleus* began to wonder, why not switch over to the winning side—that of Brown and the Reformers—and thereby keep hold of the perks of patronage? Moreover, while Macdonald had spotted the possibility that he might be reduced to an opposition rump by a loss of *bleu* support, so had Brown.

After the humiliation of the double shuffle—and the taunt that he had headed "His Excellency's most ephemeral Administration"—Brown's career had gone into decline. He seemed even to have lost power at the *Globe*, where the editorials were being determined by the editor, George Sheppard. The anti-French Sheppard repeatedly called for an end to "French domination" and demanded that the problem be solved by an outright dissolution of the Union that would release Upper Canada from "Romish" and "Jesuitical" scheming.

Brown began his march back to leadership by organizing a huge Reform convention for the fall of 1859 in Toronto; its six hundred delegates made it easily the largest Canada had seen. Sheppard delivered a powerful speech and moved a resolution calling for the "unqualified dissolution" of the United Province of Canada. Brown's turn came a day later. He agreed with Upper Canada's complaints about the dominance of its smaller partner,*

---

* The imbalance wasn't simply one of political representation in proportion to population. About three-quarters of all Canada's tax revenues came from the Upper Canada "section."

admitted that dissolving the union might resolve the problems, but then offered a brighter alternative: "What true Canadian can witness the tide of immigration now commencing to flow into the vast territories of the North West without longing . . . to make our own country the highway of the traffic to the Pacific." The one way to achieve this was to keep the United Province together, so that it "may at some future date readily furnish the machinery of a great confederation." Brown had found for himself a new voice as a moderate advocate of Confederation.

Brown, though, was no politician. After the convention, one Reform member recalled meeting his leader several times and never being recognized; a few days later, he had encountered Macdonald, who grasped his hand, slapped him on the back and declared how glad he was to see him. Brown's ideas remained remote, abstract—and confusing. The resolution eventually passed by the Reform convention called for a federation composed only of the two existing "sections" of the United Province, Upper and Lower Canada, each separating to form new provinces, with, over them, "some joint authority." The populist Grits rejected such a scheme as tame, and, far worse, as failing to be certain of ridding them of the French Canadians. By the summer of 1860, Brown's hold on the party had weakened again, and he began to talk about resigning.

At the same time as Brown was losing control over his own party, so was Macdonald over his group. Besides having to tug back into line the ever-growing number of Conservatives now openly supporting Rep by Pop, he had to cope with rising disaffection with his leadership among the Orange Order, which had always provided him with a large number of his electoral foot

The young Prince of Wales, Canada's first royal visitor. On the far left is Governor General Sir Edmund Head, a great admirer of Macdonald's. John Rose organized the prince's tour.

soldiers. The divisive force here was that, in the summer of 1860, a spectacular royal tour of Canada—the first ever of its kind—had been made by Queen Victoria's son Albert Edward, the Prince of Wales, at the request of Macdonald's government. While the prince's progress had been overwhelmingly successful, it had been marred by one jarring confrontation involving the Orange Order.

Only eighteen years old, Prince Edward was generally judged to be handsome in the way, then as now, a special indulgence is always extended to royal princes. He had the reputation of being a good dancer and a stylish dresser—too stylish perhaps, because Victoria's consort, Prince Albert, complained that his eldest son took "no interest in anything but clothes. Even when out shooting, he is more occupied with his trousers than with the game."

But no matter—parades, pageantry and pomp always please the masses. For the colony to put on its best show—as Macdonald observed, "Our administration is more familiar with cocktails than cocked hats"—he picked his friend John Rose, at this time the minister of public works. And it went splendidly. The colonials were ecstatic and awed. There was one terrible gaffe, in London, where an overeager citizen had the audacity to "seize the hand of his Royal Highness and shake it like a pump-handle." More generally, as the *Ottawa Citizen* reported, "Ottawa appeared lovely and anxious as a bride awaiting the arrival of the bridegroom to complete the joy." Everywhere, there were triumphal arches, red, white and blue bunting, patriotic banners, fireworks and illuminations achieved by the new marvel of gas. And there were newly minted ditties: "For hark, the trumpets / hark, the drums / The Princely Heir of England comes!"*

Then it all unravelled in Macdonald's hometown of Kingston. It was the most loyal town in the country, not only because of the Loyalists but even more because the Loyal Orange Order was so strong there. To greet their prince who had come over the water, Kingston's Orangemen built two large arches of firs, which they covered with their own regalia and symbols. Then they gathered en masse to await him. Premonitions of trouble came from complaints by Kingston's Catholics that the prince should not and could not be welcomed by a sectarian political organization that was banned in England itself. To stir things up, the *Globe* pointed out that when the prince began his tour in Quebec City, he had not only been greeted in French but visited Roman Catholic

---

* In his *Royal Spectacle: The 1860 Visit of the Prince of Wales to Canada and the United States,* from which much of the material in this section is drawn, Ian Radforth observes that one problem for the tour's organizers was that the towns and cities of then underdeveloped Canada lacked any of the "grand avenues and parade grounds" so necessary for ceremonial spectacles.

The prince's tour was a huge success, with one exception. In Kingston, the Orange Order massed to greet "their Prince." Because the Lodge was banned in England, he refused to come ashore and walk beneath their triumphal arch.

institutions such as Laval University and the Ursuline Convent. To head off a confrontation, Macdonald met with the colonial secretary, the Duke of Newcastle, who was accompanying the prince.* Macdonald argued that Upper Canadians felt that the Catholics "had had it all their own way in Lower Canada" and that the same courtesy should be extended to Upper Canada's Protestants. Newcastle replied that there was no comparison between the Catholic artifacts in Quebec City, "which were emblematical of a faith," and the paraphernalia of Orangemen, "which were those of a rancorous party."

On the afternoon of Tuesday, September 4, 1860, the prince entered Kingston Harbour aboard the steamer *Kingston.* It drew

---

* Newcastle thus became the first colonial secretary to visit the most important of the colonies he was responsible for, and the only one to do so during the nineteenth century.

close to the official landing place, where the Orangemen had massed—some fifteen thousand of them—in their costumes and with their banners. At the last minute, the ship changed course and moved off into mid-harbour. The standoff continued into the next day, with the Orangemen refusing to leave, but making no disturbances other than singing such songs as "Water, water, holy water. / Sprinkle the Catholics everyone. / We'll cut them asunder and make 'em lie under." Late in the morning of the 5th, despite last-minute appeals by Macdonald, the *Kingston* weighed anchor and chugged off to the prince's next engagement in Belleville, and then on to Cobourg.

The incident earned Canada an international black eye, including the comment in the *New York Times* that nowhere in Canada could the prince find "a rational population before reaching the American frontier." The *Globe* put it all down to Macdonald's hypocrisy and incompetence. In fact the blame rested principally with the Duke of Newcastle, who, concerned only with domestic British politics, ignored the fact that the Orange Order was a legal organization in Canada. In the United States, where he next went, the prince had no problems: newspapers pronounced him a "heart smasher," and many of the young ladies at balls and receptions wrestled each other to get near to him. In Philadelphia, a production of *La Traviata* came to a halt because "the leading ladies on stage could not keep their eyes off the royal youth."*

---

* Years later, the Prince of Wales encountered a Canadian MP in London who answered the prince's inquiry by saying that he came from Kingston. "Ah," replied Edward in a deft reference to his aborted visit, "it looks very well from the water." Later still, on Queen Victoria's death in 1901, he succeeded to the throne as Edward VII. Throughout his life, he remained exceptionally close to a great many ladies.

To recover from this fiasco, which had left him furious with British officials at the same time as the Orangemen were angry with him, Macdonald resorted to a political innovation that served as a response to Brown's mass convention of the summer before, as well as a platform for him to tell his side of what the newspapers were calling "The Siege at Kingston." He embarked on a cross-country speaking tour.

No one had done that before—except Americans. Stump speeches were exceedingly rare then, as Canadian politicians limited themselves to orations in the legislature, to church congregations and dinners organized by businessmen. Manifestos like Macdonald's *Address* were the standard way of spreading the word. In one critical respect, Macdonald was quite unlike most politicians of the time: he was entirely at ease with ordinary people. He dealt with people not by lecturing them or by orating at them but by talking colloquially with them, telling stories, exchanging repartee—all in everyday language.

Not for many decades would Canadians again encounter a politician so completely at ease with ordinary people. Once, after Macdonald had clambered onto a piece of farm machinery to better address a gathering, word was passed to him that he was actually standing on a manure spreader. His instant reply: "This is the first time I've stood on the Liberal platform." When a passerby stopped him on Toronto's King Street to tell him that a friend had said Macdonald was "the biggest liar in all Canada," he looked gravely at his interlocutor and answered, "I dare say it's true enough." Mostly, people—even those intending to vote against him—clustered around Macdonald at his meetings for the uncomplicated reason that he was fun.

So off he went on his speaking tour, travelling from town to town—first in Brantford, and then in a succession of meetings, from Toronto to Hamilton to St. Catharines, from St. Thomas to

London to Guelph, from Belleville to Simcoe to Kingston. At times, the crowds topped eight hundred listeners. Usually there was a dinner or lunch, typically of six or more courses. There were speeches and toasts, jokes and stories, and more speeches—typically eight or ten speakers. Macdonald frequently was funny, but in a way that got across a message. He referred to the "some joint authority" resolution passed at the Reform convention and asked, "Is it a legislature, or is it a bench of bishops?" He set out his case: "I am a sincere Unionist. I nail my colours to the mast on that great principle." He used the flag to salute two masters at the same time: "I say that next to the Union with Great Britain, next to having our Queen as ruler, I look to the Union of the two Canadas as most essential." He turned maudlin: "Whatever may have been the antecedents of any man in Canada, whether he has acted with me or against me, if he becomes a disunionist, I disown him; and I don't care what may have been the antecedents of another, though he may have struggled fiercely against me, if he enters himself as a supporter of the union with England . . . and of the union of the two Canadas, I hail him as a brother. God and nature have joined the two Canadas, and no factious politician should be allowed to sever them." The argument didn't make much sense, but it abundantly served its purpose: Macdonald had put Brown and the Reformers on the defensive as would-be dividers of the nation and of the Empire, and he had positioned himself as the protector of the nation and, better yet by far, of the Queen.

As for the recent royal tour, Macdonald took credit for its overall success: "It had called the attention of the world to the position and prospects of Canada." He admitted that although the prince's visit "had been a source of great pleasure to the people, it had been accompanied in some respects with disappointments, in some degree with heart burnings, in some degree with mistakes." The fault lay with the Duke of Newcastle for interfering in a way that upset Canada's careful balance between French and English, Catholics and Protestants. It was an adroit defence, and a courageous one, given that he was directly criticizing no less a power than the colonial secretary.

Macdonald delivered his most important speech in Caledonia. There he addressed directly the central issue of the coming election and of the Canadian political system. "It has been said that I and my Upper Canadian colleagues sacrificed the interests of Upper Canada to Lower Canada; and that we hold to our Lower Canadian colleagues simply for the sake of office. They say we are traitors to our race; that we knuckle to the Frenchmen; that we are faithless to our religion; and that we are under Roman Catholic influences." Then he offered his reply. He and Cartier had attempted, "in our humble way, to advise the head of the Government for the good of the whole country and the equal interest of all." In itself, his argument was unremarkable. What was remarkable was that Macdonald, in the heartland of English-speaking Protestantism, could tell his audience that much of what they were thinking was wrong in itself and, equally, wrong for the country.

Afterwards, Macdonald told a friend that he had found this pre-campaign swing "wearisome beyond description." But not so wearisome that he didn't add jauntily, "I never took to the stump before, & find that I get on capitally." Macdonald's legend as a man of the people had begun to take root.

⌒

Impending elections focus the minds of politicians as, to all others, the prospect of being hanged is said to do. Any frustration felt by Macdonald or any intimation of attenuated accomplishment immediately vanished. From early 1861 on, he became a whirlwind of energy. He bombarded Hamilton businessman Isaac Buchanan with arguments why he shouldn't step down as a member (Buchanan stayed on). He dispatched confidential letters to candidates tipping them off to the date of the election. He encouraged (successfully) Sidney Smith, a friend, to remain as a Reformer, so that a shred of substance would adhere to the label Liberal-Conservative. And he wrote to Egerton Ryerson—"No time must be lost in calling on the Wesleyan Methodists in every constituency"—to try to swing those of his faith to come over (quite a few did).

The results of all this activity could not have been better. Through the summer of 1861—elections were then held over several months—Macdonald won his first ever (and only ever) Conservative majority in Upper Canada. The simultaneous loss of a few seats by Cartier's *bleus* was, by comparison, a minor setback. Most admirable of all, Brown lost in his own riding.

In fact the election result changed nothing. The Rep by Pop challenge still remained to be dealt with. The double-majority convention still stalled national action. No sooner was the election over than Macdonald was complaining in a letter to a supporter about "violent Tories who are fools enough to think that a purely Conservative Gov-t can be formed. Now I am not such a fool as to destroy all that I have been doing for the last 7 years."

In fact, Macdonald's world, as well as Canada's, had already changed beyond recall.

⌒

Four months before that election was held, a single mortar shot fired on the morning of April 12, 1861, had signalled the start of the bombardment of the small federal garrison in an unfinished fort, Fort Sumter, at the mouth of Charleston Harbor, South Carolina. A day and a half later, the garrison's commander, Major Robert Anderson, surrendered to the Confederate commander, Brigadier General P.G.T. Beauregard. One of the most bloody, brutal and tragic of civil wars in history had begun. It would go on for four relentless years. Out of it would come a totally different America, pulsating with energy, confidence and drive, never pausing on its way first to industrial supremacy and thereafter to military and geopolitical supremacy. Out of it too would come a radically different Canada. The crisis that could dislodge everyone from their fixed positions had happened at last.

Interior of the badly damaged Fort Sumter by John Kay (1863). From out of the Civil War came a transformed United States and also a transformed Canada.

FIFTEEN

Canada's First Anti-American

~

Long may that principle—the Monarchial principle—prevail in
this land. Let there be "No Looking to Washington."
John A. Macdonald

For the premier of a country whose next-door neighbour had just been convulsed by a murderous domestic conflict, Macdonald's reaction to the start of the
American Civil War was remarkably calm. Through
the balance of 1861, he made no comments about the war in any
of his letters. For quite a time, his principal concern was only the
war's potential effect on Canadian politics. In his June 1861
Address to the Electors of the City of Kingston, Macdonald put forth
this analysis: "The fratricidal conflict now unhappily raging in
the United States shows us the superiority of our institutions
and of the principle on which we are based. Long may that
principle—the Monarchial principle—prevail in this land. Let
there be 'No Looking to Washington,' as was threatened by a
leading member of the opposition."

As was by no means always the case, there was actually some
validity to Macdonald's accusation. In the legislature, a leading
Grit, William McDougall, had blurted out that unless Rep by Pop

was enacted, he and other populists might look southwards for support. A jugular having been offered up to him, Macdonald went straight for it. During that summer's election, a crowd of six hundred Conservatives at Whitby burned McDougall in effigy, as the figure's straw-filled hand held up a placard reading, "Look to Washington." The Conservatives hurried out a pamphlet warning of "Clear Grit treason."

The start of hostilities at Charleston came as no great surprise to Macdonald. Close observers of the U.S. scene—so far as Canadians were concerned that really meant the British ambassador in Washington—had long regarded Southern secession as all but inevitable, particularly since the Supreme Court's famous, and infamous, 1857 Dred Scott ruling in favour of the legality of slavery. Overwhelmingly, Northerners refused to accept this judgment. The remaining issue became whether the North would allow the South to secede. This choice was determined by the victory in the November 1860 presidential election of the comparatively little-known Republican candidate Abraham Lincoln, who, although not prepared—yet—to free the slaves, was committed to an "indivisible union." Soon after Lincoln's election, Southern senators and congressmen streamed out of Washington. The new Southern Confederacy was proclaimed on February 11, 1861. Lincoln dismissed the secession as "legally void" and declared that the federal government would maintain control over all military installations throughout the country. Lincoln's policy was blown to pieces by the Confederate guns at Fort Sumter.

During this period, Macdonald expressed no opinions about Lincoln in his private correspondence. (In a later letter, of November 1864, he referred to Lincoln as "a beast," but in a jokey way, his full comment being that, for Canada's sake, "Abe Lincoln, beast as he is, should be elected.") The prevailing Canadian view about Lincoln was conveyed by the *Globe*'s dismissal of him as "a fourth-rate lawyer."[*] Canadian insiders, though, regarded Lincoln as a plus. That wasn't because of Lincoln's as-yet-untested qualities, but rather those of William Seward, the politician who, most unexpectedly, had lost the Republican presidential nomination to Lincoln. Seward, a former New York senator, able and supremely confident, a man likened to "a huge bird chiseled in stone," now became secretary of state rather than president. He was also an unabashed annexationist—and an astute one. He espoused the "ripe fruit" doctrine,

William Seward, U.S. secretary of state. A strong annexationist, he believed that Canada would sooner or later join the United States peacefully and passively, like a "ripe fruit."

which held that Canada would fall naturally from Britain's grasp into the handily available and incomparably more attractive basket of the United States.[†] Once the Civil War began, Seward searched for ways to speed the process by provoking Britain into some intemperate action that could justify a retaliatory invasion of Canada. Macdonald's concerns about Canadians who looked to Washington seemed justified.

The summer of 1861 witnessed repeated alarms and excursions. In June the British prime minister, John Russell, sent a

---

[*] The unofficial official British view of Lincoln was even wider of the mark. Lord Lyons, the ambassador (minister) in Washington, informed London that Lincoln was "a rough westerner of the lowest origin and little education."

[†] Seward had formed this view as a result of an extensive trip he made in 1857 across the British North American colonies, even north to Labrador.

coded telegram to Governor General Head warning that "a sudden declaration of war by the United States against Great Britain appears to me by no means impossible." The *New York Times* declared that Canada's union with the North was a certainty, and the New York *Herald* reassured readers there would be "no necessity for hostilities," because Canadians themselves overwhelmingly favoured annexation. Offstage, Massachusetts senator Charles Sumner, chair of the Senate Committee on Foreign Relations, talked up the advantages to the North of letting go the South in exchange for getting Canada. Ambiguous evidence exists suggesting that, in London, William Gladstone, then the chancellor of the Exchequer, may have been considering the same kind of swap to head off a possible war between Britain and the United States.* The ire of Americans had been raised by Britain's declaration of neutrality, meaning that it treated the South as a legitimate belligerent.

About the Civil War itself, Canadian public opinion was deeply divided. Taverns became meeting places for either pro-Northerners or pro-Southerners. (One bar in Montreal served mint juleps.) Anti-slavery sentiments were strong, led by George Brown, who penned denunciatory editorials in the *Globe* and donated generously to organizations that looked after runaway slaves. The historian Sidney Wise has observed astutely that Canadians didn't so much favour one side or the other, but rather were either anti-South or anti-North. The South was slave country, yet it had a British social quality to it and was a safe distance away. Canadians knew the North quite well, many had worked

---

* The evidence is questionable. In a book published in 1904, Goldwin Smith claimed that Gladstone had written to him during the war proposing that "if the North thought fit at this time to let the South go, it might in time be indemnified by . . . Canada." Smith said that he had later destroyed Gladstone's letter because it might "prove embarrassing."

there, and some forty thousand enlisted in the Northern armies, for the pay or for the excitement.* It was the North, though, that threatened Canada. A song sung by Union soldiers to the tune of "Yankee Doodle" included the lines: "Secession first he would put down / Wholly and forever, / And afterwards from Britain's crown / He Canada would sever."

As a conservative and a believer in hierarchy, and one who was always silent on the slavery issue, Macdonald appears to have favoured the South. At the war's start, he expected the South to succeed in its attempt to break away: "If they [Americans] are to be severed in two, as severed in two I believe they will be," he said in the legislature in his first post–Fort Sumter speech on April 19, 1861, "they will be two great, two noble, two free nations [that] will exist in the place of one." And his principal concern was always the North. He wrote to a friend that all the Canadians who had joined the Northern armies "will return to Canada sadder and wiser men, with a good deal of military experience that they may perhaps be able to use hereafter against their teachers." His public stance, though, was always strict neutrality. When, early on, some Conservative members cheered the news of the Southern victory at the First Battle of Bull Run, Macdonald angrily silenced them.

By the fall of 1861, it appeared that the cross-border threat had passed. The North, now losing engagement after engagement, could not risk a wider war. As well, Britain that summer hurried over an extra two thousand troops, deliberately doing so in the most public possible way by transporting them in *Great*

---

* More than half of these Canadian volunteers were Canadiens. Mass migration from Quebec to the United States during the nineteenth century dates from the Civil War years, in large part because of the classic "pull" factor in migration— those who've already gone to or already know a new country always attract others to follow them.

Eastern, the world's largest steamship.* As always, the unexpected then happened.

On November 8, 1861, the U.S. warship *San Jacinto* came upon the Royal Mail steamship *Trent* in the Bahamas Channel. On information received from federal spies in Havana, its last port of call, but without any orders from Washington, the *San Jacinto*'s commander, Captain Charles Wilkes, forced the *Trent* to stop and sent marines aboard; they found there, and brought back to their own ship, two Confederate officials who were on their way to England to order supplies and arrange for them to be brought back by blockade runners. This action was outright piracy on the high seas. The Northern newspapers, delighted to have even a small victory to report, cheered, and Wilkes was celebrated at public dinners. Canadian newspapers, naturally loyal to Britain, answered with outrage. Even if limited in itself, the affair was the most serious diplomatic incident between the United States and Britain since the War of 1812. As the giants glared at each other, Canadians, caught in between, could only blink nervously.

Sometimes, bad communications can lead to good decision making. The news took three weeks to reach London. Another three weeks passed before the British government's official response—a demand for the release of the prisoners and for a formal apology—reached Washington. By this time, heads in the White House had begun to cool. After fierce cabinet debates,

---

* *Great Eastern* raced across the Atlantic in a new record of eight days and six hours, going full speed through icefields—as would, less successfully, another "world's largest ship" a half-century later.

Lincoln ruled, "one war at a time." With deft timing, the Confederate pair was released around Christmas, when the newspapers were distracted; just as deftly, the Imperial government "forgot" that it had ever called for an apology. By luck, Alexander Tilloch Galt, Macdonald's finance minister, was then in Washington to discuss trade matters; he got an unexpected call to come to the White House; there, Lincoln reassured the visiting Canadian that he and the Northern government had no hostile intentions towards their neighbour. The assurance only partially reassured, because both Macdonald and Galt remained worried that public opinion might yet force Lincoln to take precipitate action.

That risk did exist. The New York *World* pronounced, "The simple fact is, Canada hates us." More threatening still was the Cleveland *Leader*'s declaration that, in a reference to the vast Northern Armies, "six hundred thousand men will want something more to do" once they had done with the South. To placate his public, Lincoln ruled that all visitors to the United States would henceforth have to carry passports, a rule that hit Canadians by far the hardest. Fortunately, American public opinion cooled quickly, and the passport regulation was quietly lifted.

On first hearing the news of the *Trent* crisis, the British cabinet had decided that a show of force had to be made. Some eleven thousand additional redcoats were rushed out. By the time the ships had reached the St. Lawrence, the freeze-up had begun. The boats hurriedly swung round to Saint John, where the soldiers disembarked. Using a kind of snowshoes called "creepers," they marched over the snowbound, hilly roads of New Brunswick to the St. Lawrence River. Britain had done its bit; it was now Canada's turn.

Responsibility for the defence of Canada rested at the time not with its premier and his government but with the governor general. Responsibility for Canada's doing what it could to help rested with its minister of militia. It was a new portfolio, created by Macdonald on December 18, 1861, in the midst of the *Trent* crisis. He appointed himself to the position, thereby making himself, already attorney general and premier, a triple minister.

In some ways Macdonald's assumption of this role was questionable. He had no military experience whatever, other than in 1837, when, as a member of the Sedentary Militia, he took part in the attack on Montgomery's Tavern in the countryside north of Toronto which crushed William Lyon Mackenzie's rebellion. Macdonald never fired a shot himself, claiming only to have "carried my musket." More intriguingly and reflective of his attitude towards the military, a half-century passed before Macdonald mentioned to anyone that he had actually seen action.* He learned from the brief experience that a soldier's lot was not an easy one. As he recounted, "The day was hot. My feet were blistered. I was but a weary boy and I thought I would have dropped with weight of the old flint musket which galled my shoulder, but I managed to keep up with my companion, a grim old soldier who seemed impervious to fatigue." More surprisingly still, unlike many in public life, Macdonald had never sought a commission as an officer in the militia for the sake of the status. If anything, he was actively suspicious of the military; Macdonald would later discourage his son, Hugh John, from following a military career. And he wrote back to an

---

* Not until 1887, in a conversation with his friend Judge Gowan, did Macdonald disclose for the first time his front-line experience, or, more accurately, his near to the front-line adventure. His company was placed safely behind the artillery that levelled the tavern and killed eleven of the hapless rebels.

inquirer, "There is no chance of there being any such thing in this country for a long time as a Profession of arms."

This indifference is a bit puzzling, given that the military was British and hierarchical—two of Macdonald's favourite qualities. He seemed to have a distaste for warfare itself. In no way was he a pacifist (as, then, almost no one was), but he never evinced any interest in the lives of heroes like Caesar or Napoleon. Although he loved the Empire, he was in no way an imperialist, and he later rejected appeals from London for Canadian troops to be sent to this or that patch of Imperial sand or rock.

In other respects Macdonald's self-appointment was well merited. He knew more about British politics, as was now of critical importance, than anyone else in Canada. He was also well regarded by Britain's representative—Lord Monck, who had just succeeded Head as governor general, was an admirer of Macdonald, although far from an uncritical one. Macdonald had already acted as virtual militia minister before creating the portfolio, sending regular memorandums to Monck suggesting, for instance, an increase in militia strength from 5,000 to 7,500 and proposing that railway workers be excluded from militia service, because "the withdrawal of any of them would weaken our lines of communication." Once minister, Macdonald poured out memorandums on all kinds of militia topics and early in 1862 set up a high-level commission with himself as chair to recommend ways to improve the country's defences.

~

For Canadians in the early 1860s, defence meant resisting any cross-border incursion. Yet, as few people had begun to recognize, the real threat was not that vast numbers of blue-uniformed Union soldiers might one day march across the border and, in the words of the New York *Herald*, "overrun the Province in three weeks"—as, most certainly, they could have done. It was, instead, that as soon as the Civil War was over, a transformed and powerful United States would emerge from the carnage.

The first appearance of this new United States was in its military guise. On the eve of the opening cannon-shot at Fort Sumter, the total U.S. army strength was nominally about thirteen thousand, but effectively was a good deal less, because the desertion rate was high and many soldiers were tied down by wars against the Indians. By comparison, there were then about four thousand redcoats in Canada, incomparably better trained and experienced. The odds were pretty even, particularly since more redcoats could be dispatched from elsewhere in the Empire. Less than two years later, the Federal Army had grown to more than eight hundred thousand—larger than any of Napoleon's armies. It would grow eventually to more than two million men, well provisioned and with excellent weapons. Militarily, this United States was unbeatable within North America. And that was only the start. Given the power and energy it was displaying in the Civil War, the new United States would not only rearrange the geopolitical order on the North American continent but extend its reach far overseas. A new world order was taking shape, and Canada was going to be the first country to have to figure out how to accommodate itself to it.

Canada was no longer situated next door to a larger, richer neighbour. It was huddled alongside a colossus in the making—a colossus of unprecedented dynamism which, while waging the largest civil war in history, could still take in vast numbers of immigrants and begin to build a transcontinental railway. Soon after the war ended, all this dynamism would be applied to extending the country westwards to the Pacific, and a few decades later to building it up towards the sky. All this energy, much of it generated by a new entrepreneurial form of capital-ism, would never flag: within half a century, the United States would be the world's leading industrial power.

Macdonald was slow to appreciate the scale of the change. Unlike other Canadian leaders such as Brown and McGee, he had never worked in the United States. As a young lawyer, he had gone on holidays in northern New York State with clients, and he had carried Isabella on that long pilgrimage to Savannah. But all his political, commercial and social contacts were in London rather than in Washington or New York.

This orientation was the real limitation to Macdonald's southwards gaze. He saw the United States through British eyes. During that 1845 trip south with Isabella, he went to a political meeting in Savannah at which a U.S. senator spoke. Afterwards he recounted to Margaret Greene, "He is evidently an able man, with great fluency and force of expression, but has the great fault of American speakers . . . of being too theatrical in his manner and turgid in his style." Consistently, he saw just about any bot-tle south of the border as half-empty. As he commented to a friend, "one soon tires of Yankee humour—except in a book when you can lay it down if it wearies you." About major mat-ters, Macdonald could be crashingly wrong—as in his view of the presidency: "By the election of the President by a majority and for a short time, he is never the sovereign and chief of the nation," he declared. "He is never looked up to by the whole pop-ulation as the head and fount of the nation. He is at best but the successful leader of a party."

By comparison, the British (and Canadian) system was near perfect, to Macdonald: "We shall have a Sovereign who is placed above the region of party. . . . Representatives of the Sovereign [the governors general] can act only on the advice of his minis-ters, those ministers being responsible to the people through

Parliament." He took for granted that just about anything British had to be the best: "I do not think there is anything in the world equal in real intellectual pleasure to meeting the public men of England. Their tone is so high and their mode of thinking is so correct that it really elevates one." As for the equivalent Americans, "the standard of excellence is far lower than the English one."

Macdonald did sometimes look clearly across the border. From the start of the Civil War onwards, he repeatedly described the U.S. Constitution as "defective" because it was so decentralized, treating its member states as if they were sovereign and thereby giving legitimacy to the South's secession. But he also appreciated that something out of the ordinary was being attempted there. "It has been said that the United States is a failure," he said in one major speech. "On the contrary, I consider it a marvellous exhibition of human wisdom. It was as perfect as human wisdom could make it, and under it the American states prospered until very recently; but being the work of men, it had its defects." Yet he could not help noticing all the defects below the border. American conventions to elect party leaders were "immoral" and "horrid," resulting in presidential candidates being chosen "by cliques of the lowest politicians." To reinforce his conviction of British superiority, many of the recent presidents produced by that system during his time—Millard Fillmore, Franklin Pierce, James Buchanan—had indeed been nonentities.

To Macdonald, the United States was Canada's "other"— the alien, the threat, or to put it most simply, the enemy. To him, Britain was Canada's elder brother, at once protector and role model.

To appreciate the magnitude of what was happening south of the border required an observer with the imagination of a poet, or at least with the trend-spotting capabilities of an alert journalist. D'Arcy McGee saw straight into the future: "It is not the figures [of soldiers] which give the worst view. . . . It is the change which has taken place in the spirit of the people of the Northern states themselves. If we do not desire to become part and parcel of this people, we cannot overlook this, the greatest revolution of our times. . . . We run the risk of being swallowed up by the spirit of universal democracy that prevails in the United States."

Macdonald and McGee disagreed on the way Canada could best accommodate itself to the challenge of living and surviving beside a colossus. McGee was now calling for "a new nationality," or for common social and cultural characteristics that would make Canadians a distinct people. Macdonald's solution was more narrowly political: Canada should remain as British as possible.

This disagreement was about means, not about the end they sought. Macdonald and McGee, who had started out as opponents, were now well on the way to becoming political allies and personal friends. Politically, they were both anti-Americans. Macdonald, because of his incomparably greater power, merits the title of Canada's first anti-American; before Macdonald, lots of Canadians had disliked and feared the United States, but none, like him, raised it to the level of his principal political policy. What is really striking about Macdonald's anti-Americanism was that the overwhelming majority of Canadians agreed with him.

In the mid-nineteenth century, anti-Americanism was one of two forces that held this "crazy-quilt" country together. The other, to be discussed later, was the mirror-image force of loyalty to Britain.

Anti-Americanism was one of the very few things that Canadians then agreed on—English Protestants no different from Canadien Catholics.* Its comprehensiveness defied common sense. A great many in Upper Canada were in fact Americans, not just the Loyalists but the ordinary settlers who early in the century constituted three-quarters of the province's population. There were also many Irish, whose only pre-Canadian experience of the English had been of them as oppressors and occupiers. Yet the loyalty of these Americans and French and Irish never wavered—not even among the Green Irish, many of whose kin across the border were enlisting in the Federal Army to acquire military skills to be exercised later, either in Ireland or in Canada. At the same time, the idea of Canada uniting with the United States attracted astonishingly little support, given that it would obviously benefit Canadians economically. Only in the extremities, in British Columbia and in New Brunswick, was there any substantial support for annexation, and even there only by a minority.

The historic roots of anti-Americanism were straightforward. The Americans were revolutionaries who had rebelled against their King. They had tried twice to tear Canadians away from their loyalty to the Crown—in 1775, at their start of their Revolutionary War, when armies led by Generals Benedict Arnold and Richard Montgomery invaded Quebec, capturing Montreal and besieging Quebec City; and again, and within living memory, during the War of 1812. Thomas Jefferson never entirely accepted the drawn outcome of the 1812 war, holding out in the peace negotiations for annexation to "liberate" Canada.

---

* The most powerful expression of Canadien sentiment about Americans was Premier Taché's famous prediction that "the last cannon which is shot on this continent in defence of Great Britain will be fired by the hand of a French-Canadian."

Memories of the 1812 War had a powerful effect on Canadians' consciousness. In the 1820s, soon after the Macdonald family arrived, strong public pressure developed to designate all American immigrant settlers, even those who had fought on Canada's side during the war, as "Aliens" ineligible to run for office or to hold property. A watered-down Naturalization Act was finally passed in 1828, granting citizenship to all Americans who had settled in the country before 1820 but requiring an oath of allegiance from all newcomers.

The increased confidence in the loyalty of Americans living here wasn't matched by any waning of suspicions about the intentions of America itself. The most forceful expression of this view was McGee's: "They coveted Florida, and seized it; they coveted Louisiana, and purchased it; and then picked a quarrel with Mexico, which ended by their getting California. They sometimes pretended to despise these [British North American] colonies as prizes beneath their ambition; but had we not the strong arm of England over us, we should not have had a separate existence."

Some of the sources of mid-nineteenth-century anti-Americanism in Canada would surprise and disconcert those in the twenty-first century who harbour the same views. Then, few felt any need to justify their attitude by attributing it to the doings of a particular president. Few felt any need to deny being anti-American themselves—particularly at a time when public debate was so decidedly ungenteel that explicit accusations of "traitor" were hurled routinely across the floor of the legislature.

One of the root sources of the shock and horror on this side of the border was Canadians' concern about Americans' lack of religiosity. Many Canadians—especially the Canadiens—regarded with deep misgivings the absolute division of church and state in the United States. There, no public money could be used to support faith-based schools. Deeply unsettling, further, was the fact that several of the Founding Fathers, Jefferson among them, had expressed doubts about the divinity of Christ. Most shocking was the discovery of the questionable Christianity of President James Polk.* On Polk's death in 1849, the New York press reported that he had received a last-minute baptism. The *Church* magazine of Toronto commented: "For four years the neighbouring republic was governed by an *unbaptized* President. . . . The anomaly must bring disgrace with it, and possibly something worse, to a nation professing to honour Christianity at all. . . . What would be thought of the Monarch of the British Empire, if he or she had never been baptized? Could such a thing happen in our Monarch, or in any other Christian Kingdom in the world? No!" Then there was Archdeacon A. N. Bethune of York, who declared in a sermon that republicanism meant "the extravagant wanderings and neverceasing cravings of an unbridled ambition," while monarchy meant "the inestimable blessings of law, order, quiet and true religion."

There was also lively concern in Canada about the experiment in multiculturalism being attempted south of the border. The Nova Scotia humorist Thomas Haliburton, author of the highly successful Sam Slick series, put into the mouth of one character a complaint about the "human refuse" in American cities. And, near the century's end, the popular historian George R. Parkin wrote in disgust about "those pouring into the United States. Who were they? Icelanders, Greeks, Armenians, Bulgarians, the Latin races of the South. People unaccustomed to self-government."

As is more familiar, Canadians worried that Americans were inherently violent. Canadians were aghast at the gangs in U.S. cities, at the lynchings of Negroes, at the wars against Indians. It

---

* Polk's name still lingers among Canadians as the author of the slogan "Fifty-Four Forty or Fight," meaning that the border should be pushed way up north from the forty-ninth parallel.

was widely held by Canadians that Americans were licentious, the far greater frequency of divorce there being blamed on an excess of female independence. The cross-border differences were real; on its northern side there was no equivalent, even remotely, to the slaughter by the U.S. Army of forty-five thousand Indians during the nineteenth century; nor was there any equivalent to the slave system. (In Canada's early years there had been some slaves, brought in by Loyalists or held over from the French regime, but the system was abolished in 1793,* two-thirds of a century ahead of the United States.)

The cardinal attitude of Canadians towards Americans in this century was crystal clear: they took for granted that they were morally superior. They also took for granted that their political and legal systems were superior. About other matters, from commerce to trade to education to scientific invention to the arts, they talked rather less. Not that all the talk north of the border was glib: the journalist Nicholas Flood Davin wrote shrewdly that, in an egalitarian democratic community, "where there is nothing to differentiate one man from another but wealth, nothing to aim at but wealth, character becomes materialized."

This Canadian conviction of moral superiority is the answer to one of the most puzzling questions about nineteenth-century Canadians. It was posed by Sydney Wise and Craig Brown in their book *Canada Views the United States*. In it they described as "a seeming contradiction of nature, environment and proximity" the fact that "the bulk of Canadians, standing on the very threshold of liberty, were so little susceptible to American institutions."

Not only were nature and the environment identical on both

---

* In 1793 Governor Simcoe prohibited the importation of slaves into Canada. Existing owners were allowed to retain their slaves, but most were freed not long afterwards.

sides of the border, so were the people themselves. In the mid-nineteenth century, Canadians and Americans were almost exactly the same people: both were overwhelmingly Anglo-Saxon, except for the large number of black slaves in the United States. They were not just the same people but were often of the same families. Few Canadian families did not have a relative south of the border (in Macdonald's own case, his cousin Margaret Greene). Many, including many Canadiens, had lost a son or nephew or cousin to migration across the border in search of a better job; in reverse, most of the Loyalists and the American settlers had left kin behind. Most Canadians, therefore, for all their protestations of loyalty to the Queen and genuine belief in the superiority of British law and British politics, were perfectly well aware that the United States was incomparably richer, more advanced and developed, possessed a far superior education system (Harvard University dated back to 1636), and boasted grander buildings, roads, canals, railways.

To gain all the abundant benefits of being American, Canadians then needed to do little more than to declare collectively, "We want in." Britain wouldn't have stood in their way, its leaders having declared repeatedly that they would accept Canadians' choice of independence. The succeeding step would have been, sooner or later, that of a "ripe fruit" dropping, passively and effortlessly, into the Union. But it never happened.

Macdonald did stand in the way. He possessed an instinctual understanding that the choice would be determined by passion, not by reason. That was why he so often escalated the emotional content of the public debate on the subject by accusing opponents not just of being wrong but of "treason" and even of "veiled treason"—this phrase being almost his trademark, although in fact its actual author was Disraeli. In the early 1860s, though, Macdonald was only the latest in a line of leaders, rather than the iconic, national leader he would become. The X factors that decided the issue were Canadians' certitude of moral superiority and, as much, their certitude that British was best. These attitudes did stand in the way of annexation; neither of them, though, could have stopped an army.

Describing Macdonald as an anti-American, although it evokes a contemporary echo, doesn't position him properly. Ultimately, the United States was simply irrelevant to him, except on the occasions when it specifically threatened Canada. In the huge library that he eventually accumulated at Earnscliffe, his home in Ottawa, there were almost no American books. Except for his early sorties to Upper New York State, he always holidayed in Rivière-du-Loup, or in Prince Edward Island, or in England. During all his post-Confederation years as prime minister, he went only once to Washington on government business, and to no other city. He met only one president, Ulysses S. Grant, by accident at a reception. He took no interest in U.S. politics. He never showed any understanding that one reason many Americans favoured annexation was far less expansion for its own sake— although obviously an imperative—than that they believed, genuinely, that Canadians would be better off once Americans; Richard Cartwright, in his *Reminiscences*, was much closer to the mark when he observed that Americans "have always found it very hard to believe that we honestly preferred our own institutions to theirs." As well, Macdonald was oddly unwilling to accept the legitimacy of, and most certainly the consequences of, American anger with Britain (and by extension with Canada) for the way that, during the Civil War, Confederate commerce raiders were allowed to be built under contract in British yards and then cross the Atlantic to sink Federal merchant ships. To

Macdonald, the United States was a *terra incognita* about which he had no desire, and felt no need, to learn anything.

Rejecting the United States didn't make him British. It made him a British-American, at a time when the descriptor "Canadian" was seldom used—other than by Canadiens. It made him, in other words, wholly British and at the same time wholly North American. While Macdonald went often to England, he never considered moving there, as many Canadians like him did, once they had retired—including the two first presidents of the Canadian Pacific Railway, George Stephen and Donald Smith; his political rival of the 1870s and 80s, Edward Blake; and, in his plans for the future, his own close ally Cartier. To them and to many other Canadians for quite a while yet, Britain was "home." To Macdonald, although he loved to visit London, Canada was home.

For Canada to remain his home, it had to remain British. Had Canada ever become American during his time, it's just about certain that Macdonald would have left for the other side of the Atlantic.

The leitmotif of Macdonald's career and life was to preserve Canada's un-Americanness. To him, the perpetuation of its Britishness was essential to that cause. So too would be the Confederation project. The handily available tool he used to lever himself towards both these objectives was anti-Americanism.

That most Canadians thought the same way made his task that much easier—up to a point. Being Canadians, the fact that they overwhelmingly rejected the United States didn't prevent huge numbers of them from voting for it with their feet. By the end of the nineteenth century, one in five Canadians would be living in the United States.*

---

* There was a small reverse flow, mostly of Northern draft dodgers, or "skeedadlers" as they were called, but most of them returned home once the Civil War was over, as did most of the runaway slaves. Late in the century, after

⌒

Besides stirring up the underlying anti-Americanism, the *Trent* crisis stimulated a pan-Canadian consciousness. Nova Scotia was then a separate colony, and especially emotionally close to Britain, because it was protected by the Royal Navy. Yet in the winter of 1861–62, Nova Scotians enlisted in their militia in proportionately greater numbers than did Canadians. The crisis also prompted the first serious debates about a long-discussed railway—the Intercolonial—to connect the Maritimes to inland Canada. (These discussions had been going on, entirely fruitlessly, since 1851.) The railway's justification was that it could be used to rush British reinforcements to Canada in winter rather than have them plod through the backwoods.* The Imperial government now began to consider the possibility of guaranteeing the loans needed to build a railway that in itself would be uneconomic. The crisis marked the first instance of all British North Americans reaching out to each other.

⌒

It was Macdonald himself who helped abort this nascent pan-Canadianness. He did so by botching a piece of major legislation and then seeming not to care about the consequences—one of which was the defeat of his own government.

The previous March, the commission on defence that he had

---

the Midwest was filled up, American farmers moved north in search of land, particularly in Alberta.

* A further defence problem revealed by the *Trent* crisis was that the telegraph line from Halifax to Montreal was being tapped by the Americans.

set up and chaired handed in its report. The findings were startling: there should be "an active force of 50,000 men of all arms, with a reserve of the same kind." This goal was extraordinarily ambitious. More startling still, the commission recommended that if voluntary enlistments proved insufficient, conscription should be instituted. During the *Trent* crisis, that might have been acceptable. But with that alarm well past, everyone, Macdonald included, took it for granted that Canada was secure until at least the Civil War was over.

Macdonald drafted legislation to implement his commission's recommendations. In the House, though, he came across as confused, at times offering different estimates of the costs. The best estimate amounted to a staggering one-tenth of Canada's entire revenues. To make these costs even more unacceptable, Macdonald was, at the same time, having to explain a nine-hundred-thousand-dollar overrun in the cost of the Parliament Buildings in Ottawa.

His defeat was determined by his own *bleu* supporters, many of whom bolted rather than share ownership of a measure that might result in conscription, however limited in its extent. The vote was held on May 20, 1862, and the Militia Bill was defeated 61 to 54. A day later, Macdonald and Cartier resigned. He "took the matter very quietly," reported Edward Watkin, general manager of the Grand Trunk Railway, who knew him well. "I am at last free, thank God, and can now feel as a free man," Macdonald wrote to his sister Margaret. "I have longed for this hour & only a sense of honour has kept me chained to my post . . . I have now fulfilled my duty to my part & can begin to think of myself." After Macdonald had stepped down, the governor general invited his namesake, John Sandfield Macdonald, a Reformer, to form a new government.

One good reason existed why defeat was the best possible outcome for Macdonald at this time. In the middle of the debate on his Militia Bill, the *Globe* had broken one of the unwritten rules of nineteenth-century journalism by informing its readers on May 15 that Macdonald "has had one of his old attacks."* The newspaper was entirely correct. Claiming illness, Macdonald was absent from the legislature for more than one week of the debate on his Militia Bill, and Galt had to substitute for him.

The *Globe*'s use of the phrase "old attacks" signalled its readers that Macdonald had been in the same condition—drunk, that is—before. A few days later, the paper renewed the attack: "It must be confessed that Mr. Macdonald's 'illnesses' occur at very convenient times." At the same time, Governor General Monck, in a confidential dispatch home, did his duty and informed the colonial secretary that Macdonald had been absent from the House for an entire week during the critical militia debate, "nominally by illness, but really, as everyone knows, by drunkenness."

There had in fact been quite a few earlier "attacks." The previous April, Macdonald had a heated exchange with a leading Reformer, Oliver Mowat, in the House in which he had threatened to "slap your chops." That fall, a visiting Englishwoman who met him at a dinner party at the governor general's residence, wrote afterwards, "The cleverest man of the lot, distinguished himself by getting completely drunk." After the *Globe*'s reports, Macdonald's secret was known not merely to insiders but to just about everyone in the colony.

Macdonald's "vice," as it was called then, has become since one of the best-known facts about him, almost as well known as his role in Confederation or his achievement in spanning the country with a railway. It's time to hold up this particular aspect of his life story to closer inspection.

---

* The *Globe*'s first reference to Macdonald's habit, in February 1856, was in the correct, coded form of describing him as speaking in the legislature "in a state of wild excitement."

The first recorded instance of Macdonald's drinking to excess occurred back in 1839 when a legal client and relative, Alan Macpherson, left a note on his door: "I called at your office twice on Tuesday but could not gain admittance. I suppose you were doing penance for the deeds of the previous day." That incident was nothing but a young man's boisterousness. During the years since, however, Macdonald had gained a reputation as one of the legislature's most convivial members, staying up as late as anyone in the Smoking Room and topping all of them with his repartee and anecdotes—and by his taste for champagne.

Macdonald's loss of control during the critical Militia Bill was quite different: it provoked, as Macdonald had to have known it would, highly critical comments from senior British ministers as well as a blistering editorial from the influential *Times* (London): "If Canada will not fight to protect its independence, neither will England. . . . If they are to be defended at all, they must make up their minds to bear the greater part of the burden of their own defence. This will be the case if they separate from us. This will be the case if they remain by us." The difference, very simply, was that Macdonald had by now really lost control over his drinking.

Both friends and enemies identified the same period as the time his behaviour changed—the time when it had become obvious that Isabella would never recover and that he was condemned, whether she lived or died, to bleak solitude. His secretary, Joseph Pope, wrote in his biography that Macdonald's lapses were "particularly true for the period of his widowerhood, between 1857 and 1867." Richard Cartwright, originally a Conservative and later a Liberal minister, wrote in his memoir that Macdonald was "leading a very dissipated life from 1856 to 1863, and afterwards."

Isabella's illness and death didn't cause his drinking; her condition intensified a pre-existing inclination. From Macdonald's earliest years, it was always probable that he would drink a lot. His father did. So did many Scots, and many politicians. George-Étienne Cartier was a heavy drinker, and D'Arcy McGee drank even more than Macdonald. The behaviour of these men, and a great many others like them in all occupations in Canada, was in no way out of the ordinary.

In the middle of the nineteenth century, drinking heavily was as common in Canada as smoking would be in the middle of the twentieth century. An 1842 municipal survey in Kingston counted 136 taverns for a population of fewer than five thousand people. In his 1846 book *Canada and the Canadians*, Richard Bonnycastle described Canada as "a fine place for drunkards; it is their paradise." Rotgut whisky cost 25 cents a gallon; in many houses a pail of whisky stood handy in the kitchen, much like a pail of water, for any visitor to ladle out however much he wanted At the end of a ride in a horse-drawn cab, it was common to "treat" the driver with a shot of whisky—a substitute for today's practice of tipping, which didn't then exist. At elections times, "treating" was a near-universal practice.

Few social sanctions existed to inhibit anyone from drinking heavily in public. As Susanna Moodie noted in *Life in the Clearings*, "Professional men were not ashamed to be seen coming from the bar-room of a tavern early in the morning." Her sister, Catharine Parr Traill, observed that heavy drinking was more prevalent among the "better classes" than among ordinary people. Drinking didn't mean then, as in today's "social drinking," a few glasses of wine spaced out over an evening; it meant getting totally, stupidly, drunk. Being an important public figure was no bar to getting inebriated in public. Indeed, of the U.S. presidents who were Macdonald's contemporaries, two, Franklin Pierce and Ulysses S. Grant, were well known as drunkards. Formal occasions provided no restrictions. The senior civil servant Edmund Meredith recorded in his diary, "Captain Sparks was hopelessly drunk while escorting the Governor General to the House: he fell off his horse while essaying to draw his sword." Lady Monck, the wife of the governor general at the time of Confederation, wrote home about a cousin having his coattails "nearly torn off" at a grand ball in Quebec City and reporting, "such drunkenness, pushing, kicking and tearing he says he never saw."*

As for Macdonald's own lack of inhibition about getting drunk on the most inappropriate occasions, he once got blind drunk while waiting for one newly arrived governor general's ship to dock, and an another occasion told the aide to another governor general sent to check on his prolonged absence from official duties either to "go to hell" himself or to tell the Queen's representative to go there.

At the time that Macdonald's "vice" became general public knowledge, the only real alternative to heavy drinking was total abstinence. Temperance organizations—the leading one, based in the United States, was the Order of the Sons of Temperance— lobbied fiercely against any drinking at all. Their crusade was justified: a Legislative Assembly committee reported, "One-half of all the crime committed . . . three-fourths of all the pauperism, are ascribable to intemperance." So, of course, was a great deal of the domestic violence and family breakdown.

It needs to be remembered here that the Victorian Age, in the sense we now use that term—repressed, dark, overstuffed— didn't spring into existence in 1837 when the young Victoria

---

* Even the term "alcoholic," applied to a person, didn't exist then. It was not coined until 1891, the year of Macdonald's death.

ascended to the throne. Much as the 1960s' "Peace and Love" era didn't really get going until the middle of that decade, the Victorian Age really only took hold around the 1870s. Over time, Macdonald fell behind the times. When he started out, though, his behaviour was closer to that of the preceding Regency era—incomparably freer in all respects. Lord Kimberly, the colonial secretary, was undoubtedly thinking of this time lag when he remarked of Macdonald, "He should have been in the good old times of two bottle men, when one of the duties of the Secretary of the Treasury is said to have been to hold his hat on occasion of the First Lord when 'clearing himself' for his speech."

But while Macdonald, for a time, was one of the crowd, he was always one of a kind. He was always a public drunk, in that term's exact sense. Macdonald's manner of drinking was unique to him. Increasingly, from his widowerhood on, it became uninhibited, ugly, out of control. The decisive change was in his openness. Henceforward, Macdonald would get drunk on the most public and the most important occasions without any apology or self-consciousness or shame. It became as much a defining fact about him as his crinkly hair or his inexhaustible wiliness. From this time on, and for quite a time, heavy drinking *was* Macdonald.

He never made the least attempt to hide his drinking—unlike, say, his contemporary William Gladstone, with his sallies across London to save prostitutes, or Mackenzie King, with his crystal-ball gazing. Not only was Macdonald entirely unashamed about his behaviour but he actually drew attention to it. Once, when a heckler at a public meeting accused him of being drunk, he responded, "Yes, but the people would prefer John A. drunk to George Brown sober." And indeed they did. They applauded his deft recovery from throwing up on the platform at an all-candidates' meeting by saying, "Mr. Chairman, I don't know how it is but every time I hear Mr. X speak, it turns my stomach."

There was no hypocrisy in Macdonald's makeup, and no fear.

Macdonald wasn't so much a heavy drinker as a binge drinker; he could go for long periods without a drop. Once he had started, though, it often took complete insensibility for him to stop. A common trigger for this kind of "tear" was some combination of pressure and tiredness; actual political setbacks or disappointments, though, appeared to have little effect on him. Macdonald thus didn't so much drink to relieve a fear of failing but more to relieve the tensions generated by his attempts to succeed. The best single comment about the nature of his drinking was made by the visiting governor of the Hudson's Bay Company, Sir Henry Northcote, who recorded in his diary, "People do not attribute his drinking to vice, but to a state of physical exhaustion which renders him obliged sometimes to have recourse to a stimulant, and which gives the stimulant a very powerful effect. When he once begins to drink he becomes almost mad and there is no restraining him till the fit is over."

Here is as good a place as any to clarify the record that although he was a Scot, Macdonald's favourite choice for something that would get him drunk was not Scotch, except in his earliest years, but champagne, claret, port and brandy.

As soon as Macdonald stepped down, Canadian newspapers speculated eagerly that he might carry right on and leave politics entirely. The easiest of all outs for him appeared just at this time, when the positions of chief justice and chancellor of Upper Canada fell vacant. Yet Macdonald refused them both. In a revealing letter to a supporter, he explained why he'd stepped down so quickly as premier rather than attempt some variation on his old double-shuffle escapade: by stepping down, he wrote, "we have shown that we do not wish to cling to office for its own sake." He wanted to make an elegant exit, that is to say, to make it easier for himself to slide right back in again.

That fall, Macdonald took ship to England, for the first time in twelve years. He was made an honorary member of the Athenaeum Club, met with the colonial secretary and the Duke of Newcastle, and was generally favoured and petted. In February 1863 he was back again in Canada, "in very good health and spirits, and eager for the fray." So eager indeed was Macdonald that year that he went to the extreme limit of joining the Sons of Temperance in Kingston. It probably won him some votes but had no discernible effect on his drinking.

SIXTEEN

The Will to Survive

For the sake of securing peace to ourselves and our posterity, we
must make ourselves powerful. The great security for peace is to
convince the world of our strength by being united.

John A. Macdonald

After his return from England in February 1863,
Macdonald set to work to ease his namesake out of
office and return himself to the premiership. The
deed was done just over a year later: on March 21,
1864, John Sandfield Macdonald resigned in advance of certain
defeat on a non-confidence vote. The intervening months were
probably the least useful of any in the United Province of
Canada's parliamentary history: no legislation of consequence
was passed; a second attempt to enact a Militia Bill failed;
Canadien members became more and more suspicious that Rep
by Pop was going to be imposed on them no matter what they
did; and an election in mid-1863 changed nothing at all—Cartier
won back some of the *bleus* he had lost in 1861, but Macdonald
was reduced to just twenty supporters in Upper Canada, in large
part because of suspicions he was "soft" on the French.

In an attempt to avoid yet another election, Governor General
Monck invited in succession two senior legislature members to try

to form a government. Both reported failure. Next he turned to Macdonald, who approached his former co-premier, Étienne-Paschal Taché. Between the two of them they cobbled together a bare majority in the legislature. Two months later, the Taché-Macdonald alliance lost a confidence vote. Another election was unavoidable.

Within the space of less than three years, there had now been four governments and two inconclusive elections, with a third one due. Canada's political system had degenerated into paralytic deadlock.

Amid the gathering gloom there were a few points of light. One was that Macdonald's old opponent George Brown had got married—at the mature age of forty-three. His bride, Anne Nelson, the daughter of an Edinburgh publisher, was a woman of substance. They met when he had gone north to Scotland during a trip late in 1862. Anne was intelligent, sophisticated, well travelled (she was fluent in French and had studied in Germany), calm and confident, and the marriage proved to be one of unalloyed love. Whenever he was away from home, Brown wrote to Anne almost every day—and repeatedly with unabashed affection. "Already I long to be back with you," he penned on one occasion, "and will grudge every day I am kept from your side." In the winter of 1863, when Anne informed him she was pregnant,

Anne Nelson Brown. After he married her, Brown turned into a moderate. Had she been around earlier, he might have won his contest with Macdonald.

Brown pronounced himself as "frisky as a young kitten."

Brown got himself back into politics at a by-election early in March 1863 and soon re-established himself as the leader of the Reformers. His former angry moralism had mellowed. Phrases such as "French domination" dropped from his speeches, to be replaced by softer musings about the need for "constitutional reform." Brown's biographer, J.M.S. Careless, described Anne Brown as "the Mother of Confederation,"* meaning that she so influenced Brown to view the world more even-handedly that, provided some nation-saving crusade was at stake, it actually became possible that he and Macdonald might be able to work together in a partnership—temporarily. At the time, Brown's most important political supporter and ally, Oliver Mowat, wrote that under Anne's influence, "the softer side of his nature has been developed." To Brown, she was "the best wife that ever lived." No story is ever perfect. While she may have been Confederation's mother, Anne disliked the child itself. "You must never speak of settling down here for life," she wrote to Brown, "The idea of being buried here is dreadful to me." (After Brown's early death, Anne moved back to Scotland.)

Brown's new attitude of moderation showed that some movement had begun beneath the hardened crust of Canadian politics. Macdonald made two attempts to find out what Brown was up to, one with the assistance of a Liberal-Conservative member who had connections to both camps, and the other by making use of Charles Brydges, the new general manager of the Grand Trunk Railway. In his meeting with Brown, Brydges offered him the bait

---

* The first to make this observation was Frank Underhill. In a paper he presented to the Canadian Historical Association in 1927, Underhill, in the terminology of those less-evolved times, described Anne Brown as "perhaps the real father of Confederation."

of the chair of the Canada Board of the Hudson's Bay Company, stirring up some interest in Brown. The reports of both intermediaries suggested that Brown was looking for what Brydges called an "omnibus arrangement," or some kind of comprehensive new political rearrangement. By no means, though, had he lost his suspicions of his old rival. During the 1863 session, Brown got off a splendid shot at Macdonald, calling him a "grimalkin" crouched "at the door of the pantry, watching for mice to come in and out."

Movement had begun elsewhere as well. By now, Macdonald and McGee were allies. In a key by-election early in 1863, they campaigned and caroused together; one of the songs they bawled out in taverns went, "A drunken man is a terrible curse / But a drunken woman is twice as worse." The Conservative candidate won handily. McGee brought Macdonald a lot of Catholic Irish votes; he also brought with him his passion for Confederation. In a series of articles that summer, McGee put forward his argument for a "new nationality." Later he toured the Maritimes—the first Canadian politician to do so—to tell audiences in Halifax and Saint John about "the fortunate genius of a united British America." When Macdonald formed his March 1864 government with Taché, McGee became its minister of agriculture.

The most significant change in the Canadian political scene took place in the early summer of 1863, but outside the country. That June, General Robert E. Lee followed up a sweeping victory at Fredericksburg, Virginia, by sending the seventy-five-thousand-strong Army of Northern Virginia swinging up into the Shenandoah Valley. At the hamlet of Gettysburg, Pennsylvania, Lees' troops met the ninety-thousand-strong Army of the Potomac. The two vast forces clashed on July 1. Two days later, Lee turned his shattered army back towards Virginia, followed almost immediately by the surrender of Vicksburg, the last Confederate fort on the Mississippi. The Confederacy was now cut in two. Gallantry and dash could no longer overcome numbers and industrial productivity. The South hung on, despite Lincoln's expectations of its collapse, but the war's eventual outcome could no longer be doubted. Once that happened, the question would then become, what would happen to Canada?

During the months after Gettysburg, Macdonald plotted his way through all the post–Civil War possibilities. They encompassed everything from an actual cross-border invasion, to nothing happening at all but with the U.S. colossus completely overshadowing the small and poor Province of Canada, to Britain reassessing its position on the North American continent and withdrawing its troops. The *Times* (London) commented, perceptively but embarrassingly, that the redcoats stationed in Canada were "numerous enough to irritate but not numerous enough to intimidate or to defend." Macdonald revealed the product of his ponderings in a remarkable speech—more exactly, a remarkable portion of a speech dealing mostly with other matters—that he gave in the fall of 1864, a year and a bit after Gettysburg.

To describe the key section of this speech here involves fast-forwarding past a cluster of political events in which Macdonald played a critical part, and afterwards winding back to recapture the skipped-over parts. This, though, is the only way to make sense of the sequence of events and to understand why Macdonald should have abruptly abandoned his long indifference to Confederation and then gone on to become first its main cheerleader and then its impresario.

The date of this speech was Tuesday, October 11, 1864. By then, the Confederation process was already well under way. Macdonald spoke at the start of a conference in Quebec City at which delegates from all the colonies of British North America debated whether to create a new, pan-Canadian government and how best to do it. Macdonald used part of his speech to explain why success at the conference mattered so much. The issue, he argued, was not a new constitution, important and indeed essential as that obviously was. Rather, it was Canada's survival. Macdonald was expressing here the leitmotif of his life—to ensure that Canada did not become American.

From Macdonald's perspective, Confederation and the new constitution that would go with it were means to an end. That end was Canada's survival as a distinct, un-American society in North America. To remain distinct, Canada had to remain British. To keep the British connection, Canada had to impress a doubting Britain by an expression of its national will to survive. And the way to do that was Confederation, because it involved a commitment to national unity across British North America on a scale never before attempted.

In trying to communicate such thoughts to an audience, Macdonald was hobbled by his customary and considerable handicap. As a debater, he was quick, skilled and often lethal; as a speaker, though, he was little better than average. He had little aptitude for, and was actually suspicious of, oratory or eloquence. Unlike Lincoln, he never attempted to summon up "men's better angels." Most times, Macdonald preferred to act rather than talk, expressing himself by deeds rather than by words. He did, however, possess one highly effective oratorical device: every now and then he would use candour to get people to pay attention. This device sent out a signal that whatever he was saying, he actually meant. So people listened.

"It is stated [by some opponents of Confederation], that in England . . . federalism will be considered as showing a desire for independence," Macdonald began this part of his speech at the conference. He himself didn't believe that, he continued, but rather that "the people of England are strongly bent on keeping her position as a mighty empire, which can only be done by helping her colonies." Yet, he admitted, "the value of the colonies has never been fairly represented to the people of England." He cited some of the important British figures who publicly questioned the worth of the colonies—for instance, the influential journalist Goldwin Smith, then still a professor at Oxford. Many of the delegates, few of whom ever looked much beyond their own county or town, would have been surprised and shocked to hear their most senior politician admit openly that doubts existed in high places in England about the value of holding on to Canada. Macdonald hammered home his point: "Our present isolated and defenceless position is, no doubt, a source of embarrassment to England." He speculated that "if it were not for the weakness of Canada, Great Britain might have joined France in acknowledging the Southern Confederacy."

Having identified the problem—Canada's weakness might motivate England to pull back from North America—Macdonald then presented his solution: "We must, therefore, become important, not only to England but in the eyes of foreign states. And most especially to the United States. . . . For the sake of securing peace to ourselves and our posterity, we must make ourselves powerful. The great security for peace is to convince the world of our strength by being united."

Macdonald was using these passages in his speech to appeal to Canadians to send out a clear, collective signal of their will to survive. Doing this—by Confederation—would give a message that would be noticed and respected in the two places that mattered to Canada—London and Washington.

What Macdonald was telling the delegates in Quebec City was, as most of them must have recognized, the truth itself, harsh and unvarnished. U.S. power was the new continental reality. Britain could still help and would continue to do so, but increasingly from a distance. Ultimately, Canada was on its own. Either it made a convulsive effort to survive or it just might vanish.

When and how Macdonald underwent such a eureka moment has to remain a mystery—indeed, no proof exists that he ever experienced it. He left no writing describing it; no colleague ever claimed later to have been there when he blurted out, "Now I see!" Intellectual epiphanies were not, anyway, his style; Macdonald favoured action, not angst. And to him action included the seeming inaction of waiting for the exact moment when all the stars were aligned. That Macdonald eventually committed himself to Confederation at about five minutes to midnight doesn't mean that he had not recognized its necessity a good deal earlier. What mattered is that, once he had intuited that the moment was ripe, Macdonald hurled himself into action, never again glancing back. We were made, this is to say, by a man who, once he knew what do to, knew how to get it done.

Other commentators have argued for different interpretations of the sequence of events. To some, Donald Creighton above all, Macdonald moved stealthily towards Confederation for years before he committed himself to it publicly. The predominant view is that he took up Confederation's cause only when he realized that unless he joined the project he would put at risk his own and his party's future. That interpretation is, of course, far from being wholly wrong. But it amounts to a one-dimensional analysis of a leader with a multilayered mind—something akin to treating as the complete Lincoln the very limited leader that Lincoln amounted to at the start of the American Civil War.

That speech by Macdonald at Quebec City was the first time Canada's politicians had been told the truth about the "double" threat that Canada faced from across the Atlantic and from across the border. It's uncertain how many of his contemporaries understood what Macdonald was attempting to do. Galt did, as a later letter of his will show. And so did Goldwin Smith, who at the time wrote that the only way to defend Canada was "to fence her round with the majesty of an independent nation." What was happening, though, was that the Confederation stakes were being transformed from merely those of finding a way to end a political deadlock to that of finding a way for Canada to survive.

That Britain might, if not actually abandon Canada, then gently but firmly pull itself back from a close embrace in order to position itself nearer to the United States, challenges the generally presented view of Canada as the nineteenth-century linchpin of the British Empire. After all, without Canada, the Empire would no longer stretch around the world in an unbroken chain on which the sun never set. At the time, though, such a gap would not have mattered that much—simply because the Empire did not matter that much to the British themselves.

The British Empire of the mid-1860s was not at all the Empire of bugles and banners and thin red lines that has been handed down in the history books. These flummeries existed then, but the Empire itself did not really exist. It did physically, of course. Britain was the global hegemon: it accounted for one-third of the world's industrial output; its Royal Navy policed the seas; and London was easily the world's largest and richest city. Moreover, the British Empire possessed the aura of having defeated Napoleon (a glory now fading fast) and the moral aura of having deployed the Royal Navy to sweep slavery from the high seas.*

---

* In counterpoint to whatever credit Britain gained by its abolition of slavery in the Empire in 1833, it incurred the off-setting discredit of initiating the Opium Wars at about the same time, employing the Royal Navy to blast open China's ports to the opium trade.

But it didn't exist psychically. Rather than an empire, what Britain owned then was an agglomeration of territories acquired or conquered or bought or swapped or stolen "in a fit of absence of mind," to use the famous phrase.* The British Empire, in the term's ordinary meaning—the one it took Canada until the Statute of Westminster of 1931 to gain full independence from—didn't come into being until the 1870s. Its birth is commonly dated to Disraeli's purchase of the Suez Canal shares in 1875, although a better date might be 1872, when Disraeli turned imperialism into Britain's political litmus test—and not coincidentally won power for himself—by attacking the Liberals, and his arch-rival Gladstone, for seeking "the disintegration of the Empire of England."†

Before this time, the British were quite uncertain whether they wanted to have an empire. The country was divided between "Big Englanders" like Disraeli and "Little Englanders," who reckoned that any empire imposed far greater costs on Britain than benefits. Intellectually, the Little Englanders made all the running; they won a key argument over free trade in the 1840s, after which Britain's trade no longer followed the flag but chased after profits anywhere. Disraeli himself spoke at times in the tones of a Little Englander; in 1852 he described the colonies

---

* Accident played a large part in determining that nineteenth-century Canada was among the blotches of red on the map. In the negotiations for the Treaty of Paris of 1763, Prime Minister Pitt the Elder came close to handing Canada back in exchange for France's sugar-rich islands of Guadeloupe. In the end, he held on to Canada largely out of fear of public outrage at the abandonment of the conquest for which the dauntless hero General James Wolfe had given his life.

† In 1872 Disraeli made imperialism the central tenet of Conservative Party policy. He was drawn to this stance because he had realized that working-class Britons, newly enfranchised by the 1867 Reform Act, were strong supporters of the Empire, perhaps as a source of colour in their hard lives.

as "a millstone around our necks." As late as 1866 he reasoned from the emergence of a united Germany and a rising Russia that "power and influence we should exercise in Asia, consequently in Eastern Europe, consequently in Western Europe; but what is the use of these colonial deadweights *which we do not govern?*" (The peak of the Little Englanders came in 1868–72, when such views were held not just by Gladstone, then the prime minister, but also by his chancellor of the Exchequer, the foreign secretary and the colonial secretary.)

Little Englanders made the economic case—men including Manchester School Liberals such as Richard Cobden,* John Bright and Goldwin Smith. The press fired more shots, as in the *Edinburgh Review*'s description of the North American colonies as "productive of heavy expense to Great Britain, and of nothing else." Such opinions were common among the most knowledgeable Britons of all—those in the Colonial Office. In 1864 John Taylor, one of the influential officials there, dismissed all the British North American colonies as "a sort of *damnosa hereditas.*" Taylor and the top official, Sir Frederic Rogers, were "separatists" who believed that the best solution was to gently nudge the colonies towards independence.

Those who wanted the Empire retained evoked glory and honour. Prime ministers in particular held this view: Lord Melbourne proclaimed that "the final separation of these colonies might possibly not be of material detriment. . . . But it is clear it would be a serious blow to the honour of Great Britain"; Sir Robert Peel's

---

* Cobden could lay a claim to be the father of the "Narcissism of small differences," that practice whereby some Canadians stare intently across the border to identify differences between themselves and their neighbouring Americans. After a tour of the two countries in 1859, he proclaimed that Canadians "looked more English than those on the other side of the American frontier—they are more fleshy and have ruddier complexions."

view, specifically about "the Canadas," was that "the tenure by which we hold [them] is most precarious, & that sooner or later we must lose them"; Lord John Russell warned that "the loss of a great portion of our Colonies would disrupt our imperial interests in the world, and the vultures would soon be getting together"; and Lord Palmerston felt that "it would lower us greatly, for 'if reputation is strength' then the reverse would weaken us much." Until Disraeli won the day, the Big Englanders' case was defensive: while no particular colony might be worth keeping, a domino effect might precipitate the loss of all the rest. (The real concern of those who wanted to keep the colonies was that if Canada went, so, sooner or later, would Ireland.)

It was only *after* Confederation that the British really embraced their empire, and so embraced Canada. During the earlier years, Macdonald had no assurance that his own loyalty and that of other Canadians would be reciprocated. Indeed, it was during this period of uncertainty that he made some of his sharpest comments about Canada-British relations: he pronounced that Canada had the right "to raise revenue in [its] own fashion," that is, to impose whatever tariffs it saw fit on British goods; he protested strongly to the governor general, as "a matter of the gravest importance . . . directly affecting the independence of our Courts and of our people" and as "an unseemly and irritating conflict of jurisdiction," the decision of a British court to issue a writ of habeas corpus to protect an accused person in Canada.* Macdonald praised the action itself as done for "praiseworthy motives" but insisted that "the English Courts of Justice

---

* The accused was a runaway slave charged with murder in the United States whom the British Anti-Slavery Society was seeking to protect from being extradited from Canada.

shall have no jurisdiction in Canada, and that no writ or process from them shall run into it."

The possibility of a split should not be exaggerated. The British aristocracy and political class always supported the Empire—it created jobs for those troublesome younger sons. Some did so for high-minded reasons: Edward Cardwell, the colonial secretary, argued in a January 1865 speech at Oxford University that while "lynx-eyed logicians" might dismiss the colonies, in contrast to other empires that had clung on to their holdings, "it has been given to England alone to be also the mother of great and free communities."* There was also the powerful emotional argument that imperialism's real purpose was to create converts to Christianity; prime ministers always wanted to keep the colonies, because none of them wanted to go down in the history books as the leader who had "lost" them. And at no time did anyone ever suggest giving up India, that jewel in Britain's crown, or naval bases such as Gibraltar and Malta—or Halifax.

Support for keeping all the other colonies, though, remained suspect until the 1870s—particularly Canada, because with it came the risk of a clash with the United States. The Colonial Office itself was a second-rank portfolio and remained so until almost the end of the century.† Its staff was tiny; its offices—at 14 Downing Street—were crumbling and so damp that fires had to be kept going all year round to prevent the files from going mouldy. Colonial Office clerks passed their time playing darts with pen-nibs attached to literal red tape.

---

* *The Times* went on to comment sourly, "We put no great trust in the 'gratitude' of colonies."

† The earliest first-rate colonial secretary—to everyone's amazement, and even more so because he had insisted on the portfolio—was Joseph Chamberlain— but he didn't take office there until the post-Macdonald year of 1895.

Among the colonies, Canada, while the richest and most advanced politically, attracted little sentiment. "Who is Minister, at Quebec City or any other seat of British government in America, we none of us know," observed the *Times*. "If we knew today, we should forget tomorrow." New Brunswick's lieutenant-governor, Arthur Gordon, described Canada as "a last resort for people who have ruined themselves at home." According to the *Times*, Canada came second to Australia, because those going there came from "a wealthier and more completely English class"—by which it meant that, blessedly, few Irish went to Australia. Outside politics, Canada could count on few friendly voices or pens: the novelist Anthony Trollope had his eponymous hero Phineas Finn declare, "Not one man in a thousand cares whether the Canadas prosper or fail to prosper."* Mind you, a number of Canadians— Macdonald conspicuously absent from their ranks—felt the same, in reverse. A legislature member, Philip VanKoughnet, wrote home from London that he "felt himself like a cat in a strange garret." George Brown, while in England on the trip during which he met Anne, wrote home that "after all I have seen, I say now as earnestly as I can—Canada for me!" Still, there was that crushing, dismissive judgment of the authoritative *Times* that whether Canadians opted for independence or not was hardly "considered a matter of great moment to England."

From this conflicting raw material, Macdonald had to forge a counterweight to the colossus next door. Two comments capture the outer limits of the possibilities available to him. One was by the colonial secretary, the Duke of Newcastle. The other was by an unknown editor of a backcountry weekly. While in

---

* Trollope had his finger on the public pulse. He had Phineas Finn go on to say that the British did care "that Canada not go to the States because although they don't love the Canadians, they do hate the Americans."

Wilfrid Laurier. As the editor of a small rural newspaper, Laurier dismissed the argument that Confederation would secure Canada from invasion by comparing its effect to trying to stop a bullet with an eggshell.

Washington at the end of 1860, following the Prince of Wales' North American tour, Newcastle sought out the future secretary of state, William Seward. They talked about the possibility that Canada, just by being there, might accidentally precipitate a Britain-U.S. conflict. Seward said he couldn't believe Britain would risk so much for so little. "Do not remain under such an error," answered Newcastle. "Once touch us on our honour, and you will soon find the bricks of New York and Boston falling about your heads"*—in other words, the Royal Navy would use the Atlantic ports of the United States for target practice. The other comment was contained in a small Lower Canada newspaper, *Le Défricheur*, in an editorial about whether, as Macdonald and many others claimed, a confederation of the British North American colonies would actually improve Canada's military security. Such dependence on a piece of paper, wrote the young editor, would be like being "armed with an eggshell to stop a bullet." The editor's name was Wilfrid Laurier.

The duke in private and the country editor in an unknown newspaper were saying what Macdonald had told the Quebec

---

* Back home, Newcastle gave a level-headed analysis of the implications of what he had said to Seward: "The injury to our own trade of burning New York and Boston would be so serious we ought to be as reluctant to do it as to destroy Liverpool and Bristol," he reported. He added, though, "but they know we must do it if they declare war."

City delegates. There was only so much that Britain could or would do for Canada. It would do even that almost entirely for the sake of its honour, and do it on its own terms. Canada really was on its own.

⌒

Credible or not, useful or not, some sort of attempt to improve Canada's military security had to be made, if only as a gesture. In 1863 Britain sent out a Lieutenant-Colonel William Francis Drummond Jervois to recommend improvements for defence. Jervois's report, made public early in 1864, touched off a political storm because he had quite clearly concluded that Upper Canada was indefensible. Hope remained only for those places the Royal Navy could reach, such as Halifax, Quebec City and perhaps Montreal. The effect of his report, said Macdonald, had been to create "a panic" in Upper Canada. Jervois later turned in a second, more optimistic report calling for heavy spending on fortifications and, to reassure Upper Canadians, for a fleet on Lake Ontario. The Canadian legislature approved the spending of one million dollars, though little work was actually done. Macdonald refused to take the plans seriously. After two years, he forecast, "a hole may be made in the mud opposite Quebec, and the foundation of single redoubt built." Implicitly, Macdonald agreed with Laurier.

⌒

Something else was needed. What it might be, Macdonald as yet had no idea. But he did understand the nature of the problem that had to be solved—Canada had to find a gap, no matter how narrow and twisting it might be, between the opposed risks of "forcible annexation and abandonment by Britain," as he phrased it in a letter to a Maritime supporter. What Macdonald could not know was that Queen Victoria had been discussing the very same conundrum with her ministers at the same time. This was, as she recorded, "the impossibility of our being able to hold Canada, but we must struggle for it; and by far the best solution would be to let it go as an independent kingdom under an English prince."* The problem was defined. The next step, long overdue, was to define a solution and then implement it.

---

* A rough precedent existed in the creation of Brazil, which broke away from Portugal in 1822 and remained an independent kingdom, under Pedro I and Pedro II, until it became a republic in 1899.

SEVENTEEN

Irreplaceable Man

~

> Everybody admits that the union must take place some time. I say
> now is the time. If we allow so favourable an opportunity to pass, it
> may never come again.
>
> John A. Macdonald

The political minuet that followed the defeat of Macdonald's government on June 14, 1864, was well practised. After he had lost the non-confidence vote, Macdonald called on Governor General Monck at Spencer Wood, his residence in Quebec City, where the government was now located, to ask for a dissolution of the legislature so an election could be held. This Monck agreed to. Here, though, the familiar ritual was halted; it was interrupted first by George Brown, and soon afterwards by Monck himself.

A month earlier, the resolution Brown had moved at the start of the session—for a legislative committee to look at all the alternative proposals for some form of federation—had at last come to a vote; to general surprise it passed, 59 to 48. Those opposed were mostly Canadien *bleus*, but they also included John A. Macdonald, Alexander Tilloch Galt and George-Étienne Cartier, all of them suspicious of what Brown was up to. On May 20 the committee assembled—Macdonald as a member—to begin its work. To make certain that all present stayed and really worked, Brown strode over to the door, locked it, and told the group, "Now gentlemen, you must talk to me about this matter, as you cannot leave this room without coming to me." Another seven meetings followed, with Cartier playing an active part—an unusual role for him when constitutional changes were being discussed.

By a fluke of fate, the committee's report was finished on the same day, June 14, that Macdonald's government fell. Brown read out its conclusion to the House: "A strong feeling was found to exist among members of the committee in favour of changes in the direction of a federative system, applied either to Canada alone or to the whole British North American Provinces." Its sole recommendation—opposed by just three of the twenty members, among them Macdonald—was that yet another committee look again at the matter. This was tepid stuff.

Late that night, though, Brown spoke to two Liberal-Conservative members. Could the crisis not be used to address directly the great constitutional questions? he suggested. The pair asked if they could pass this comment back to Macdonald and Cartier. Brown agreed. The members hurried off.

The next morning, there was a slight alteration in the customary steps of the minuet. Macdonald asked the House for an adjournment to give him time to consult the governor general. When Macdonald and his delegation arrived, Monck assured them that his approval for a dissolution and an election still stood. He asked, though, why they did not talk to the opposition leaders to see whether an all-party government might be formed to address the constitutional options. One day later, members of the legislature were astonished to see Brown and Macdonald having a brief, urgent yet seemingly amicable conversation in the chamber's centre aisle. They were discussing when and where

Macdonald and Galt should meet Brown to talk about a possible coalition government.

The challenge before the old enemies was to agree on what such a government should stand for and, scarcely less consequential, who should be in its cabinet. They met, at one in the afternoon on the 17th, in Brown's room in the St. Louis Hotel, overlooking Quebec City's harbour. For Macdonald and Galt, harking back to their own agreement of 1858, the new government's first priority had to be a pan-Canadian federation. For Brown, it had to be Representation by Population. The differences between them had to be fudged, and getting there took time and immense care by both sides as they struggled not to look back at old battles and wounds. The fudge proved to be that Brown, no less than Macdonald and Galt, was committed to the "federative principle"—a term that conveniently could mean almost anything and could also be applied as easily to the United Province of Canada alone, as Brown wanted, or to all of British North America, as was Macdonald and Galt's choice. They were still arguing about details when they had to hurry back to the chamber for Parliament's three o'clock opening.

Macdonald spoke first. His government had initiated negotiations with a leading opposition member, he disclosed, and as a result of progress in these talks the dissolution of Parliament was being delayed. After a pause to heighten the suspense, Macdonald revealed that the opposition member he was negotiating with was "the member for South Oxford"—Brown. There were gasps of disbelief. Then Brown spoke. He had never imagined himself negotiating with such a government, but "the repeated endeavours year after year to get a strong government formed have resulted in constant failure." Out of this crisis, he continued, a chance had been created "to consider the interests of both sections of the Province, and to find a settlement of our differences." With great grace, Brown singled out Cartier as having done "a most bold and manly thing" by agreeing to the project. The chamber rang out with cheers, shouts, exclamations, slaps on the back. At one in the morning, alone at last in his hotel room, Brown wrote home to tell Anne all about it: "You never saw such a scene . . . but as the whole thing may fail, we will not count our chickens yet." The *Canadien* newspaper expressed its opinion that the Macdonald-Brown accord "comptera parmi les plus memorable de notre histoire parlementaire." In the town now known as Kitchener, the *Berliner Journal* expressed, in the primary language of the people of that area, its delight that the project could lead to the incongruity: that "George Brown mit John A. Macdonald, Cartier und Galt Hand in Hand zu gehen—daran nätte, gewiss Niemand in Traume gedacht."[*]

It was the most dramatic instance of political reconciliation in Canada's parliamentary history since 1848, when Governor General Lord Elgin had followed his reading of the Throne Speech in English with, for first time, a re-reading in French. As on that earlier occasion, some Canadien members rushed up to Brown to kiss him on both cheeks—a challenging feat given his height of more than six feet. Brown and Macdonald had fought over everything from Rep by Pop to the double majority to the choice for Canada's capital. Besides their multiple combats, they shared a mutual animosity, thickening towards contempt, matched only a century later by that between Prime Ministers John Diefenbaker and Lester Pearson. Yet here they were, doing what they had promised never to do—joining hands with each other.

---

[*] A rough translation, provided by a bilingual friend, would be: "Certainly no one would have dreamed of Brown walking hand in hand with Macdonald, Cartier and Galt."

The explanation each gave at the time was "deadlock." That was true enough: the journalist Goldwin Smith would later describe deadlock as having been the "true Father of Confederation." The Canadian political system had become stale and sterile. The Conservatives and the Reformers were like punch-drunk fighters, still upright only because they each propped the other up, too depleted now to take more than the occasional swipe at each other over stale quarrels.

Brown in particular was displaying an out-of-character generosity for which Anne Brown surely deserves a share of the credit. The newspaper owner had a first-rate mind, but as a politician he was of the third rank; yet he was now putting himself into Macdonald's supple and deviously articulated hands.

Macdonald's own explanation for embracing Brown and Confederation, given in a letter to a Conservative supporter two years later, was straightforward: "As leader of the Conservatives in Upper Canada, I then had the option of forming a coalition government or of handing over the administration of affairs to the Grit party for the next ten years." That admission of opportunism is persuasive—Macdonald's political circumstances were indeed parlous. His count of Conservative supporters was down to twenty. He had misjudged until the very last moment the readiness of politicians in all corners of the House to find a way out of the legislative inertia made unavoidable by the double-majority rule.

An entirely new political threat also confronted him. Now that Brown had stopped denouncing "French domination," an alliance between Brown and Cartier's *bleus* became a real possibility. Brown could bring to such a grouping many more elected members than remained with Macdonald. The "mini-confederation" that Brown favoured, of separating Upper and Lower Canada into autonomous provinces with some minimal "joint authority" over them, would give Cartier what he most wanted—protection against Rep by Pop. And Macdonald knew it would be far easier merely to reshape the existing government in this way than to recreate the entire country as he now wanted to do.

It fact, though, Brown had for too long said too much that was hateful for Canadien members ever to fully accept him. His "mini-federation" would be far more difficult to bring off than it might seem at first glance. It would leave the English in Lower Canada (now one-quarter of Montreal's population) isolated in a quasi-separate province dominated by the French. Cartwright wrote in his *Reminiscences* that he thought the English in Lower Canada would have responded by seeking union with the United States (as they had advocated in 1849). To prevent such an unhinging of all its British North American colonies, the Imperial government would almost certainly have intervened to disallow the "mini-federation."

Yet something was going on between Brown and Cartier, and if it ever came to anything, the victim would be Macdonald. Cartwright wrote later that there existed at this time a perfectly good understanding between Mr. Cartier and Mr. Brown about forming "a new ministry"—and he claimed that Governor General Monck had told him this. In the end, all this backstage plotting came to nothing, except that thereafter Macdonald and Brown circled each other even more warily.

Nevertheless, a transformational change had taken place. Macdonald and Brown had reversed their roles. Brown, the impatient moralist, was now the cautious conservative. The scheme he was advocating amounted only to a rejigging of the existing system. Macdonald, the scheming opportunist, had turned visionary. He had not only committed himself to Galt's 1858 plan for a new Confederation extending to the Maritimes but had added to it an entirely new goal of stretching this new nation west to the Pacific. His leitmotif of maintaining Canada as an un-American nation was at work. As Macdonald expressed it in a letter to British railway promoter Edward Watkin, "If Canada is to remain a Country separate from the United States, it is of great importance that they should not get behind us by right or force and intercept the route to the Pacific." Not only was Macdonald now calling for a much more ambitious federation than that proposed by Brown but he was calling also for a much more ambitious national government than Brown's minimalist "some joint authority." Of the pair, one wanted only to spring clean the existing house, while the other wanted to build an entirely new mansion.

It was this formula for national survival that, six months later, Macdonald would lay before the delegates at the Quebec Conference when he challenged them to "convince the world of our strength by being united."

In the immediate future, the boldest of the three was Cartier. He was risking the bird he already had in his hand—the effective veto on national affairs exercised by his *bleu* members—on a good-faith assumption that Quebec's distinctiveness would continue to be respected even when it was surrounded by an entire transcontinental flock of English-speaking fowl. Between Macdonald and Brown, though, there was no question who now was the bolder. Indeed, Brown at times seemed curiously self-doubting. Asked how he saw the way ahead, he replied, "I am not so well informed as to all the bearings on the question of a union of all the British North American Provinces that I could at once pronounce a final option on that question." Brown's *Globe* echoed his timidity: "Efforts are to be made to induce the Lower Provinces [the Maritimes] to join confederation, but the success of the scheme, so far as Canada is concerned, is not to be contingent on their assent."

A timeout is needed here to justify the argument being presented that Macdonald, despite the judgment of most historians, was acting strategically as well as tactically for the sake of his own partisan advantage. True, Macdonald seldom went in for big ideas or "visions." But that's not the same as saying—as has been said many times—that he had no ideas at all.

The world over, politics then had precious little to do with ideas. There were exceptions, of course, such as the daring ones that came out of the French and American revolutions, ideas that found their source in the eighteenth-century Enlightenment. But the sweeping economic and social concepts that lay ahead—Karl Marx published the first volume of *Das Kapital* in the Confederation year of 1867—were prompted largely by the search for a response to the human dislocations caused by the Industrial Revolution and the growth of huge, impersonal cities, neither of which had happened yet in overwhelmingly rural Canada. Other than going to war or, the Canadian equivalent, trying to build a nation, governments did precious little. Only the most occasional politician—the high-minded Gladstone in Britain or Bismarck in Germany—thought much about social change and reform. As Goldwin Smith, the Regius Professor of History at Oxford before he transplanted himself to the colony, wrote in sad resignation about Canada, "In this country, what is there for Conservatives to conserve, or for Reformers to reform?"

Macdonald's Scottishness should never be discounted: Scots didn't go in for intellectualizing or for attitudinizing. Essentially, they get on with the job at hand. Inside almost every Scot, though, there is, somewhere, an urge handed down across the generations to behold the Hebrides in dreams. Confederation, while about such practical matters as ending political deadlock, was at its core an absurdly romantic project. Its end objective was to create a new nation that might actually survive in North America without becoming American. At some level that Macdonald would never allow himself to show, man and mission had to be as one.

Some of Macdonald's often-expressed contempt for the utility of ideas was a pose. He read far too much, from literature to philosophy to politics to history, to have been in the least timid about ideas in themselves. It's a rare reader who does not think.

Yet Macdonald has usually been portrayed as having no political ideas at all: the two historians who studied this specific part of his record—T.W.L. MacDermot in 1931 and Peter Waite in 1968—reached this conclusion.* The single contrary view is that of political scientist Rod Preece, who in a 1980 article made a spirited argument that Macdonald did have a political philosophy. He traced Macdonald's philosophy to Edmund Burke, writing that "Macdonald practised the Burkean principles of prudence and experience combined and it is these which have been confused with pragmatism by Macdonald's numerous commentators." In one especially fine phrase, Preece writes: "What distinguished Macdonald from the commonplace political leader was that he understood in a philosophical manner why he should be expedient."

Waite, the leading post-Creighton scholar on Macdonald, doesn't in any way dismiss him as merely an opportunist. "For Macdonald, the supreme test of any policy was in the results. . . . No Canadian politician, except perhaps [Mackenzie] King, had

---

* In one article, MacDermot criticized Macdonald for failing to show any awareness of having read, among others, "the Fabians." Since the Fabian Society was formed only in 1884, this seems a critical reach too far. In fact, the Fabian leaders Sidney and Beatrice Webb did come to Canada, in 1897, and didn't much like what they saw: a "complete lack of thinking" about social problems in a "nation of successful speculators in land values."

such a grasp of the art of the possible." He goes on to discuss the central characteristic about Macdonald's concept of the exercise of political power: "For Macdonald, the word 'reform' was largely devoid of political significance. . . . He distrusted the reforming temperament; he distrusted the view of society, which sees in changes of institutions or of laws, the panacea for the problems of human society. . . . The reason for that assumption was his view of human nature. Human beings do not change, and since they do not, the root character of human life cannot change much either. Reform this, or reform that; but human beings will find holes in any system."

Waite's analysis is brilliant and is absolutely correct. In fact, Preece was saying much the same thing in describing Macdonald as the embodiment of Burkean prudence and experience. Both are different ways of saying that politics is about people, not about ideology—and that, of course, is an ideology in itself.

Besides his belief in the cardinal values of prudence and experience, and his idea that politics is about the nature of human beings writ large, Macdonald had a second line of consistent thought. This thought was about Canada itself. Today, Canadianness has acquired a kind of cult status. Contemporary politicians and all those involved in public life in any way compete to be more Canadian than anyone else, to be more passionate about the nation's potential than others. Some end their speeches with the words, "God bless Canada." In the mid-nineteenth century, few people loved Canada. Their love was for Britain (or, for Canadiens, for Quebec). The constitution that the Confederation project eventually gave birth to was not the Constitution of Canada but the British North America Act.

Whatever the constitution's formal title, its defining characteristics were that it was a British-inspired document crafted for an un-American Canada. It would be only one step of many that

Macdonald would take to preserve the un-Americanness of Canada—the National Policy of protecting domestic manufacturers, the building of a railway from sea to sea, and his unceasing opposition to cross-border free trade. What is so striking about these policies is their consistency. Macdonald committed himself to this course with his first declaration on entering politics in 1844; his last war cry a half-century later was "A British subject I was born, a British subject I will die." Among Canadian leaders, perhaps only Trudeau matched his consistency. Macdonald, though, unlike Trudeau, never paraded his intellect before the crowd like a cape. Rather, he went out of his way to appear to have no ideas: "I am satisfied to confine myself to practical things . . . I am satisfied not to have a reputation for indulging in imaginary schemes and harbouring visionary ideas . . . always utopian and never practical," he said during the Confederation Debates of 1865. He sent out to ordinary Canadians the reassuring signal that he was just like them, and to his opponents the equally reassuring signal that they didn't need to worry about overestimating his intellect.

He just got on with the job, occasionally smiling sardonically at those who preferred merely to talk about the job. In Creighton's fine phrase, "he thumped no tubs and he banged no pulpits." In his *Reminiscences*, *Globe* editor Sir John Willison gave a wonderful description of Macdonald keeping himself at a distance from ideology: "For the evangelical school of reconstructionists who would remake the world in their own image and reform mankind by legislation, he had only a complacent tolerance." Except that Macdonald then went ahead and reconstructed Canada in his own image.

Macdonald seldom allowed his feeling about Canada to show through his pose of unruffled pragmatism. It happened once in the small Upper Canada town of St. Thomas during his speaking tour in November 1860. There he said, "I am like those who hear me, a Canadian heart and soul. I heard the gallant officer who returned thanks for the army and navy say he was. That, I believe, is the feeling that exists in every breast here; and though I have the misfortune, like my friend the deputy adjutant-general, to be a Scotchman, still I was caught young and was brought to this country before I was very much corrupted. [Laughter] Since I was five years old, I have been in Canada. All my hopes and dreams and my remembrances are Canadian; not only are my principles and prejudices Canadian but what, as a Scotchman, I feel as much as anyone else, my interests are Canadian. [Applause]"

Not until Laurier would another Canadian leader talk with such feeling about his country, and, after Laurier, there was a long gap until Diefenbaker.

It's time now to return to the story itself.

⌒

The backroom bargaining about the policies and composition of the new coalition government went on for another week. Brown made a last attempt to secure a commitment that the new government would work for an immediate federation of the Province of Canada alone, but yielded to Macdonald's insistence that a pan-Canadian federation had to be considered first. Incomparably more difficult was the bargaining over cabinet posts. Macdonald insisted that the six Upper Canada portfolios be split evenly between Conservatives and Reformers, even though Brown's party was far larger. He insisted also that Brown himself fill one of those coalition posts. "I have the offer of office for myself and two others to be named by me," Brown wrote to Anne. "I am deeply distressed at having this matter thrust on me now—but dare not refuse the responsibility with such vast interests at stake. How I do wish you had been here to advise me." During the bargaining, Macdonald at one point offered to step aside himself if this would induce Brown to come in; the offer was rejected, as Macdonald undoubtedly knew it would be. Brown, before making his final decision, consulted his caucus and the governor general and read all the letters that came pouring in. One from D'Arcy McGee advised, "How *can* you hope to secure the settlement without your own personal participation?" Monck similarly told Brown that success or failure "depends very much on your consenting to come into the Cabinet." Finally, on Wednesday, June 22, Brown made up his mind, explaining to Anne, who had been hoping he would return home to Toronto, "There was no help for it—and it was such a temptation to have possible the power of settling the sectional troubles of Canada forever."

That day, Macdonald informed the House that a new government had been formed—the Great Coalition it would come to be called—for the specific purpose of attempting a confederation of all the British American colonies, and, if that failed, of the United Province of Canada alone. The new premier was—again—Sir Étienne-Paschal Taché, by now close to seventy years old and serving in the Legislative Council. Taché's Upper Canadian ministers would be Macdonald, Alexander Campbell and McGee, and, from the Reformers, Brown, Oliver Mowat and William McDougall. His Lower Canadian ministers would be led by Cartier and would include Galt. The only group not represented was Antoine-Aimé Dorion's *rouges*.

Relations between Macdonald and Brown were never easy. Just six weeks after the coalition was formed, Brown was complaining about overspending on the new Parliament Buildings, exactly as he had done repeatedly from the Opposition benches but now, as a minister, fully informed that "it will cost half the revenue to the province to light them and heat them and keep them clean. Such monstrous folly was never perpetrated in the world before." More smoothly, that same August, Macdonald advised an inquiring newspaper editor that "Brown and myself are going to sit down immediately to arrange the names of the newspapers deserving of Government patronage."

Convincing Conservatives and Reformers to work together after years of clawing at each other was a constant trial. As early as July, Macdonald had to plead with a supporter "that I may call on you to lay aside, for the present at least, party feeling . . . and to ask you to support Mr. McDougall, and will feel very much obliged by your doing so." To McDougall, one of Brown's supporters now in the cabinet and running in a by-election, Macdonald wrote reassuringly that he shouldn't "suspect McGee of acting against you merely because he was seen talking to his countryman and co-religionist Moylan [an old opponent of McDougall's]." Macdonald added that Brown, by saying that the Great Coalition was only "a temporary junction for a temporary purpose, which being attained[,] old party lines would be re-drawn," had made many Conservatives unwilling to "dissolve their organization and be powerless at the next general election." The Conservatives followed their chief, but reluctantly. "I scarcely know where I am or who I am," one wrote plaintively to Macdonald.

The work that mattered, of drafting proposals for a confederal constitution, did get done, nevertheless, and at remarkable speed. Luck helped, by confining these internal debates, carried on in the cabinet offices in Quebec City, to an inalterable deadline. It so happened that the Maritime provinces were already scheduled to meet, in just over two months, in Charlottetown, on

September 1. Their agenda was to discuss Maritime Union, a scheme being pushed on them by the Colonial Office. Monck asked London whether a Canadian group could come down and add its ideas to the mix. London said yes, and the request to attend was made and accepted.

Over a span of less than six weeks, the cabinet ministers discussed, and made decisions about, what they would say about federalism to the Maritime politicians, along with the specific proposals they would make about a confederation of British North America. No record survives of how they accomplished this task, or of any disagreements among them and how they resolved them. There certainly were difficult moments. Macdonald, with the extreme pressure and ongoing exhaustion as factors, was now hitting the bottle hard. As Brown recounted to Anne, a key meeting set for noon was delayed until three, when Macdonald finally arrived, "bearing symptoms of having been on a spree." Having at last joined the others, who were waiting impatiently, Macdonald promptly went over to the lunch table and poured himself one glass of ale after another, until he was "quite drunk." Yet somehow the discussion began and the business got done.

There were also easier times: Macdonald and Brown went together to a party at the governor general's residence and, as Brown reported to Anne, "John A. and I were the only civilians—we had a very good fun." The driving force behind them all was the sense of history. As Brown told Anne, "For the first time in my political life, I indulged in a regular chuckle of gratified pride. . . . It will be a tremendous thing if we accomplish it. . . . There is no other instance of a colony peacefully remodelling its own constitution—such changes have always been the work of the parent state."

A distinctively Canadian attribute of the process by which Confederation was achieved was that the motivating force which enabled it to happen was, as often as not, that of separating Canadians as of uniting them. Thus, the United Province of Canada was to be disassembled into its two original provinces— soon to be renamed Ontario and Quebec—in order to separate English Protestants from French-Canadian Catholics. London's foremost interest, though never stated in public, was that Confederation would give Britain an excuse to separate itself militarily from North America. To the Maritimers, a determining attraction of Confederation was that it would keep them separate from each other rather than compacting them together into a Maritime Union. The Colonial Office strongly advocated this scheme, but Arthur Gordon, New Brunswick's lieutenant-governor, understood Maritime culture better. He reported home: "The different counties [of New Brunswick] hate each other, and they all unite in hating Halifax."*

On August 29, seven senior ministers, among them Macdonald, Cartier, Brown, Galt and McGee, and also three secretaries (including Hewitt Bernard, Macdonald's principal civil servant), boarded the government steamer *Queen Victoria* for the sail down the St. Lawrence to Charlottetown, Prince Edward Island. *Queen Victoria* was a gay little ship of two hundred tons and with a three-hundred-horsepower engine.

⌒

Fortunately, for this part of the story, an insider's report on Confederation does exist. It deals not with politics but with

---

* During the century and a half since, Maritime Union has remained a topic of academic interest, but of none whatever to Maritime people and politicians.

A twentieth-century painting by Rex Woods of the ship Queen Victoria, *which brought the Canadian delegates to the Charlottetown Conference. Macdonald stands on the landing at the top of the ladder.*

people. In his almost daily letters to Anne, Brown described how the voyage downstream was a succession of sunny, calm days, with the delegates relaxing under an awning, reading, playing chess and backgammon, and sometimes taking saltwater baths. The *Queen Victoria* arrived at Charlottetown on September 1 and lowered its two boats, each packed with ministers accompanied by four oarsmen and a boatswain. They were met by a single oyster boat, flat-bottomed and with a barrel of flour in the bow and two jars of molasses in the stern, and, in between, the Prince Edward Island provincial secretary, William H. Pope. He reported that no official reception was immediately possible, because everyone was attending a performance of Slaymaker and Nichols' Olympic Circus. Because of this attraction, all the hotels were filled. Most of the Canadians, Macdonald included, had to sleep on their own boat.

Brown described to Anne the "shake elbow, and the how-d'ye-do" of their first encounter with the Maritime delegates, who immediately informed them that Maritime Union was being held over for later so that Canada's Confederation proposal could be first on the conference agenda. All business was then set aside until the next day, which included a state dinner given by the island's governor, followed by dancing. Brown sat outside as he wrote, telling Anne about "the sea washing up gently to the very door" and how "there is something to the sea."

The next day, in the small red-sandstone building that housed the island's Parliament, the real work began. Cartier started, making a general case for Confederation. Macdonald followed with a long exposition on the benefits of union and the different types of federalism, along with their faults and virtues. That evening there was a buffet that, according to the Charlottetown *Islander*, included "substantials of beef rounds, splendid hams, salmon, lobster . . . all vegetable delicacies peculiar to the season, pastry in all its forms, fruits in almost every variety." All these dishes were generously washed down with the ample supplies of liquor, principally champagne, that the Canadians had cagily brought with them on their boat.

The next day Galt delivered a closely argued analysis of the finances of federalism, laying special stress on how the new central government would compensate the Maritime provinces for their revenue losses—primarily from giving up their tariffs on entering Confederation. There followed a long lunch aboard *Queen Victoria* at which, in Brown's description, "the ice became completely broken, the tongues of the delegates wagged merrily." That night, PEI's premier, Colonel John Hamilton Gray, gave a dinner, followed by dancing. To his astonishment, Brown found himself talking there to one lady who, in her entire life, had never crossed to the mainland; he later advised Anne that

In this cabinet room in Charlottetown's Parliament Buildings, the two sides agreed on the principles of Confederation. Macdonald took time out to sign his name as a "Cabinet maker" in the visitors' book.

Prince Edward Islanders were, nevertheless, "amazingly civilized." After the break on the Sunday, Brown spoke about the division of powers and the new national judiciary.

By Tuesday, the Canadians were done. On Wednesday, the Maritimers gave their answer. "They were unanimous," a delighted Brown wrote home, "in regarding Federation of all the Provinces to be highly desirable—*if the terms of union could be made satisfactory.*" To celebrate their success, they gathered together for a grand ball at Province House. John Ross of *Ross's*

Weekly described the closing gala: "The fascinating dance goes merrily, and the libidi[n]ous waltz with its lascivious entwinements while in growing excitement; the swelling bosom and the voluptuous eye tell the story of intemperate revel." Ross may have been getting a bit intemperate himself.

Macdonald would have been too canny to get overexcited while still in the company of the Maritimers. But he must have been as pleased as Brown was with their progress. To augment his pleasure, he had acquired in Charlottetown a political asset that would prove invaluable in the future. Among the Canadians, no one knew the Maritimes as well as McGee did. In addition to all his visits, he had that summer organized and led a tour of approximately one hundred Canadian businessmen, journalists and politicians around the principal Maritime cities. He would have briefed Macdonald that both of the two most important Maritime premiers, Nova Scotia's Charles Tupper and New Brunswick's Leonard Tilley, were strong Confederates. In Charlottetown, Macdonald began developing friendships with these powerful regional figures as potential recruits for the Liberal-Conservative Party.

The wind was blowing full in the sails of the Canadians. The Maritimers had not only agreed in principle to Confederation but had also agreed to attend a second conference to be held in Quebec City just one month later. There, they and the Canadians, and as well delegates from Newfoundland, would attempt to draft an actual constitution for a confederation. Moreover, while the agreements reached at Charlottetown had been only an agreement in principle, those there had in fact settled on many draft clauses that could go on for final approval at Quebec City.

During one of the breaks in the conference, when Macdonald took a tour of Province House, the island's legislature building, he came upon the visitors' book. He signed his name and, in the column for occupation, wrote "Cabinet maker."

From Charlottetown, the delegates went on as planned to Halifax, some by train and others, Macdonald among them, by the *Queen Victoria*. The press commentary was highly laudatory. As the Halifax *Witness* remarked, almost in bewilderment at the change in Maritimers' attitude towards the Canadians, "There is less aversion to Canada. Indeed, there seems to be a positive desire for union."

At a dinner in the Halifax Hotel on September 12, Premier Tupper proposed a toast to "Colonial Union." In his reply Macdonald talked about his twenty long, dreary years in provincial politics. He mentioned the distance that Canada and the Maritimes still had to go to form a real nation: while all were part of the Empire, he said, "there was no political connection, and we were as wide apart as British America is from Australia. . . . We had only the mere sentiment of a common allegiance, and we were liable, in case England and the United States were pleased to differ, to be cut off, one by one." He outlined the mistakes that the American constitution makers had made in giving too much power and sovereignty to the constituent states—an arrangement that, in his view, had made the American Civil War, or dissolution, inevitable. He claimed that the makers of Canada could avoid these dangers, "if we can agree upon forming a strong central government—a great central legislature—a constitution for a union which will have all the rights of sovereignty except those that are given to the local governments."

He talked, again with the almost unnerving frankness he sometimes employed, about the Intercolonial Railway, that great lure to attract the Maritimes to Confederation; the truth here, said Macdonald, was that "as a commercial enterprise [it] would be of comparatively little advantage to the people of Canada. Whilst we have the St. Lawrence in summer, and the American ports in time of peace, we have all that is requisite for progress."* But, Macdonald went on, this railway would provide for a common defence, and, once the West was opened up, "all [its] great resources will come over the immense railways of Canada to the bosom of your harbour." He described how the new nation would be "a great British monarchy, in connection with the British empire, and under the British Queen." And he said the time to do all this nation-building had to be now: "Everything, gentlemen, is to be gained by union, and everything to be lost by disunion. Everybody admits that the union must take place some time. I say now is the time. If we allow so favourable an opportunity to pass, it may never come again."

The cheers went on and on and on. Three months earlier, Macdonald had been a defeated premier leading a dwindling band of Conservative members. He was now British North America's irreplaceable man.

---

* In fact, the Intercolonial enabled Canadian manufactures to capture the Maritime market from local companies. At the time Macdonald spoke, though, the Reciprocity deal with the United States had made east-west traffic incidental to the huge flow of north-south traffic.

EIGHTEEN

A Pact of Trust

~

*In giving ourselves a complete government we affirm our existence
as a separate nationality.*
La Minerve (Montreal)

Four weeks after the close of the Charlottetown
Conference, the *Queen Victoria* was again chugging
around the Gulf of St. Lawrence, this time to Pictou
and Shediac and once again to Charlottetown to pick
up the Maritime delegates to transport them to Quebec City for
the second Confederation conference. The return trip, unlike the
downriver one, was stormy and cold; they arrived on October 6,
amid an unseasonably early snowstorm. The conference's purpose
was to move beyond pleasantries and generalities by drafting a
constitution, which would be sent over to London for enactment
by the Mother of Parliaments.

A little more than two weeks later, between October 10 and
October 27, with only two days off for rest, the deed was done.
Seldom can so much work of this kind have been done so quickly.
By the end of the conference, the delegates had agreed to
seventy-two resolutions spelling out the rules of governance for a
new nation, down to minutiae such that the "general government"

would be responsible for "quarantine" but the "local" ones for immigration. With remarkably few changes (for example, to make immigration and agriculture joint jurisdictions), these resolutions would be translated into the clauses of the British North America Act that established Confederation. To this original constitution, no substantial change would be made until 1982, when

The Quebec City Conference. In less than three weeks, the Canadians and Maritimers agreed on seventy-two resolutions that, with few changes, became Canada's founding constitution. Macdonald emerged as the clear leader.

Pierre Trudeau's new Constitution Act* added to it the Charter of Rights and Freedoms. In a fundamental sense, all of Canada's prime ministers have functioned as managers of the estate that Macdonald created, Trudeau alone expanding it significantly.

D'Arcy McGee later credited Macdonald with the authorship of fifty of these seventy-two resolutions. Macdonald himself claimed to a friend, "I ha[d] no help. Not one man of the Conference (except Galt on finance) had the slightest idea of Constitution making." Warming to his theme, he wrote, "I must do it all alone as there is not one person connected with the government who has the slightest idea of the work."† Both were exaggerating, but not by that much. Macdonald was the gathering's orchestra conductor, cheerleader, bookkeeper (of the law, not the finances), entertainer and diplomat. At times, he performed as a clown, cooling tempers by his antics: "Feo" Monck, the governor general's sister, who was visiting from Ireland, recorded in her diary, "He is always drunk now, I am sorry to say, and when someone went to his room the other night, they found him in his night shirt with a railway rug thrown over him, practicing Hamlet."‡

The best description of Macdonald's performance was made later by the Colonial Office's top official, Sir Frederic Rogers. He made these comments about the last of the Confederation confer-

---

* As a consequence of the 1982 Constitution Act, the BNA Act was renamed the Constitution Act, 1867.

† To improve his own knowledge, Macdonald in this letter asked for a copy of a standard work, G.T. Curtis's *History of the Origin, Formation, and Adoption of the Constitution of the United States*.

‡ In the published edition of Feo Monck's journal, Macdonald's name was left a discreet blank, but her original page contains the handwritten note "Macdonald afterwards Premier."

ences, held in London at the end of 1866, which he attended and where Macdonald once again did just about everything except cut the sandwiches for the luncheon breaks. They provide an excellent insight into how he operated throughout the entire Confederation project: "Macdonald was the ruling genius and spokesman, and I was very much struck by his powers of management and adroitness," wrote Rogers. "The French delegates were keenly on the watch for anything that weakened their security; on the contrary, the Nova Scotia and New Brunswick delegates were very jealous of concessions to the *arrière province;* while one main stipulation in favour of the French was open to constitutional objection on the part of the home government. Macdonald had to argue the question with the home government on a point on which the slightest divergence from the narrow line already agreed on in Canada was watched for—here by the English, and there by the French—as eager dogs watch a rat-hole; a snap on one side might have provoked a snap on the other; and put an end to all the concord. He stated and argued the case with cool, ready fluency while at the same time you saw that every word was measured, and that while he was making for a point ahead, he was never for a moment unconscious of the rocks among which he had to steer."

The clear, deep water beyond the shoals towards which Macdonald was steering the delegates at the Quebec Conference was Confederation itself. Just getting the deal on the constitution mattered far more than its specific legal arrangements. As Macdonald wrote to Matthew Crooks Cameron shortly after the conference, on December 19, 1864, "I am satisfied that we have hit upon the only practical plan. I do not mean to say the best plan, but the only practical plan for carrying out the Confederation." About the value of constitutional rewrites in order to solve fundamental political and economic problems,

Macdonald had always been deeply skeptical. A constitution, he told the Quebec City delegates, "should be a mere skeleton and framework that would not bind us down. We have now all the elasticity which has kept England together." He wanted the best possible constitution, and he wanted a strongly centralized one. But just gaining a constitution itself would be the declaration of will that Canada needed to make to become a nation that others would respect as a nation.

Luck helped. Chilly rain fell day after day, leaving the delegates with nothing better to do than get on with the work. As a further inducement to stay indoors, the delegates soon found that while Quebec City was charming and historic, its streets were new and horrible. "Bump-thump-jump you go from one stick to another— out of one deep hole into another till you are well nigh shaken to pieces," was the account of a ride in a horse-drawn calèche by a reporter from Halifax's *Morning Chronicle*. The work itself was done in a plain, three-storey, grey-stone building, originally intended as a post office and used temporarily as a parliament building after the original one had burned down.* The second-storey parliamentary reading room, now crowded with a huge table, had been refashioned into a conference chamber. The incessant rain was hard to take; for some reason the pitch of the roof, combined with three awkward skylights, magnified the noise of the rain to a constant drumming. What made up for this was the conference's location: through the windows of their chamber, the delegates could look down at the St. Lawrence River, at the rafts

---

* Within a year, as the government moved to the new, permanent national capital in Ottawa, Quebec City would lose even its temporary parliament building.

of logs a little upstream, and then the shipyards and docks, and then the river flowing eastwards, past thin strips of farms on either bank, the magnificent Montmorency Falls as a white wisp in the distance, and the water gradually becoming ever more saline as, now out of sight, it widened into the Gulf, there to wash against all four of the Lower Provinces now represented at the conference. The delegates worked exceedingly hard, initially from 11 a.m. to 4 p.m., and soon through two full sessions each day, the first from 10 a.m. to 2 p.m., and the second from 7:30 on, sometimes to midnight. Lunches, usually so leisurely, lasted just fifteen minutes. The Canadians worked harder still, meeting each day at 9 a.m. to discuss tactics and, again, from 4 to 6 p.m. After the close of the conference sessions, Canadian ministers retired to their rooms to catch up on their correspondence and go over their draft resolutions.

Careful planning and several dollops of canniness helped as well. In advance of the arrival of the Maritimers in Quebec City, the Canadians leaked to the *Morning Chronicle* a summary of most of their intended resolutions, thereby minimizing the surprises while leaving themselves free to deny authorship should controversy break out over any of them. They paid for all the hotel expenses (totalling some fifteen thousand dollars) of the delegates, and of their wives and daughters. To keep everyone amiable, there were constant balls and dinners and receptions, principally hosted by the governor general but also by railway lobbyists. Mercy Coles, the daughter of a Prince Edward Island delegate, recorded in her diary that her father returned home from one of these balls "with every stitch of clothing wringing wet with perspiration." Feo Monck wrote of Cartier flirting with her, saying that his favourite occupation was "the *activity* of the heart." (Neither woman paid the least attention to the work of the conference itself.) The Prince Edward Island delegate Edward

Whelan sent regular stories to his newspaper, the *Examiner*, informing readers that "the Cabinet ministers—the leading ones especially—are the most inveterate dancers I've ever seen" and that "the French ladies here give a delightful tone to society. . . . They make no difficulty in falling in love—or appearing to do it—with a dozen gentlemen at a time."

As with Charlottetown, a good deal more is known about who danced with whom at Quebec City than who bargained what with whom. The sessions were closed, and no briefings were held for the press. (Among the journalists were a half-dozen from Britain and the United States.) All that was ever made public were the texts of the seventy-two approved resolutions. Official minutes were kept by Macdonald's deputy minister, Hewitt Bernard, but they were prosaic and terse. Unofficial and abbreviated notes were taken by a Prince Edward Island delegate, A.A. Macdonald, who did record the snippet that Newfoundland delegate Frederick Carter had expressed the hope that Confederation might encourage wealthy fish merchants not to "retir[e] to the Old Country to spend their fortunes."

After a brief formal opening by the premier of the United Province of Canada, Étienne-Paschal Taché, Macdonald took the floor. He delivered a speech that said little that was new— Confederation should not repeat the American mistake of being too decentralized, and all residual or unspecified powers should revert to the federal government, not to the states, as had happened south of the border—but he said it persuasively. When Macdonald finished, those outside the chamber could hear a burst of applause from inside. His speech done, Macdonald moved the first general resolution, to establish a "federal union" with a government based on the British system and with the monarch as its head of state. The actual work now began.

In hindsight it is remarkable how much the delegates accomplished—and also how little they did. Issues that have dominated Canadian politics ever since, such as the division of powers between the two levels of government, were barely discussed at all; Macdonald suggested a list of federal powers, and Oliver Mowat a list of provincial ones, and both were passed quickly with little argument or debate. Matters fundamental to the functioning of any federal system, such as how to amend the constitution, were not debated. A satisfactory explanation has never been constructed for the absence of so vital a piece of constitutional machinery. Speculatively, Macdonald may have worried that an amending system, which merely by existing implied that the constitution might need improving later on, might open the way for critics calling for changes before the constitution was carved into legislative stone, but whose real purpose was delay for its own sake. What is remarkable is that no one in Quebec City commented on the absence of an amending formula, even though one existed in the United States and was known to be working well. The Nova Scotia anti-Confederate Joseph Howe (who was not present at Quebec City) was one of the few in the entire country to raise the issue.

Premier Étienne-Paschal Taché. He served as the titular leader whom both Macdonald and Brown could accept.

What interested the delegates most was the Senate. One full week was spent on a debate (which came close to breaking up the conference) about how many senators* each section (Upper Canada, Lower Canada, the Maritimes) should have. "Everyone here has had a fit of the blues," reported the Toronto *Globe*. At Charlottetown, it had been agreed that every section would have twenty-four senators. The possible addition of Newfoundland meant that the Maritime colonies as a whole would end up with fewer senators than either of the Canadas. Eventually Macdonald concocted a compromise—Newfoundland would get four senators all of its own, if and when it joined. That said, the work resumed.

It was now October 19, and progress had been slow. From this point on, as Prince Edward Island delegate Edward Palmer reported in a newspaper article, "the current seemed to set with the Canadians." Contentious matters remained: Prince Edward Island asked for a special grant of £200,000 to buy up the extensive holdings of absentee landlords (mostly British) but was refused, and its delegates thereafter effectively dropped out of the discussions. Mistakes were made: on New Brunswick's behalf, Leonard Tilley managed to get an extra $63,000, but Charles Tupper forgot to ask for a matching amount for Nova Scotia.

The turn of the tide towards the Canadians meant a turn at the same time towards the strong central government that Macdonald had always called for. Words like "unity" and "nation" gained a magical quality. During a debate about criminal law, Mowat declared, "I quite concur in the advantages of one uniform system. It would weld us into a nation." A quote from a popular pamphlet, *The Northern Kingdom*, written by S.E. Dawson—"Never was there such an opportunity as now for the birth of a nation"—was reprinted in a Quebec City newspaper

---

* The term used then was Legislative Council, but for simplicity's sake, Senate and senators are here used throughout.

and commented on by many delegates. When a New Brunswicker, E.B. Chandler, protested that the provinces would be reduced to "merely large municipal corporations," he was almost shouted down. Macdonald was now so confident of success that he was able to dismiss as invalid another delegate's claim that the provisions of New Zealand's 1842 constitution, which had ended with the provinces there being abolished, could be used in Canada. A Newfoundland delegate, Ambrose Shea, caught the mood of many when he said the scheme would enable British North Americans to escape from the "wretched broils of our colonial life." Out of Quebec City came the first sense of Canada as a national community.

On Wednesday, October 26, the conference held its final full sessions—which extended until midnight. They met again on Friday to tidy up the details. That evening there was a huge ball, attended by one thousand guests. For the first time in history, a band of colonists had drafted a constitution for themselves. The deed was done.

The first reward of this constitutional success was financial. "The immediate effect of the scheme was such on the public mind that our five per cents [government bonds] rose from 75 to 92," Brown reported to Anne.

~

The new draft constitution was in fact an unrelievedly prosaic document, more like a car repair manual than a prescription for building a nation. The London *Times* commented, unkindly but accurately, on its "practical and unpretending a style." Only one resolution contained even a hint of poetry. It called for Canadians to move ahead by means of "the perpetuation of our connection with the mother country and the promotion of the best interests of the people of these provinces [who] desire to follow the model of the

British constitution," with, since this was a Canadian document, the closing qualifier "so far as our circumstances will prevail."

Macdonald understood the significance of what had been achieved. During the brief debate on the division of powers, he intervened to say that if the mix was too decentralized, a "radical weakness" would be introduced into the constitution that would "ruin us in the eyes of the civilized world." To gain respect and acceptance, the new nation had to let the world know, and its own people know, that it was united and capable of being daring. To do that took a strong central government. By contrast, Brown's understanding was much more parochial: "Constitution adopted—a most credible document—a complete reform of all the abuses and injustices we have complained of," he wrote to Anne right after the conference's close. He then added, "Is it not wonderful? French-Canadianism is entirely extinguished." (He meant by this that French Quebecers would no longer be able to intervene in the politics of English Ontarians.)

~

To be fair to the Quebec City delegates, they had to cobble together a federal constitution at the very time when the world's best-known federation had dissolved into a horrendous civil war. The temptation was strong to assume that federations were inherently flawed and that only a "legislative union," or a unitary state like Britain, could work. They were also hemmed in by circumstances. The United States' solution to the challenge of representing the regions at the centre—two senators from each state, no matter their size—was indeed well known in Canada. But Canada was too oddly sized for such a system to work here. The three Maritime provinces together contained only a fifth of the total population; a U.S.-style equal allocation of Senate seats would give

them a majority in that chamber, growing to a two-to-one majority once Newfoundland joined. This said, any solution would have
served better the need for a national balance than the one the delegates settled on—a Senate supposed to represent the regions,
but with all its members appointed by the federal government.

There was, nevertheless, a fair amount of shrewd sense in the
delegates' preference for the pedestrian. Thus, the Canadiens
were conspicuous by their silence about the rights of French
Canadians outside Quebec, in particular entirely ignoring the
interests of New Brunswick's Acadians. Any vocal defence of the
pan-Canadian interests of French Canadians, though, would have
triggered demands for extra protections by English Canadians in
Quebec. The silence was unbrotherly, and even cowardly, but it
preserved for Quebec's Canadiens what they wanted.

To contemporary eyes, the aspect of the Quebec City resolutions most difficult to comprehend is that the delegates took
almost no interest in the respective powers of the federal and
provincial governments. Ever since, there have been long periods
when the only matter of consequence in Canadian politics seems
to be which level of government is responsible for what, and who
should pay for it. While unsatisfying, the explanation for this constitutional amnesia is easy: governments then did so little because
people wanted them to do little. Pre-Confederation, the share of
government revenues expended on what are now the principal
activities of government—education, public charities and social
services—was just 9 per cent of the total.* Neither governments
themselves nor ordinary Canadians expected them to do much
more. Then, some 80 per cent of Canadians were farmers and fishermen, and they looked after themselves and their families.

---

* Today, the equivalent share of government spending on education, health and
social programs would be around 70 per cent.

Also, there was a general assumption that setting down lists of federal and provincial responsibilities would pre-empt all the jurisdictional problems. This attitude was odd, given that delegates were familiar with the contortions that had bedevilled the quasi-federation of the United Province of Canada. But the naïveté about federalism was widespread. Macdonald would later proclaim, "We have avoided all conflict of jurisdiction and authority." The *Globe*, in that tone of plaintive exasperation at the follies of others so distinctive to editorial writers, would ask with unconcealed impatience, "We desire local self-government in order that the separate nationalities of which the population is composed may not quarrel. 'We desire at the same time a strong central authority. Is there anything incompatible in these two things? Cannot we have both? What is the difficulty?"

The delegates were practical men, not visionaries or scholars. Just one of the thirty-three Fathers of Confederation at Quebec City—Nova Scotia's Charles Tupper—had a university education, in his case in medicine from the University of Edinburgh.* By contrast, of the fifty-five at Philadelphia in 1787, more than half were university trained or had studied at the Inns of Court in London. The composition of the Senate interested the delegates for the sake of regional balance, but scarcely less so for their personal career prospects.† Few had bothered to study federal

---

* To confirm the indistinguishable interconnectedness of law and politics, of the thirty-three Fathers, two-thirds, or twenty-one, were lawyers, but, like Macdonald, lawyers who had learned the trade on the job.

† The interest the delegates took in the Senate would have reached fever pitch had they known that serious consideration would be given later to granting to all the Confederation senators "the rank and title of Knight Bachelor." Macdonald scotched this idea by pointing out to the colonial secretary that quite aside from the possibility of an errant senator lowering the tone of knighthood, it "would entail a title on his wife, which might not in all cases be considered desirable."

systems. The proceedings of those American colonists were available at the conference, and Macdonald had brought along his well-annotated copy of James Madison's *Debates in the Federal Convention of 1787*, which included Alexander Hamilton's *Draft of a Constitution for the United States*. But really only Macdonald, Galt, Mowat and, less so, Brown understood the complexities and subtle tradeoffs inherent in any federal system.

Practical men—even pedestrian ones as most of them were—the Quebec City delegates did one thing that was more imaginative than anything attempted at any federal-provincial conference since: most of the delegations were composed of representatives of both the government and the opposition in the home colony, as Christopher Moore pointed out in his excellent book *1867: How the Fathers Made a Deal*. (The one exception was the opposition *rouges*, who refused to take part.) Also, half hidden beneath all the workaday clauses of the resolutions, there was one radical new notion that was little appreciated by most of the drafters: in the new nation, linguistic and cultural differences would be protected.* This promise had never been made before, not even in the constitution of the original Swiss federation, which, if only by historic circumstance, was based on cantons that were all linguistically and ethnically German.

Here resides one of the great mysteries of the achievement of Confederation. It was built on the understanding of a pact between Canada's two founding races. Yet this fundamental

---

* No protection was provided for French Canadians as such or for any ethnic group, Aboriginal people excepted. The protections were all to religion and to language.

building block of the national architecture was, for all practical purposes, never discussed.

.   The extent of this pact is not at all easy to decipher. The actual provisions for bilingualism agreed on at Quebec City were exceedingly limited. There was no ringing proclamation of the equality of the two languages: the Quebec Resolutions merely declared, permissively, that "both the English and French languages may be employed by the general parliament . . . and also in the federal courts." There was no mention of bilingualism in the federal government, or anywhere in Canada outside Quebec.

Just once did Macdonald appear to accept that French should be a national language rather than one limited, outside Quebec, to Parliament and the federal courts. During the Confederation Debates that immediately followed the Quebec Conference, Macdonald said that "the use of the French language should form one of the principles upon which the Confederation should be established." Here, he linked French to Confederation itself rather than only to the new central government. This statement, though, was made only during a debate; he made no similar statement (so far as is known) during any of the conferences at which the new constitution was drafted. And his phrase "the use of" was imprecise. Yet the *bleu* members were satisfied. More striking, because Confederation could never have been implemented without his approval, Cartier was satisfied.

Cartier's confidence wasn't misplaced. Much would be gained by Confederation: the Canadiens would have their own legislature and government. In them, the dominant language would of course be French, in a return to the situation that existed before the Conquest. To reinforce the sense of assurance so gained, there was also the force of rising expectations. The eventual British North America Act would be the sixth constitutional construct by which French Canadians had been ruled—the earlier

five being the Military Government of 1760, the Royal
Proclamation of 1763, the Quebec Act of 1774, the Constitutional
Act of 1791 and the Act of Union of 1841. Whatever the particular constitutional system, French Canadians had found ways to
use it not merely to survive but progressively to enlarge their
self-rule, gaining recognition of their religion, their language and
their right to a full share of the patronage of the national government. If this much had been won already, why not more, later, by
other constitutional changes and rearrangements?

These ambitions were expressed quite openly. *La Minerve*
(Montreal), a strong supporter of Cartier, used the evocative
phrase "maîtres chez nous" to describe what Confederation
would accomplish for the francophones of Quebec. *Le Journal de
Québec* said that French Canadians "can and must one day aspire
to being a nation," adding that premature independence would
lead to annexation by the United States. Other than "nation,"
probably the most common word in the commentaries on the
Confederation project in Quebec newspapers was that of "separation." The most explicit declaration was in *La Minerve*, which
in its issue for Confederation Day, July 1, 1867, advised readers,
"As a distinct and separate nationality, we form a state within a
state. We enjoy the full exercise of our rights, and the formal
recognition of our national independence." The magazine
Contre-poison wrote that Quebec was to be "completely separated
from Upper Canada" and praised the leaders who had "turned
us over into our own hands, who have restored our complete
autonomy." And *La Minerve* observed, "In giving ourselves a
complete government we affirm our existence as a separate
nationality."

Quebecers—as they soon would be called—were saying to
each other, or at least were being told by their newspapers and
political leaders, that Confederation's purpose was not to create

some new Canadian nation but to create a political system in which they could not only continue to be what they always had been but grow into something larger—perhaps, to quote *La Minerve* again, into a "state within a state," or, eventually, into "national independence." And their understanding of Confederation itself was quite different from that of English Canadians. At the same time, English Canadians were being told by leaders such as Macdonald and Brown that Confederation's purpose was to create a "new nation." *Le Canadien*, by contrast, informed its readers that Confederation's purpose was to create "un certain nombre d'États souverains, déléguant une partie définie de leurs droits et leurs pouvoirs à un gouvernement central."

Few if any English Canadians, in Upper Canada or the Maritimes, read any of these commentaries. In the mid-nineteenth century, the two solitudes were wholly disconnected from each other and wholly self-absorbed. But for this mutual ignorance, the bliss of Confederation, such as it is, simply could not have been achieved.

To some extent, the use of terms such as "separation" and "nationality" in *bleu* newspapers was just a tactic to reassure Quebec francophone voters. Some of it was wish-fulfillment. A large part of it, though, was real. It was an expectation about the future that arose directly out of the past and the present.

The concept of Canada as a political pact between the two races derived from the alliance years between Robert Baldwin and Louis-Hippolyte LaFontaine. Macdonald and Cartier had picked it up a decade later, and so it had remained in the public discourse. The Confederation pact itself was now Macdonald and Cartier's pact. Once it was achieved, both of them would still be there to implement it. Many Canadiens must have taken for granted that the pair of them could, and would, make it work. It wasn't a legal compact but rather a pact of trust.

Nothing was ever said about this pact during any of the Confederation conferences, and no evidence exists that Cartier and Macdonald ever discussed the nature of the pact between them. Whether they even sketched out a deal is unknowable. Most of Cartier's personal papers were destroyed after his early death in 1873, almost certainly deliberately to protect him (and Macdonald) from any further disclosures about Canadian Pacific Railway funds being used in Conservative election campaigns. Macdonald and Cartier were so close, though, that they would hardly have needed to commit to paper any agreement between them about Confederation's future.

Macdonald, nevertheless, is on the public record as committing himself to a pact with both Cartier and *les Canadiens*. In reference not to Confederation but to its predecessor, the United Province of Canada, he said in a speech he gave in Toronto, which was quoted in the Toronto *Leader* on April 30, 1861, that union had been "a distinct bargain, a solemn contract." During the Confederation Debates of 1865, Macdonald again used the term "Treaty of Union" to refer to the practices followed in the legislature of the United Province, and he intriguingly admitted that, although a single unit according to its constitution, it had been, "as a matter of fact . . . a Federal Union"—or little different in its reality from what the proposed Confederation would be.

Legally, no such treaty or contract between the French and English ever existed. But in Macdonald's mind, and equally in Cartier's, a "distinct bargain, a solemn contract" existed between them, and so between the English and the French. Confederation didn't create this bargain between the two founding peoples, as has often been claimed. Instead, it arose out of a pact of trust that predated Confederation and had, by the time of Confederation, been made into part of Canada's DNA by Macdonald and Cartier.

Between Cartier and Macdonald there was one dramatic Confederation-era public exchange that revealed how they understood their respective roles. In March 1864, on the eve of the formation of the Great Coalition government, Macdonald, then not yet committed to Confederation, spoke briefly on Brown's motion to set up a legislature committee to consider all federal options. "The sad experience on the other side [the United States]," Macdonald said, "proved that it must not be merely a federal one; that instead of having a federal one, we should have a Legislative Union, in fact, in principle, and in practice." Sitting beside him, Cartier interjected grimly, "That is not my policy," meaning he would never accept a unitary state in which his Canadiens would have no government of their own to protect them. Just a few days later, Macdonald showed that he understood Cartier's objection, and that he accepted it, by coming out in support of a pan-Canadian federal union. The mutual trust between these two men was the unwritten pact that made Confederation possible.

At Quebec City, there was one revealing public discussion of this existential issue between French and English, though it involved neither Macdonald nor Cartier. It occurred right at the start of the conference, and it's very likely that only Macdonald among the English-speaking delegates understood the significance of what was being said. Sir Étienne-Paschal Taché made a brief opening statement in his role as nominal premier of Canada. After pleasantries, he informed the delegates that Confederation would be "tantamount to a separation of the provinces, and Lower Canada would thereby preserve its autonomy together with all the institutions it held so dear." Not one member of the "other" solitude rose to challenge or inquire about what the words "separation" and "autonomy" meant; by their silence, English Canadians sealed the pact.

Here is the place for a footnote too important to be tucked away at the bottom of the page. Taché, avuncular in his appearance and genial in his manner, was highly regarded by his English counterparts as one of the gatekeepers between themselves and the near-invisible Canadiens. But Taché was also a passionate patriot. He showed this side of himself in a remarkable 1858 letter to a fellow Canadien politician. "The important thing to remember is that the unity we have just consolidated in Lower Canada ensures that *we are the de facto rulers of the entire province* [of Canada]," he wrote. "It may come that, in their impotent rage, we will soon be hearing weeping and gnashing of teeth from the Upper Canadians. . . . All the blustering of our enemies will vanish into thin air, while we go forward, *govern*, progress. . . . And we will do more: we will safeguard our institutions and preserve them from impure contact." Fortunately for Macdonald, and for Canada, neither Brown nor the *Globe* ever learned about this other side of their gatekeeper.* Equally fortunately for Canada, no Canadien leader learned of Brown's triumphant declaration to Anne that Confederation's great accomplishment was that French Canadianism had been extinguished.

~

Macdonald achieved all he really wanted just in getting the Confederation deal itself at Quebec City. Prince Edward Island pulled out from the pact later, as did Newfoundland, neither of these island colonies having any interest in the Intercolonial Railway or any fear of Americans attempting to invade by running the gauntlet of the Royal Navy. The approval of the Nova

---

* This revealing letter is reproduced in full in Alastair Sweeny's *George-Étienne Cartier: A Biography*.

Scotia and New Brunswick delegates, though, meant that Macdonald had in his hand one-half of a continental-sized nation that would stretch to the Atlantic; the addition of the second half, stretching all the way to the Pacific, was specifically provided for in the Quebec Resolutions.

⁓

Macdonald didn't get what he had said on several occasions he personally would prefer to a confederation or federation—a "legislative union." Such an arrangement was highly attractive to Britain, itself a "legislative union," or unitary state, and one that had forged a "Union" with Scotland and had rejected repeatedly, and violently, any attempts at Home Rule, or self-government, in Ireland. Midway through the conference, Macdonald wrote to the businessman-politician Isaac Buchanan, "My great aim is to strengthen the general Legislature and Govt. as much as possible, and approach as nearly to a Legislative Union as is practicable." Shortly after the conference ended, he wrote to a supporter, Malcolm Cameron, "If the Confederation goes on, you, if spared the ordinary age of man, will see both local Parliaments and Governments absorbed in the General Power." Macdonald added, as hardly needed to be said, "But of course, it doesn't do to adopt that point of view in discussing the subject in Lower Canada."

While Macdonald kept on saying this kind of thing, he may not have meant it. He may have been playing another set of his "long game." He once even showed his hand in public. In the Confederation Debates in the Canadian legislature that followed the Quebec Conference, Macdonald engaged in an intriguing exchange with the High Tory M.C. Cameron, who challenged Macdonald that he would have "better shown [his] patriotism by waiting a little longer to accomplish it." Macdonald interjected,

"Accomplish what?" Cameron answered, "A legislative union of all the provinces." Macdonald then gave his colleague a lesson in *realpolitik*. "I thought my hon. friend knew that every man in Lower Canada was against it, every man in New Brunswick, every man in Nova Scotia,* every man in Newfoundland and every man in Prince Edward Island. How, then, is it to be accomplished?" The "long game" that Macdonald thus was playing was to position himself at a constitutional extreme from which he could gracefully retreat, while using his concessions to gain in exchange yet more bits and pieces of a highly centralized federal system.

That in fact is exactly what happened. Before the Confederation project was completed, Macdonald won a succession of important additions to the central power. Immigration and agriculture became joint jurisdictions rather than exclusively provincial concerns, and Ottawa gained the right to appoint the provincial lieutenant-governors, officials considered so powerful at the time that Macdonald described them as "chief executive officers." Moreover, during the negotiations at the Quebec Conference, even though many delegates favoured a legislative union rather than a confederation—Brown† and Galt among the Canadians, and, among the Maritimers, Tupper and some senior men—Macdonald made no attempt to win approval for a legislative union. By not attempting seriously the impossibility of a legislative union, he got the possible—namely, as he expressed it

---

* Macdonald was exaggerating for effect. Tupper, Nova Scotia's premier, denounced the "absurdity" of provinces claiming any sovereignty and said that Confederation would instead make Nova Scotia "a large municipality under the Central Government; but just as clearly a municipality as the City of Halifax now is under our Provincial Government."

† Brown so doubted the usefulness of provincial governments that he said they "should not take up political matters."

and believed he had achieved, that "the Central Government assumes towards the local governments precisely the same position as the Imperial Government holds with respect to each of the provinces."

The constitution that emerged from Quebec City, and that went on to become the BNA Act, was almost certainly the most centralized constitution for a federation or confederation that's ever been assembled. Macdonald secured all the four centralizing measures Alexander Hamilton had attempted to insert into the U.S. Constitution at Philadelphia in 1787—appointment of senators for life; federal appointment of state governors; the federal right to disallow state laws; and the granting of residual powers to the federal government. He also secured one centralizing authority, over "banking, incorporation of banks, and the issue of paper money," that Hamilton never even thought of.

Macdonald's "long game" had another objective, one far more critical to his purpose than creating a strong central government for the sake of governmental efficiency. Confederation's prime purpose was to impress Britain and the United States by a statement of national will; gathering together the British North America colonies was merely a means to that end. A central government that possessed, as he put it, "all the powers which are incident to sovereignty" would impress as the government of a nation rather than of some upgraded province or colony. To impress further, it would avoid what Macdonald saw as the "fatal error" that had almost sundered the United States—that of "making each state a distinct sovereignty, and giving to each a distinct sovereign power." In the nation-state he was creating, therefore, sovereignty would reside, as in all real nation-states, at its centre.

As it turned out, Macdonald would lose this part of his "long game"—in later sets. Quirky decisions by the Judicial Committee of the Privy Council in London during the latter part of Macdonald's post-Confederation term were an early cause. The underlying reason was that Canadians themselves wanted a decentralized confederation rather than Macdonald's centralized one. Another reason was the most obvious one of all: immense distances kept the people of British North America apart from each other and turned them to their own local governments and away from the remote national one. Above all, Canadiens, soon to become Québécois, located their true national government not in Ottawa but in Quebec City. As to the future of federal-provincial relations, rather than Macdonald's benign confidence about federal dominance, the shrewdest guess was the one made by that unnervingly perceptive critic Christopher Dunkin: the "cry" of the provinces, he predicted in 1865, "will be found to be pretty often and pretty successfully—'Give, give, give.'"

A closing note about the Quebec Conference. The most famous painting in Canadian historiography is Robert Harris's *The Fathers of Confederation*. Macdonald dominates the picture— because he's in the centre, he's standing rather than sitting, he's tall (at five foot eleven he was above the average height for the time), he's wearing a dashing white waistcoat inside his black frock coat, and, in contrast to the ponderous gravitas of most of the others, his posture is alert, watchful, purposeful. Harris painted it in 1884. By that time the building in which the event had taken place had burned down, and Harris improved the vista by painting in delicate arched windows in place of the square wooden casements of the original.

This painting was lost in the 1916 fire that destroyed the Parliament Buildings in Ottawa. Harris, by then seventy, refused a second commission but did touch up his original cartoon, or charcoal sketch. In 1964 the insurance company Confederation Life commissioned Toronto artist Rex Woods to recreate Harris's 1884 version and presented it to Parliament as a Centennial gift. It now hangs in the Railway Committee Room of the Parliament Buildings.*

———

Macdonald's mood after the comprehensive success at Quebec City was confident to the point of being cocky. Within a fortnight of the conference's end, he was treating Confederation as if it were already an accomplished fact and was looking beyond to the administrative details of a post-Confederation government. On November 14, 1864, he wrote to Premier Tilley of New Brunswick, "Have you thought over the formation of the Govt— the Federal Govt I mean?—i.e. as to the number and composition of the Executive, the number and nature of the Departments & the general system of administration?" He made the same request to Nova Scotia's Tupper the same day, adding, "I intend to commence next week to draft the Bill to be submitted for the consideration of the Imperial Govt."

His personal correspondence communicated the same assurance. A day after his letters to Tilley and Tupper, in a letter to Judge James Robert Gowan, Macdonald claimed the entire constitution as "mine." In another letter at this time, he declared, "We

---

* A nine-foot-long oak-and-basswood table in the Saskatchewan Legislative Library at Regina may be the same one around which the Quebec City delegates bargained for the resolutions. It was used in the Privy Council at Ottawa from 1865 to some date in the 1883–92 period, when it was brought to Regina. It probably came to Ottawa from Quebec City, and so may have been used at the Confederation conference, but no certain connection has been established.

do not pretend that it is at all perfect, or even symmetrical, but it was the result of a series of compromises which were necessary to secure the support of all classes."

To heighten his high spirits, events kept breaking his way. Midway through the Quebec Conference, the delegates heard worrisome news that two dozen Southern Confederates hiding in Canada had staged a cross-border raid on the northern Vermont town of St. Albans, taking two hundred thousand dollars from three banks, killing one person and wounding another before fleeing back to Canada. The general commanding the American forces in the region gave his troops an order that if other Confederates made a similar sortie, they were to give hot pursuit right into Canada. President Lincoln refused to confirm the order, which would have breached Canada's neutrality, and waited to see how Canada would respond.

By bad luck, that response could not have been more thoroughly bungled. Most of the Confederates were arrested as soon as they arrived back in Canada from St. Albans. On December 13, their preliminary trial came up before Montreal magistrate Charles-Joseph Coursol. The defence lawyer made a convoluted argument for the prisoners' temporary release; a confused Coursol assented, and the Confederate raiders instantly vanished. American newspapers, and many American politicians, were certain it was an anti-North plot. Four days later Washington gave notice that all Canadians would have to have passports to enter the United States. Privately, Macdonald expressed his fury at "the unhappy and mistaken decision of Coursol." To an inquiring businessman, Macdonald's response was nuanced adroitly. On the one hand, Macdonald wrote, there was no reason why "individuals or incorporated companies like Railways should not join in their exertions with Americans from the Western Frontier to procure its [the passport order's] withdrawal." On the other, "it would be extremely impolitic, and, indeed, defeat our object, if the Canadian Government went on its knees to the United States government." Macdonald then gave the businessman a lesson in governance: an intervention by the Canadian government itself, he wrote, "would give Mr. Seward [the secretary of state] an exaggerated idea of the inconvenience and loss suffered by Canada and it [the order] would be kept up as a means of punishment or for purposes of coercion."

In fact, the released raiders were quickly rearrested and retried by a different judge, who subsequently ruled (very likely after being prompted by Macdonald) that they should be extradited to the United States.[*] To forestall future raids, Macdonald called up two thousand volunteers to stand guard along the border. As a further precaution, he organized a detective force, headed by Gilbert McMicken, "a shrewd, cool and determined man who won't easily lose his head," to provide intelligence on what was happening across the border. The flap died down, although, as always, not without calls by American newspapers, especially the New York *Herald*, for Canada's annexation, if necessary by force. Of lasting consequence, though, was the decision by Congress not to renew the Reciprocity Treaty when it reached its due date in 1866, in reaction to what was seen to be Canadian favouritism towards the South. The combination of this cross-border free-trade pact, together with the immense demand generated by American military mobilization, had led to the growth of Canada's economy at a faster rate than ever before in the nineteenth century.[†]

---

[*] To further mollify the Americans, the Canadian government compensated the St. Albans banks for their losses with thirty thousand dollars in banknotes and forty thousand in gold.

[†] In June 1864, the value of the Canadian dollar reached $2.78, a peak never even approached since.

The immediate consequences of this mini-crisis, though, were all positive. Even the passport rule was soon withdrawn. As always, an external threat drew people together. Further, the St. Albans affair reminded Canadians of the threat about to be posed by the imminent victory of the North over the South. About the war itself, Macdonald now insisted on the strictest neutrality, urging it on a colleague with just a hint of regret: "We can't help the South[,] and a naked expression of sympathy would do it no good and greatly injure us." Nevertheless, the fact remained that once the American Civil War ended, the vast Federal armies might be demobilized—or, perhaps, mobilized to march northwards.

To this threat, actual or perceived, two responses were possible: Confederation, which would signal Canada's will to survive; as well, a helping hand from Britain. Macdonald now set out to secure both.

NINETEEN

Parliament vs the People

⌐

If we do not represent the people of Canada,
we have no right to be here.
John A. Macdonald

The sweeping success of the Quebec Conference was
followed by the double afterglow of a triumphal
tour of Canada by the Maritime delegates and the
plaudits for the accomplishment expressed by
British newspapers from the *Times* on down. Macdonald's
response to all this praise was to go on a prolonged binge. He performed like a tightly wound spring that, once released, flies all
over the place and then collapses in a heap.

The post-conference tour, which had the dual purpose of
showing Canada to the Maritimers and showing off the
Maritimers to Canadians, began in Montreal with a gala dinner
hosted by Cartier. To encourage the delegates to complete their
good work, the program of toasts included the verse "Then let us
be firm and united / One country, one flag for us all; / United,
our strength will be freedom / Divided, we each of us fall." The
cavalcade then moved to Ottawa, where Macdonald was to act as
host. It began well: the crowds were huge and they escorted the

visitors in a torchlight procession to the Russell Hotel, where they were to dine. As the gala's principal speaker, Macdonald got to his feet, said a few words, then stopped and fell silent.* Galt had to fill up the vacuum with an extemporaneous speech. Macdonald rejoined the group when it left by train for Kingston, with succeeding stops planned at all the communities— Belleville, Cobourg, Port Hope—on the way to Toronto, where Brown would be host. But Macdonald never left Kingston. It's safe to guess that he spent most of his time at Eliza Grimason's tavern, periodically collapsing into the bed kept for him there.

As all who knew him realized well, Macdonald, from this period on, would every now and then go on one of these binges and be unable to do anything until they were over. Then suddenly he would reappear as though nothing had happened, as full of vigour and zest as ever. His constitution was a minor marvel. Macdonald did enjoy walking, but he never undertook any strenuous exercise. He ate lightly, not because he drank heavily as is frequently the case, but because he always ate lightly. A photograph of Macdonald taken at around this time—in 1863 by the famed William Notman of Montreal, and the front cover of this book—portrays him as lean and fit and impressively erect.† The photo also captures perfectly the distinctive quality of his eyes— amused, observant, commanding. It may have been Notman's magic (all the more magical because he used only natural light),

---

* In his report on the Charlottetown and Quebec conferences, published in 1865 under the title *The Union of the British Provinces*, the pro-Confederation Prince Edward Island delegate Edward Whelan dealt delicately with Macdonald's performance: "Illness induced by fatigue from assiduous devotion to public affairs, compelled him to curtail his observations."

† It's possible there was a concealed brace behind Macdonald, as was often used to enable a client to last out the minute and a half or more of motionlessness required for the exposure.

but absolutely nothing about the photo suggests a public figure with a single care in the world, least of all that of his having become, if irregularly, an out-of-control public drunk.

After Macdonald had finished wrestling with whatever devils were assailing him, he went right back to the job at hand. With the Quebec Conference over and a constitution agreed on, the way ahead was clear. Macdonald needed now to get approval for the Confederation scheme first from Canada's legislature, and then from the legislatures of the key Maritime provinces, Nova Scotia and New Brunswick. As the climactic step, he needed the approval of the Parliament at Westminster. Thereafter, he could come back home with Confederation's constitution in his pocket.

One intervening step was required, though. The British press had indeed been laudatory, but it had also expressed some disquieting notes. The *Edinburgh Review*, while applauding the accomplishment, had gone on to describe it as the "harbinger of the future and complete independence of British North America," while the *Saturday Review* judged the achievement as "not so much a step towards independence as a means of softening the inevitable shock." The *Times*, in its more orotund way, declared that while "nothing could be more in correspondence with the interests and wishes of this country" than Confederation, nevertheless "the dependency that wishes to quit us has only to make up its mind to that effect." What Macdonald needed, then, was an official stamp of approval to Confederation from the Imperial government that could be waved in front of the Canadian and Maritime legislatures, and, as an additional reassurance, a cessation of talk in London about possible Canadian independence.

For this vital but delicate mission, Macdonald chose Brown. It was a deft choice. Brown's key qualifications were that he wasn't Macdonald and that he was the leader of Canada's largest party. He would carry in his person to London the message that support for Confederation was widespread. He would also allow Macdonald to get on with his immediate task of assembling the legislature and of figuring out how to secure as quickly as possible its agreement to the scheme.

For Brown, this transatlantic trip had to be one of the most agreeable he ever made, not least because Anne went along with him. They travelled first to Edinburgh, and then Brown went on alone to London.

On December 3, 1864, Brown called on the colonial secretary, Edward Cardwell, who received him almost as a brother. Cardwell had already drafted a memorandum setting out his views on the Quebec Resolutions; this, if Brown approved of it, he intended to dispatch to the governor general in Ottawa and to the Maritime lieutenant-governors. Brown not only approved but was ecstatic. "A most gracious answer to our constitutional scheme. Nothing could be more laudatory—it praises our statesmanlike discretion, loyalty and so on," he wrote afterwards to Macdonald.

Cardwell had one more bit of news of even greater import to pass on. Confederation, he told Brown, was a subject "of great interest . . . in the highest circles." Brown immediately picked up the reference that Queen Victoria herself wanted Confederation for her distant colonies. He was so overcome by this confidence that he asked whether the Queen might come to Canada to open the first post-Confederation Parliament. Cardwell's reply, no doubt couched in the correct circumlocutory phrases, was that Victoria, a grieving widow ever since the recent death of her beloved Prince Albert, was so emotionally shattered that it was "totally out of the question" for her even to open Parliament in next-door Westminster.

Nothing else was denied Brown, and so by extension Canada's Confederates. He went to Prime Minister Lord Palmerston's country house in Hampshire and took a long stroll with the prime minister through the gardens. He met the foreign secretary and the rising political titan and fellow-Liberal William Gladstone. A bit carried away, Brown afterwards told Anne of his encounter with Gladstone: "Though we had been discussing the highest questions of statesmanship—he did not by any means drag me out of my depth." Then hastily he added, "Don't for any sake read this to Tom or Willie, or they will think I have gone daft."

Brown did have one concern to report to Macdonald: "There is a manifest desire in almost every quarter that ere long the British colonies should shift for themselves, and in some quarters evident regret that we did not declare at once for independence." The cause, Brown said, was "the fear of invasion of Canada by the United States," an affront that might compel Britain, for the sake of honour and of face, to make the futile gesture of intervening to try to save its colony. In fact Brown and Macdonald would have been even more concerned had they known of a letter sent at this time to Governor General Monck by the junior minister for the colonies, C.B. Adderley. In it, he reported, "Gladstone said to me the other day: 'Canada is England's weakness, till the last British soldier is brought away & Canada left on her own. We cannot hold our own with the United States.'"

Britain was onside all right, but in its own way.

~

Brown landed back in Canada on January 13, 1865. Two days earlier, Macdonald had passed a significant milestone—he'd reached the age of fifty. He either paid no attention to his birthday or marked it by consuming a bottle in his room in some boarding house. But for cronies, Macdonald was now alone. Hugh John, at the age of fifteen, was distant from his father, both because he had been brought up by Margaret and James Williamson in Kingston and because he was now beginning to feel the strain of being the son of a famous father. That fall, Hugh John entered the University of Toronto as an undergraduate.*

Macdonald in his prime. This photo was taken by the famous William Notman of Montreal in 1863. The two minutes of motionlessness required for a photograph at the time did nothing to dim his energy and vivacity.

At this same time Macdonald was becoming increasingly concerned about the condition of his law practice. His law partner Archibald Macdonnell had died the previous spring, and ever since Macdonald had been discovering just how deeply his company was in debt, with some of the debts resulting from transactions of highly questionable probity, but for which he would be personally responsible. Brown, in one letter to Anne at this time, confided that "John A.'s business affairs are in sad disorder, and need more close attention."†

Macdonald's two escapes from solitude now were the Confederation project and drink.

---

* That Hugh John should have gone to university at the age of fifteen was not in the least unusual. Some undergraduates then were a year younger. No high schools existed until the 1870s, and bright students were prepared for university entrance exams in special schools. See A.B. McKillop, *Matters of Mind: The University in Ontario, 1791–1951*.

† As must have galled Macdonald, Brown at this time made himself wealthy for life by selling his farm and lands in southwestern Ontario for a handsome $275,000.

The Legislative Assembly met unusually early that year—on January 17, following Macdonald's request to Governor General Monck. The members would need the extra time to debate and, all going well, approve the seventy-two Quebec Resolutions. Thereafter would come the debates in the New Brunswick and Nova Scotia legislatures about the same draft resolutions to establish Confederation.

As if in anticipation of his impending triumph, Macdonald was advised of a tribute soon to be extended to him—he was to be given an honorary degree by Oxford University, the first Canadian to be so recognized.* It is probable, although not certain, that Monck also gave Macdonald early notice that, when it came time to form a government for the new nation (in about a year, it was generally expected), he would invite him to be its first prime minister. At Quebec City, Macdonald had raised himself to the status of the irreplaceable man; he was about to become *the* man.

About winning approval of the draft constitution from Canada's Legislative Assembly, Macdonald had no qualms. "Canada on the whole seems to take up the scheme warmly," he wrote to Tilley. About opinion in his own Upper Canada, he was absolutely right: the only naysayers were a few Tory Conservatives worried that Confederation might weaken the country's ties to Britain. In Lower Canada the prospects were more mixed, yet still predominantly

---

*Macdonald had received his first honorary degree in 1863 from Queen's University; it was also the first honorary degree awarded by Queen's, which he had helped to found.

positive. *Rouge* leader Antoine-Aimé Dorion had already published an anti-Confederation manifesto charging that the Quebec Resolutions would produce not a "true confederation" of sovereign provinces but a disguised legislative union in which the provinces would be mere municipalities and so unable to protect their electorates. As an example of the way Confederation lurched along, one step forward, one back, Galt at this same time was reassuring audiences of his fellow Lower Canada English-speakers that, precisely because the provinces would be merely "municipalities of larger growth," controlled by a strong central government, there was no need for them to worry about being reduced to a minority in a French-dominated province. Fortunately, none of Cartier's *bleu* members had blinked at any of these concerns, and this was all that really mattered in Lower Canada—soon to become Quebec.

And then some of them did blink. The cause wasn't a real problem but an apparent one—in politics, no different from a real problem. The Throne Speech read by Monck at the opening of the legislature included a call for Canadians to "create a new nationality." This ambition was logical enough: everywhere, the reason for creating new nations, as in Italy, which had come into existence just four years earlier, was either to create a new nationality or to liberate an old one from oppression. McGee had been calling for years for a "new nationality." During the Quebec Conference, Prince Edward Island delegate Edward Whelan had got so caught up in the national vision that he dismissed his own province as "a patch of sandbank in the Gulf." Even the cautious Oliver Mowat got into the nationalist spirit, although his exuberance may have been for show because, right after the conference, he announced he was leaving politics to become a judge in the chancery court. (Macdonald filled the vacant Reform cabinet slot by appointing the little-known W.P. Howland.)

The problem was that all this talk about a Canadian nation and a Canadian nationality threatened the national distinctiveness of Canadiens. Adroitly, Dorion moved a resolution calling on members to disavow plans for a new nationality. It was defeated, predictably, but it gained the support of twenty-five French-Canadian members. If Dorion could find another hot button, he might yet be able to whip up an anti-Confederate storm in Quebec.

On February 3, Macdonald moved that the House adopt the Quebec Resolutions. He made a brief explanatory statement, following up three days later with a two-hour speech. Subsequently, all the leading pro-Confederates—Brown, Cartier, Galt and McGee—had their say, as well as some of the far smaller number of anti-Confederates, notably *rouge* leader Dorion and Independent Conservative Christopher Dunkin. All these words, filling 1,032 double-columned pages, became known as the Confederation Debates.

It was in his short statement that Macdonald made his key new contribution to the Confederation project. He had already anticipated the now well-known difficulty of implementing a new constitution or of making major changes to an existing one: that all those unhappy for any reason particular to themselves can vote No, and that all the Noes may add up to a deal-breaking majority, even though the reasons for many of them contradict each other. In Canada—inevitably—there was a further problem. Any division in an overall vote on a constitution can cause frictions to national harmony; a division caused by confrontations between races or religions, though, can shatter national unity. Two values were thus put into conflict—democracy and national unity. Macdonald's choice, naturally, was for national unity over democracy.

In his statement of February 3, Macdonald set out first to reduce to a minimum the extent of the legislature's debate on the constitution. Rather than a discussion and a vote on each of the seventy-two clauses, there should be only a single vote, for or against the entire document.* The entire Confederation package "was in the nature of a treaty," he said;† each of its clauses had already been fully discussed and either agreed to or amended after compromises. "If the scheme was not now adopted in all its principal details as presented to the House," he informed the members, "we could not expect it to be passed this century."

That mission accomplished, Macdonald moved on to his main argument: approval by the legislature's members was all that was needed for the constitution to be passed. "If this measure received the support of the House," he said, "there would be no necessity of going back to the people." There was no need, that is, for the people to say what they felt, either in an election or in a plebiscite.

That Macdonald wanted to avoid delay and division was the immediate, practical motive for his stance. But it was by no means the only one. He believed also, entirely genuinely, that the

---

* Before his speech, Macdonald had already rejected a suggestion by Brown that he should move a series of resolutions on the scheme.

† This purely tactical use by Macdonald of the term "treaty" was later seized on by advocates of the "Compact Theory" of Confederation. They held that it was a compact or treaty negotiated between the provinces, with the federal government set up by them to perform certain functions. But the provinces, as colonies, had no power to negotiate anything. Further, Ontario and Quebec didn't exist before Confederation and had no one to negotiate on their behalf. A supposed compact or treaty that no one signed, and whose two largest participants (representing four-fifths of the population) didn't exist, is difficult to take seriously.

decision was the exclusive responsibility of the members of Parliament whom the people had elected to represent them, rather than that of the public at large. Canada's constitution was to be for the people, but not of the people.

On the same day that he spoke, Macdonald sent a letter to a supporter, John Beattie, setting out the philosophical justification for his policy. The constitutional package, he pointed out, had received "general if not universal favour." The government had the right, therefore, "to assume, as well as the Legislature, that the scheme, in principle meets with the approbation of the Country, and as it would be obviously absurd to submit the complicated details of such a measure to the people, it is not proposed to seek their sanction."

Today, after the Meech Lake and the Charlottetown accords, no politician would advance such an argument, except one wishing to commit instant political suicide. Oddly, though, the constitutional change cherished most highly by the majority of Canadians, that of the Charter of Rights and Freedoms, was never submitted for approval in a referendum.

In the mid-nineteenth century, however, nothing that Macdonald said was in any way novel or shocking. Then, representative democracy was the norm. He was taking his stand on the side Edmund Burke had taken in his famous declaration to the electors of Bristol: "Your representative owes you, not his industry only, but his judgment; and he betrays, instead of serving you, if he sacrifices it to your opinion." It was the duty of elected members to make the decisions they judged the best; it was the duty of voters to elect those they judged best able to make those decisions.

Today, most of that is an archaism. On almost all occasions

now, MPs make the decisions that their party has already decided they should make. Voters today insist on contributing themselves—the system is known as direct democracy—to the making and the implementing of decisions. It could be said that the era of the divine right of kings was followed, comparatively briefly, by an era of the divine right of Parliament, and this is now giving way to an era of the divine right of the people.

The mid-nineteenth century, though, was still the era of parliamentary supremacy. The Canadian version of it might have been small and parochial, yet it was a branch of the majestic Mother of Parliaments in London stretching back, often gloriously, at times bloodily, over the centuries. And the Canadian version had won for its people the great victory of Responsible Government. Its debates were widely followed, and reported nearly in full, in the newspapers. Its leading men—Macdonald, Cartier, Brown and McGee—were national celebrities, the only ones there were then. The widespread distaste for "partyism," or for disciplined, organized parties, reflected the presumption that individual members would—certainly should—speak out for and vote for their personal beliefs, even their conscience, rather than just the partisan interests of their party. The doctrine of parliamentary supremacy was as much a part of all people's upbringing as were the doctrines of their particular Christian faith. When Macdonald said, "Parliament is a grand inquest with the right to inquire into anything and everything," everyone, except perhaps the dwindling number of populist Grits, would have agreed.

The alternative doctrine of democracy not only had few supporters but was widely suspect. A prime reason was that democracy was an American idea. To Canadians, what was happening south of the border was not democracy but mob rule. Canadians, by contrast, assumed that they themselves enjoyed real liberty because their ultimate ruler was a constitutional monarch rather than an elected president who might become a dictator. That their head of state was essentially powerless was the reason, so hard for Americans to comprehend, why anti-democratic Canadians were genuinely convinced that they enjoyed more real freedom and liberty than their neighbours. Nor were critics of democracy without good arguments: in France it had led to the Terror, then to the dictatorship of Napoleon; in the United States, to the Revolution, then to the Civil War. And Macdonald's arguments were persuasive. The Confederation project had got this far only because of "a very happy concurrence of circumstances which might not easily come again." He appealed to members to "sacrifice their individual opinions as to particular details, if satisfied with the government that the scheme as a whole was for the benefit and prosperity of the people of Canada."

As thought Macdonald, so did almost everyone else. If, in Macdonald's judgment, Americans were subject to "the tyranny of mere numbers," to the Toronto *Leader* U.S. presidents were "the slave of the rabble," to the *Globe* democracy was "one of those dreadful American heresies," and to Brown American elections were a sham, because "the balance of power is held by the ignorant unreasoning mass." McGee, during his speech in the Confederation Debates, said, "The proposed Confederation will enable us to bear up shoulder to shoulder, to resist the spread of this universal democracy doctrine." In Lower Canada politicians thought the same way; so, still more vociferously, did the Catholic hierarchy. In Canada there were conspicuously no great debates about democracy as there had been in Britain during each of its Reform Laws.*

---

* Although democracy, as a grand theory, had few supporters in Canada, the country's political system was quite respectably democratic in practice. While the franchise was limited to property-owning males, as in Britain, there were many more of them here than there, and the vote was extended to Roman Catholics and Jews much earlier here. Walter Bagehot, the great British political

There nevertheless was a debate in Canada's Legislative Assembly about whether a constitution should be sanctioned by the people or only by those few who happened to be members of the legislature. A Reform backbencher, James O'Halloran, addressed the issue directly. "When we assume the power to deal with this question, to change the whole system of government, to effect a revolution peaceful though it may be, without reference to the will of the people of this country," he said, "we arrogate to ourselves a right never conferred upon us, and our act is a usurpation." He went on, describing the people as "the only rightful source of political power." Another backbencher, Benjamin Seymour, supported O'Halloran,* as did a few newspapers, such as the Hamilton *Times*, which declared forthrightly, "If their [the people's] direct decision on the confederation question is unnecessary . . . we can imagine none in the future of sufficient importance to justify an appeal to them. The polling booths thereafter may as well be turned into pig-pens, and the voters lists cut into pipe-lighters."

A second debate on the issue of democracy occurred after the Confederation Debates had ended, when a Conservative member, John Hillyard Cameron, moved a motion calling for an election to be held before the constitution was enacted. The motion was defeated easily. The brief debate that followed, though, inspired Macdonald

---

analyst, wrote in *The English Constitution* (published in 1867) that while "the masses in England are not fit for elective government," because too little educated, "the idea is roughly realized in the North American colonies."

* O'Halloran's speech is quoted in that excellent source book *Canada's Founding Debates*, edited by Janet Ajzenstat. One chapter, "Direct Democracy: Pro and Con," contains an extended analysis of both sides of the argument. O'Halloran himself suffered one serious handicap as an advocate of democracy: he had been educated at the University of Vermont and had served in the U.S. Army, all of which put him under severe suspicion.

to muster his most extended and considered arguments to justify parliamentary supremacy over the will of the people.

The only way to determine the people's will on a single issue would be to hold a referendum, declared Macdonald. In a letter to a supporter, Saumel Amsden, he argued that a referendum would be "unconstitutional and anti-British"; anyway, "submission of the complicated details to the Country is an obvious absurdity." In the Parliament, he based his argument on the nature of Parliament itself. "We in this house" he told the members, "are representatives of the people, not mere delegates, and to pass such a law would be robbing ourselves of the character of representatives." The idea itself was dangerous, because "a despot, an absolute monarch" could use referendums to win public approval "for the laws necessary to support a continuation of his usurpation." The strength of Macdonald's feelings came through in his unaccustomed eloquence: "If the members of this house do not represent the country—all its interest, classes and communities—it never has been represented. If we represent the people of Canada . . . then we are here to pass laws for the peace, welfare and good government of the country. . . . If we do not represent the people of Canada, we have no right to be here."* Macdonald genuinely believed what he was saying; as a desirable bonus, his argument ensured that the Quebec Resolutions would be approved as quickly as possible.†

---

* Macdonald used the phrase "peace, welfare and good government" rather than the now familiar "peace, order and good government." See Chapter 22 for a fuller explanation of this iconic phrase.

† Macdonald—predictably—could switch his arguments against democracy to suit his political convenience. In one letter he denounced constituency nominating conventions as "immoral and democratic," but then went on to advise his preferred candidate that "if a respectable and influential body of delegates is likely to be called together, you must exert every energy to have your friends chosen."

One other factor may have influenced Macdonald's arguments against democracy: he knew that referendums produce losers as well as winners, and that turning some people into losers always comes at a cost. Macdonald had anticipated this point in the speech he delivered at the beginning of the conference in Quebec City. The effect of the constitution, he told the delegates, would be to create "a strong and lasting government under which we can work out our constitutional liberty as opposed to democracy, and be able to protect the minority by having a powerful central government. . . . The people of every section must feel they are protected." One of the constitution's purposes would be specifically to protect minorities—religious, ethnic and linguistic. Here Macdonald was feeling his way towards the thoroughly modern and pre-eminently Canadian concept that democracy must balance its own defining rule—the will of the majority—with the needs, and the rights, of minorities.

Contemporary sensibilities are still bruised by Macdonald's exclusion of Canadians from any say in making their own constitution. If he had included them, though, it might not have made that decisive a difference. Then, no more than 15 per cent of adults in Canada had the vote. And the turnout might well have been low. A systematic search of Macdonald's correspondence during the key years of 1864 and 1865 reveals how few letters he sent out expressing his views about and arguments for the constitution. The explanation is disconcerting: he wrote few letters about the constitution because he received very few asking for his thoughts. The truth is that at the same time they were excluded from constitution making, Canadians willingly excluded themselves. Moreover, there was always the risk that a referendum might indeed have made a decisive difference: Confederation might well have lost.

Macdonald's main speech, two hours in length, given on February 6, wasn't one of his best. He was tired, suffering an illness of some kind that was caused or exacerbated by heavy drinking. Anyway, he had said everything many times before. He declared that he had always favoured a legislative union—"the best, the cheapest, the most vigorous, and the strongest system of government we could adopt"—but accepted that a federation of some kind was needed to protect "the individuality of Lower Canada." In addition, both of the Maritime provinces now committed to Confederation were not prepared to "lose their individuality as separate political organizations."

He did broach one fresh topic of potentially great importance. Some Canadians, Macdonald noted, opposed Confederation out of fear that "it is an advance towards independence." He himself had no such concern; he did, though, expect the transatlantic relationship to change. "The colonies are now in a transition state. Gradually a different colonial system is being developed— and it will become[,] year by year, less a case of dependence on our part, and of overruling protection on the part of the Mother Country, and more a case of healthy and cordial alliance. Instead of looking on us as a merely dependent colony, England will have in us a friendly nation to stand by her in North America in peace or in war."

Among all the speakers in the six-week debate, no one identified the dilemma inherent in Canada's ongoing relationship with Britain with more devastating accuracy than Christopher Dunkin.* Small and whip-smart—perhaps too smart for his own

---

* As noted earlier, Dunkin predicted that the constant cry of the provinces would be "Give, give, give." On defence, he commented with equal acuity, "The best thing Canada can do is to keep quiet and give no cause for war." Dunkin joined Macdonald's cabinet in 1869.

good, because he generated more bright ideas than his hearers could absorb—Dunkin asked rhetorically, "What are we doing? Creating a new nationality, according to the advocates of this scheme. I hardly know whether we are to take the phrase as ironical or not. It is a reminder that, in fact, we have no sort of nationality at all about us. . . . Unlike the people of the United States, we are to have no foreign relations at all to look after . . . therefore, our new nationality, if we could create it, could be nothing but a name." Cruelly, but unanswerably, Dunkin commented, "Half a dozen colonies federated are but a federated colony after all."

In response to the contradiction identified by Dunkin—of creating a nation that would have no nationality—Cartier did his best, very possibly, since he was no intellectual, by repeating ideas suggested to him by Macdonald. "When we were united together, if union were attained, we would form a political nationality, with which neither the national origin nor the religion of any individual would interfere," said Cartier. Some complained that Canada was too diverse, but, he continued, "the idea of unity of races was utopian—it was impossible. Distinctions of this kind would always exist. Dissimilarity in fact appeared to be the order of the physical world, of the moral world, as well as in the political world." Britain itself was composed of several nations. Likewise in Canada, the English, French, Irish and Scots would each, by their "efforts and success[,] increase the prosperity and glory of the new confederacy." In his rough way, Cartier was talking about a nation whose unity would be its diversity.

Cartier's principal purpose was to mollify Quebecers' anxieties about a "new nationality." Nevertheless, his comments were one of perhaps only two genuinely original insights to emerge during the prolonged debate. The other insight has almost vanished from the history books, but it merits being revived. Its author,

Alexander Mackenzie, that worthy but dull rawboned Scot, later a Liberal prime minister, commented in the midst of an otherwise routine speech, "I do not think the federal system is necessarily a weak one, but it is a system which requires a large degree of intelligence and political knowledge on the part of the people."

As the days passed, it became clear that those opposed to the scheme, principally the *rouges*, had nothing to suggest in its place. A mood of inevitability took hold. At times, there were only twenty members in the chamber. In the description of the *Stratford Beacon*, the House had deteriorated to "an unmistakably seedy condition, having as it was positively declared, eaten the saloon keeper clean out, drunk him entirely out, and got all the fitful naps of sleep that the benches along the passages could be made to yield."

The vote on the main motion was called at last, at 4:30 a.m. on Saturday, March 11, 1865. The result was 99 to 33. The Nays included nineteen French Canadians—a half-dozen fewer than those who had voted six weeks earlier for Dorion's motion opposing a "new nationality."

Except for the legislatures in New Brunswick and Nova Scotia, Confederation was now a done deal.

Four weeks later, the long agony south of the border ended when General Robert E. Lee called on Lieutenant General Ulysses S. Grant at Appomattox Court House, Virginia, bringing with him the signed surrender of the Army of Northern Virginia. Thereafter, the North began demobilizing its vast armies with remarkable speed. Fear of an invasion northwards receded rapidly, in Canada as well as in Britain. In Macdonald's judgment, either the huge Northern armies, "full of fight," would invade almost immediately or, if not, "we may look for peace for a series of years."

One substantive concern did remain. Among those soon to be released from the Northern armies were tens of thousands of Irishmen, all now trained in the arts of war. A new word entered the Canadian political vocabulary—*Fenian* (from the Fenian Brotherhood, originally created in 1858 for the purpose of liberating Ireland). Macdonald charged his intelligence chief, Gilbert McMicken, to keep a close eye for any possible cross-border raids. He took seriously the declarations by Fenian leaders that one effective way to deliver a blow at Britain would be to attack the lightly guarded Canada. "The movement must not be despised," he wrote to Monck. "I shall spare no expense in watching them."

Before the Confederation Debates ended, other news—this time deeply discouraging—reached Macdonald. It came from New Brunswick's small capital of Fredericton. The result of a provincial election there, even though not yet completed, was almost certainly going to be the defeat of Premier Leonard Tilley's pro-Confederation government. Shortly afterwards, Nova Scotia's premier, Charles Tupper, sent word to Macdonald that support for Confederation was slipping fast there.

Patching these pieces back together now became Macdonald's principal mission. It would remain so for far longer than he, or anyone, imagined.

TWENTY

The Administration
of Strangers

~

[Take a Nova Scotian to Ottawa], where he cannot view
the Atlantic, smell salt water or see the sail of
a ship, and the man will pine and die.
Joseph Howe, Nova Scotia anti-Confederate leader

The news from New Brunswick, once it had been handed over to Macdonald from the telegraph office, was far worse than the initial reports. Premier Leonard Tilley had not merely lost the government; he had lost his own seat. His party had not just been defeated but trounced, winning fourteen seats against the twenty-seven captured by the incoming anti-Confederation premier, Albert James Smith. Even if Nova Scotia could be kept on side—Charles Tupper by now was thoroughly gloomy—there would be no continuous chain of provinces extending out to the Atlantic. With such a gap in its middle, Confederation would be all but unattainable; without it, Britain and the United States would have no reason to believe that Canadians possessed the will to be a nation.

In the House, Macdonald accepted without argument the choice that New Brunswickers had made; the result, he admitted, represented a "declaration against the policy of Confederation."

In contrast to D'Arcy McGee, who claimed that American money had determined the outcome, Macdonald made only a glancing reference to that possibility. He remained defiant, though, rejecting "any signs of weakness, any signs of receding on this question," and telling Tupper, "there was nothing left for us but the bold game." To one alarmed supporter he counselled, "stick with the ship until she rights." He was particularly concerned that George Brown might use the setback to argue once again for his "mini-federation," applying only to the United Province of Canada. Macdonald was able to forestall that. In private, though, he let his frustration show, telling a Prince Edward Island supporter that Tilley had been "unstatesmanlike" to allow an election to happen without first putting the Confederation scheme to his legislature to ensure that "the subject had been fairly discussed and its merits understood."

By the end of March, he was already planning a counterattack. "We will endeavour to convince the Catholic Bishop of the benefits to be derived from Confederation," he told Tupper, while he himself would arrange "to get the communication you speak of from the Orange Grand Lodge to the same body in New Brunswick." These tactics were premature, though. The news soon got bleaker. On April 10, 1865, Tupper informed his legislature in Halifax that "under existing circumstances, an immediate Union of the British North American Colonies has become impractical." He stopped

Nova Scotia premier Charles Tupper. He was the only Father of Confederation with a university education (Edinburgh, in medicine). He was bold and blustery, an even stronger advocate of a centralized Confederation than Macdonald.

trying to bring the issue to a vote. Inevitably, anti-Confederates in Canada itself joined in. *Rouge* leader Antoine-Aimé Dorion declared triumphantly, "This scheme is killed. I repeat that it is killed." And a new player now came onto the stage. He was Joseph Howe, a former Nova Scotia premier and easily its most exceptional politician of the century. He was also the strongest anti-Confederate that Macdonald would ever face.

Howe was the third of the three Maritime politicians who were by now becoming familiar names to newspaper readers across the country. The others were Tupper and Tilley. Since both men would have long terms in post-Confederation Ottawa, a snapshot of each will suffice for now. Tupper was a medical doctor— ebullient, bombastic, bold. He practically challenged observers to employ purple ink while describing him, as in "broad-shouldered, self-contained, as vigorous-looking as Wellington's charger" and "oratorical and obstetrical"—these latter words by Lord Rosebery, later the British prime minister. Tupper was not just pro-Confederate but an ultra Confederate: he outdid even Macdonald in his advocacy of a full legislative union with minimalist provinces, rather than merely the kind of centralized confederation Macdonald aspired to. Tilley was a druggist, and a most successful one. Never popular because of a self-righteous streak, particularly as a

New Brunswick premier Leonard Tilley. He led the fight for Confederation in his province, and for a time lost it.

Joseph Howe, the anti-Confederate leader in Nova Scotia. He was the one "anti" to propose a serious alternative. The odds were against him and he lost, but Macdonald later praised him as "the most seminal mind" he had met.

prohibitionist, he was widely respected for his intelligence and integrity. It's because of Tilley that for a long time, as we shall see, our title was that of a dominion. Between them, Tupper and Tilley began the tradition of the Maritimes exporting its political talent to Ottawa.

Of all the men who fought against Confederation, and so against Macdonald, Howe was the one Macdonald respected the most. Years later, he told his secretary Joseph Pope that Howe possessed "the most seminal mind" he had ever met. Yet Howe was the tragic figure of Confederation. He opposed it, and lost. The true source of his pain, though, was that he lost his faith in Britain. His father, John Howe, who had been living in the United States at the time of the rebellion by the American colonies, had been the only member of his family to come north as a Loyalist. He passed on this almost mystical attitude towards Britain to his son.

Self-educated, Howe edited a journal, the *Novascotian*, which was way ahead of its time in calling for such grand notions as "more of rational freedom" and, as early as 1838, for a union of the British American colonies. Howe sent letters to the colonial secretary suggesting how best to reform the Empire, into a sort of super-confederation of Britain and its colonies strikingly similar to the concept developed decades later as Imperial Federation. Elected to the legislature, Howe took up the cause of Responsible

Government and played a major role in its attainment in 1848, a few months ahead of the United Province of Canada. He became premier, a post he lost to Tupper, regained and then lost again to Tupper in 1860. Short of money, he accepted a minor patronage post as a fisheries commissioner. In 1864 he gave a fiery speech to the touring group of Canadian businessmen and journalists organized by McGee, calling for a sea-to-sea union; the alternative, he said, was to "live and die in insignificance."

Then, in January 1865, Howe burst out as a fully fledged anti-Confederate. He wrote eleven long articles, the "Botheration Letters," which played a substantial part in stoking Nova Scotian fears of what Confederation might bring. Disappointment at his own career was a factor: when his poorly paid patronage job came to an end, Howe would face virtual penury at the age of sixty. Jealousy of Tupper, who had forced him out of politics, was also a factor; invited to be a Nova Scotia delegate to the Charlottetown Conference, Howe refused, saying he wouldn't "play second-fiddle to that damn'd Tupper." He assumed that the conclave would fail, then watched from the sidelines as Confederation took off—and Tupper with it. Howe's core reason for opposing Confederation was his love of country—far less for Nova Scotia than for Britain. As he wrote, "I am a dear lover of old England, and to save her would blow up Nova Scotia into the air or scuttle her like an old ship."

He opposed Confederation so fiercely because he feared it would tug Canada, and so Nova Scotia, away from the mother country. He talked more often about Britain than about his own province, as in his speech in Yarmouth in May 1866: "You go down to the sea in ships, and a flag of old renown floats above them, and the Consuls and Ministers of the Empire are prompt to protect your property, and your sons in every part of the world." And, in another speech, "London [was] large enough—

London, the financial centre of the world, the nursing mother of universal enterprise, the home of the arts, the seat of Empire, the fountainhead of civilization." Who could think of giving all that up for a capital in Canada's backwoods "with an Indian name and any quantity of wilderness and ice in the rear of it"?

When Howe did talk to Nova Scotians about themselves, it was about their past. To take any Nova Scotian to Ottawa, "away from tidewater . . . where he cannot view the Atlantic, smell salt water or see the sail of a ship, and the man will pine and die." Rule by Canada, he said, would be "the administration of strangers." And he simply didn't believe that so polyglot and divided a country as Canada could possibly work: "The builders of Babel were only a little more ambitious than these Canadian politicians."

Howe's interventions made a difference. But the prime source of Maritimers' hostility to Confederation was something quite different and almost unresolvable. This was that they were so distant from Canada and so near, relatively, to Britain. In his speech in Halifax after the Charlottetown Conference, Macdonald had said, jokingly, that Canada was almost as far from the Maritimes as from Australia. (Later, Howe remarked, entirely correctly, that the Maritimes were no nearer to Canada than was Britain to Austria, across half of Europe.) Less than 3 per cent of Canada's exports went to the Maritimes, and the return flow was even smaller. A letter from Halifax took as long to reach Ottawa as it did to cross the Atlantic to Liverpool. There were no Canada–Maritime rail or road connections; just the St. Lawrence River, and it only in summer. Few Canadians had any commercial or personal reasons to make the laborious journey; nor, in reverse, did Maritimers. The *Acadian Recorder* of Halifax summed it all up: "We don't know each other. We have no facilities or resources to mingle with each other. We are shut off from each other by a wilderness, geographically, commercially, politically and socially.

We always cross the United States to shake hands." By contrast, any Maritimer could travel to England in one of the steamships that now made the voyage in as little as ten days.

Differences in self-perception widened the physical distance. The Maritime provinces were small: 350,000 inhabitants in Nova Scotia, 250,000 in New Brunswick, 80,000 in Prince Edward Island. But they were already mini-nations. Just as in the United Province of Canada, they had Responsible Government. In politics, they were ahead in some respects: New Brunswick had the secret ballot, and Nova Scotia had experimented with universal suffrage. It was the Maritimers who, at Charlottetown and Quebec City, had taken the innovative step of including opposition members in their delegations.

Maritimers felt themselves superior to Canada, looking dubiously on its jumble of immigrants and its disturbing qualities of dynamism and brashness—an almost mirror image of the way Canadians viewed the United States.* They were, in other words, defensively superior. British North America's first real theatre had opened in Halifax in 1787, and its first literary periodical began there twelve years later. The Royal Navy, with its base in Halifax, gave the small city a distinct social life. Confederation, if it happened, would bring the Maritimes no new gifts except the Intercolonial Railway, which would create short-term jobs but over time bring new competition for the small and inefficient local business class. Tupper warned Macdonald that "a great body of the trading men comprising the most wealthy merchants" opposed Confederation.

Just as critical, all three Maritime provinces were booming, due chiefly to Reciprocity with the United States and the demand

---

* Howe himself on one occasion argued that "deadly weapons, so common in the streets of Montreal, are rarely carried in Nova Scotia, except in pursuit of game."

created by the Civil War. These, too, were the great days of the sailing ship: one in three ships entering Boston Harbor started out from Nova Scotia. That Maritimers were living on borrowed time was not yet realized, with the steam engine, the screw propeller and the iron hull all soon to turn even the finest wood and sail ships into museum pieces. Why risk any of this prosperity, they argued, for what Howe called "this crazy Confederacy with a mongrel crew, half-English, half-French"? Why give up John Bull for Jack Frost?

There was a good reason to make such a switch, one that Howe undoubtedly realized as it became the principal cause of his anger and his anguish. John Bull was showing clear signs of wanting to get rid of the Maritimes by thrusting them into the arms of Jack Frost. Confederation would enable Britain to distance itself from Canada, most certainly so militarily. Of lesser consequence, yet still useful, Confederation would enable Britain to rid itself of the Maritimes—except for the vital Halifax base, which was considered as important to the Empire as Gibraltar or Malta.

As Howe would have been the first to understand, and so have wanted to rage against the dying of the light, the Maritimes in the end had nowhere to go other than into a union with Canada. Alone, they would be lost. The only alternative was Maritime Union, something New Brunswick and Prince Edward Island feared even more than union with "mongrel" Canada. Ottawa, unlike Halifax, was at least not next door.

The Maritimers who struggled against Confederation were major contributors to their own defeat. They failed to unite themselves, so they never spoke with a single, magnified voice. They trusted Britain. They failed to do their homework until it was too late. At the Quebec Conference, Brown wrote dismissively that "we hear much talkee-talkee" from the Maritimers, "but not very much administrative ability." And they deluded themselves that they could outfox Macdonald.

Before Macdonald appears back on stage, it's necessary to describe the scenery against which this particular act unfolded. This backdrop was not something physical but a force far more substantial—a psychological attitude that had hardened into an utter conviction.

~

During the twenty-first century, Canadians have come to define themselves by their tolerance—a quality now accepted almost universally as the feature that makes us a distinct people. The acceptance of difference—indeed, its outright celebration—has gained a talismanic power among contemporary Canadians. To be tolerant is to be a Canadian. To be intolerant is not just to be personally racist or exclusionary, but to possess the attribute of someone who is not a real member of the Canadian community.

The equivalent talismanic virtue in nineteenth-century Canada was loyalty. To be disloyal, even to doubt the centrality of the importance of loyalty, was to be something less than a full Canadian. Expressions of disloyalty divided the community and threatened its identity. Loyalty distinguished the nation from its neighbour even more definitively than tolerance does today. Canada was loyal; the United States was disloyal, or had been when it rebelled. No other cross-border differences needed to be identified or constructed.*

---

* Over time, as may be only a coincidence, there has been a displacement of one nationally unifying virtue by the other. In the nineteenth century, there was little tolerance in Canada—hence the sectarianism and open religious hatreds. Today, there is little loyalty to institutions, from marriage to employers.

The object of Canadians' loyalty was Britain, the Empire, the Crown, personified so alluringly by Queen Victoria. Even more so, Britain was exemplified by such institutions as the parliamentary system and the judicial system, and by British values of fair play, a stiff upper lip and a man's words being his bond, no matter whether they were for real or just for boasting.

Loyalty wasn't only about being British. Loyalty was a cardinal virtue—its near kin being fidelity—and extended to loyalty to family, to the marriage vows (there were incomparably fewer divorces in Canada than in the United States), to friends, to tribe or clan or community, and to religion (Canadians who exchanged one faith for another faith were called "perverts"). As the educator Egerton Ryerson put it, "it is a reverence for, and attachment to, the laws, order, institutions and freedom of the country."

Being loyal was seen as synonymous with being God-fearing. Ryerson observed that if "a man does not love the King, he cannot love God." And the Reverend J.W.D. Gray informed his parishioners that the "spirit of *submission to lawful authority . . .* lies at the foundation of your loyalty to your earthly Sovereign."

The potency of the ethic of loyalty, conjoining as it did an earthly sovereign with a heavenly one and with the rule of law, was overwhelming. It made Canadians not just proud to be who they were (and not to be Americans) but ebulliently, braggartly proud. There was not the least shyness about Canadians' loyalty. Flags were waved, songs were sung and public figures competed in their expressions of devotion to Crown and Queen. Canadians in the mid-nineteenth century may well have been more patriotic than were Americans, but to the mother country rather than to their own country. Macdonald, the great loyalist, heightened the stakes, and advanced his partisan cause, by accusing his opponents of "treason."

It all began with the Loyalists. There were only about fifty thousand of them, but their spirit defined Upper Canada, Nova Scotia, New Brunswick and Prince Edward Island, and the far larger number of British immigrants who followed took over the torch from them. That torch was the Loyalist Myth—the chronicles of their suffering and sacrifice for the sake of their loyalty to the Crown. It was much embellished, as all national foundational myths always are. In his book *The Sense of Power*, historian Carl Berger makes two perceptive points. One is that "nationalistic history was just as much an instrument for survival for the British-Canadian Loyalists as it was for the French-Canadians." The other is that the Loyalists brought with them not so much British institutions as "its inner spirit"—assumptions such as "the primacy of the community over individual selfishness, society conceived as an organism of functionally related parts . . . religion as the mortar of the social order, and the distrust of materialism." The British connection has long vanished, but it takes only a short dig down to the sedimentary layer once occupied by the Loyalists to locate the sources of a great many contemporary Canadian convictions and conventions.

Perhaps the most eloquent expression of the force of loyalty in Canada among English Canadians was made by a British Columbia Legislature member, T.L. Wood, in a debate about possible entry into Confederation. "The bond of union between Canada and the other provinces bears no resemblance to the union between England and her colonial possessions," Wood said. "There is not natural love and feeling of loyalty. The feeling of loyalty towards England is a blind feeling, instinctive, strong, born with us and impossible to shake off."

If the loyalty of English Canadians was so potent and deeply rooted because it was instinctual, that among Canadiens was as strong, even if unemotional, precisely because it was self-interested and calculated. Cartier summed it up during the Confederation Debates when he said that the reason the Canadiens "had their institutions, their language and their religion intact today, was because of their adherence to the British Crown." Back in 1846 Étienne-Paschal Taché had famously proclaimed that "the last cannon which is shot on this continent in defence of Great Britain will be fired by the hand of a French Canadian." Here resided the magical, however paradoxical, effect of the creed of loyalty among Canadians: being loyal to another nation and to an absent monarch kept Canadians loyal to each other.

Macdonald, to return to the theme of this book, was not merely a loyalist: he embodied it in his very person. In his 1883 biography of Macdonald, the journalist J.E. Collins wrote that "more than any other Canadian statesman . . . [he] taught us the duty of loyalty." In his lifelong battle to keep Canada un-American, Macdonald's most potent instrument was Canadians' loyalty to Britain. No less valuable was the particular nature of his own loyalty to Britain.

His was fiercely loyal, of course; but there was no deference in his posture. Macdonald was exactly the kind of colonial, or foreigner, who could break through English reserve and snobbery simply because there was not a trace of colonial cringe about him. As the journalist Nicholas Flood Davin, himself a British immigrant, observed, Macdonald was "the type of politician who has never failed to delight the English people—the man who, like Palmerston, can work hard, do strong things, hold his purpose, never lose sight for a moment of the honour and welfare of his country, and yet crack his joke and have his laugh. . . . There is nothing viewy about Sir John Macdonald." In short, whenever in Britain, Macdonald regarded himself as an equal, and he was accepted as one.

Only when the British Empire began to fade and fall apart did loyalty lose its magnetic appeal to Canadians; thereafter, as was incomparably more challenging, Canadians had to find reasons to be loyal to themselves.

~

In the task of turning around public opinion in the Maritimes, loyalty constituted Macdonald's secret weapon. In Nova Scotia, loyalty to Britain, beginning with that of the tortured Joseph Howe, was even deeper than in Canada. In New Brunswick, attitudes were more ambiguous. After an 1864 visit there, the editor of the Kingston *British American* wrote, "They are more American [than Canadians]—more democratic in their tastes— have more of the 'free' swagger in their manners . . . more flash-dressed ladies at Theatres and Concerts."

What Macdonald now had to do was make certain that Maritimers understood what it was that Britain wanted of them— to join Canada. This, therefore, is what he proceeded to do.

TWENTY-ONE

The Turn of the Screw

⁓

The left arm is then extended a little, and the Queen laid her
hand upon it which I touched slightly with my lips.
Alexander Tilloch Galt, describing his presentation to the Queen

S ometime in the spring of 1865, Macdonald figured out how to haul the Maritime provinces onto the side of Confederation. He would appeal to their sentiments about Britain. To do that, a Fathers of Confederation mission would call upon the Great White Mother.

No real reason existed for Macdonald and the other Canadian leaders to go over to London. In the legislature, Macdonald described the group's purpose as "to take stock . . . with the British Government"—about as vague a description as he could concoct. For a time Macdonald even protested that he was too busy to go. This excuse was blatantly untrue, because he was due to go to Oxford to collect his treasured honorary degree. But once Macdonald had committed himself to the trip, a doubting Brown agreed to go along as well. The actual topics to be discussed while they were in London were not easy to compile: the Imperial government had already made clear its wholehearted support for Confederation, and although there were defence matters to go over—the Canadian government had just voted one million dollars for new defence works—no one in London had the least interest in provoking the United States by new military projects. Nevertheless, off went the Big Four—first Cartier and Galt in a ship that made a stopover in Halifax, giving them time for discussions on railway matters there, and then Macdonald and Brown shortly afterwards on a different vessel. The real purpose of their mission was to use the Imperial government to get the Maritimers to turn around and face in the right direction.

The softening process has already begun. The colonial secretary, Edward Cardwell, after his meeting with Brown the previous December, had dispatched to Canada the laudatory memorandum on Confederation that had so pleased his visitor. Still more useful was the covering note attached by Cardwell to the copies he sent to the Maritime lieutenant-governors. "Our official dispatch," he wrote to Arthur Gordon in New Brunswick, "will show you that Her Majesty's Government wish you to give the whole [Confederation] scheme all the support and assistance in your power." Britain's general policy, he explained, was "to turn the screw as hard as will be useful, but not harder." Two discrete turns of the screw were then applied. Gordon was reminded that his career depended on his shepherding New Brunswickers towards voting for Confederation. His counterpart in Nova Scotia, Sir Richard MacDonnell, who had made no secret of his opposition to Confederation, was pulled out completely and sent to Hong Kong. He was replaced by a soldier hero, Sir William Fenwick Williams, who knew how to take orders. Less successfully, Prince Edward Islanders were warned that the bill for the salary of their lieutenant-governor might be transferred from London to Charlottetown, but this pressure made them only more truculent than they already were.

For the Big Four, the reception in London was at least as agreeable as had been the earlier one for Brown alone. The Colonial Office chose the moment of Macdonald's arrival to send word to the Maritime capitals that Maritime Union was no longer discussible; all that was left on the Maritimes' negotiating table, therefore, was Confederation.

The quartet did have diligent discussions with the appropriate British politicians on matters such as defence, Confederation, the prospects for Canada's renewing the Reciprocity Treaty with the United States and the future of the Hudson's Bay Company and the North-West. At the only meeting that actually mattered, none of these topics was raised. That was the meeting with Her Majesty.

On May 18 the four went excitedly to Buckingham Palace in a carriage that picked them up at the Westminster Palace Hotel. On arriving, they discovered, to their mixed pride and terror, that Queen Victoria had asked for them to be presented first. "Dukes and Duchesses had to give way and open up a passage to us," Brown reported to Anne. The procedure that followed was a trifle more complicated: it involved, as Galt described it to his wife, going "down on the right knee (a matter involving, in my own case, a slight mental doubt as to the tenacity of my breeches), the left arm is then extended a little, and the Queen laid her hand upon it which I touched slightly with my lips." That ordeal completed, the quartet was kept together so the Queen could engage them in small talk, including an exchange with Cartier in French. Then she glided away.

Back across the Atlantic went a report that amounted to a command: Her Majesty and her Canadian ministers were as one.

Earlier, the four had spent little time at the Westminster Palace Hotel, because night after night they were out dining at the mansions of dukes and lords and cabinet ministers and railway magnates, or they went to balls where coiffed, bare-shouldered ladies exhibited a remarkable interest in the details of Canadian politics, economics and culture. No less deeply interested in Canadian doings was the Prince of Wales. He had them over to dinner at Buckingham Palace, drew them into an inside room filled with a specially selected group of one hundred of the two thousand guests, and while chatting with them smoked cigars and showed off his new Turkish dressing gown. (In an exercise in re-gifting, Galt was given one of these cigars, which earlier had been presented to the prince by the King of Portugal.) Less interested in

Queen Victoria. The last British monarch with real political influence, she used it to give Confederation the push it needed to overcome Maritime opposition.

the Canadians and in Canada was Bishop Wilberforce, who, as Brown reported to Anne, asked "whether Darwin believed that 'turnips are tending to become men.'"

They also went to the Epsom Downs on Derby Day, taking with them a hamper of food and wine from Fortnum and Mason. The *Times*'s famed war correspondent from the Crimean War, William Russell, took them around, getting them into one of the most socially fashionable of tents, where they sipped turtle soup and champagne cup. They took in the races (Macdonald won twenty guineas) and gazed, as Galt reported to his wife, at "the sights of the course, gypsies, music, mountebanks, games of all kinds, menageries of savage animals, and shows of Irishmen disguised as savage Indians." On the jam-packed road driving back, they used the roof of their carriage as a mobile platform from which to fire dried peas through a peashooter at passersby, who, as was customary, fired back balls of flour. Brown and Macdonald also went together to the opera *Lucrezia Borgia*.

That was it. Official replies to their queries about specifics such as defence were exasperatingly vague. There was one significant shift in their own attitudes, though. The people they had met, Brown reported home, "are a different race from us, different ideas, different aspirations, and however well it may be to see what the thing is like, it takes no hold on your feelings, or even of your respect." Galt was more easily impressed, writing back, "We were treated as if we were ambassadors and not as *mere Colonists*," yet even he added warily, "it bodes no good no matter how flattering it may be."

Three of the four returned home on June 17. Macdonald stayed a week longer to go up to Oxford for his honorary degree of Doctor of Civil Law. "This is the greatest honour they can confer, and is much sought after by the first men," Macdonald reported in delight to his sister Louisa. He made it back to Canada early in July.

While little or nothing specific had been accomplished, things could hardly have gone better. Before the Canadians left, Cardwell gave Governor General Monck the green light to employ "every proper means of influence to carry into effect without delay the proposed confederation." Above all, Confederation had been given de facto Royal Assent.

The Confederation project now resumed its forward motion, if still creakily. A shift in Maritime public opinion began. To help

it along, Cardwell began to dangle before the Maritimers the possibility of improvements in the terms agreed to in the Quebec
Resolutions. Those most attracted by this bait were the
Maritime Roman Catholic bishops, who set out to secure guarantees for their separate schools.

On closer scrutiny, Confederation's election defeat in New
Brunswick turned out to be less crushing than it had first
seemed. The Saint John *Telegraph* calculated that the vote had
been 15,979 for the anti-Confederate Smith against 15,556 for
Tilley. A key by-election was due that fall. To help New
Brunswickers make the right judgment about what to do, Tilley
wrote to Macdonald, estimating first that victory would require
"an expenditure of 8 or ten thousand dollars," and then asking,
"Is there any chance of the friends in Canada providing half the
expenditure?" On the back of this letter, Macdonald scribbled to
Galt, "Read this. What about the monies?" Later, Charles
Brydges of the Grand Trunk Railway reassured Macdonald that
he had "sent the needful to Tilley" and had "kept all our names
here off the document." Down went Canadian money; in came
the votes for the pro-Confederate candidate.* By the fall, New
Brunswick's Lieutenant-Governor Gordon was able to brag to
London, "I am convinced I can make (or buy) a union majority in
the Legislature."

A new problem had arisen. On July 30 Étienne-Paschal Taché
died, sending Macdonald his last poignant note: "J'aimerais à
vous voir encore une fois avant le long voyage que je vais bientôt

---

* Brown very generously contributed five hundred dollars to the by-election
fund and wrote, "[I] will not be behind if further aid is required."

entreprendre." The day after Taché's funeral, Monck asked Macdonald, as the most senior of the quartet, to head the ministry. Brown, when called in to see Monck, would have none of it; while denying he had any "personal aspirations whatever," he pointed out that his own Reformers were twice as numerous as Macdonald's Conservatives. He and Macdonald then met one on one. They reached no meeting of minds, despite an offer by Macdonald to step down for Cartier. Given that those two were joined politically at the hip, Brown naturally rejected it. Eventually they reached a compromise: the new premier would be an anonymous, long-serving Canadien, Sir Narcisse-Fortunat Belleau. He was sworn in on August 7.

Then came another complication. Brown, always quick to identify a slight, had already complained that Macdonald had given Galt public precedence over him. He also harboured suspicions—justified, no doubt—that Macdonald and Cartier were dispensing patronage that ought to have been his to allocate. From that point on, Brown refused to speak to Macdonald, dealing only with Cartier.

The malaise continued. A mid-summer government statement on Confederation made to the legislature in August had nothing new to say. Macdonald himself was often absent, supposedly on doctor's orders, but in fact because he was drinking heavily.

Yet while Macdonald was drinking far too much at the worst possible time, his antennae remained as alert as ever. In July a large conference was held in Detroit, organized by the Detroit Chamber of Commerce, to discuss and if possible reverse Washington's decision to end the Reciprocity Treaty with Canada in the spring of 1866. No fewer than five hundred American businessmen attended, as well as fifty Canadians, all worried deeply by the impending loss of cross-border trade.

During the meeting the American consul general in Montreal, J. R. Potter, chose to declare in his speech that the entire problem could be resolved by the United States annexing Canada. News of this extraordinary behaviour by the principal representative of the U.S. Government in Canada took time to reach Ottawa. Macdonald invented an occasion for himself to deliver a speech in Ottawa (press releases didn't exist then), and on September 28 gave his reply in a way that revealed a great deal about his personal feelings on Canada's future in North America. First he talked about Confederation, actually a bit optimistically: "The union of all the Provinces is a fixed fact." Then he talked about himself: "The mere struggle for office and fight for position—the difference between the 'outs' and 'ins' have no charms for me," he said, "but now I have something worth fighting for—and that is the junction of Her Majesty's subjects in all British North America as one great nation." Macdonald knew fully what his own leitmotif was.

As fully, Macdonald now knew precisely what he was doing for himself. The month before, in a letter to Monck on June 26, 1866, he described Confederation as "an event which will make us historical." He then added, almost as if warning Brown to stay out of his way, "—not with my will would another person take my position in completing the scheme for which I have worked so earnestly."

As was now inevitable, relations between Macdonald and Brown went from bad to worse. In November, Brown took umbrage at Galt's having been sent alone to Washington to try (unsuccessfully) to negotiate an extension of the Reciprocity Treaty. Macdonald got Galt to explain that his mission had been unofficial and that, on a second trip, a Reform minister would accompany him.

A parting could no longer be prevented. On December 17 Brown sent in his resignation. Afterwards, he wrote to Anne, "Thank Providence—I am a free man once more." Macdonald got Galt "*without fail* to prepare at once" an account of what had happened between him and Brown so he could show it to the other Reform ministers, in the hope that he could convince them to stay rather than leave with Brown. The tactic worked: there were no other defections from the Great Coalition, and a third Reformer took Brown's place in the government.

The long, intensely personal duel between Brown and Macdonald had reached its end. The clash of personalities made their parting inevitable, as did the fact that their objectives were fundamentally at odds. Brown wanted a "mini-federation" within just the United Province of Canada, to separate the French and the English. He had exulted at the end of the Quebec Conference that French-Canadianism had been extinguished and was delighted when he heard in the spring of 1865 that New Brunswick's pro-Confederation government had been defeated in the election. This result, he wrote to Anne, "is a very serious matter for the Maritime provinces, but magnificent for us." Macdonald's purpose, by contrast, was a transcontinental nation, with Confederation as its essential first building block, one based on a pact of trust between French and English. Brown's last comments about Confederation before it actually happened, during a debate in the legislature in the summer of 1866, showed how distant he was from Macdonald. There, Brown condemned as "a most inconvenient and inexpedient device" any attempt to use the constitution "to bind down a majority . . . to protect a minority"; rather, he argued, the majority should be left free "to act according to their sense of what is right and just."

Nevertheless, Brown fully deserved McGee's encomium to him for having displayed "moral courage" in bringing his followers with him into the Great Coalition government that would bring about Confederation. While many of his political views were narrow, Brown was an exceptional public figure. There was even an expansiveness to his later explanation for quitting: "I want to be free to write of men and things without control. . . . Party leadership and the conducting of a great journal do not harmonize." Most certainly he deserved from Macdonald a great deal more than the crabbed, ungracious compliment he later paid him: "[Brown] deserves the credit of joining with me; he and his party gave me that assistance in Parliament that enabled us to carry confederation."

~

From this point on, the tide began to turn decisively. Through the winter, New Brunswick's Premier Smith and his government progressively lost their way. By the spring of 1866 he had been pushed back so far onto the defensive that the Throne Speech actually contained a description of Confederation as "an object much to be desired." Not long afterwards, his government was defeated in the House and an election called. At that instant, there appeared exactly the political reinforcements that Macdonald most needed: the Fenians appeared on New Brunswick's borders.

~

In fact, Canada-U.S. relations had improved considerably by this time, if for the worst of all possible reasons. The previous April, just one week after Lee's surrender at Appomattox Court House, President Lincoln had been assassinated while attending a play at

Ford's Theater in Washington. Unanimously, Canadian politicians and the press recognized that a giant had been struck down, and they mourned the loss to the United States as well as to the world. The day after, the Toronto *Globe* appeared with its front page bordered in black; Toronto sent two municipal representatives to attend the funeral, and during the two hours that the service was being held, church bells throughout the country pealed unceasingly while ships in the ports of British North America lowered their flags to half-mast. The most moving and the most deeply grieving services for Lincoln were those held in the small wooden churches of Canadian blacks.

At the same time, the rapid demobilization of the North's armies provided relief from the threat of a possible invasion. Just one lingering cause for alarm remained: demobbed soldiers had been allowed to buy back their rifles for six dollars; noticeably, many of those doing so had been Irish Americans. Macdonald was kept well briefed about the Fenians' doings by his intelligence chief, Gilbert McMicken. At least as much, he was kept well briefed by the Fenians themselves. They were talkative, boastful, combative (with each other) and, while brave soldiers individually, hopeless as an organized force. They did have one good marching song: "Many battles have been won / Along with the boys in blue / And we'll go and capture Canada / For we've nothing else to do."

As St. Patrick's Day, March 17, 1866, approached, nervousness mounted in Canada. Some ten thousand militia men were mobilized. Nothing happened. Then on April 7, the streets of the Maine seaport of Portland were suddenly crowded with Irishmen, most carrying revolvers and with long knives in their belts; they went on to the town of Eastport to hold a "convention." Their objective was the island of Campobello, New Brunswick. Two British warships hastily sailed from Halifax, followed by two troopships from Malta. Soon there was a mini Royal Navy fleet off the Maine coast, together with some five thousand British and New Brunswick militia soldiers. The Fenians straggled out of Eastport, leaving behind unpaid hotel bills and around fifteen hundred rifles. Actual action was limited to one boatload of Fenians who made it to an offshore Canadian island and burned down a customs warehouse.

That the Fenian raid had been a fiasco didn't change its consequences but only multiplied them. Canada had been threatened. Britain had fulfilled its obligation to rush to its aid. Most disturbingly, American authorities had allowed the invasion to be attempted from its territory (no Fenian was ever charged afterwards for violating the neutrality laws). Everything that had happened reinforced the argument that Confederation was essential to national security.* Governor General Monck sent home the word that the militia's performance had ended forever the accusation so often hurled at the North American colonies of "helplessness, inertness and dependence." Indeed, the Fenian expedition had been so counterproductive that some people speculated that Macdonald had stage-managed the entire affair with McGee's help.† Not a scrap of evidence suggests that was so. There was, though, something ominous. One of McMicken's detectives reported he had been told that "one thousand dollars is offered in gold to anyone that will bring in D'Arcy McGee's head."

For the time being, Macdonald could not have asked for more than he already had. In Nova Scotia, Tupper was able finally to get the Legislative Assembly to approve a pro-Confederation resolution, which cleverly asked not for approval of Confederation but only for

---

* The militia's adjutant general, Colonel Patrick MacDougall, later wrote that the Fenians had functioned as "invaluable, though involuntary, benefactors of Canada" by giving its people "a proud consciousness of strength."

† The Fenian who had actually proposed the raid was accused of being a Canadian agent and expelled from the movement.

Nova Scotia delegates to take part in negotiations that could "effectually assure just provision for the rights and interests of Nova Scotia."*

A month later, Tilley won the New Brunswick election, winning even more decisively—33 seats to 8—than had his anti-Confederate opponent the previous year. One factor was the support of the Roman Catholic bishops. But money talked even more loudly than did the faith. In June Tilley had written to Macdonald, "Telegraph me in cipher saying what we can rely on. . . . It will require some $40,000 or $50,000 to do the work in all our counties." A few days later, he wrote again, even more urgently, "To be frank with you, the election in this Province can be made certain if the *means* are used." He suggested that the exchange of cash be made outside the province, in Portland, Maine. Monck then got into the act, telegraphing Macdonald: "I think it is very desirable that he [Galt] should undertake the journey to Portland." In counterpoint, Galt wrote to Macdonald, saying, "That *means* had better be used—I think we *must* put it through," adding that he would go to Portland together with Brydges in order to meet with Tilley and consummate the exchange. The use of the "means" did achieve its end. This exercise, undertaken for the higher cause of Confederation and one fully approved by a governor general of the highest probity, introduced Macdonald to the art of extracting election campaign funds from a large railway company.[†]

---

* Anti-Confederates argued that a referendum should be held before any final commitment to Confederation was made, but Tupper retorted that the same legislature had approved negotiations to create a Maritime Union—with no provision for a referendum.

† New Brunswick's Governor Gordon, as so often, summed up the electoral chicanery perfectly: "Confederation has hardly any friends here, but it will be carried by large majorities nonetheless."

Review Extra.

Fenians are coming

(BY TELEGRAPH.)

PORT COLBORNE,
JUNE 1, 1866.—3.30 p. m.

Refugees from Fort Erie report the burning of a Bridge 4 miles back of Fort Erie by the Fenians.

They have possession of Taylor's Heights, one mile and a half below Fort Erie, near a place called Waterloo, and the highest land in the vicinity. They have commenced throwing up earthworks there, and have struck towards Brantford road. This you can rely on.

There were reports this morning about the capturing of Port Sarnia and Welland Canal.

FROM COBOURG.

The following telegram was received by Capt. Poole from Brigade-Major Patterson at Cobourg this afternoon :—

"All the Companies in my District are to assemble at Cobourg at once. Tell Captains Kennedy and Rogers, and send word to Capt. Leigh, Lakefield.

ALEX. PATTERSON,
Brigade-Major."

Cobourg, June 1, 1866.

The Fenians decisively helped Confederation. As American Irish trying to end British rule in Ireland, they invaded Canada—and so reminded Canadians of the threat to them from the south.

The Fenians had not yet completed their contribution to Confederation. On June 1, one of McMicken's detectives sent an urgent telegram from Welland: "1,500 Fenians landed at Fort Erie." Inaccurate in some details, it was correct in substance. About half that number of Fenians, many wearing Union or Confederate uniforms, had been ferried across the Niagara River led by a capable officer, John O'Neill. Canadian authorities, made complacent by the earlier fiascos, were slow to respond. O'Neill's men occupied Fort Erie and cut the telegraph wires. A clash with the Canadian militia took place at the village of Ridgeway, in Welland County. The ill-trained militia were overwhelmed, suffering nine killed and thirty-eight wounded. Another clash with militia units outside Fort Erie ended in a second victory for O'Neill's Fenians. None of the promised reinforcements from the United States arrived, though, so O'Neill ferried his troops back across the Niagara River. The U.S. authorities persuaded them to "abandon [their] expedition against Canada" in exchange for free transportation to their homes. The *Globe* proclaimed, "The autonomy of British America, its independence of all control save that to which its people willingly submit, is cemented by the blood shed in the battle." To intensify Canadians' anger, and to magnify their sense of aggrieved nationalism, three of the militia men killed had been teenaged students from the University of Toronto. Never again would Macdonald treat a threat of Fenian invasion as probable comedy.

~

With approval now from both New Brunswick and Nova Scotia, with Canadians having just shown they were ready to fight for their country and, far from least, with the Imperial government having committed itself to guarantee five million pounds in loans for the Intercolonial Railway, Confederation stretched out ahead like a broad, flat highway.

A bump soon appeared. In London, the government of Lord John Russell went down to defeat on its key Reform Bill. The new prime minister, Lord Derby, would have to replace Cardwell, by now an authority on the Confederation file. The new colonial secretary was announced as Lord Carnarvon, just thirty-six years old, but, as was unusual, happy to have the post because he was a strong believer in the Empire. Carnarvon moved quickly. By July 21 a complete British North America Bill had been drafted in London, and it merely awaited the arrival of the Canadian and Maritime delegates to agree on its details before the document would be submitted to the Westminster Parliament.*

Then came another bump, and a considerably larger one. The Maritimers arrived in London as planned, at the end of July 1866,

---

* This first version of the BNA Act contained only twenty-two clauses and, unlike the Quebec Resolutions and the final act, did not specify the powers of the central government, relying instead on its general enabling power to make laws for "the peace, order and good government."

but neither Macdonald nor any Canadians appeared.

One of the lesser mysteries of the Confederation chronicle resides in Macdonald's failure to exploit the momentum built up by the middle of 1866 to rush a British North America Act through the British Parliament by that fall. There were some technical considerations. The constitutions for the soon-to-be created provinces of Quebec and Ontario had yet to be approved by the Canadian legislature. Also, Macdonald was convinced that the government needed first to lower Canadian tariffs to ease Maritime fears about high taxation before the climactic negotiations began. The new Derby government was weak, though, and the longer the delay, the greater the risk that the political crisis absorbing the British Parliament would halt Confederation's progress and give its critics a chance to regroup.

Macdonald remained gripped in his inertia. He ignored a June 17 warning from Tupper reminding him that an election in Nova Scotia—of which the outcome was far from certain— had by law to be held before May of the next year, 1867. Tupper pleaded, "We *must* obtain action during the present session of the Imperial Parliament or all may be lost." Governor General Monck was at least as anxious. To get Macdonald moving, he sent him a stinging letter on June 21. In it, he bluntly told Macdonald that "valuable time is being lost and a great opportunity in the temper and disposition of the House is being thrown away by the adoption of this system of delay." Monck then showed the mailed fist inside his habitually well-padded glove: "I have come to the delicate conviction that if from my cause this session of Parliament should be allowed to pass without the completion of our portion of the Union scheme . . . that my sense of duty to the people of Canada myself would leave me no alternative except to apply for my immediate recall." A bit disingenuously, he added that he

wasn't mentioning his possible resignation "by way of threat."

Macdonald's reply, one day later,
began by saying that Monck's letter
had "distressed" him greatly. Thereafter, he conceded nothing. "The proceedings have arrived at the stage
that success is certain and it is now
not a question of strategy. It is merely
one of tactic," he wrote. This tactic
involved picking "the proper moment
for projecting the local scheme [the
provincial constitutions]." Macdonald
then showed his own mailed fist:
"With respect to the best mode of
guiding the measure through the
House, I think I must ask Your
Excellency to leave somewhat to my

Governor General Monck. He and Macdonald had their disagreements, but they worked well together, making sure that Tilley had enough money to win the key election in New Brunswick for Confederation.

Canadian Parliamentary experience." The fist having been shown,
Macdonald offered a conciliatory hand: Monck must not resign
because "to you belongs . . . all the kudos and all the position (not
to be lightly thrown away) which must result from being a founder
of a nation." After that delicate reminder of the relationship
between Monck's prospects for future Imperial employment and
the achievement of Confederation, Macdonald ended jauntily, as he
so often did, "My lame finger makes me write rather indistinctly. I
hope you can read this note."

Monck's reply, written the day he received Macdonald's letter,
was almost as deft. While he accepted without question "your
right as a leader of the Government to take your own line," he
nevertheless reserved the right to advise Macdonald against "a
course of conduct which I consider injudicious." He retained his

right to resign should Macdonald continue to "hang back now when all other parties to the matter are prepared to move on." Thereafter, Macdonald moved no faster than before, but some of the tensions each felt had been released. And their relationship remained as cordial as ever, even surviving Macdonald's spectacular misdemeanour of so losing control during one visit to the governor general's residence as to vomit over a newly upholstered chair Lady Monck had installed in her drawing room.*

A major cause of Macdonald's shilly-shallying was the most obvious. He was drinking more heavily, more continually than he had ever done before, at times having to grip his desk so he could remain standing in the House. Tiredness and stress made him vulnerable. So did D'Arcy McGee. Night after night they caroused together at Ottawa's Russell Hotel. After one such binge, while Macdonald managed to make it back to his room, McGee wandered off into the night and was found the next morning curled up on the desk of the editor of the *Ottawa Citizen*. Cabinet finally addressed the matter, one minister calling the behaviour of the pair a "disgrace." In response, Macdonald sought out McGee and informed him, "Look here McGee, this Cabinet can't afford two drunkards, and I'm not quitting."

Both continued to drink heavily. On August 6, Brown, now an ordinary member, reported to Anne that "John A. was drunk on Friday and Saturday, and unable to attend the House. Is it not disgraceful?" The *Globe* went into attack mode: Macdonald had not been sober for ten successive days and was unfit for his duties as minister of militia. In fact, it was not until the legisla-

---

* This crashing fall from grace is reported in the biography by Elisabeth Batt, *Monck: Governor General, 1861–1868*. She hedges her bets by saying that although this story is told by Monck's descendants, it should be remembered that "the Irish were ever loath to spoil a good story for lack of a ha-porth' of exaggeration."

ture had adjourned in September that he began to regain control over his drinking. He was able to handle a mini-crisis caused by Galt's resignation from the cabinet after he failed to win his long-sought guarantees for Protestant education in Quebec. After shuffling the ministry, Macdonald still persuaded Galt to come to London as one of Canada's constitutional delegates. In the meantime, though, McGee in particular continued to drink heavily.

That Confederation was now so close yet still remained vulnerable was undoubtedly a major cause of Macdonald's prolonged drinking. But cool calculation may also have influenced his behaviour. As people kept blaming Macdonald for his misdeeds, they paid less attention to the fact that time was indeed slipping steadily by. And that is precisely what Macdonald wanted to happen.[*] His objective was to shrink to a bare minimum the span of time between the moment when the Confederation delegates finally agreed on a revised constitution and the actual introduction of the document into the British Parliament. The longer the gap between those two events, the greater the risk that Confederation critics would learn of any last-minute changes to the original Quebec Resolutions and demand a reopening of the entire debate on the grounds that Canada's Legislative Assembly had approved a different version of Confederation.[†] Macdonald explained his stratagem to Tilley in a letter on October 6: "The Bill should not be finally settled until just before the meeting of

---

[*] An apt description of what Macdonald was doing would be "ragging the puck," except that hockey was then so new that the phrase had yet to be minted.

[†] In fact, the *Globe* got hold of a summary of the BNA Bill and published it in late February 1867, fiercely attacking the shifts in jurisdiction to favour Ottawa and the increase in subsidies to the Maritimes. By that time, though, it was all too little, too late.

the British Parliament"; the measure had to be "carried *per saltum*—with a rush. No echo of it must reverberate through the British provinces until it becomes law." Premature disclosure could "excite new and fierce agitation on this side of the Atlantic." But, he promised, "the Act once passed and beyond remede, the people will soon be reconciled to it."

Not until the end of November 1866 did the Canadians finally make it to London. They—Macdonald, Cartier, Galt, Hector-Louis Langevin (a rising Quebec *bleu*) and two Reform ministers, William McDougall and William Howland—all stayed at the now-familiar Westminster Palace Hotel, looking out on Westminster Abbey and with the Houses of Parliament across the road.* Already ensconced there were the two five-member Maritime delegations, headed by Tupper and Tilley. In getting them to join this final, climactic phase of a project that by now had been going on for more than two years, Macdonald and the Fenians had played critical roles. For the Maritimes, though, the decisive force had been that of Britain—far less by its "turn[ing] of the screw" than by the irresistible pull of loyalty. In the end, what caused Maritimers to come in was their realization that in order to remain British, they had to become Canadians.

---

* One of the particular attractions of the Westminster Palace Hotel was that it had been equipped with that new technological marvel, an elevator.

TWENTY-TWO

The Man of the Conference

~

I had a merry Xmas alone in my own room and my
dinner of tea & toasts & drank all your healths.
John A. Macdonald, in a letter to Louisa

The last of the three Confederation conferences began on December 4, 1866, at London's Westminster Palace Hotel, in an elongated ground-floor room used most of the time for lectures and concerts. The delegates' first order of business was to elect Macdonald as chairman. It was his performance here that prompted Sir Frederic Rogers, the senior Colonial Office mandarin, to describe him as "the ruling genius." Hector-Louis Langevin, the senior Canadien after Cartier, sketched out a similar judgment in a letter to his brother: "Macdonald is a sharp fox. He is a very well informed man, ingratiating, clever and very popular. He is *the man* of the conference."

The conference's second item of business was to keep anti-Confederate critics in a state of sullen ignorance by making sure that everything done inside the room stayed there. At Macdonald's urging, the delegates agreed that "no minutes of the various discussions should be taken, and no record, therefore,

The London Conference was the last of the three conferences that drew up the constitution. The Canadians and the Maritimers were quartered at the grand Westminster Palace Hotel—so grand that it had an elevator.

exists of them."* Macdonald also urged the new colonial secretary, Lord Carnarvon, to "avoid any publicity being given to the resolutions," since this might "tend to premature discussion on imperfect information of the subject both in this country and America." A key reason for this manoeuvring was that Joseph Howe had come over to London and was telling everyone he could persuade to meet him that the project should be halted and that Macdonald was a helpless drunkard. Howe himself, though, was now a forlorn figure. The Halifax *Morning Chronicle* dismissed him as "vanity struck," and he even described himself as "lonely, weary and vexed." He was simply being shunted aside.

Until the conference began, Macdonald used his time to get briefed on the latest twists and turns in British politics caused by

---

* Hewitt Bernard did keep some scanty minutes.

the looming crisis over the Reform Bill and to catch up on news at the Colonial Office. He also got to know the colonial secretary. Despite the gap in their ages, they shared a mutual enthusiasm for the Empire and, from this point on, remained lifelong friends. Carnarvon, while fully briefed about Macdonald's "notorious vice," and angered that Macdonald was "occasionally so drunk as to be incapable of official business for days altogether," yet judged him "the ablest politician in Upper Canada" and reckoned that, without him, the entire Coalition would collapse.

In fact, Macdonald succumbed spectacularly to his "vice" on at least one occasion in London. On December 27 he reported to Louisa that "for fear that an alarming story may reach you, I may as well tell you what occurred." He had come back from a weekend at Lord Carnarvon's country house, took the newspapers to his bed to read, fell asleep and awoke to discover his "bed, bed clothes & curtains all on fire." Macdonald tore down the curtains, dousing them with water, then tore the "blazing" sheets and blankets from the bed and stomped out the flames. With Cartier's help, he made certain that the flames were entirely out. Only then did Macdonald realize that his "hair, forehead & hands [were] scorched." But for wearing a thick flannel shirt under his nightshirt, "I would have been burned to death."* A bad wound on Macdonald's shoulder caused the doctor to order him to bed for three days, and he had to stay on in the hotel for an extra eight days. He ended his note jauntily: "I had a merry Xmas alone in my own room and my dinner of tea & toasts & drank all your healths."

---

* Macdonald was wearing so many garments in bed simply because British buildings in those days were heated only by open fires, windows were single paned and doors gaped.

From the start of the conference, Macdonald's objectives were clear. He wanted the work done as quickly as possible to minimize the risk that a defeat of Lord Derby's government on the Reform Bill would force an election and so delay Confederation's passage beyond the May deadline, when Nova Scotia had to go to the polls. If that happened, there was a distinct possibility that Tupper would be defeated, bringing down with him the entire Confederation project. Indeed, to delay the constitution's passage until after May was the specific reason for Howe's presence in London. No less urgently, Macdonald wanted as few changes as possible to the already agreed upon Quebec Resolutions: each change could lead to others being demanded, and to the potential unravelling of the entire package.

Debate itself could not be avoided. Unlike Canada's Legislative Assembly, neither the Nova Scotia nor the New Brunswick legislatures had approved the Quebec Resolutions; their delegates' mandate was to secure improvements, and only then to sanction Confederation's go-ahead. To negotiate around those obstacles, adroitness was required. Tupper initiated a debate about just how binding were the Quebec Resolutions. Delegates argued both sides of the question. At the right moment, Macdonald pulled them together by declaring that both were right, but within definite limits: "We are quite free to discuss points as if they were open," he said, "although we may be bound to adhere to the Quebec scheme." Macdonald thereby managed to quiet restive Maritimers while keeping any actual amendments to a minimum.

A number of changes were made. Immigration and agriculture were redesignated as joint responsibilities of both levels of government; coastal fisheries and penitentiaries were added to Ottawa's list; and the solemnization of marriages was given to the care of the provinces. There was a long debate about whether, and how, additional senators might be created to resolve a dead-lock between Parliament's two houses, the Senate and the Commons.* The Maritimes won for themselves an increase in their subsidies from Ottawa, although Tupper, probably from overconfidence, gained far less for Nova Scotia than the less-showy Tilley did for New Brunswick. "Confederation" was agreed on as the official term rather than "federation," but con-fusingly the term used throughout the resulting act was "union." The names agreed on for the two Canadian provinces were Quebec and Toronto, the latter being changed later to Ontario.

The single substantive change was to strengthen—a little—Ottawa's role as defender of the educational rights of minorities across the country. This correction came about at the insistence of Galt on behalf of the English minority in Quebec, supported by Archbishop Connolly of Halifax, who lobbied on behalf of his separate schools. The change was small: the federal government was granted the power to intervene in educational matters, but only on occasions when there was a need for "remedial laws." Even this limited authority applied only to school systems already in place before Confederation.

All this work was done in a couple of weeks; indeed, twenty-nine of the Quebec Resolutions were dealt with on the first day. Revised clauses were hurried over to the legal draftsmen at the Colonial Office. There, the chief draftsman, F.S. Reilly, complained at one time, "I can't make bricks without clay, to say nothing of straw."

One change that might have greatly altered Canadian history never happened. A year earlier, when Confederation had seemed

---

* The British authorities insisted on adding a provision authorizing the cabinet to appoint extra senators under exceptional circumstances. This power was first used by Prime Minister Brian Mulroney in 1990 to secure passage of the Goods and Services' Tax Bill through a Liberal-dominated Senate.

Inside this room at the hotel, the delegates settled the last clauses of the British North America Act. A top British official described Macdonald as "the ruling genius."

imminent, a legal draftsman at Westminster, Henry Thring, had drawn up draft legislation by which Canada could opt to become independent from Britain at any time by a two-thirds' vote in both the Commons and Senate. At around the same time, a British politician, Lord Bury, who had served in Canada as an aide to the governor general, proposed that an agreement be negotiated that would allow either Canada or Britain to terminate the colonial connection by its government giving a year's notice. So far as can be determined, this possibility was never discussed at the London Conference. Macdonald would very likely have vetoed it, because of his own attachment to Britain and out of concern that it might provoke a backlash in Canada against Confederation. Indeed, Howe at this time was reporting to Nova Scotia anti-Confederates his dismay at "the almost universal feeling . . . that *uniting the provinces was an easy mode of getting rid of them.*" In fact, Canada's status as a colony would not be ended—legally—until the Statute of Westminster in 1931. Had the constitution included from its start an agreed way to achieve independence, it's more likely that the leap to national maturity would have been taken a lot earlier.

The most significant change was one made to prevent another change from happening. All along, Macdonald had intended that the new nation should be called the Kingdom of Canada.* In one speech during the 1865 Confederation Debates, he had gone further, suggesting that the Queen should be represented in the new nation by "one of her own family, a Royal prince, as a Viceroy to rule over us." (The Queen, as it turned out, had been musing similarly about how "dearest Albert had often thought of the Colonies for our sons.")[†] At one stage during the London Conference, Macdonald tried out alternative titles, writing in the margin of a handwritten draft of the bill: "Province, Dependency, Colony, Dominion, Vice-Royalty, Kingdom." This last title was used in all the drafts of the constitution sent by the delegates to the Colonial Office until early February.[‡]

---

* Feo Monck, in her diary about the 1864 Quebec Conference, recalled Macdonald telling her teasingly that the new nation might be called "Canadin" and, as might well have actually happened, that "in some speeches he had said that, to please the Nova Scotians, it should be called 'Acadia.'" She concluded, "John A. is very agreeable."

[†] At the time, it was widely assumed that the likeliest sibling to be sent to rule Canada as its King was the third son, Prince Arthur. He did in fact make it, although in a lesser role. In 1911, Prince Arthur, by then the Duke of Connaught, was appointed governor general, serving until 1916. He died in 1942, at the age of ninety-one.

[‡] Quite different, though, was the first draft of the British North America Bill as sent from the Colonial Office to the delegates at the Westminster Palace Hotel. To the fury of the Canadians, this version used the word "colony" throughout, declaring that the provinces were to be "united into one colony." The offending word was struck out and never used again.

Just before the bill's final version—there were seven drafts in all—the nation's title was changed to the Dominion of Canada.* It was done by Prime Minister Lord Derby on the advice of Carnarvon,† who feared that Americans would interpret monarchical nomenclature as a deliberate provocation. There were, in fact, grounds for this worry: the British minister at Washington reported that newspaper speculation that Canada might become a kingdom had provoked "much comment of an unfriendly character." Macdonald never forgot or forgave this dismissal of his dream. In 1889 he wrote to the then colonial secretary, Lord Knutsford, recounting that he had once described to Disraeli what had happened, and that Disraeli's response had been, "It is so like Derby—a very good fellow but who lives in a region of perpetual funk."

The well-known story about "dominion" is that its author was Tilley, who informed the conference delegates that he had come upon in the Bible, in Psalm 72, verse 8, the evocative phrase, "And he shall have dominion also from sea to sea." This account is certainly correct.‡ The full story may have been a bit more complicated. The use of the term "dominion" for such a purpose was

---

* A problem with the chosen title, "Dominion," overlooked by the London Conference delegates, was that no ready translation for the term exists in French. The one most often used, "La Puissance," is hardly satisfactory.

† Carnarvon reached this judgment despite Monck's counter-argument that "Kingdom" would meet "the natural yearning of a growing people to emerge . . . from the provincial phase of existence."

‡ Tilley's authorship was confirmed by his son, also called Leonard, in a letter he wrote on June 28, 1917, on the eve of Confederation's half-century, to the High Court registrar in Toronto. He recounted that his father had told him how he came upon the phrase in his daily Bible reading, and, "When he went back to the sitting of the convention that morning," he had suggested the title, "which was agreed to."

not in fact new. It was applied to the brief confederation of American colonies, known as the Dominion of New England, which lasted from 1686 to 1689. As well, Virginia, until it became a state, was known as "The Old Dominion."

All these details were marginalia. The central fact was that Confederation had been agreed to by all the constituent provinces. The later "compact" theory, that Confederation constituted a treaty negotiated by the provinces, was pure myth; none of them, as colonies, had the power to sign treaties. Lord Carnarvon, on behalf of the enabling power, Britain, explained in his parliamentary speech that the new dominion "derives its political existence from an external authority"—namely, the Imperial government.

The constitution itself, as Macdonald had wanted from the start, amounted to a prescription for a highly centralized confederation, very likely the most centralized confederation ever conceived (not least because it granted to the central government the power to disallow provincial legislation). Indeed, as the historian Peter Waite has written, "One might almost say that Canada has become a federal state in spite of its constitution."* It was indeed plausible, as Macdonald kept saying in private letters, that the provinces might wither away to municipalities.

The fact was, though, the provinces *did* exist. They were accountable to their voters through political mechanisms—of organized parties, elections and parliamentary debates—identical to those of the "senior" government. They were also, as

---

* Waite included this sentence in his 1953 doctoral thesis, "Ideas and Politics in British North America, 1864–66."

was inherent in so vast a country, incomparably closer to their people. As Macdonald had schemed for all along, the federal government was accorded not just extensive powers but all the unassigned powers, and as well a national override power. Yet although the newcomers, Nova Scotia and New Brunswick, lost some of their existing powers on joining Confederation, they still wielded considerable ones. The two reborn "internal" members, Quebec and Ontario, gained powers greater than their institutional ancestors had ever possessed (if only because, back then, all power resided with the governors general).

Macdonald, moreover, failed to anticipate the consequence to his centralized scheme of the absence from federal jurisdiction of one vital power. Post-Confederation, just as before, Canada was still only a colony; responsibility for foreign affairs remained in London. Ottawa, unlike Washington, could not summon up national support on the grounds that it was responsible for Canadians' doings and reputation in the wider world. In the absence of any shared sense of national identity across the country (really, until the 1960s), the vacuum was bound to be filled by provincial identities. This flaw in Macdonald's concept of the new nation was recognized by Goldwin Smith in an almost eerily perceptive article for *Macmillan's Magazine* in March 1865. There he wrote that while "the sentiment of provincial independence among the several provinces of British North America is at this moment merged in the desire of combining against the common danger [the United States] . . . [w]hen the danger is overpast, divergent interests may reappear and the sentiment of independence may revive . . . especially in the French and Catholic province." It was because national identity was pallid for so long that provincial identities commanded so much support.

In no sense was the British North America Act a constitution made for the people. There was nowhere in it any ringing "We, the people" proclamation. It was, instead, a constitution made for governments. Over the decades, the balance between centralization and decentralization of governmental powers has settled down into pretty much what most Canadians want. Pragmatism has triumphed over principle, and muddling through over theory. Macdonald would disagree with the resulting decentralization, but as a pragmatist and as a believer that politics is about people, he would be delighted by the process.

~

Today, just one part of the British North America Act—now the Constitution Act, 1867—is familiar to any number of Canadians. It is widely known that the Fathers of Confederation defined their new nation by the talismanic mantra of "Peace, Order and good Government." It is also widely known that this self-description contrasts radically with the idealistic but aggressive aspiration laid upon Americans by their constitutional call to "life, liberty and the pursuit of happiness." In fact, this phrase occurs not in the constitution of the American people but in their Declaration of Independence. But it's the contrast between these two rallying cries, and the illumination it provides about national differences, that matter.

Except that most of this is untrue. More exactly, it is true symbolically, but untrue substantively.

The phrase actually contained in the documents laid before the delegates at the Quebec Conference of 1864 (from which came the greatest part of the BNA Act), and at the start of the Confederation Debates in the Canadian Parliament in 1865 and at the London Conference, was "Peace, Welfare and good Government." The second, unfamiliar, term, "Welfare," was used here in the sense of well-being. It was only at the last moment before the constitution was introduced into the Parliament at Westminster that "Welfare" was replaced by "Order."* The actual change was most probably made by the British legal draftsman Francis Reilly; and no evidence exists that Reilly ever discussed his choice of words with Macdonald or with any Canadian.

To get to the heart of the matter, no evidence exists that at any time throughout any of the three Confederation conferences, or during the long debate in the Canadian legislature, anyone paid the least attention to the phrase itself. The more than one thousand double-columned pages of the published Confederation Debates contain only a handful of references to "Peace, Welfare and good Government" (as it then was); moreover, it was raised almost always in discussions about the narrow issue of marriages and divorces.†

The reason why no one paid any attention to the phrase was straightforward: it actually meant very little. It amounted to a kind of legal boilerplate that was inserted routinely into all kinds of British colonial constitutions—from Newfoundland to New Zealand to New South Wales, from Ceylon to the Cape Colony (of South Africa), from Sierra Leone to St. Helena. The use of this

---

* Not until January 23, 1867, does the familiar "Peace, Order and good Government" triad appear in a draft. This version reappears in the later drafts of January 30 and February 2 and then in the actual BNA Act.

† One of the very few substantial references during the entire Confederation process to the phrase "Peace, Order and good Government" was made not by any Father of Confederation but by its godfather, Colonial Secretary Lord Carnarvon. In his speech in the Lords introducing the British North America Bill, he said that the powers of the federal government "extend to all laws made for the 'peace, order and good government' of Confederation"—a term he described as having "an ample measure of legislative authority."

The author has been able to find only one early use of "peace and order" in its contemporary descriptive sense. The anti-Confederate Howe once described phrase can be dated all the way back to 1689.* It appeared in every Canadian constitution before Confederation, from the Royal Proclamation of 1763† to the 1841 Act of Union, which conjoined Upper and Lower Canada. The phrase that Canadians now embrace as distinctively their own was thus employed in the service of just about any entity in the Empire for which a constitution was needed.

Perhaps the most insightful comment ever made about the ways by which national communities acquire their particular character was from British-born international scholar Benedict Anderson. According to him, almost all of them amount to "imagined communities." Few citizens in any of these societies know many other citizens personally, "yet in the minds of each," wrote Anderson, "lives this image of communion." People, that is to say, become what they are by the way that they think they are.

Not long after the Second World War, Canadians took cognizance of the fact that the British Empire was vanishing from the map and that its role as global hegemon had been taken over by the United States. Canada was threatened by being absorbed into this new imperium, of being reduced to a kind of virtual colony. Cross-border differences therefore became central to national existence itself, because if no differences existed, survival became pointless. In 1961 the historian W.L. Morton published *The Canadian Identity*, a book composed of four major lectures that he had given. In this work, Morton expressed the notion of a rad-

---

the Maritimes as "accustomed to peace and order," in contrast to the belligerent, boastful Canadians. And he made this remark back in 1849.

* The phrase's origin is most probably in John Locke's *Two Treatises of Government* of that same year of 1689, where Locke described government's purpose as "the Peace, Security and publick good of the people."

† The form used in the Royal Proclamation of 1763, the earliest appearance of the phrase in Canada, was "Public Peace, Welfare, and good Government."

ical difference between Canada and the United States from their very beginnings. "Not life, liberty and the pursuit of happiness," wrote Morton, "but peace, order and good government, are what the national government of Canada guarantees." So far as this author has been able to determine, Morton was the first person to present the concept that the "Peace, Order and good Government" of Macdonald's constitution *is* Canada, in the same way that Jefferson's "Life, liberty and the pursuit of happiness" *is* the United States.

Not long afterwards, "Peace, Order and good Government"— known to Ottawa insiders as POGG—was elevated into a defining national invocation. It has gone on to become the one item of our original constitution that almost every Canadian can recite—and holds to fiercely.[*]

It's as though, when Canadians learned of the phrase "Peace, Order and good Government" for the first time in the sixties, they, in the mysterious way by which the collective will can exert itself, said more or less simultaneously, "That's us." The constitution's real patriation can thus be dated from the early sixties rather than from its formal enactment in 1982. It was during those years that the people of Canada made the constitution—at the very least one vital part of it—*their* constitution. Maybe it's coincidence, maybe it's karma, but Macdonald, as a conservative, could not have defined the purpose of a constitution better than as "Peace, Order and good Government."[†]

---

[*] To appreciate why Morton's insight should have had such a consciousness-raising effect, it should be remembered that right afterwards—in 1965—George Grant published his seminal *Lament for a Nation*, which itself had so powerful an effect among Canadian nationalists.

[†] Much of the material for this section was provided by the research staff of the Library of Parliament. A number of the facts are drawn from a groundbreaking article by the historian Stephen Eggleston in the *Journal of Canadian Studies*.

At the time, Macdonald won just about everything he wanted. All the last-minute changes made in London strengthened the power of the central government. The federation would indeed be as close to a "legislative union" as was politically practical. These, though, were tactical accomplishments. In themselves, Confederation and the constitution that necessarily accompanied it amounted to not much more than a political fix of a political problem—"deadlock"—that the politicians, Macdonald included, had created themselves. That purpose could have been achieved as easily, almost certainly more so, by a "mini-federation" encompassing just the United Province of Canada. Such a nation, though, would have been a rump of a nation. What was being created instead was, at least potentially, a continental nation—one that would be, or could be, a real nation, marked at its birth by the extravagant ambition both of its geographical reach and of its commitment to British law and British political institutions. As such, it made a commitment to be and to remain that most improbable of all political communities—an un-American nation within North America. First, Macdonald had imagined a Canadian community of this kind; then, in London, he realized it.

All that remained now were details. Howe took his arguments for delay to as many people as he could secure introductions to in Britain. Lord Carnarvon heard him out politely, but without response; almost all the others showed the same indifference. All that remained between Macdonald and his final triumph was a thin red line of British MPs—few of them interested in the colonies at the best of times, and all of them now totally absorbed by the crisis over the Reform Bill and the prospect of an imminent election.

In Macdonald's circumstances—he knew by now he would soon be invited formally to become the first prime minister of the new nation—many would have gloated or at least have celebrated. Instead, Macdonald stayed close to Carnarvon, fussing and worrying over the last details. His one celebratory gesture was to slip over to France for a few days' holiday when things had quieted down.

Once the delegates had finished their last fixes, Francis Reilly, the legal draftsman, worked overtime through the first week of February to render it into proper parliamentary form. The bill was set in type under conditions of strict confidentiality through the nights of February 6 and 7. On February 12 it was introduced into the House of Lords—there, rather than the Commons, because that's where Carnarvon had his seat. The debate was scheduled for February 19, 1867.

TWENTY-THREE

Two Unions

My diaries as Miss Bernard did not need such precautions but then I
was an insignificant spinster & what I might write did not matter; now
I am a great premier's wife & Lady Macdonald & "Cabinet secrets and
mysteries" might drop unwittingly from the nib of my pen.

Lady Macdonald, in the first entry of her new diary, July 5, 1867

In the brief gap between the last few days of haggling over
the clauses of the constitution and the document's actual
introduction into the Parliament at Westminster in the
form of the British North America Bill, Macdonald found
time for one other assignment. He got married. His second wife
was Susan Agnes Bernard, the sister of Hewitt Bernard, his principal civil service aide, originally his private secretary, and now
head of his staff at the Attorney General's Department—and
also his friend and apartment mate at the "Quadrilateral," a
house on Daly Street in Ottawa.

Their marriage was a union of mutual self-interest. He, now
on the verge of becoming prime minister of the Dominion of
Canada, would soon need a hostess and a chatelaine. She, by now
aged thirty-one, needed to escape a future of ever-diminishing
choices. Besides asymmetric needs, they possessed in common
one defining quality: each revelled in the exercise of power.
Agnes, in the diary that she began right after the first Dominion

Susan Agnes Bernard. She is still five years away from marrying Macdonald, young and slender here, unlike in later photographs. She appears to be wearing a costume.

Day,* expressed her addiction the more self-critically: "I also know that my love of Power is strong, so strong that I sometimes dread it; it influences me when I imagine I am influenced by a sense of right." To Macdonald, power was like a comfortable old suit he had no need to apologize for wearing. "I don't care for office for the sake of money, but for the sake of power; for the sake of carrying out my own view of what's best for the country," he once said.

They differed in quite a few respects, from religiosity, of which Agnes possessed an excess, and he little if at all, to her far greater capacity for physicality, as in the epic ride she would take through the tunnels and curves of the Rocky Mountains on the cowcatcher of a Canadian Pacific Railway engine while, most of the time, her grumpy husband, the prime minister, remained rooted in his seat in the special car laid on for them.

The difference between them that defined their relationship was that, while Macdonald respected Agnes, was always polite and considerate, and never deviated in his loyalty, she adored him, if not at the start of their union, which was in no sense a love match, then soon after, and ever after, completely and joyously and defencelessly. Although strong and confident in so

---

* Lady Macdonald's diary covers the years 1867 to 1869 with some regularity, but later entries are few and far between. Her diary is the only known one kept by a Canadian prime ministerial spouse.

many respects, as Agnes Bernard most certainly was, at times not merely cajoling him but outright bullying him, and later ruling Ottawa society like a moralizing martinet, she, in her relationship with Macdonald, seemed always to be running to catch up to him while trying never to show how hard she was trying. "I have found something worth living for—living in—my husband's heart and love," she wrote in the diary. Her most revealing comment about herself to herself was "I often look in astonishment at him," referring, surely, both to astonished delight in his almost infinite variety, and even more to her delighted amazement that he should be hers.

Although the marriage was arranged with speed, the courtship between them extended over more than a half-dozen years and may have included an earlier offer of marriage. The original obstacle to any union was, of course, Macdonald's drinking. Bernard would later tell his fellow deputy minister Edmund Meredith that he had done "everything to dissuade his sister from the marriage." To resolve the obstacle, Bernard got Macdonald to sign a marriage contract that committed him to pay sixteen thousand dollars into a trust for Lady Macdonald, thereby protecting her and any children of theirs, but also benefiting Macdonald, since this money could no longer be claimed by his creditors.* To raise the initial funds, Macdonald sold one hundred acres of land in Kingston and deposited his life-insurance policy into the trust. As dowry, Lady Macdonald brought neither money nor looks. A contemporary described her as "tall, tawny, and . . . rather 'raw-boned' and angular."

---

* Marriage contracts of this kind were quite common—most particularly when the woman was bringing property into the union and would immediately lose control over it to her husband—until the passage of the Married Women's Property Act of 1887.

In later photographs, particularly as she became, at one and the same time, stouter and more commanding, she comes across as stern and censorious. In the one early photograph taken before their marriage, she is much slimmer and, if not exactly attractive, wholly agreeable rather than the gorgon she came to be. One photograph of her inclining backwards over a chair conveys not just her physical exuberance but a clear awareness of her own sexuality. (Mid-nineteenth-century photographs showed women to disadvantage: the long period of motionlessness required for the exposure invested men with a portentous gravitas but diminished women's natural animation.) She was highly intelligent, well travelled, well read, accustomed to social situations and fluent in French. Bilingualism, though, didn't cause Agnes to share Macdonald's partiality to French Canadians: "The French seem always wanting everything, and they get everything," she wrote crossly. She was also strong, determined and thoroughly bossy.

She was born in Jamaica in 1836, the only daughter among the four sons of a wealthy sugar-plantation owner, Thomas Bernard.* Following her father's death from cholera, Agnes and her mother moved to England and then, in 1854, to Barrie, Ontario, where her brother Hewitt was practising law. There, just turned twenty, she revealed her fearlessness about physical adventure by ice-fishing and by tobogganing even at night, "tearing down a steep forest roadway and scudding away, breathless, disheveled and nearly shaken to death, over the frozen surface of some lonely pine-fringed lake," as she later portrayed it in a magazine article. Agnes may have been describing here one of her attractions to Macdonald: her physical boldness and athleticism would have

---

* Her ancestry, through her mother, was Scottish.

reassured him that she would not turn into another wifely invalid like Isabella. The decisive influence on her girlhood had surely been her mother, Theodora, a deeply religious woman of demanding and domineering piety. Theodora's death, in 1875, caused the minister who broke the news to a distraught Agnes to "fear for [her] sanity."

In 1858, Hewitt had become Macdonald's secretary, and the future couple—Macdonald by now a newly bereaved widower—had a brief encounter at a concert in Toronto. Agnes's later recollection was acute: "A forcible, yet changeful face, with such a mixture of strength and vivacity, and his bushy, dark peculiar hair as he leaned on his elbows and looked down." Macdonald's recollection had about it a distinct dollop of his "soft sawder": he praised her "very fine eyes," while taking care to avoid getting their colour wrong by not mentioning it. (Agnes's eyes, like her hair, were in fact a striking jet black.)

When the government moved to Quebec City, the Bernards moved with it. They both attended the Valentine's Day Ball that Macdonald organized with such panache in 1860. Some kind of relationship appears to have developed as a result, with Macdonald later calling on Theodora at Hewitt's suggestion that he meet his mother—his unmarried sister being of course the real reason for the arranged encounter. There were rumours of a marriage proposal made but rejected. While Macdonald was by now famous and powerful, besides being charming and witty, he was also a notorious drunk. It's easy to guess that Theodora put her foot down and that Hewitt, despite his loyalty to Macdonald, confirmed the damning reports. Anyway, Macdonald had no pressing need then for a chatelaine and hostess. In 1865 the distaff Bernards moved on to London, where they occupied a grand house on Grosvenor Square. Of life in England, Agnes commented shrewdly that it was "a delicious country for the rich, but I should hate it for the poor," while the middle class had to "toady and fawn."

She and Macdonald met by happenstance, on December 8, 1866, while both were sauntering down Bond Street. However it happened, the relationship developed with lightning speed, much as it had between Macdonald and Isabella. By Christmas they were engaged.

They wed six weeks later, at St. George's Anglican Church in Hanover Square, on February 16, 1867. (It was a most fashionable church. Two British prime ministers were married there, Disraeli and Asquith, and one American president, Theodore Roosevelt). It was all done so quickly that there was no time for reading the banns, for which a special dispensation had to be secured from the Archbishop of Canterbury. For the occasion, Macdonald wore a "Superfine Black Dress Coat with sleeve linings [and] corded silk

Registration record of the February 16, 1867, marriage of John A. Macdonald, "widower," and Susan Agnes Bernard, "spinster," both being of "full" age.

breast facing," as well as a sword. Agnes wore a long dress of white satin and a veil of Brussels lace. The bridesmaids included the daughters of three of the Fathers of Confederation. After the service, Hewitt Bernard hosted a breakfast for ninety at the Westminster Palace Hotel; the *Ottawa Citizen* reported that "a bunch of violets and snow-drops" adorned each plate. In his speech, Macdonald compared his union with Agnes with the one he was on the verge of completing with the provinces. In the marriage register, Macdonald changed his "profession" from that of "cabinet-maker," as he'd given in Charlottetown. Here, with surely a twinkle in his eye, he listed it as "Hon-ble"—Honourable.*

The happy couple honeymooned in Oxford. Then they returned hurriedly in time to hear the British North America Bill being introduced into the House of Lords.

Agnes and John A. were always husband and wife, rather than partners in the manner of the Disraelis† or of George and Anne Brown. But they connected intimately at two vital points. Macdonald possessed a first-rate mind: he read omnivorously, had an exceptional memory and would quote in the legislature and Parliament from novelists such as Dickens and Trollope, from Shakespeare, and from parliamentary greats such as Pitt and Peel and Sheridan and Walpole. Agnes, similarly, was highly intelligent and read at least as much (certainly more novels, often reading them while waiting in his office for him at the end of a long

---

* The details about Macdonald's self-designation as "Honourable" and of the other distinguished marriages at St. George's Church were uncovered by the journalist Arthur Milnes on a research trip to London.

† Disraeli once paid his wife, Mary, the highest-possible matrimonial compliment by telling her she was "more a mistress than a wife." At the end of a long day in the Commons, Disraeli returned home to find Mary had stayed up waiting for him with a bottle of cooled champagne and a pork pie from Fortnum and Mason.

day in the Commons). In the provincial Canada of those days, there weren't many like this pair. Agnes provided Macdonald with an opportunity to stretch his intellectual wings beyond the usual politician's fare of government reports and newspapers and campaign anecdotes. She gave him someone he could talk to about ideas and literature, and about such un-Canadian topics as beauty. They were partners as well in another joint enterprise. It took Agnes a long time, it wasn't in the least easy, and there were many setbacks, but because of her care and watchfulness and bullying, Macdonald eventually broke the grip of alcohol on himself. If the biographer E.B. Biggar is right, Agnes may have extended his life by two decades.

Nevertheless, Macdonald for most of the time was a politician, with political jobs to be done. Agnes, for her part, had to set out now to learn the tasks and tricks of being a political wife. One learning experience came quickly. Just over a week after becoming Mrs. John A. Macdonald, Agnes, accompanied by Lady Carnarvon, was presented to the Queen in a general audience at Buckingham Palace. Macdonald afterwards wrote to Louisa, "My wife likes it from its novelty to her, but it rather bores me as I have seen it all before." His indifference was pure posture; Agnes, though, had yet to learn to pretend that she wasn't impressed.

The passage of the British North America Act through the Parliament of Westminster began, in the House of Lords, on February 12. In his speech, Carnarvon laid it on lavishly: "We are laying the foundation of a great State—perhaps one that at a future day may even overshadow this country . . . we have shown neither indifference to their wishes nor jealousy of their aspirations." Macdonald heard it all from the gallery, with Agnes beside him. He was surely reassured by the almost complete absence of any expressions of dissent. But he must also have been worried that the crisis in the government caused by Disraeli's insistence on introducing a new version of the Reform Bill to extend the franchise yet more widely might cause the government's defeat and Parliament's closure for an election. Even if a breakup were avoided, the crisis would make it ever harder for the British parliamentarians to find the time to deal with so minor a matter as a new constitution for an old colony.

On February 26, the British North America Bill slipped through the Lords, despite the appeals of some members that the measure should be temporarily set aside so that Parliament could address "a prospect which affects its own existence"—namely, the Reform Bill. Just one day later, the bill was hurriedly introduced into the Commons.

A brief moment of release from the pressure came Macdonald's way. He and four of the delegates were presented to the Queen in a private audience. Macdonald knelt and kissed the extended hand. As he later wrote to Louisa, "On rising, she said, 'I am very glad to see you on this mission.'" He told her how loyal Canadians were to the Crown: "H.M. said—'It is a very important measure, and you have all exhibited so much loyalty.'" Queen Victoria could influence many things, but not how Parliament did its business.

In the Commons, responsibility for piloting the bill through the chamber fell to the junior minister for the colonies, C.B. Adderley. To head off attempts to amend specific clauses in the bill, he described the measure as "a matter of a most delicate treaty and compact between the Provinces," thereby providing ammunition for generations of Canadian constitutional lawyers.*

---

* Earlier, Carnarvon, for the same purpose of limiting debate, had called the bill "in the nature of a treaty." *The Daily News* commented tartly that it was, in fact, "merely an inter-colonial project."

Criticism came from the Radical John Bright, an ardent advocate of liberating the colonies to look after themselves. As must have delighted Macdonald, Bright gave an indifferent speech and failed to attract any support.

On March 4 the House went into committee to study the details. Almost no changes were asked for or even mentioned. That same day the crisis over the Reform Bill broke: Disraeli had presented to the cabinet his radical scheme for increasing the franchise—the start of his rise to the prime ministership as the champion of an alliance of the aristocracy and the working class against their common enemy, the new middle class. Three Conservative ministers, Carnarvon among them, resigned in protest at this dangerous sally into democracy.

Adderley, though, remained at his post. Suddenly, it was all over. On Friday, March 8, the bill passed third reading without a single word of debate and with the Commons clerk gabbling through the clauses so fast that few MPs could have understood a word of what it was they were voting on. On March 29 the Queen granted Royal Assent.

In fact, it had all happened too easily and too quickly. An anti-Confederate Nova Scotian watching the scene from the gallery wrote home, "The great body of the house was utterly indifferent, even the [Canadian] delegates seemed chagrined at the lazy contempt with which a thin House suffered their bill to pass unnoticed . . . this utter indifference was more mortifying to me than positive opposition. . . . It showed they considered Colonist beings so little related to them as the inhabitants of some nameless Chinese mud village."

Macdonald, in his 1889 letter to the then colonial secretary, Lord Knutsford, looked back with regret and anger: "This remarkable event in the history of the British Empire passed almost without notice." The British politicians had been "quite unable, from the constitution of their minds, to rise to the occasion." Confederation had been treated "much as if the B.N.A. Act were a private Bill uniting two or three English parishes."* Macdonald's rage at the diminution of his and of Canada's historic achievement was understandable, even if allowance is made for the fact that the obsession of the British MPs with the crisis over their Reform Bill was also valid. Of course, being British, the instant the British North America Bill was done with, the MPs switched to debate enthusiastically a bill to reform the system of funding homes for "Destitute Dogs." D'Arcy McGee understood best what had happened: "Everyone knew the result was a foregone conclusion, and they are not apt in England to debate matters already decided."

There were, inevitably, some serious flaws in the constitution that would govern the Canadian Confederation from its birth. No provision was made for amendments to the constitution. The most vital part of any federation, and always its most contentious—the allocation of different powers to the different levels of government—was done quickly and negligently (no thought given to the status of cities, for example), and with scarcely any debate at all. The Aboriginal people were entirely overlooked. Whereas the Royal Proclamation of 1763 had declared that Indians "should not be molested or disturbed" on their historic hunting grounds, no mention of them was made in the British North America Act, except to identify Indians as a subject of federal jurisdiction.

---

* British MPs were famously uninterested in colonial affairs. On one occasion a debate was held in the Commons to determine why this should be so: few attended, and the debate ended inconclusively.

MAP OF
THE CONFEDERATE PROVINCES
OF
BRITISH NORTH AMERICA.
Engraved expressly
for the
CANADIAN ALMANAC,
1867.
Published by
W. C. Chewett & Co.
17 & 19 King Street East, Toronto.

The Canada Macdonald Made

Lastly, two provinces—Prince Edward Island and Newfoundland—remained outside Confederation and so outside its constitution. Typically, the Newfoundlanders said no with a flourish: Confederation was roundly rejected in an election in 1869, with the leading anti-Confederate, Charles Fox Bennett, warning that if they joined, their sons would end up as cannon-fodder, "leaving their bones to bleach in a foreign land."

Still, the act encompassed substantial achievements. It was the first ever constitution to be written by the colonials themselves. It enshrined protection for a minority people, even if only in the limited, permissive form of declaring that the French language "may" be used in Parliament and federal courts. It created a strong central government, and also—not an easy feat to pull off simultaneously—provincial governments with the potential to be strong. It created, or so everyone at the time assumed, a new Canadian common market: Clause 121 provided that "All Articles of the Growth, Produce or Manufacture of any one of the Provinces ... shall be admitted free into each of the other Provinces." It was used later as a blueprint for the 1877 draft confederation of the South Africa Act and for Gladstone's 1886 proposed Home Rule for Ireland.

At the time, all that really mattered was that the deed was done. Canada was about to emerge in the world as a confederation. Once so reconfigured, it could, as its constitution provided for specifically, extend itself right across the entire top half of the continent, initially eastwards, subsequently westwards. This achievement wouldn't make Canada's survival certain, but it would transform Canada's geopolitical character. Until then, the British-American colonies had added up to little more than the accidental detritus of empire—semi-detached statelets somehow left behind in a remote nest of the mother country when the American colonies struck out on their own. In their place there now would be a state with the inherent logic of a community bordered on three sides by salt water and, within these boundaries, stretching out unbrokenly "from sea to sea." The old scattered colonies could never have amounted to more than states in transition; the new one would have the potential to be a permanent state, provided only that its people so willed.

Canadians themselves had created this new state by an exercise of political will that matched almost exactly the one Macdonald had laid down at Quebec City just over two years earlier: "We must, therefore, become important, not only to England but in the eyes of foreign states. And most especially to the United States. . . . The great security for peace is to convince the world of our strength by being united."

The single most important decision taken by Canadians in the nineteenth century was not to form a confederation but, rather, not to become American. Confederation mattered decisively, of course: it was the necessary means to achieve a national unity, and a national ambition, that others would notice and respect. But it was only a means, not an end. That end was a non-American nation-state in North America with enough of the stuff, of will and nerve, to survive—and, no less, with an unbroken connection to Britain. It was, moreover, an uncommonly ambitious nation. Included in its constitution was a pledge—indeed, "a duty of the Government and Parliament of Canada"—to build a railway to Halifax and to the Atlantic, and to begin this construction within six months in order to bind the Maritimes to Canada's heartland. Even more ambitious, and again included in the very constitution of the new nation, was provision for adding to this new nation the vast expanse of "Rupert's Land and the North-Western Territory." It was to be a union not so much of those provinces that joined Confederation but of all the top half of the North American continent.

It was by making this union that Macdonald made us. He made us in the way he had intended to all along—and he made us his way.

TWENTY-FOUR

Idea in the Wilderness

~

A brilliant future would certainly await us were it not for those
wretched Yankees who hunger & thirst for Naboth's field.
John A. Macdonald

Macdonald and Agnes were back in Canada by early May 1867, proceeding directly to Ottawa. They moved into the "Quadrilateral," the large house that Macdonald had shared with Hewitt Bernard and two legislature members (one of them Galt) ever since the government had moved from Quebec City to Ottawa late in 1865. The members moved out, but Bernard stayed on. These departures created room—sort of—for Macdonald and Agnes, and her mother, Theodora, too. In an instant, Macdonald had gone from solitude to being enfolded within the bosom of a family.*

Marriage hadn't altered Macdonald's best-known personal habit. He had made a solemn marital vow to drink less, but not to

---

* That Agnes's mother and brother lived with her at the start of her marriage prompted historian Keith Johnson to write one of the niftiest footnotes in Canadian historiography—"Macdonald had in-laws the way other people had mice."

never drink at all; "less," as Macdonald undoubtedly reminded himself while taking this vow, can only be a subjective measurement. Soon after Macdonald was back, Deputy Minister Edmund Meredith noted in his diary, "John A. carried out of the lunchroom, hopelessly drunk. What a prospect Mrs. John A. has before her!" On the brighter side of his condition, Macdonald was now being cared for, and was eating more or less regularly. He didn't have to worry about arranging to get the house cleaned or laundry seen to. And Agnes was there to express her own views about how "less" should be measured.

The Ottawa they had come to, and where Macdonald had so far lived only spasmodically between his many recent trips to England, was a lumber town of just under twenty thousand people. Its principal characteristic was to be the most verbally abused town in the country: visitors and its own citizens competed to excoriate the place. No one was ever able to top journalist Goldwin Smith's well-known dismissal of Ottawa as "a sub-Arctic lumber village transformed by royal mandate into a political cockpit." But many tried their best. Feo Monck, the governor general's sister, made two diary entries about Ottawa, one describing it as "squalid," the other as "beastly."* Governor General Monck himself persisted in forecasting that Ottawa would be abandoned as the capital within a few years. Edmund Meredith, glancing back nostalgically at Quebec City, which he had just left, wrote in his diary, "The more I see of Ottawa, the more do I dislike and detest it. . . . Possibly the place may be fit for habitation in 50 years from now."

Meredith was being no more than a pinch pessimistic. Ottawa had no sewers, no gas system, no water supply. Water, so-called,

---

* When the diary was published in 1873, Feo Monck's "beastly" was toned down to "horrid."

was delivered in barrels by door-to-door carts; the contents of one barrel when opened turned out to include a dead cat. The streets were like country roads, so that even a central street like Sparks challenged shoppers to make it from one side to the other through three inches of mud. No trees were planted anywhere within the town.* The river was chock full of logs; there were huge piles of sawdust on its banks; and the three hundred or more sawmills created an incessant noise. It was a rough town: Irish and French loggers engaged in repeated drunken brawls. The handful of "respectable" people ranged from lumber barons to a few professional men. There was an acute shortage of housing, due to the arrival from Quebec City of the politicians and some 350 civil servants, soon to become federal civil servants. Joseph Howe, the anti-Confederate Nova Scotian, called Ottawa "a shabby imitation of Washington"; the *Ottawa Citizen* responded that he was grossly unfair.

There was another deficiency to Ottawa. It was about to become a one-industry town, that industry being politics. No less so, its entire social life and the vital decisions about who was up or down or in or out, and about what should be talked about and what mattered, would henceforth be determined exclusively by politicians, or by their spouses. Goldwin Smith made a shrewd analysis of the consequences: because Ottawa lacked "the tempering and restraining influences which the mixed society of a real capital affords," he wrote, the result would be "an unadulterated element of professional politicians, devoting their whole time to the undivided work of corruption and intrigue."†

---

* This was by no means a failing only of Ottawa. Anna Jameson, in her *Winter Studies and Summer Rambles in Canada of 1838*, noted, "A Canadian settler *hates* a tree, regards it to be destroyed, eradicated, annihilated. . . . The idea of useful or ornamental is seldom associated here even with the most magnificent timber trees."

† Smith was in fact anticipating things. In 1867, the entire new dominion civil service numbered just 2,660. As for the "professional politicians," only a few

Amid all the dross, there was one shining and quite astonishing exception: the three Parliament Buildings—the East Block, West Block and Centre Block—situated on what was then called Barrack's Hill and soon to be renamed Parliament Hill, looking down at the churning Ottawa River far below and, northwards, out to the distant, dark blue rim of the Gatineau Hills. The site was spectacular, and so were the buildings. "The noblest architecture in North American . . . I know of no modern Gothic purer of its kind," pronounced the novelist Anthony Trollope, happening by on a lecture tour in 1861. Most other visitors agreed with him.

Inevitably, though, there were defects. The buildings were too hot in summer and too cold in winter, because—inexplicably—the air vents had been placed close to the ceiling of each room. The main building, designed originally for the 130 members of the old United Province of Canada Legislature, was already too small for the 180 who would be coming in from the now four provinces. And, predictably, the buildings had cost far more than expected: the original estimate at the start of construction in 1860 had been an impressively exact $688,505; by Confederation Day, 1867, it had risen to just under $2.6 million; by completion, the figure topped $4.5 million, a sevenfold increase from the original estimate. Macdonald's reaction was more practical: the buildings were at least largely finished, even if the towers still lacked roofs, and the Hill had been cleared of all the construction debris. He did complain privately that the tower of the West Block looked "like a cow bell."

---

dozen actually lived in Ottawa. Most members of Parliament got by in boarding houses during the three months or so that Parliament met each year. Not until after the Second World War did Ottawa become a politics-obsessed, one-industry town.

*By sheer luck, the magnificent, if magnificently expensive, Parliament Buildings were com-
pleted by Confederation Day. This photo shows a military review in front of the West
Block, on May 24, 1867.*

Nevertheless, the grandeur and scale of the Parliament
Buildings cast its defects deep into the shade. By building it,
Canadians had pulled off "a visionary, if slightly uncertain, idea
in the wilderness," in the words of historian Sandra Fraser
Gwyn in her splendid book *The Private Capital: Ambition and Love
in the Age of Macdonald and Laurier.* They had, that is, actually
dared to dare.

Macdonald's immediate concern on entering the capital that
would be his home for the next quarter-century was far less how
best to arrange the celebrations for the new country's birthday
than—naturally—the politics of Canada's now imminent
accouchement. Once Governor General Monck had advised him
officially that he would become Canada's first prime minister,

Macdonald knew he would have to form a government. To do that, he would have to form a cabinet. When it assembled, the first item of business would be to call an election soon after Confederation Day. Only after Macdonald had won an election would he become Canada's real prime minister, possessing a mandate rather than just the title.

About his cabinet, Macdonald had long ago settled on its single most important characteristic—it would include Reformers. Their presence would enable him to claim that the old Liberal-Conservative coalition still breathed. At a minimum, the side benefit would be to infuriate the opposition, now more and more calling themselves Liberal-Reformers, or just Liberals; the maximum benefit could be to divide them. Macdonald therefore retained in his new cabinet the three holdover Reformers from the Confederation administration, the most important being William McDougall, originally a Grit, now a Reformer, and well on his way to becoming a Conservative, a progress across the political map that earned him the nickname Wandering Willie. The freshman Maritime provinces would each have two ministers. To further constrain Macdonald's manoeuvring room, Cartier was adamant he would accept nothing less than three posts for *bleu* Quebecers. As well, one Quebec spot had to be kept open for Galt to re-enter the cabinet as finance minister. In these circumstances, no Quebec cabinet seat would be left for Confederation's poet laureate, D'Arcy McGee. Excluding him would be a severe blow to McGee's pride; he had already written to Macdonald that he would "give way neither to Galt, nor to a third Frenchman, 'nor to any other man.'"

To soften McGee's sense of rejection, Macdonald resorted to the device of rejecting another senior member of the Confederation team so that McGee would not twist alone in the wind. His choice was Charles Tupper. Macdonald already owed him a great deal. He now owed him even more, because this Nova Scotian, with great generosity, agreed to stand aside. On Tupper's advice, Macdonald telegraphed an amiable but otherwise anonymous backbencher, Edward Kenny, the unexpected news of his elevation to cabinet. A dry-goods merchant known as "Papa," Kenny had the great virtue of being a Catholic, so could compensate for the exclusion of his co-religionist McGee. Kennedy only just made it to Ottawa from Nova Scotia in time for the swearing-in.* Among the other Maritime representatives was of course New Brunswick's Leonard Tilley.

By his first cabinet choices, Macdonald showed that he understood a cardinal function of Canadian cabinet making: that the duties of the ministers would be not only to run the country but to represent the country to itself. In a tacit admission that the Senate he had just constructed could never serve, unlike its U.S. equivalent, as the regions' representative at the centre, Macdonald fashioned his cabinet into a rough simulacrum of the nation's regions and religions. This practice—ever more finely tuned to accommodate an ever-expanding spectrum of ethnic and other identity claims—has been followed since. Macdonald's handicap was that, while contemporary prime ministers can stretch their cabinets to almost any size, he had to squeeze his choices into a Procrustean bed of just thirteen cabinet portfolios. For himself, Macdonald chose the new portfolio of minister of justice. In a radical change from the past, this post now encompassed the duties of both of the previous attorneys general, for Upper and Lower Canada. The salary for all ministers remained at the pre-Confederation level of five thousand dollars a year.

---

* Kenny's career continued in anonymity, but of a most agreeable kind. After resigning from the cabinet in 1870, he was appointed a senator and later gained a knighthood.

Composing the cabinet by no means ended Macdonald's tasks as national personnel manager. If Canada needed a government, so, no less, did Ontario and Quebec, neither of which yet existed legally. As well, neither of these two new, but old, provinces had a lieutenant-governor. Macdonald, who had called these officials "chief executive officers," looked on them as key performers in his plan to perpetuate a strong central government that would, besides other accomplishments, reduce the provinces to "mere municipalities." Viewed thus, his choice for Ontario was decidedly odd. Its first lieutenant-governor was Major-General Henry Stisted, a British officer whose most considerable attainment was to have married the sister of the celebrity explorer Sir Richard Burton. Not until one year later, when Stisted resigned and returned to Britain, did the reason for Macdonald's choice become apparent. He then filled this much-sought-after post with William Howland, a Reformer who, by accepting a cabinet post in advance of the 1867 election, had helped insinuate a minimal credibility into Macdonald's claim that his government was a Liberal-Conservative one. Filling the lieutenant-governorship post in Quebec was easy: Macdonald's choice was Sir Narcisse-Fortunat Belleau, who had served Macdonald as titular premier of the Great Coalition. The choice for Quebec's first premier was made by the Quebec Conservatives themselves: he was Pierre-Joseph-Olivier Chauveau, a cultured intellectual who implemented some important educational reforms but was politically a naïf. He too ended up in the Senate, but missed out on a knighthood.

The appointment that took everybody by surprise was Macdonald's choice for the first premier of Ontario. A good deal more useful than being merely surprising, his selection involved one of the most adroit political seductions that Macdonald ever consummated. His choice for the post was his own namesake,

John Sandfield Macdonald. As the first Conservative premier of Confederation's largest province, "Little John" Macdonald harboured two substantial disqualifications: he was a lifelong Reformer (he had firmly rejected earlier attempts by Macdonald to seduce him), and he had been Upper Canada's best-known anti-Confederate. His compensating assets were yet considerable. As a former premier, he commanded credibility. As a Catholic, he brought Irish votes to the Conservatives, federally as well as provincially, along with the other Irishmen Macdonald had already bonded to the party by his alliance with the Orange Order. Most desirable of all, John S. Macdonald's appointment as Ontario premier not only infuriated the Liberals but divided them.

One other political matter needed to be sorted out. Back in London, the British had become convinced, for reasons difficult to comprehend, that when the new dominion was proclaimed officially, the document should include the names of all those who had won the ultimate Canadian lottery of appointment as senators—at that time a life appointment, unlike today's unkind cutoff at the tender age of seventy-five.* Macdonald, looking ahead to the impending first election after Confederation, protested to Lord Carnarvon that "if the list were settled now, every man . . . who is omitted, rightly or wrongly, would vote against the Government." The senatorial announcements were delayed until the fall, safely past the election's date.

The date for the Confederation celebrations was fixed for July 1. Macdonald would have preferred July 15, fearful that not all the preparations could be completed in time, but Monck

---

* The super winner of the Confederation senatorial lottery had to have been New Brunswick's David Wark. Called to the Upper House in October 1867, Wark remained a senator for forty years, leaving the chamber only by death in 1905, at the age of 101.

insisted on the earlier date. He quietly passed the word to Macdonald that he was to receive a knighthood, as Knight Commander of the Bath; the lesser honour of the Companion of the Bath would be accorded to Cartier, Galt, Tupper and Tilley, as well as to "housebroken" Reformers like McDougall and Howland. Of all the people on Monck's list, the most conspicuous, by his absence, was George Brown, now back running the *Globe* and de facto leader of the Reform-Liberals. The list had been compiled on Macdonald's recommendations, and his choices showed him at his least gracious and most vengeful. A year later, Monck wrote to Brown apologizing with great grace: "I will confess to you that I was mortified and disappointed that circumstances rendered it impossible for me to recommend for a share in these distinctions *the* man whose conduct in 1864 had rendered the project of union feasible."

Two of the others, Galt and Cartier, protested strenuously that they too should have been awarded knighthoods. Cartier declined the lesser honour on the grounds that it was an insult to French Canadians for their leader not to have been put in the front rank. Galt similarly refused his reward, telling his wife, "It is an ingracious and most unusual thing to refuse an honour publicly conferred, but if Lord Monck is an ass, I cannot help it." Galt, and several of the others, eventually received the knighthoods they sought while Cartier was appeased with the higher honour of baronecy, although Galt, always hypersensitive, accepted only after writing to the colonial secretary that he actually opposed all titles and believed instead that Canada should become independent from Britain.

One story that went the rounds was that Macdonald learned from Monck only on Confederation Day itself of his own impending, solitary elevation to the knighthood. Very probably Macdonald was the source of this tale, letting it circulate in order to distance himself from blame for the hurt the incident had caused several of his cabinet colleagues. It's easy to guess that the reason all of them learned of their rewards only at the very last moment was because Macdonald, foreseeing the outcome, had advised Monck to maintain secrecy to the end.

With the Confederation bandwagon now at high speed, more and more people clambered aboard. In June, four of Quebec's five bishops praised Confederation's virtues in pastoral letters that were read for two Sundays from all the pulpits they commanded. Montreal bishop Ignace Bourget, at this time quarrelling with Cartier over his support of the liberal Sulpicians, delayed his pastoral letter until after July 1; in it he enjoined "l'obeissance à l'autorité constituée," a formula that avoided any praise of Confederation.

The most revealing pastoral letter was that of the bishop of Saint-Hyacinthe: he favoured Confederation, he told his flock, because "the fate awaiting us if God suffered us at some future date to enter the great American republic, would be exactly comparable to that of so many tributaries which have come to be swallowed up in the great St. Lawrence." Cartier had made exactly the same point in his speech in the 1865 Confederation Debates: "The question is reduced to this: we must either have a British North American federation or else be absorbed into the American federation." Canadiens had come to accept Confederation because, at the very least, it was better than the probably inevitable alternative of annexation, and at best could—just—prevent that national disappearance. If Macdonald understood this gut sense among French Canadians in a way that few other English-Canadian politicians then did, there was one obvious and decisive reason why: his own gut sense told him the same. Besides instinct, Macdonald by now possessed ample evidence of the United States' mood of expansiveness, northwards.

As Confederation approached, dramatic news came from Washington: the American government had just announced the takeover of a major piece of territory in North America. This territory was Alaska, whose Panhandle, stretching far southwards, cut off much of northern British Columbia from the sea. A steep purchase price of $7.2 million (U.S.) was agreed on between the territory's owner, Russia, and the United States, and the treaty was signed by President Andrew Johnson on March 29—by coincidence the same day that Queen Victoria signed the British North America Act. The New York *Herald* praised the purchase as "a hint" to England that it had "no business on this continent." The New York *Tribune* described it as "a flank movement" on British Columbia by surrounding "a hostile cockney with a watchful Yankee on either side of him." About Confederation itself, the *Tribune* said, "When the experiment of the 'dominion' shall have failed, as fail it must, a process of peaceful absorption will give Canada her proper place in the great North American Republic."

Comments by circulation-chasing editors counted for relatively little. Quite different was the fact that the principal advocates of the Alaska purchase should have been the United States' two well-known annexationists—Secretary of State William Seward and Senator Charles Sumner, the chair of the Senate Committee on Foreign Relations. On April 7, during Senate hearings on the Alaska purchase, Sumner described the takeover as "a visible step to the occupation of the whole North American continent." Seward, in a speech in Boston on the eve of Confederation, said, "I know that Nature designs that this whole continent, not merely the thirty-six states, shall be, sooner or later, within the magic circle of the American Union."

At the same time, a U.S. agent in Canada, E.H. Derby, suggested in a report to Seward that Britain should be asked to cede its possessions in the far west—the then separate colonies of Vancouver Island and British Columbia—as payment for damages to the United States during the Civil War. This damage had been caused by Confederate raiders that had been built in and launched from British ports. From St. Paul, Minnesota, another agent, James W. Taylor, reported to Washington on the steady Americanization of the Red River region of Manitoba; he recommended that "events have presented to the people of the government of the United States the opportunity—let me rather say have developed the duty, of interposing an overture to the people of the English colonies . . . to unite their fortunes with the United States."

These were private communications, about which Macdonald could have no knowledge, although he would have known about the judgment of the *Nor'Wester* newspaper in Red River that "Americanism has become rampant with all classes, ages and conditions." Other private communications, had he been aware of them, would have worried him a good deal more. They would have revealed that similar opinions existed in high places on the far side of the Atlantic. Early in 1867 the foreign secretary, Lord Stanley, wrote to the British ambassador in Washington, Sir Frederick Bruce, to say that Confederation had made Canada even more of a risk to Britain: "Many people would dislike the long boundary line with the United States (they look now to an early separation of Canada)." In March 1867 Stanley wrote again to Bruce: "The Colonies will remain Colonies, only confederated for the sake of convenience. If they choose to separate, we on this side shall not object; it is they who would protest against this idea. In England, separation would be generally popular."

Perhaps most disturbing of all to Macdonald, had he been

aware of it, would have been the private comment by C.B. Adderley, the junior minister for the colonies, who had steered the British North America Act through the Commons: he told some of his colleagues, "It seems to me impossible that we should long hold B.C. from its natural annexation." Nor were these views wholly private. The authoritative *Times* broadcast them by its editorial comment (read, regularly, not just by Canadian officials but no less so by American ones): "We look to Confederation as the means of relieving this country from much expense and much embarrassment." And of Britain's need to pull back its troops still stationed in Canada, the *Times* observed, accurately but embarrassingly, that these served only as "hostages . . . for British good behaviour."

An indication of just how seriously Macdonald took this mood is contained in a letter he wrote shortly before leaving England. Dated April 9, 1867, it was addressed to a prominent English lawyer, Henry Maine, who had received an honorary doctorate from Oxford at the same time as Macdonald the previous June. "I sail in four days for Canada with the act uniting all British America in my pocket," he wrote. "A brilliant future would certainly await us were it not for those wretched Yankees who hunger & thirst for Naboth's field—War will come some day between England & the United States."

In facing this challenge, Macdonald could really count on only one influential political ally who thought as he did. Unexpectedly, that was Galt, highly intelligent but highly volatile too. (There was also the passionate nationalist McGee, except that his political career was now in steep decline because of his insensate drinking.) Back in January 1867, Galt, while still in London and working to get the BNA Act through Westminster, wrote a letter to his wife that indicates a great deal about the threat to Canada from the east as well as the south, or from Britain as well as the United States—at least as that threat was perceived. Galt's letter reveals also an exceptional appreciation of Macdonald's determination to stand on guard for the Canada that was about to be born.

"I am more than ever disappointed at the tone of feeling here as to the colonies. I cannot shut my eyes to the fact that they want to get rid of us . . . and would rather give us up than defend us, or incur the risk of war with that country. Day by day I am more oppressed with the sense of responsibility of maintaining a connection undesired here, and which exposes us to such peril at home. I pray God to show me the right path. But I much doubt whether Confederation will save us from Annexation. Even Macdonald is rapidly feeling as I do." He continued, "Except Macdonald, I know none of the Delegates who really think enough of the future that is before us, and he considers that our present immediate task is to complete the Union, leaving the rest to be solved by time."

Galt had grasped the nature of the "long game" of national survival that Macdonald was playing. It's a shame, in hindsight, that the two never really became partners.

In fact, Macdonald was dead wrong about the readiness of the government of a war-weary America to risk a new conflict, even if against a lion now starting to show signs of its age. The vast armies mobilized during the Civil War had been demobilized down to a minimalist fifty thousand. He was right absolutely, though, that Canada was passing through a period of exceptional peril in which, at the same time that some American leaders were looking expectantly northwards, their equivalents in Britain were doing their best to look the other way. Among possible remedies, Macdonald possessed just one: Confederation itself, or, more exactly, making Confederation serve as a synonym for a nation's will to survive.

As Confederation Day neared, Macdonald wrote to Monck, arguing that it would be "gratifying to the people" if Canada's new national status could be marked by elevating the title of the Queen's representative from governor general to viceroy, the same honorific held by his counterpart in the Empire's "crown jewel" of India. He made the argument that "British North America is now merely a geographical description" and that elevating it to a vice-royalty would reinforce the entity's status. Back from London came word that governor general was as high a title as Imperial protocol could accommodate.

Then, suddenly, there was nothing more for Macdonald to do apart from watch Canada become a Confederation.

Eighteen sixty-seven was something of a banner year for the creation of confederations. There was the North German Confederation, encompassing all the states north of the Main River, which came into being on July 1, and out of which would come Bismarck's Prussian-controlled German Empire. There was, in February of the same year, Austria's *Ausgleich*, or "compromise," which turned the Austrian Empire into the Austro-Hungarian Empire, giving each component state its own parliament and prime minister under a single monarch. And in the wings, rather than on the international stage itself, there was what happened in Ottawa.

July 1, 1867, was "a hot dusty day," as Agnes recorded four days later in the diary she had begun to mark her elevation to Lady Macdonald. She continued in her lively and observant style, "This new Dominion of ours came into existence on the 1st, and the very newspapers look hot and tired with the weight of announcements and of cabinet lists. Here—in this house—the atmosphere is so awfully political that sometimes I think the very flies hold Parliament on the kitchen tablecloths."

As always happens, glitches occurred. The Royal Canadian Rifles assembled on Ottawa's Sparks Street to fire a *feu de joie*, pulled their triggers on command and watched their ramrods, which they had forgotten to remove, make a graceful arc across the street. In Whitby, Ontario, a cavalry troop staged a mock attack on a square of militiamen, but as the Oshawa *Vindicator* reported, "some of them rush[ed] so closely upon the bayonets as to receive severe thrusts."

Inevitably, not everyone regarded the occasion as a festive one. In Halifax, the *Morning Chronicle*, in a front-page editorial edged in black, mourned, "Died! Last night at twelve o'clock, the free and enlightened Province of Nova Scotia," while in Yarmouth, no guns saluted the new nation, the ammunition being preserved for use three days later to mark the United States' Independence Day. The Nova Scotia government went so far as to refuse to allow the Queen's printer in the province to publish the official proclamation sent down from Ottawa by the governor general. In the new province of Quebec, the *bleu* newspaper *La Minerve* reassured its readers that all would be well because Confederation constituted "la seule voie qui nous soit offerte pour arriver à l'indépendance politique."

Although mostly confined to Ontario, there was some genuine excitement, even pride, in the achievement. In Toronto, a whole ox was roasted, carved up and distributed to the poor. In Hamilton, huge bonfires burned for hours on the Mountain. The crowd in Whitby swelled to seven thousand. In town after town there were band concerts, parades, picnics, free ice cream, cricket games, croquet matches and lots of speeches. Montreal sponsored

In Kingston, the Market Square was jammed as the Proclamation was read on July 1, 1867.

a spectacular fireworks display, and there were special celebrations in Macdonald's home town of Kingston. There were artillery salutes everywhere, usually of twenty-one guns, but in Ottawa, starting at midnight, of 101. George Brown stayed up late writing a nine-thousand-word article that filled the *Globe*'s entire front page and many of the inside pages. In fact, Brown had little new to say, expressing himself inelegantly in his opening paragraph: "With the first dawn of this gladsome midsummer morn, we hail the birthday of a new nationality."

At Ottawa, the formal ceremonies were headed by Governor General Monck. He disappointed everyone by turning up in a plain business suit instead of the plumed hat and gold braid people had looked forward to. Accompanied by a single aide, he drove in a carriage to Parliament Hill and then sauntered off to the Privy Council Chamber, where judges, dignitaries, militia officers, senior civil servants and Macdonald were waiting. Monck

was sworn in by a judge as the first governor general of the
Dominion of Canada, following which he handed over for safe-
keeping the new Great Seal of the new nation. Afterwards,
Monck, accompanied by the newly sworn-in prime minister, Sir
John A. Macdonald, reviewed the troops drawn up on Parliament
Hill. That evening there were fireworks displays, and the
Parliament Buildings blazed with illuminations.*

Real emotion, though, was rare. Surprisingly, perhaps the
most uninhibited expression occurred in the Maritimes. The *New
Brunswick Reporter* declared on July 5, "From Halifax to Sarnia, we
are one people—one in laws, one in government, one in interests." In these details, little was actually true. Macdonald's
description of Canada as only "a geographical expression" was far
closer to reality. *The Times* of London came unnervingly close to
identifying the limitations and the downright fragility of the
new nation: "It supposes a nationality able to command the two
oceans it touches, and to raise a barrier of law and moral force
extending near three thousand miles between itself and the most
powerful and aggressive state in the New World." For such a task,
The Times added, "we look in vain for the body, the vital organs,
the circulation and the muscular force that are to give adequate
power to these wide-spread limbs." *The Times* was being a bit
severe: Canada's population at birth would be close to four million, a bare tenth of that of its giant neighbour but roughly the
same as that of the thirteen American colonies when they had set
off on their own national journey.

---

* The celebrations staged by Canadians were outclassed, inevitably, by the great
Exposition Universelle held in Paris in that same year of 1867. It attracted ten
million visitors. Several Canadian companies even won prizes for their goods;
the prize that mattered, though, was the victory by a crew from Saint John, NB,
at the World Rowing Championships held on the Seine.

There was a good deal more to the country than just a new administrative interconnectedness across the immense expanses of geography. For the first time anywhere, colonials had written their own constitution. It was an usually difficult constitution to construct, because it was a federal constitution, one of only four in the world—in the United States, Switzerland and the new North German Confederation. And even if still only a colony—as the independent member Charles Dunkin had pointed out, accurately if cruelly—there was something of the stuff of a nation in this curious new entry on the world's stage. Just by achieving Confederation, its citizens had shown they did indeed possess some of the will and nerve it would take to survive.

They possessed another asset. Their leader was Macdonald. Soon his last name would become superfluous: he was about to become known universally as Sir John A. No one else in the country knew politics as well, by a wide margin, as he did. With Lincoln now gone, he knew as much as any leader anywhere about managing a people and a country. He had large and easily visible flaws, and few condemned them more thoroughly than the British-born journalist Goldwin Smith. Yet no one understood better than Smith the sheer impossibility that Macdonald had somehow defied by achieving Confederation. Macdonald, wrote Smith, had been obliged "to hold together a set of elements, national, religious, sectional and personal, as motley as the component patches of any 'crazy quilt,' and actuated each of them by paramount regard for its own interest."

Macdonald hadn't so much created a nation as manipulated and seduced and connived and bullied it into existence against the wishes of most of its own citizens. The best description of the role Macdonald had played came from his friend Judge James Gowan, who called him Confederation's "artificer in chief." By whatever combination of deviousness and magic it took, he had done it. He had made Confederation out of scraps and patches and oddments of thread and string, many frayed and few fitting naturally, but at last it actually existed.

Now that Confederation was done, Macdonald would have to do it all over again. Having conjured up a child-nation, he would have to nurture it through adolescence towards adulthood. How he did this is another story, and its telling, up to his death in 1891, awaits the second volume of this chronicle.

The man who made us, just after he had made us, c. 1868.

Acknowledgements

A great many individuals made important, and in some instances critical, contributions to this work. My first expression of thanks, though, has to be to someone who played no direct part in the process at all—Donald Creighton, author of the two-volume biography of Macdonald, *The Young Politician* and *The Old Chieftain*, published in the mid-1950s. These books are the two greatest achievements in Canadian historiography; no other work even approaches them in the scale of their ambition, in the comprehensiveness and originality of their research and, most distinctively, in the power and persuasiveness of their narrative drive. In later years, Creighton's stature shrank: his opposition to national bilingualism and biculturalism—"francophobic" was one term hurled at him—isolated him from the mainstream. He died in 1979, despairing of Canada's future, convinced that it had become "just a nice place to live . . . but that's all Canada is now." Belatedly, revisionism is under way. The historian Donald Wright is now writing Creighton's biography, only the second ever of a Canadian historian. Creighton indeed could be difficult—prickly, thin-skinned, hot-tempered, if also generous and hospitable. There's no rule, though, that great artists have to be nice— Picasso is a kind of negative role model. That Creighton was a great historian, there is not the least doubt. He did me the exceptional service of stimulating me, challenging me and at times intimidating me; no writer could ask more of another than to be driven by him or her to stretch to the limit.

~

All the causes of my other thanks are more conventional. The best way to express them may be in a rough chronological order.

This book exists because Louise Dennys, executive publisher of Knopf Canada / Random House of Canada, and Anne Collins, publisher of Random House, decided jointly to defy one of the embedded rules of Canadian publishing—that Canadians don't read Canadian history. If this book succeeds in its objective of re-introducing Canadians to their past, and so to themselves, with John A. Macdonald performing as a kind of tour guide, these women will have guessed right that rules exist not so much to be broken as to be rewritten. In helping to persuade them to make this decision, my agent John Pearce played a critical role.

Post-Creighton, with infrequent exceptions, works of Canadian history intended for the general reader have most often been written by generalists—first, and forever the foremost, by Pierre Berton, then by Peter C. Newman and Sandra Fraser Gwyn, and today by Charlotte Gray, Christopher Moore, Ken McGoogan and others. All these writers are filling a niche that the professional historians have, largely, stepped back from in order to concentrate on more specific studies. Yet the expertise and the scholarly standards of the professionals remain the foundation on which the generalists must build.

Beyond any doubt, the preceding pages contain errors that I should have excised before surrendering the manuscript or never have put to paper in the first place. That there are not many more is due principally to two individuals. George Ekins, reference librarian at the Library of Parliament, was indefatigably imaginative, not just in looking out for what was wrong but in looking for what I should have known about in the first place—everything from Governor General Head's remarkable memorandum on how Canada should be governed (so reminiscent of Macdonald's own views) to pinning down for me the genealogy of that supposedly distinctive Canadian mantra, "Peace, Order and good Government." My debt to George Ekins is immense, not least because he also read an early draft of the text. My debt to the historian Keith Johnson, now retired from Carleton University and the principal authority on pre-Confederate Macdonald, is almost as considerable. He saved me from multiple embarrassments by reading both the first rough drafts and the near-final text.

Others were as forthcoming. Historian Roger Hall, who played a major role in the process; political scientist David Cameron; social historian Charlotte Gray; and Andrew Smith, just appointed as professor of history at Laurentian University, performed similarly as readers of the early drafts, doing both the grunt work of identifying errors and the creative job of suggesting improvements. Later, I was able to tap the expertise of two historians, Brian McKillop of Carleton University and Donald Smith of the University of Calgary, on important specific topics. Earlier, the geographer Brian Osborne and architectural historian Jennifer McKendry took me on a detailed tour of Macdonald's Kingston. The journalist Arthur Milnes, himself an outstanding researcher, guided me both through Kingston and into Macdonald's personal life. I spent a delightful afternoon with Donna Ivey and Norma Kelly going through their Macdonald memorabilia at his one-time residence, 110 Rideau Street in Kingston.

Those whose job it is to help responded with equal generosity. Maureen Hoogenraad of Library and Archives Canada went out of her way to respond to all my requests. Likewise Paul Banfield, archivist at Queen's University; Robert Paul of the Diefenbaker Canada Centre Archives; Barbara Pilek of the Library of Parliament; and David Brown of LAC's Cartography Division. Those responsible for collections of visual material were every bit as responsive, among them Dorothy Farr of Queen's University's Agnes Etherington Art Centre, Steven McNeil of the National Gallery of Canada, and Heather Home of Queen's University Archives.

It goes without saying that none of those mentioned above bears any responsibility for errors that may remain.

Research is the fun part of any undertaking of this kind; writing is a self-imposed sentence to hard labour interspersed with the occasional epiphany. There can be few more agreeable ways of researching than sitting in Library and Archives Canada poring over a book or learned journal, or the contents of a cardboard box, and every now and then looking out through the ceiling-high windows at the Ottawa River below and the far-off blue line of the Gatineau Hills. The exceptional Robarts Library of the University of Toronto has no views at all but instead offers the stimulation of students scurrying about in search of data to stuff into essay assignments, and the side benefit of researchers being allowed to explore the stacks and so, sometimes, to come upon an unknown book that may contain long-sought details about some scene or personality. An additional research asset I enjoyed was the work done for me by archival consultant Elizabeth Vincent. A medical friend, Dr. Byron Hyde, applied his expertise to trying to diagnose the mysterious illnesses of Isabella. A brother-in-law, Gordon Fulton, took the photograph of me that's on the back cover.

This work went through multiple drafts. Anne Collins first suggested ways to reshape chapters to better fit the narrative through-line. Rosemary Shipton, senior editor for Knopf Canada and Random House Canada, then took over, initially performing the same function and becoming almost a partner in the process of revision and rewriting; working with her was a delight. My copy-editor, Alexander Schultz, and my proofreader, Alison Reid, saved me from yet more embarrassments of detail and grammar.

The person I'm indebted to by far the most is Carol Bishop-Gwyn. During the three years the project took, and most especially during the nine, obsessively focused months of the actual writing, she protected me from daily reality by weaving a cocoon around me and only occasionally interrupting to interpose a hand between me and the screen and, after the premonitory warning "Earth to Richard," bringing me up to date on the latest misdemeanour of the dog or on the social obligation that started half an hour earlier. (A comparable sustaining role was performed by a dear friend, Moira Dexter, during my intense research stints in Ottawa.) Carol was also a full partner in the project itself. All the illustrations are of her choosing, her one regret about them being that the mid-nineteenth century predates both the widespread use of photography and the development of newspaper cartoons. The dedication better expresses my thanks.

A Note on Sources

These source notes are comparatively short. One reason is that the bibliography of books and articles used during the research is so long. More to the point, the endnotes that customarily identify the sources for quotations and other information in the text have been placed on the website of Random House Canada—to save some trees and to lighten this book's heft.

The purpose of these source notes is comparatively modest—to steer readers who are interested in going more deeply into particular topics towards material that should be useful to them. As a side benefit, this approach enables me to identify writers whose insights set me off in especially productive directions. These notes are therefore indicative rather than definitive. They also use the short-form reference style, so readers should consult the bibliography for the full reference.

For the detailed source notes, see the website at www.randomhouse.ca/johnamacdonald.

Overview

The essentials of John A. Macdonald's story can be found in fewer than ten books. The times themselves—political, social and economic—are recounted in the Canadian Centenary Series, the relevant volumes being Careless's *The Union of the Canadas, 1841–1857* and Morton's *The Critical Years, 1857–1875*. Two contemporary works are invaluable: Biggar's *Anecdotal Life* and Pope's *Memoirs*. The foundation text is, of course, Creighton's *The Young Politician*. Johnson's *Affectionately Yours* is insightful about relationships within the family. Waite's *Life and World* is an elegant essay that includes some interesting information about daily life. Waite, again, in his *Life and Times of Confederation* has provided the best detailed account (if rather Maritime-centric) of the way we were made.

Chapters 1–3 (*Youth*)

Besides Pope, Biggar and Creighton, there's some useful information in Pennington Macpherson's otherwise vacuous biography. Johnson's article, "British Immigration to North America, 1815–1860," is a good source for that topic, with reinforcement provided by Harper's article, "Image and Reality in Early Emigrant Literature." The best review by far of Kingston's past is Tulchinsky's *To Preserve and Defend*. On conditions in early-nineteenth-century towns, nothing comes close to Fingard's article, "The Winter's Tale." A good account of pioneer life is contained in Harris's *Canada Before Confederation*; Susanna Moodie, Catharine Parr Traill and Anna Jameson are musts. About the Scots, Herman's *How the Scots Invented the Modern World* is a captivating read in itself.

Chapters 4–5 (*Young man*)

The best source for Macdonald's years as a full-time lawyer is Teatero's thesis, "A Dead and Alive Way Never Does." Sources about the general state of nineteenth-century law and of crime and punishment include McGrath's *Crime and Its Treatment in Canada* and Waite's *Life and World*. Information about Macdonald's business ventures comes primarily from Johnson's long article, "Macdonald, the Young Non-Politician." Family information is available in Phenix's *Private Demons*. Macdonald's February 1, 1845, speech on primogeniture is in the *Debates* of the legislature, as are all his other contributions up to 1856.

Chapter 6 (*Marriage*)

The prime source is the family letters in Johnson's *Affectionately Yours*. Additional material is in Phenix's *Private Demons* and in Cohoe's articles in

Historic Kingston. Prevailing attitudes towards death are well described in Luella Creighton's *Elegant Canadians*.

Chapters 7–8 (*Early politics*)

Donald Creighton is especially good on this period, while Stewart's *Origins* serves almost as a foundation text. The "miracle" of the revival of post-Durham French Canada is recounted well by Wade's *The French Canadians*, by Monet's *The Last Cannon-shot*, and by Heintzman in his article "The Political Culture of Quebec." A good comparison of French and English attitudes is contained in Morton's *Shield of Achilles*. Bodelson's *Studies in Mid-Victorian Imperialism* and Shippee's *Canadian-American Relations* are useful (if a bit dated) on issues such as Responsible Government and Reciprocity; up to date is Hyam and Ged Martin's *Reappraisals*. *The Dictionary of Canadian Biography* is the place to go for mini-biographies, amplified by sources such as, on Ogle Gowan, Akenson's biography, *Orangeman*; and, on Baldwin, Careless's essay in *Pre-Confederation Premiers*. Ged Martin's "Sir John Eh?" explores Macdonald's speech habits, including whether he had a Scots accent.

Chapter 9 (*The "Big Tent"*)

The (former) National Library's two volumes of Macdonald's letters to the end of 1861, and its third, unpublished, one are an essential source in the years up to Confederation. Much of the argument about Macdonald's ability to speak French is in Ged Martin's "The Canadian Question." The principal source on George Brown is, of course, Careless's *Brown of the Globe*. Willison's *Reminiscences* are a wonderful read.

Chapter 10 (*"Forms Are Things"*)

The argument that Macdonald was a competent administrator is made by Sowby in her thesis, "Macdonald the Administrator," and by Johnson in his article, "John A. Macdonald." Bellomo's "Upper Canada Attitudes towards Crime and Punishment (1832–1851)" is a fine source on exactly that topic. Good material on Macdonald's judicial appointments is contained in Stewart's article "Macdonald's Greatest Triumph."

Chapters 11 and 13 (*Political manoeuvres*)

Macdonald's political stratagems, especially those concerned with patronage, draw substantively on Noel's *Patrons, Clients, Brokers*, Stewart's *Origins* and Simpson's *Spoils*. The development of organized parties is well described in Underhill's article "National Political Parties." The expansive mood of nineteenth-century Canada is covered exceptionally well in Fallis's essay in Morton, *The Shield of Achilles*; McKillop's *Disciplined Intelligence* is good here, while Keefer's *Philosophy of Railroads* is a delightful read in itself. Macdonald's extravagant Valentine's Day ball is well described in Lena Newman's *Album*. For Macdonald's relationship with women, turn to Willison's *Reminiscences* and to Waite's essay "The Man."

Chapter 12 (*The death of Isabella*)

Johnson's *Affectionately Yours* is the principal source. Dr. McSherry's two articles on Isabella's ailments are a fascinating exercise in historical medical sleuthing.

Chapters 14–15 (*The Americans*)

For a fuller understanding of D'Arcy McGee, see Slattery's *McGee*, along with Burns's article, "The Economic Aspects of the New Nationality." For Galt, the source is Skelton's biography. A fine description of the West's first entry onto the Canadian scene is contained in Zaslow's *Canadian North* and Morton's *The West and Confederation*. The early notions for some form of confederation are reviewed in Upton's article, "The Idea of Confederation." The Prince of Wales's tour is well covered in Radforth's *Royal Spectacle*. For Canadian attitudes to the United States, the essential source is Wise and Brown's *Canada Views the United States*, its one defect being that it's too brief. The source for facts and details on this topic is Winks's *The Civil War Years*. On liquor, Ged Martin's "Macdonald and the

Bottle" is an excellent summary. Burnet's article "The Urban Community and Changing Moral Standards" provides a good overview of the social consequences of widespread drinking.

Chapter 16 (*The Brits*)
The prime source for Canada-British relationships throughout this period is Ged Martin's *Britain and the Origins of Canadian Confederation*. Farr's *Colonial Office and Canada* provides good supporting material. Useful also is Waite's "Cardwell and Confederation" and his *Life and Times of Confederation*.

Chapters 17–18 (*The start of the Confederation project*)
The best sources for the creation of the Great Coalition are Careless's *Brown*, Waite's *Life and Times* and Creighton's *The Young Politician*. Ged Martin's *Britain and the Origins of Canadian Confederation* is also useful. The discussion of Macdonald's ideas is drawn from Preece's article on "Political Philosophy" and from Waite's articles "Political Ideas" and "The Man." The *Reminiscences* of both Willison and Cartwright are useful. The story to Charlottetown can be followed in Morton's *Critical Years* and in Waite's *Life and Times*. Louella Creighton provides some delightful fresh details in *The Elegant Canadians*. Careless's "George Brown and the Mother of Confederation" is first class. At the Quebec Conference, Feo Monck in her journal was an astute observer, as was Mercy Coles, while Waite's "Ed Whelan's Reports" is a lot of fun. A fine overview is provided by Moore's *1867: How the Fathers Made a Deal*. Munro's small work, *American Influences*, has good material on Macdonald's thought processes. Smith's "Canadian Confederation" provides some good insights. Useful also is Ged Martin's *Causes of Canadian Confederation*.

Chapter 19 (*Democracy*)
The familiar sources, such as Waite's *Life and Times*, Whelan's *Confederation of the Provinces*, Careless's *Brown*, Ged Martin's *Britain and the Origins of Canadian Confederation*, are all relevant. A new source of great value, espe-

cially on the debate about democracy, is the insightful *Canada's Founding Debates*, edited by Ajzenstat.

Chapters 20–21 (*The Maritimes*)

The Maritime scene is well described in Beck's *Howe* and in Pryke's *Nova Scotia and Confederation*, as well as in Waite's *Life and Times*. There's considerable useful material in Chester Martin's *Foundations of Canadian Nationhood*. The nature of the loyalty issue in Canada is well covered in Berger's *The Sense of Power*, and Mills's *The Idea of Loyalty* is a useful supplement. The Fenian threat is described in Senior's books as well as in Stacey's article "Fenianism." The best way to keep tabs on what Monck was doing is Batt's *Monck*.

Chapter 22 (*The London Conference*)

Moore's *1867* and Waite's *Life and Times* are useful, as is Batt's *Monck*. A good overview of the Confederation pact is contained in Frank Scott's long article, "Political Nationalism and Confederation." The magic moment when "Peace, Order and good Government" became the essence of Canada is in Morton's *Canadian Identity*.

Chapter 23 ("*Two Unions*")

The best source on Macdonald's second courtship and wedding is Reynold's *Agnes*, the first-ever biography of a prime ministerial wife. On matters constitutional, good sources are Peter Russell's *Constitutional Odyssey* and, from the British perspective, Hyam and Martin's *Reappraisals*.

Chapter 24 (*Confederation Day*)

The prime source for descriptions of life in early Ottawa is Sandra Gwyn's *Private Capital*. The rise in cross-border tensions prompted by the purchase of Alaska and by Confederation is well described in Shippee's *Canadian-American Relations*. Skelton's *Galt* contains important relevant material, while Louella Creighton has some charming anecdotes in *The Elegant Canadians* about the celebrations.

Notes

These notes provide source citations for quotations and facts contained in the text. The specific sources are described here in summary form. Thus, the first entry below, referring to a quotation on page 1 of the text, reads: "P. 1 Moodie, "The spirit of past ages": McKillop, *Intelligence*, p. 4." The full entry would be: "Susanna Moodie, quoted in A.B. McKillop, *A Disciplined Intelligence: Critical Inquiry and Canadian Thought in the Victorian Era* (Montreal: McGill-Queen's University Press, 1970), p. 4. A complete listing for McKillop, *A Disciplined Intelligence*, is found in the bibliography in *John A.*, under Secondary Sources, General Works Consulted. The notes provided here are thus a companion piece to the book's Note on Sources and Bibliography.

INTRODUCTION

P. 1   Moodie, "The spirit of past ages": McKillop, *Intelligence*, p. 4.

P. 2   Smith, "crazy quilt": *The Week*, April 10, 1884.

P. 3   "This frail-looking man": MacLennan, *Scotchman*, p. 108.

P. 4   "species of heiress": Prentice, *Canadian Women*, p. 86.

CHAPTER 1: LAIRDS OURSELVES

P. 8   Macdonald birthdate: Johnson, *Affectionately*, p. 2 (n).

P. 8   Macdonald birthplace: Gibson and Patterson, *Historic Kingston*,
            p. 71, letter from Dr. Govin White, University of Glasgow.

P. 10   Macdonald grandfather: Pope, *Memoirs*, pp. 2–3; and Creighton, *Young Politician*, p. 9

P. 10   Shaw-Clark-Macpherson-Macdonald clan: Johnson, *Affectionately*, p. 3.

P. 11   Helen Macdonald description: Biggar, *Anecdotal Life*, p. 82; and Creighton, *Politician*, p. 13.

P. 11 (fn)   Dornoch trial of "witch" in 1727: Ged Martin, *John A. Macdonald: Scotsman or Canadian?* Standard Life Lecture in Canadian Studies, 2004, p. 5.

P. 12   Helen Macdonald's love of jokes: Biggar, *Anecdotal Life*, p. 82.

P. 12   Helen Macdonald dances jig in street: *Weekly British Whig*, June 4, 1891.

P. 12   Helen Macdonald's love of Gaelic: Biggar, *Anecdotal Life*, p. 83.

P. 13   Helen Macdonald's prediction of "more than an ordinary man": Biggar, *Anecdotal Life*, p. 28.

P. 14   George Forbes, "we are lairds ourselves": Peter Russell, *Attitudes to Social Structures and Social Mobility in Upper Canada* (Lewiston, NY: E. Mellen Press, 1990), letter to John Forbes, April 20, 1840, Forbes Papers, Edinburgh.

P. 15   Moodie on servants: *First Drafts*, pp. 54–55.

CHAPTER 2: A BOY'S TOWN

P. 17   "I grow weary of its immensity": Parr Traill, *Backwoods of Canada*, p. 34.

P. 17 (fn)   feeding porridge to passengers: Harper, *Image and Reality*, p. 7.

P. 19   Sydenham's ride to Montreal: Robertson, *Old Toronto*, p. 295.

P. 21   Kingston epidemics: Angus, "Health, Emigration and Welfare," pp. 120–25; and *Preserve and Defend*, p. 188.

P. 22   Dickens, Kingston a "very poor town": *Preserve and Defend*, p. 109.

P. 23   Galt, "settlement in the backwoods of Canada": Skelton, *Galt*, p. 48.

P. 24   Fingard, "absence of mass demonstrations": "The Winter's Tale," p. 341.

P. 24   Preston, Kingston as "stragglingly built": Lockhardt, "Early Life," p. 26.

P. 26   Kingston Council, one drink shop for every seven or eight men: *Preserve and Defend*, p. 107.

P. 27   Hugh Macdonald's ad for "groceries, wines, vinegar, powder": Phenix, *Demons*, p. 12.

P. 27   Death of James Macdonald: Pope, *Memoirs*, p. 4; and Macpherson, *Macdonald*, p. 78.

P. 28   Montreal survey on children's deaths: Silver, "An Introduction," in Monet, *Canadian History*, p. 340.

P. 29   Three-mile walk to school with sisters: Biggar, *Anecdotal Life*, p. 23.

P. 29   Louisa Macdonald compared to her brother, "the ugliest man": ibid., p. 84.

P. 29   Macdonald, "never had a boyhood": Pope, *Memoirs*, p. 6.

P. 30   Macdonald, "university education": ibid., p. 5.

P. 31   Macdonald, "the fascination of the turkey": Macpherson, *Macdonald*, p. 81.

P. 32   Macdonald as compulsive reader, ibid., p. v.

CHAPTER 3: THE RIGHT TIME TO BE A SCOT

P. 35   St. Andrew's preceptor takes liking to Macdonald: Creighton, *Politician*, p. 39.

P. 37   Edinburgh as "self-consciously modern": Herman, *How the Scots*, p. vii.

P. 37   Scots "deal[ing] with a dominant culture": ibid., p. 115.

P. 40   Disraeli on Scots at head of poll: ibid., p. 347.

P. 42   Ross, "entire educational system of the country": McKillop, *Intelligence*, pp. 25–29.

P. 43   Macdonald in "Macdonald Soft Tartan Kilt": Martin, *Macdonald: Scotsman or Canadian*, p. 10.

P. 43   Campbell on Macdonald's "tone of voice & manner": Martin, "Sir John Eh?" p. 2.

P. 43   Journalist on "moot question where he was born": ibid., p. 3.

CHAPTER 4: HORSE DEALING, TAVERN KEEPING AND THE LAW

P. 45   Hugh Macdonald on demand for lawyers: Biggar, *Anecdotal Life*, p. 28.

P. 45   John Langton, "I know of no money-making business in Canada": *Early Days*, p. 201.

P. 46   George Mackenzie, "say nothing on business" and "A dead-and-alive way with them never goes": Lena Newman, *Album*, p. 25; Teatero, "Dead and Alive," thesis; and Creighton, *Politician*, p. 27.

P. 48   Macdonald, "The one thing I have always admired": Lockhardt, "Early Life," thes jis, p. 25.

Pp. 49–54   Macdonald law cases: Teatero, "Dead and Alive," thesis; and Creighton, *Politician*, pp. 43, 55–68.

P. 54   Macdonald in real estate in 1842: Johnson, *Macdonald*, p. 200.

P. 58   "Join the Orange Lodge and become an alderman": *Kingston Daily News*, June 8, 1891.

P. 58   Wilson, "Secure a handsome independence first": LAC, Macdonald Fonds, vol. 544, p. 257.

CHAPTER 5: A CONSERVATIVE IN A CONSERVATIVE COUNTRY

P. 61   Macdonald's wedding, exchanges gold rings with Isabella: Phenix, *Demons*, p. 60.

P. 62   Macdonald, "To fill a gap": Parkin, *Macdonald*, p. 12.

P. 62   Disraeli, "I love fame": Aldous, *Lion and Unicorn*, p. xiv; and
               Trudeau, "a great man": English, *Citizen*, p. 78.

P. 63   Macdonald's reply to nomination as candidate: Biggar, *Anecdotal
               Life*, pp. 56–57.

P. 64   Macdonald election manifesto: Pope, *Memoirs*, p. 34.

P. 67   First statute of Upper Canada re the poor: Malcolmson in
               Tulchinski, *Preserve and Defend*, p. 45.

P. 68   Estimate of 9 per cent government spending on social programs
               and education: Wallace, "Origins of Social Welfare State."

P. 68   Liberal MP, "The moment a Government is asked to take
               charge": Waite, *Life and World*, p. 37.

P. 69   Bishop Strachan on national debt "consistent" with interests
               of country: Martin, *Causes of Confederation*, p. 170.

P. 70   Insults in Legislature debates: Skelton, *Galt*, p. 203.

P. 70   Legislature debate, De Bleurey, et al.: *Debates*, May 8, 1846,
               vol. IV, part II, pp. 1296–97.

P. 71   Macdonald-Blake duel: Creighton, "Macdonald and Kingston,"
               p. 75; and Swainson, *Macdonald of Kingston*, p. 36.

P. 71   "His walk, then, as ever, was peculiar": Biggar, *Anecdotal Life*,
               p. 61.

P. 72   Langelier, "qui faisait toute sa gloire": Waite, *Life and World*, p. 6.

Pp. 72–73   Macdonald, "The law of primogeniture": *Debates*, Feb. 1, 1845,
               vol. IV, part I, pp. 1235–38.

P. 73   Macdonald's activities on behalf of Kingston: Johnson,
               Macdonald, p. 205.

CHAPTER 6: GOING HEADLONG

P. 75   Macdonald's letter to Margaret Greene, July 12, 1845: Johnson,
               Affectionately, p. 35.

P. 78   Isabella's second letter of 1848: ibid., p. 54.

P. 79 (fn)   patent medicines containing opium: Newman, *Album*, p. 41.

P. 82   Macdonald, "The weather here is so fine and warm": Nov. 20,
             1848, Johnson, *Affectionately*, p. 42.

P. 84   Macdonald, "The *Boy* is flourishing," and "I feel quite soli-
             tary": Montreal, Sept. 28, 1847, ibid., p. 53.

P. 85   Macdonald, "he is now however great friends with her":
             Kingston, July 9, 1848, Johnson, ibid., p. 56

P. 86   "grey, unrelieved tragedy": Creighton, *Politician*, p. 260.

CHAPTER 7: NEW GUYS WITH NEW IDEAS

P. 88   "failed, with astonishing uniformity": Creighton, *Politician*,
             p. 69.

P. 89   Campbell and Macdonald rewrite law partnership: ibid., pp.
             100–101; and Phenix, *Demons*, p. 61.

Pp. 89–90.   "The key to understanding the main features of Canadian
             national political culture": Stewart, *Origins*, p. 85.

P. 92   Descriptions of Lord Durham: Wade, *French Canadians*,
             pp. 180–83; Hyam and Martin, *Reappraisals*, pp. 73–74.

Pp. 92–93   Quotations from Durham Report: Bliss, *Documents*, pp. 50–62;
             Wade, pp. 184–96.

Pp. 94–95   "Miracle" of French-Canadian revival: Wade, *The French
             Canadians*, pp. 284–308; also in Heintzman, "Political Culture
             of Quebec"; and Dickinson and Young, *History of Quebec*.

P. 95   "clergy was as much a means of national unity": Trofimenkoff,
             Dream, p. 115.

P. 96   Durham Report as "the greatest state document": Hyam and
             Martin, *Reappraisals*, p. 75.

P. 96   Lord Russell, "impossible for a Governor to be responsible":
             Finlay, *Structure of History*, p. 138.

P. 97   Sydenham election tactics: Abella, "Sydenham Election."

P. 97   Bagot, "Whether the doctrine of responsible government is
             openly acknowledged": McInnis, *Canada*, p. 237.

P. 97   British attitudes to Responsible Government: Bodelson, *Studies in Imperialism*.

P. 98   Baldwin descriptions: Careless, *Pre-Confederation Premiers;* and Cross, "The Waste that Lies before Me."

Pp. 98–99   LaFontaine description: *Dictionary of Canadian Biography*, vol. XII.

P. 100   "With a kind of bacterial thoroughness": Monet, in Hamelin, *Political Ideas*, p. 27.

CHAPTER 8: A SHORT TIME BEFORE THE LONG GAME

P. 104   Macdonald, "it would make me too dependent on Govt": letter to Margaret Greene, Jan. 20, 1847, Johnson, *Affectionately*, p. 48.

P. 104   "could not be called a great speaker": Pope, *Memoirs*, p. 647.

Pp. 104–105 journalist, "careless utterance": Martin, "Sir John Eh?" p. 2.

P. 105   Fabre, "he is languid at times at stating his case": Pope, *Memoirs*, p. 658.

P. 105   "not infrequently contrived to mislay": ibid., p. 658.

P. 105   Fabre, "too clever and too well-versed": ibid., p. 658.

Pp. 105–106 Macdonald's memory for names: Biggar, *Anecdotal Life*, pp. 206–209.

P. 106   Patteson literary argument: Waite, *Macdonald*, p. 40.

Pp. 106–107 Macdonald, "an Indian once said to myself": Smith, "John A. Macdonald and Aboriginal Canada."

P. 108   Macdonald, "I returned last week from Toronto" and "She had as much to do as she is able for": Dec. 3, 1848, Johnson, *Affectionately*, p. 60.

P. 109   Macdonald, "She is like the 'Invisible Lady'" and "Since September last I have been alone": Jan. 20, 1850, ibid., pp. 67–68.

P. 110   Campbell-Macdonald partnership negotiations: Johnson, *Letters of Sir John A. Macdonald*, vol. 1, p. 158, and (fn) pp. 158–59; and Creighton, *Politician*, p. 148.

P. 110   Macdonald, "I am more than usually *tight* now": letter to Benson, Johnson, *Letters of Sir John A. Macdonald*, vol. 1, p. 178.

p. 110   Macdonald, "I haven't got a shilling to jingle": letter to Saddler, ibid., vol. 1, p. 260.

P. 111   Buchanan, "I would not have supposed it possible": Waite, *Life and World*, p. 17.

P. 111   Macdonald, "I thoroughly understand that business": Johnson, *Macdonald: Young Non-Politician*, p. 144.

P. 112   Campbell, "You will remember": Pope, *Memoirs*, p. 148.

P. 112   Macdonald, "If I don't carry a thing" and "There's no use crying": Waite, *Life and World*, p. 22.

Pp. 113–14   Rose, description: *Dictionary of Canadian Biography*, vol. XI; and Frankfurter, *Baneful Domination*, pp. 210–12.

P. 114   "personally, he was most attracted to Rose": Pope, *Memoirs*, p. 422.

P. 115   Ogle Gowan, relations with Macdonald and rape charge: Akenson, *Orangeman*, pp. 249, 295–300.

P. 116   Effect of Canada of British free trade: Finlay, *Structure*, pp. 148–50; and Shippee, *Relations*, pp. 3–6.

P. 116   Elgin, "property in most Canadians towns": Shippee, *Relations*, p. 6.

P. 117   Montreal manifesto calling for annexation: Macpherson, *Macdonald*, p. 201; Finlay, *Structure*; and Skelton, *Galt*.

P. 116 (fn)   Carnegie, "trade follows the lowest price"; Hyam and Martin, *Reappraisals*, p. 4.

P. 117   Kingston meeting: Creighton, *Politician*, pp. 140–45; and Stewart, "Imperial Policy," thesis.

P. 118   Macdonald, "all arrangements have long been made": Johnson, *Affectionately*, p. 66.

P. 119   Macdonald, "We have got Johnnie back again": ibid., p. 71.

CHAPTER 9: ENLARGING THE BOUNDS

P. 120 Macdonald, "We are a good deal hampered": Feb. 9, 1854, Johnson, *Letters of Sir John A. Macdonald*, vol. 1, pp. 200–203.

P. 123 Formation of Grit party: Careless, *Union of the Canadas*, p. 167; and Underhill, *National Political Parties.*

P. 125 Macdonald, "little ability, no political principles and no strength in numbers": Stewart, *Origins*, p. 61.

P. 125 Macdonald, "pre-Adamite Tories": letter to Charles Lyndsay, June 18, 1860, Johnson and Stelmack, *Letters of Sir John A. Macdonald*, vol. 2.

P. 126 Brown on possible Reform-Conservative alliance: Careless, *Brown*, vol. 2, p. 188.

Pp. 127–29 Macdonald letter to Brown Chamberlain: Jan. 21, 1856, Johnson, *Letters of Sir John A. Macdonald*, vol. 1, pp. 337–40.

P. 130 "They [Scots] manifested a real goodwill": Siegfried, *Race Question*, p. 55.

Pp. 130–31 Macdonald's fluency in French: From commentaries to author by historians Keith Johnson and Donald Smith. Sulte, "Macdonald was fond of reading French novels": Sweeny, *George-Etienne Cartier*, p. 102 (also fn p. 131). Ged Martin, in "Sir John Eh? Macdonald," cites a unlingual Quebec MP who claimed to have had many conversations in French with Macdonald. Smith cites a biography of Senator F.X.A. Trudel, who, in a February 1887 edition of *L'Etandard,* claims Macdonald spoke not a word of French. Martin, in "Sir John Eh?" cites the *Dictionary of Canadian Biography* as an authority that Laurier spoke English with a slight Scots accent. Taché's last letter to Macdonald, entirely in French, is quoted in Creighton, *Politician*, p. 418.

P. 132 Macdonald, "steeped to the lips in corruption": Swainson, *Macdonald*, p. 42.

P. 132   MacNab, "all my politics are railroads": Simpson, *Spoils*, p. 68.

P. 132   Macdonald, "The party is nowhere": letter by Macdonald to
              Campbell, March 8, 1855, LAC, Macdonald Fonds, vol. 194.

P. 133   Macdonald, "the Parson": Johnson, *Affectionately*, p. 15.

P. 134   Louisa's rental arrangements with Williamsons: Pope, *Memoirs*,
              p. 650.

P. 136   Macdonald, "Isabella has been very, very ill" and "desperately
              ill all last week": Johnson, *Affectionately*, pp. 75, 77.

P. 136   Macdonald, quoting Hugh John, "I like Kingston best": ibid.,
              p. 77.

P. 137   Macdonald, "I am carrying on a war": March 17, 1856, ibid.,
              p. 77.

P. 138   Macdonald, "The great reason I have always been able to beat
              Brown": Pope, *Memoirs*, p. 653 (fn).

Pp. 138–39   Brown description: *Dictionary of Canadian Biography*, vol. X;
              Careless, *Brown*, and Careless, "Brown's Political Ideas," in
              Careless at Work, pp. 67–74.

P. 138   "A campaign is George Brown in the pulpit": Willison,
              Reminiscences, p. 178.

P. 139 (fn)   Brown, "men-stealers: Careless, *Brown*, vol. 2, p. 27.

P. 140   Sheppard, "Take him on the ground of abuses": Waite, "Ideas
              and Politics in British North America," p. 100.

P. 140   Macdonald, "every man should support his own religious
              teacher": *Debates*, vol. XI, part I, pp. 546–48.

P. 141   Brown versus Macdonald re Kingston Penitentiary: Creighton,
              Politician; Careless, *Brown;* and *Debates*, 1849 (pp. 203, 207,
              208), 1850 (pp. 1507–09), 1851 (pp. 519–20).

Pp. 141–42   Macdonald, "If there is one thing to be avoided": *Debates*,
              vol. XI, part III, p. 2296, March 23, 1853.

P. 143   Brown, "What has French-Canadianism been denied?":
              Careless, *Brown*, vol. 1, p. 166; Bliss, *Canadian Historical
              Documents*, pp. 92–94.

P. 144   "Church and state could not really be separated": Morton, *Shield*, p. 316.

CHAPTER 10: FORMS ARE THINGS

P. 146   Macdonald, "You will see by the enclosed": Johnson, *Letters of Sir John A. Macdonald*, vol. 1, p. 296.

P. 146   Macdonald, "I am told there are a dozen [Conservative] candidates": letter to Henry Becher, Dec. 5, 1857, ibid., p. 466.

P. 147   A.J. Macdonnell to replace Campbell: Creighton, *Politician*, p. 208.

P. 148   "Contrary to the claims of the Liberal politicians": Sowby, "Macdonald the Administrator," thesis, p. ii.

P. 148   "He took these duties seriously": Johnson, *Macdonald*, p. 206.

P. 149   Macdonald, "I have infinitely more to do": ibid., p. 207.

P. 149   "He attached great importance to his correspondence" and "was exacting in his demands": Pope, *Memoirs*, pp. 639, 655.

P. 150   Macdonald, "the devil of a departmental reformer": Waite, *Life and World*, p. 20.

P. 152   Macdonald, "I'd as soon go to hell": Gwyn, *Private Capital*, p. 118.

P. 153   Responsibilities of attorney general: Johnson, *Macdonald*, pp. 207–208.

Pp. 153–54 Macdonald and Indian affairs: Smith, "John A. Macdonald and Aboriginal Canada," pp. 10–14.

P. 155   Macdonald and Rev. Peter Jones: Smith, ibid., p. 20.

Pp. 155–56 Lewis, "all Criminal Law should be considered a transcript of the Divine Law": Bellomo, "Attitudes Towards Crime," p. 11.

P. 156   Macdonald on sentence for attempted sodomy: letter to provincial secretary, May 7, 1864, LAC, Macdonald Fonds, vol. 587.

P. 156   Macdonald on sentencing of thirteen-year-old girl: letter to
            provincial secretary, Nov. 16, 1864, ibid.

P. 157   Macdonald on sentencing of Samuel Ross: July 12, 1858,
            Johnson and Stelmack, *Letters of Sir John A. Macdonald*,
            vol. 2, p. 65. Macdonald on poverty of another prisoner:
            June 15, 1859, ibid., p. 151.

P. 157   Macdonald, "Your natural kindness of disposition": Oct. 31,
            1871, Creighton Papers, LAC, Macdonald Fonds, MG 29,
            F 9–3.

P. 157   Brown, "the moral tomb of those who enter them": Bellomo,
            "Attitudes Towards Crime," p. 22.

Pp. 157–58 Macdonald, "Cut him dead": Gwyn, *Private Capital*, pp. 93–94.

P. 158   Macdonald, "The first duty of a Government": June 19, 1871,
            LAC, Macdonald Letters, LB-15, pp. 940–41.

P. 158   Macdonald, "We are satisfied that these requirements": letter
            to Bench, Feb. 13, 1855, Johnson, *Letters of Sir John A.
            Macdonald*, vol. 1, pp. 240–41.

P. 159   Macdonald, "to consider fitness as the first requirement":
            Simpson, *Spoils*, p. 305.

P. 159   "Sir John was always anxious": Cartwright, *Reminiscences*,
            p. 49.

P. 159   Macdonald promotion of William Ritchie to Supreme Court
            chief justice: *Dictionary of Canadian Biography*, vol. XII,
            entry for Ritchie.

P. 159   Macdonald, "He is a Grit": Stewart, "Macdonald's Greatest
            Triumph," p. 6.

P. 160   Macdonald, "Certainty of punishment": Oct. 31, 1871, LAC,
            Creighton Papers, MG 29 L9–3.

P. 160   Macdonald, "This is a country of law and order": MacDermot,
            "Political Ideas," p. 250.

CHAPTER 11: THE DOUBLE SHUFFLE

P. 162   Macdonald, "Heap as many epithets and reproaches on me":
          Debates, May 28, 1856, vol. XIII, part V, p. 2283.

P. 162   Macdonald, "I might, as you know, have been Premier": Nov.
          13, 1856, Johnson, *Letters of Sir John A. Macdonald*, vol. 1,
          p. 392.

P. 165   Campbell, "I dare say you are very busy": Swainson, *Mac-
          donald*, p. 43.

P. 165   "Ah, John A., how I love you": Cartwright, *Reminiscences*, p.
          47.

P. 165   Maclean, Macdonald "had a wonderful influence over many
          men": Willison, *Reminiscences*, p. 184.

P. 166   Macdonald, "He destroyed one or two marvellous good plots":
          letter to James Strachan, Feb. 9, 1854, Johnson, *Letters of
          Sir John A. Macdonald*, vol. 1, pp. 100–102.

P. 166   Macdonald, "It's a damned sharp curve": Waite, *Life and Times*,
          p. 324.

P. 166   Macdonald, "We are losing everywhere": letter to Becher,
          Dec. 14, 1857, Johnson, *Letters of Sir John A. Macdonald*,
          vol. 1, p. 472.

P. 167   Macdonald, "Canvass steadily and vigorously": Johnson,
          Macdonald, p. 218.

P. 167   Macdonald, "I am infinitely obliged to you": Johnson, *Letters of
          Sir John A. Macdonald*, vol. 1, p. 1.

P. 167   clientelism "long assumed to be a normal part of the political
          process": Noel, *Patrons*, p. 15.

P. 168   Zimmerman claims more members to be found in own apart-
          ment: ibid., p. 117.

P. 168   Macdonald, "keep the Whitby Post Office [position] open":
          letter to Smith, May 23, 1861, Johnson, *Letters of Sir John
          A. Macdonald*, vol. 1, p. 366.

Pp. 168–69   Macdonald, "As soon as Toronto returns Conservative members": Stewart, *Origins*, p. 65.

P. 169   Macdonald, "De L'Armitage is dying": July 12, 1856, Johnson, *Letters of Sir John A. Macdonald*, vol. 1, p. 326.

P. 169   Macdonald, "I have a letter from Noel wanting the Notaryship of the Bank": letter to Charles Ross, June 7, 1864, ibid., vol. 3.

P. 171   Macdonald, "It was of the very greatest importance": *Debates*, Oct. 27, 1854, vol. XII, part II, p. 830.

P. 171   Macdonald, "that the agitation will still be kept up" and "There is no maxim which experience teaches more clearly": *Debates*, Nov. 6, 1854, vol. II, part II, pp. 897, 942–46.

P. 173   "He should be sorry" and "if they [the opposition] could make the world all of one way of thinking": Creighton, *Politician*, p. 221.

P. 174   Queen's choice of Ottawa as capital: Gwyn, *Private Capital*, p. 37.

P. 174   Head, "the least objectionable": Memorandum, *CHR*, vol. 16 (1935), p. 417.

P. 175   Macdonald, "an insult offered to the Queen": telegram to S. Amsden, July 30, 1858, Johnson, *Letters of Sir John A. Macdonald*, vol. 2, p. 70.

P. 177   Macdonald, "Some fish require to be toyed with": Creighton, *Politician*, p. 267.

Pp. 177–78   Macdonald's comments on Cartier: Johnson and Stelmack, *Letters of Sir John A. Macdonald*, vol. 2, pp. 22, 235, 238.

Pp. 178–81   Description of Cartier: Sweeny, *Cartier*; Young, *Montreal Bourgeois*; *Dictionary of Canadian Biography*, vol. X; Best, "George-Etienne Cartier," thesis.

P. 179   "his career demonstrates the power of railways": Young, *Montreal Bourgeois*, p. xii.

P. 180   Cartier, "The prosperity of Montreal": Underhill, *National Political Parties*, p. 372.

P. 181   Cartier, "That is quite correct, I do not consult anybody": Moore, *1867*, p. 136.

P. 181   Cartier, "The activity of the heart": Monck, *My Canadian Leaves*, p. 149.

P. 181   Description of Luce Cuvillier: Young, *Montreal Bourgeois*, p. 35.

P. 181   Macdonald, "sheet anchor": letter to George Benjamin, June 4, 1861, Johnson and Stelmack, *Letters of Sir John A. Macdonald*, vol. 2, p. 342.

P. 182   Cartier's plan to retire to England: Young, *Montreal Bourgeois*, p. 45.

CHAPTER 12: ISABELLE, HUGH JOHN AND DAISY

P. 183   "grey unrelieved tragedy": Creighton, *Politician*, p. 260.

P. 183   Macdonald, "bare his bottom with dignity": Aug. 21, 1857, letter to Helen Macdonald, Johnson, *Affectionately*, p. 82.

Pp. 184–86 Dr. McSherry's diagnosis of Isabella's illness: McSherry, "The Illness of the First Mrs. John A. Macdonald," pp. 31–37.

P. 185   Dr. Hyde's diagnosis: commentary to author.

P. 187   Macdonald, "In the first place, tell Hugh that I am extremely pleased at the report": April 11, 1861, letter to Louisa, Johnson, *Affectionately*, p. 95.

P. 188   James Williamson's letters to father: Phenix, *Demons*, pp. 112–19.

P. 189   *Ploughboy* shipwreck scare: July 7, 1859, letter to Margaret: Johnson, *Affectionately*, p. 91.

CHAPTER 13: DOUBLE MAJORITY

Pp. 190–91 British commentary on Macdonald as "a distinguished statesman" and "the principal man": Stewart, "Imperial Policy,"
thesis, p. 108 (fn).

P. 191 "Whither Are We Drifting?": *Colonist*, June 29, 1858.

P. 191 Jones, "through British American territory to the Pacific":
Pope, *Day*, p. 50.

P. 192 "an almost total absence of a literature of pessimism": Fallis,
"Idea of Progress," p. 176.

P. 194 Keefer, "Steam has exerted an influence over matter": Nelles,
Philosophy of Railroads, p. xxv.

P. 194–95 "Steam conquered space and time"; Bliss, *Northern Enterprise*,
pp. 161–62.

P. 195 Keefer, "Ignorance and prejudice will flee": Nelles, *Philosophy of
Railroads*, p. xxxvii.

P. 195 *Canadian Gem*, "Canada is destined to become one of the finest
countries": Morton, *Shield*, p. 171.

P. 195 Hind, "a magnificent future . . . which shall place the
province": Fallis, "Idea of Progress," p. 172.

P. 196 "Upon my word, I do not think that there is much to be said":
Noel, *Patrons*, p. 137.

P. 196 Macdonald, "We are having a hard fight in the House": letter
to Margaret Williamson, March 29, 1858, Johnson,
Affectionately, p. 89.

P. 196 Macdonald, "We are getting on very slowly": letter to Helen
Macdonald, June, 17, 1858, ibid., p. 90.

P. 196 Pope, "I believe, [he] had fully made up his mind": Creighton,
Politician, p. 337.

P. 197 Macdonald, "When I have looked back upon my public life":
Kingston speech, November 1860, Macpherson, *Macdonald*,
pp. 296–98.

P. 197   Macdonald, "He is a very good fellow": letter to Margaret, Johnson, *Affectionately*, p. 94.

P. 198   Macdonald, "Take things pleasantly": Waite, *Life and World*, p. 18.

P. 198   Macdonald, "For twenty long years": Pope, *Memoirs*, Appendix F, pp. 526–30.

P. 199   Macdonald, "too abstract a question": letter to Brown Chamberlin, 1855, Johnson, *Letters of Sir John A. Macdonald*, vol. 1, p. 292.

P. 200   *Globe*, "Our French rulers": Sweeny, *Cartier*, p. 100.

P. 200   Brown, "a deep scheme of Romish Priestcraft": Slattery, *McGee*, p. 41.

P. 200   Macdonald, "The Elections will come off in June": letter to Ryerson, May 29, 1861, Johnson and Stelmack, *Letters of Sir John A. Macdonald*, vol. 2, p. 331.

P. 200   Macdonald, "We must soothe the Orangemen": letter to Sidney Smith, Oct. 13, 1860, ibid., vol. 2, p. 168.

P. 200   Macdonald, "politics is a game requiring great coolness": ibid.

P. 201   Macdonald, qualified double-majority: Russell, *Constitutional Odyssey*, p. 16.

P. 203   *Globe*, "The disruption of the existing union": Morton, *The Critical Years*, p. 72.

P. 203   Macdonald, "I am a sincere unionist": Johnson, *Macdonald*, p. 225.

P. 204   "was known to have an amorous disposition": Roy, *Kingston*, p. 163.

P. 204   Macdonald, "There is no wisdom below belt": Waite, "Sir John A. Macdonald: The Man," p. 151.

P. 204   "I have never met": Jameson, *Summer Rambles*, p. 139.

P. 205   Macdonald, "I forgot to tell you": letter to Margaret Greene, Nov. 3, 1845, Johnson, *Affectionately*, p. 37.

Pp. 205–206 St. Valentine's Day ball: Macpherson, *Macdonald*, pp. 38–39; and Newman, *Album*, p. 46.

P. 207   Macdonald and Agnes Bernard in Toronto and Quebec City: Reynolds, *Agnes*, pp. 28–30.

P. 207   Macdonald, "a warm, personal friend": letter to Helen Macdonald, Oct. 20, 1858, Johnson, *Affectionately*, p. 90.

Pp. 207–208 Hall, "My loved John": Dec. 21, 1860, LAC, Macdonald Fonds, vol. 545; and Newman, *Album*, p. 46.

P. 208   Macdonald, "P. S. You can make love to Polly": Johnson and Stelmack, *Letters of Sir John A. Macdonald*, vol. 2, p. 402.

Pp. 209–11 Eliza Grimason description: Newman, *Album*; Phenix, *Demons*; and Biggar, *Anecdotal Life*, pp. 238–40.

P. 210   "the shrine of John A.'s worshippers": Roy, *Kingston*, p. 193.

P. 211   "central, emotional dead spot": Johnson, *Macdonald*, p. 202.

P. 211   "because women know men": Willison, *Reminiscences*, p. 178.

P. 212   "It is not too much to say": Waite, "Sir John A. Macdonald: The Man," p. 146.

Pp. 212–13 Head, "If it is difficult for any statesman": July 16, 1857, *House of Commons Parliamentary Papers*, 1857–58, vol. 40, pp. 12–15.

P. 213   "never so intimate with any Governor-General": Pope, *Memoirs*, p. 141.

CHAPTER 14: THE SHIELD OF ACHILLES

P. 215   Macdonald, "quite willing personally": letter to Watkin, March 27, 1865, Waite, *Confederation Debates*, p. 228.

P. 216   McGee, "Who reads a Canadian book?": *Hamilton Gazette*, June 8, 1854.

P. 216   McGee, description: Slattery, *McGee*; and *Dictionary of Canadian Biography*, vol. IX.

P. 217   McGee, "I see in the not remote distance": Slattery, *McGee*, p. 137.

P. 218   McGee, "one of expedients, a succession of make-shifts": ibid., p. 82.

P. 218   Macdonald, "Never did a man throw away a fine career": letter to Henry Smith, Oct. 28, 1858, Johnson and Stelmack, *Letters of Sir John A. Macdonald*, vol. 2, p. 91.

P. 219   McGee, "ready and dextrous": Slattery, *McGee*, p. 93.

P. 219   Galt description: Skelton, *Galt*; and *Dictionary of Canadian Biography*, vol. XII.

Pp. 219–20   Macdonald, "You call yourself a *Rouge*": letter to Galt, Nov. 2, 1857, Johnson, *Letters of Sir John A. Macdonald*, vol. 1, p. 457.

P. 221   Macdonald, "unstable as water": Van den Otten, "Alexander Galt."

P. 222   Cauchon memorandum on the "Red River and Saskatchewan Country": Zaslow, *Canadian North*, p. 2.

P. 223   Report on West by Hind: ibid., p. 3

P. 225   Cartier warning to Bulwer-Lytton: Sweeny, *Cartier*, pp. 120–21.

P. 226   Early Confederation proposals: Upton, "The Idea of Confederation," in Morton, *Shield*.

P. 227   Bulwer-Lytton, "the convenience of the present Canadian administration": Careless, *Brown*, vol. 1, p. 284.

P. 228   Macdonald, *Address to the Electors:* in Johnson and Stelmack, *Letters of Sir John A. Macdonald*, vol. 2, pp. 345–51.

P. 229   Macdonald, "As you are situated": letter to Benjamin, June 4, 1861, ibid., vol. 2, p. 342.

Pp. 230–31   Brown at Reform convention: George Brown, "Reform Convention," p. 262.

P. 231   "some joint authority": ibid., p. 263.

Pp. 232–35   Prince of Wales's tour: Radforth, *Royal Spectacle*.

P. 233   Macdonald, "Our administration is more familiar": Johnson, *Macdonald*, p. 210.

P. 233   *Citizen*, "Ottawa appeared lovely and anxious as a bride": Radforth, *Royal Spectacle*, p. 48.

P. 235   Orangemen sing, "Water, water, holy water": ibid., p. 184.

P. 235   *New York Times*, "a rational population": ibid., p.198.

P. 235   Prince a "heart smasher": ibid., p. 332.

P. 235 (fn)   Prince of Wales, "Ah, it looks very well from the water":
              Cartwright, *Reminiscences*, p. 30.

P. 236   "the biggest liar in all Canada": Thompson, *Reminiscences*, p. 251.

P. 237   "I am a sincere unionist": Macdonald, speech in London, Nov.
              12, 1860, *Address to the Electors*, Appendix A, pp. 3–6.

P. 237   "It had called the attention of the world": ibid., Appendix A,
              pp. 28–35.

P. 238   "It has been said that I and my Upper Canadian colleagues":
              ibid., Appendix A, pp. 23–25.

P. 238   Macdonald, "wearisome beyond description": letter to James
              Gowan, March 12, 1861, Johnson and Stelmack, *Letters of
              Sir John A. Macdonald*, vol. 2, pp. 311–12.

P. 239   Macdonald, "violent Tories who are fools enough": Johnson,
              Macdonald, p. 222.

CHAPTER 15: CANADA'S FIRST ANTI-AMERICAN

P. 241   "The fratricidal conflict": Macdonald, *Address to the Electors*, in
              Johnson and Stelmack, *Letters of Sir John A. Macdonald*,
              vol. 2, p. 351.

P. 242   Macdonald on Lincoln as "a beast": letter to Judge Gowan,
              Nov. 27, 1864, LAC, MG27 1E17.

P. 243   "a huge bird chiseled in stone": Winks, *Civil War*, pp. 24–28.

P. 243 (fn)   Lyons, "a rough westerner of the lowest origin": Morton,
              Union, p. 88.

P. 244   Russell, "a sudden declaration of war": Winks, *Civil War*, p. 56.

P. 244 (fn)   "if the North thought fit at this time": Smith, *My Memory of
              Gladstone* (London: T.F. Unwin, 1904), pp. 43–44.

P. 245   "Secession first he would put down": Winks, *Civil War*, p. 50.

P. 245   Macdonald, "If they [Americans] are to be severed in two":
              speech in House, April 19, 1861; Pope, *Memoirs*, pp. 242–43.

P. 245   Macdonald, "will return to Canada sadder and wiser men": letter to McMicken, Feb. 15, 1865, LAC, Macdonald Fonds, vol. 587.

P. 245   Macdonald silences Conservatives cheering Southern victory: Cartwright, *Reminiscences*, p. 24.

P. 246   The *Trent* crisis: Winks, *Civil War*, pp. 71–77.

P. 247   Lincoln, "one war at a time": ibid., p. 77.

P. 247   *World*, "The simple fact is, Canada hates us": ibid., p. 99 (fn).

P. 247   Snowshoes called "creepers"; Bourne, *Balance of Power*, p. 224.

P. 248   Macdonald, "The day was hot": Pope, *Day*, p. 9.

Pp. 249   Macdonald, "There is no chance of there being": Johnson, *Macdonald*, p. 232.

P. 250   *Herald*, "overrun the Province in three weeks": Slattery, *McGee*, p. 156.

P. 251   Macdonald, "He is evidently an able man": letter to Margaret Greene, Nov. 20, 1845, Johnson, *Affectionately*, p. 42.

P. 251   Macdonald, "By the election of the President": Wise and Brown, *Canada Views*, p. 100.

P. 252   Macdonald, "I do not think there is anything in the world": letter to James Gowan, June 27, 1871, Macdonald Fonds, vol. 589, pp. 972–75.

P. 252   Macdonald, "It has been said that the United States is a failure": Martin, *Foundations*, p. 298.

P. 253   McGee, "It is not the figures [of soldiers] which give the worst view": Wise and Brown, *Canada Views*, p. 109.

P. 254   Jefferson to "liberate" Canada: Hyam, *Britain's Century*, p. 180.

P. 254 (fn) Taché, "the last cannon which is shot": *Dictionary of Canadian Biography*, vol. IX.

P. 255   American settlers as "Aliens": Errington, *The Lion, the Eagle*, pp. 166–87.

P. 255   McGee, "they coveted Florida": Wise and Brown, *Canada Views*, p. 109.

P. 256   *Church*, "For four years": ibid., p. 48.

P. 256   Bethune, "the extravagant wanderings": ibid., p. 49.

P. 257   Davin, "where there is nothing to differentiate": Berger, *Sense of Power*, p. 157.

P. 257   "a seeming contradiction": Wise and Brown, *Canada Views*, p. 94.

P. 259   "have always found it very hard to believe": Cartwright, *Reminiscences*, p. 60.

P. 262   "an active force of 50,000": Creighton, *Politician*, p. 330.

P. 262   Macdonald, "I am at last free": letter to Margaret Williamson, May 23, 1862, Johnson, *Affectionately*, pp. 96–97.

P. 263   "has had one of his old attacks": *Globe*, May 15, 1862.

P. 263 (fn)   *Globe*, "in a state of wild excitement": Martin, "Bottle," p. 166.

P. 263   Monck, "nominally by illness"; Batt, *Monck*, p. 50.

P. 263   Macdonald, "slap your chops": Swainson, *Macdonald*, p. 54.

P. 263   "The cleverest man of the lot": Martin, "Bottle," p. 167.

P. 264   Macpherson, "I called at your office twice": letter of 1839, Teatero, "Dead and Alive," thesis, p. 226.

P. 264   "particularly true for the period of his widowerhood": Pope, *Day*, p. 166.

Pp. 264–65   "leading a very dissipated life": Cartwright, *Reminiscences*, p. 32.

P. 265   Kingston's 136 taverns: Martin, "Bottle," p. 165.

P. 265   "Professional men were not ashamed": Moodie, *Life in the Clearings*, p. 45.

P. 266   Meredith, "Captain Sparks was hopelessly drunk": Gwyn, *Private Capital*, p. 189.

P. 266   Lady Monck, "such drunkenness": Batt, *Monck*, pp. 84–85.

P. 266   "One-half of all the crime": Burnet, "Changing Naval Standards." in Horn and Sabourin, *Studies in Canadian Social History*.

P. 267   Kimberley, "He should have been in the good old times": Creighton, *Old Chieftain*, pp. 158–59.

P. 267   Macdonald, "Yes, but the people would prefer John A. drunk" and "Mr. Chairman, I don't know how it is": Biggar, *Anecdotal Life*, pp. 193–94.

P. 268   Northcote, "People do not attribute his drinking": April 29, 1870, Morton, *Manitoba*, p. 98.

Pp. 268–69, Macdonald, "we have shown that we do not wish to cling": Creighton, *Politician*, p. 335.

CHAPTER 16: THE WILL TO SURVIVE

P. 271   Brown, "Already I long to be back with you": Careless, "Mother of Confederation," p. 79.

P. 271   Anne Brown, studies in Germany: ibid., p. 58.

P. 272   Mowat, "the softer side of his nature": Careless, *Brown*, vol. 2, p. 186.

P. 272   Anne Brown, "You must never speak of settling down here": ibid., vol. 2, p. 188.

P. 273   Brydges, "omnibus arrangement": Creighton, *Politician*, p. 349.

P. 273   Brown, "grimalkin": *Globe*, April 30, 1863.

P. 273   Macdonald, McGee, "A drunken man is a terrible curse": Slattery, *McGee*, p. 207.

P. 273   McGee, "the fortunate genius": ibid., p. 230.

P. 274   *Times*, "numerous enough to irritate": Martin, *Britain and Confederation*, p. 185.

P. 275–76   Macdonald, "It is stated [by some opponents of Confederation]": Browne, *Documents on Confederation*, pp. 95–96.

P. 276   Macdonald, "We must, therefore, become important": ibid.

P. 278   Britain's share of world trade: Hyam, *Britain's Imperial Century*, p. 99.

P. 280   Disraeli, "a millstone around our necks": Alice Stewart, "Imperial Policy," thesis, p. 160.

P. 280   Disraeli, "power and influence we should exercise": ibid.

P. 280 *Edinburgh Review*, "productive of heavy expense": Slattery, *McGee*, p. 58.

P. 280 Taylor, "a sort of *damnosa hereditas*": Waite, "Cardwell and Confederation," p. 27.

P. 280 Melbourne, "the final separation of these colonies": Martin, *Britain and Confederation*, p. 166.

P. 280 (fn) Cobden, "looked more English": Morton, *Union*, p. 2.

Pp. 281 Peel, "the tenure by which we hold [them]": Martin, *Britain and Confederation*, p. 167.

P. 281 Russell, "the loss of a great portion of our Colonies": ibid.

P. 281 Palmerston, "it would lower us greatly": ibid.

P. 281 Macdonald, "to raise revenue in [its] own fashion": Johnson, *Macdonald*, p. 234.

P. 281 Macdonald, "a matter of the gravest importance": memorandum to Head, March 6, 1861, Johnson and Stelmack, *Letters of Sir John A. Macdonald*, vol. 2, pp. 306–307.

P. 282 Cardwell, "lynx-eyed logicians": Waite, *Cardwell*, pp. 20–21.

P. 282 State of Colonial Office: Farr, *Colonial Office*, pp. 33–34.

P. 283 *Times*, "Who is Minister, at Quebec City": Martin, *Britain and Confederation*, p. 147.

P. 283 Gordon, "a last resort": ibid., p. 138.

P. 283 *Times*, "a wealthier and more completely English": ibid.

P. 283 Trollope, "Not one man in a thousand": Porter, *Imperialists*, p. 110.

P. 283 "felt himself like a cat in a strange garret": ibid., p. 251.

P. 283 Brown, "after all I have seen": Careless, *Brown*, vol. 2, p. 75.

P. 284 Newcastle, "Do not remain under such an error": Martin, *Britain and Confederation*, p. 65.

P. 284 Laurier, "armed with an eggshell": ibid., p. 64.

P. 284 (fn) Newcastle, "The injury to our own trade": ibid., p.67.

P. 285 Macdonald, "a panic": Creighton, *Politician*, p. 410.

P. 285 Macdonald, "a hole may be made in the mud": Winks, *Civil War*, p. 354.

P. 285   Macdonald, "forcible annexation and abandonment": letter to Col. Gray, March 27, 1865, Pope, *Memoirs*, p. 298.

P. 286   Queen Victoria, "the impossibility of our being able to hold Canada": Stacey, "British Military Policy," p. 25.

CHAPTER 17: IRREPLACEABLE MAN

P. 288   Brown, "Now gentlemen, you must talk to me": Careless, *Brown*, vol. 2, p. 127.

P. 288   "A strong feeling was found to exist": Creighton, *Politician*, p. 355.

P. 289   Macdonald, "the member for South Oxford": ibid., p. 356.

P. 289   Brown, "the repeated endeavours year after year": Reid, *Sourcebook*, pp. 200–201.

P. 290   Brown, "You never saw such a scene": Careless, *Brown*, vol. 2, p. 135.

P. 290   *Canadien*, "comptera parmi les plus memorable": Waite, *Life and Times*, pp. 45–46.

P. 290   *Berliner Journal*, "George Brown mit John A. Macdonald, Cartier und Galt": ibid.

P. 291   Macdonald, "As leader of the Conservatives": letter to S. Lynn, April 1866, Pope, *Correspondence*, p. 31.

P. 292   Cartwright on union with United States: Cartwright, *Reminiscences*, p. 20.

P. 292   Cartwright on understanding between Cartier and Brown: ibid.

P. 293   Macdonald, "If Canada is to remain a Country": Waite, *Confederation Debates*, p. 307.

P. 293   Brown, "I am not so well informed": Martin, *Britain and Confederation*, p. 53.

P. 293   *Globe*, "Efforts are to be made to induce the Lower Provinces": ibid.

P. 294   Smith, "In this country, what is there for Conservatives to conserve": Gwyn, *Paradox*, p. 36.

P. 295   "Macdonald practised the Burkean principles": Preece,
"Political Philosophy," p. 157.

P. 295   Preece, "What distinguished Macdonald": ibid., p. 162.

P. 295 (fn) Webbs' view of Canada: Feaver, "The Webbs in Canada."

P. 296   "For Macdonald, the word 'reform' was largely devoid of political significance": Waite, "Sir John A. Macdonald: The
Man," p. 37.

P. 297   Macdonald, "I am satisfied to confine myself to practical
things": *Parliamentary Debates on Confederation*, pp. 1001–
1002.

P. 297   "he thumped no tubs": Creighton, *Politician*, p. 180.

P. 297   "For the evangelical school of reconstructionists": Willison,
Reminiscences, p. 197.

P. 298   Macdonald, "I am like those who hear me": *Address to the
Electors*, 1860, Appendix A, p. 6.

P. 299   McGee, "How *can* you hope to secure the settlement":
Slattery, *McGee*, p. 220.

P. 299   Monck, "depends very much on your consenting to come into
the Cabinet": Careless, *Brown*, vol. 2, p. 138.

P. 299   Brown, "There was no help for it": ibid., p. 140.

P. 300   Brown, "it will cost half the revenue to the province": letter to
John A., August 14, 1864, Pope, *Memoirs*, pp. 281–82.

P. 300   Macdonald, "that I may call on you to lay aside": letter, July 7,
1864, ibid., pp. 276–77.

P. 301   Brown, "bearing symptoms of having been on a spree":
Careless, *Brown*, vol. 2, p. 151.

P. 301   Brown, "John A. and I were the only civilians": ibid., p. 150.

P. 301   Brown, "For the first time in my political life": Waite, *Life and
Times*, p. 38.

P. 303   Canadians met by oyster boat: ibid., p. 75.

P. 304   Brown, "shake elbow and how d'ye-do" and "something to the sea": Careless, *Brown*, vol. 2, p. 154.

P. 304   *Islander*, "substantials of beef rounds": Louella Creighton, *Elegant Canadians*, p. 13.

P. 304   Brown, "the ice became completely broken": Careless, *Brown*, vol. 2, p. 155.

P. 305   Brown, "They were unanimous": Wilfrid Smith, introduction to "Tupper's Minutes."

Pp. 305–306 Ross, "The fascinating dance goes merrily": Waite, *Life and Times*, p. 79.

P. 307   Macdonald, "there was no political connection": Whelan, *Union of the Provinces*, p. 43.

Pp. 307–308 Macdonald, "as a commercial enterprise": ibid., p. 45.

P. 308   Macdonald, "Everything, gentlemen, is to be gained by union": ibid., pp. 46–47.

CHAPTER 18: A PACT OF TRUST

P. 311   Macdonald, "I ha[d] no help": letter to James Gowan, Nov. 15, 1864.

P. 311   Feo Monck, "He is always drunk now": Monck, *Canadian Leaves*, p. 81.

P. 312   Rogers, "Macdonald was the ruling genius": Moore, *1867*, pp. 213–14.

P. 312   Macdonald, "I am satisfied": letter to M.C. Cameron, Dec. 19, 1864, LAC, Macdonald Fonds, vol. 387.

P. 313   Macdonald, "should be a mere skeleton and framework": Waite, *Life and Times*, p. 120.

P. 313   *Morning-Chronicle*, "bump-thump-jump": ibid., p. 86.

P. 314   Delegates' working hours: Moore, *1867*, p. 98.

P. 314   Mercy Coles, "with every stitch of clothing wringing wet": ibid., pp. 98–99.

P. 315   Whelan, "the Cabinet ministers—the leading ones especially":
         Waite, "Whelan's Reports."

P. 315   Carter, "retir[e] to the Old Country to spend their fortunes":
         Doughty, "Notes on the Quebec Conference," p. 26.

P. 315   Macdonald gets applause for opening speech: Creighton,
         Politician, p. 375.

P. 317   *Globe*, "Everyone here has had a fit of the blues": Waite, *Life
         and Times*, p. 90.

P. 317   Palmer, "the current seemed to set with the Canadians": ibid.,
         p. 94.

P. 317   Mowat, "I quite concur in the advantages": ibid., p. 95.

P. 317   *Northern Kingdom*, "Never was there such an opportunity":
         ibid., p. 88.

P. 318   Chandler, "merely large municipal corporations": ibid., p. 95.

P. 318   Macdonald rejects New Zealand example: Martin, "Archival
         Evidence."

P. 318   *Times*, "practical and unpretending": Waite, *Life and Times*,
         p. III.

P. 319   Brown, "Constitution adopted—a most credible document":
         Careless, *Brown*, vol. 2, p. 171.

P. 321   Macdonald, "We have avoided all conflict": Russell,
         Constitutional Odyssey, p. 27.

P. 321   *Globe*, "We desire local self-government": Vipond, "Federal
         Principle," p. 14.

P. 321 (fn)   Senators to be knighted: Pope, *Memoirs*, pp. 727–28, including
         Macdonald letter to Carnarvon, Jan. 30, 1867.

P. 322   Macdonald's books by Madison, Hamilton: Munro, *American
         Influences*, p. 18.

P. 322   Original Swiss constitution: McRoberts, *Canada and the
         Multinational State*, p. 695.

P. 323   Macdonald, "the use of the French language": *Parliamentary
         Debates on Confederation*, p. 944.

P. 324   *Journal de Québec*, "can and must one day aspire to being a nation": Silver, "Quebec and the French-Speaking Minorities," thesis.

P. 324   *La Minerve*, "As a distinct and separate nationality": ibid.

P. 326   Macdonald, "a distinct bargain, a solemn contract": Stanley, "Act or Pact," p. 142.

P. 326   Macdonald, "as a matter of fact . . . a Federal Union": ibid., p. 8.

P. 327   Macdonald, "The sad experience on the other side": Sweeny, *Cartier*, p. 143.

P. 327   Cartier, "That is not my policy": ibid.

P. 327   Taché, "tantamount to a separation": Jennifer Smith, "Confederation," p. 454.

P. 328   Taché, "The important thing to remember": Sweeny, *Cartier*, p. 106.

P. 329   Macdonald, "My great aim": letter to Buchanan, Oct. 16, 1864, LAC, Macdonald Fonds, vol. 587.

P. 329   Cameron, "better shown [his] patriotism": Dec. 19, 1864, ibid., vol. 587.

P. 330   Macdonald, "I thought my hon. friend knew": Martin, "Archival Evidence."

P. 330   Macdonald, "chief executive officers": Glazebrook, *History of Political Thought*, p. 146.

P. 330 (fn) Tupper, "a large municipality under the Central Government": Waite, *Life and Times*, p. 204.

P. 331   Macdonald, "the Central Government assumes": Creighton, *Politician*, p. 403.

P. 331   Hamilton's centralizing measures; Munro, *American Influences*, pp. 19, 33.

P. 331   Macdonald, "all the powers which are incident to sovereignty": Vipond, "Federal Principle," p. 14.

P. 332   Dunkin, "cry will be found to be pretty often": Martin, *Causes of Confederation*, p. 31.

P. 333 (fn) "Confederation table": Turner, "Mystery."

P. 333 Macdonald, "Have you thought over the formation of the Govt": letter to Tilley, Nov. 14, 1864, LAC, Macdonald Fonds, vol. 587.

P. 333 Macdonald, "I intend to commence next week": letter to Tupper, Nov. 14, 1864, ibid.

P. 334 St. Alban's Raid: Winks, *Civil War*, pp. 311, 314–15.

P. 334 Macdonald, "the unhappy and mistaken decision of Cursol": Creighton, *Politician*, p. 392.

P. 334–35 Macdonald, "individuals or incorporated companies like Railways": letter to Thomas Swinyard, Jan. 1, 1865, Macdonald Papers, Letterbook 7.

P. 335 Repayment to U.S. banks of $70,000: Winks, *Civil War*, p. 320.

P. 335 Macdonald, "a shrewd, cool and determined man": Creighton, *Politician*, p. 393.

P. 336 Macdonald, "We can't help the South": letter to Buchanan, Oct. 16, 1864, Hamilton Public Library.

CHAPTER 19: PARLIAMENT VS THE PEOPLE

P. 337 "Then let us be firm and united": Waite, *Life and Times*, p. 98.

P. 338 (fn) Whelan, "illness induced by fatigue": Waite, "Whelan's Reports," p. 139.

P. 339 *Edinburgh Review*, "harbinger of the future and complete independence": Waite, *Life and Times*, p. 20.

P. 339 *Saturday Review*, "not so much a step towards independence": Martin, *Britain and Confederation*, p. 173.

P. 339 *Times*, "nothing could be more in correspondence": Stewart, "Imperial Policy," thesis, p. 138.

P. 340 Brown, "A most gracious answer": Careless, *Brown*, vol. 2, p. 177.

P. 341 Brown, "Though we had been discussing the highest questions": ibid.

P. 341   Adderley, "Gladstone said to me the other day": Batt, *Monck*, p. 152.

P. 342   Brown, "John A.'s business affairs are in sad disorder": Careless, ibid., p. 190.

P. 343   Macdonald, "Canada on the whole": letter to Tupper, Nov. 14, 1864, Pope, *Correspondence*, p. 13.

P. 344   Dorion, "true confederation": Waite, *Pre-Confederation*, p. 221.

P. 344   "create a new nationality": Slattery, *McGee*, p. 268.

P. 344   Whelan, "a patch of sandbank in the Gulf": Waite, *Life and Times*, p. 186.

P. 346   Macdonald, "was in the nature of a treaty": Ajzenstat, *Founding Debates*, p. 421.

P. 346   Macdonald, "If this measure received the support of the House": ibid., p. 422.

P. 347   Macdonald, "general if not universal favour": letter to John Beattie, Feb. 3, 1865, Pope, *Correspondence*, p. 21.

P. 348   Macdonald, "Parliament is a grand inquest": Lockhart, "Contribution."

P. 349   Macdonald, "the tyranny of mere numbers": Johnson, *Macdonald*, p. 220.

P. 349   "one of those dreadful American heresies": *Globe*, Nov. 5, 1864.

P. 349   Brown, "the balance of power is held by the ignorant": Wise, *Peculiar Peoples*, p. 137.

P. 349   McGee, "The proposed Confederation": Ajzenstat, *Founding Debates*, pp. 189–90.

P. 350   O'Halloran, "When we assume the power": ibid., pp. 449–51.

P. 350   Hamilton *Times*, "If their [the people's] direct decision": Martin, *Causes of Confederation*, p. 30.

P. 351   Macdonald, "We in this house": Ajzenstat, *Founding Debates*, pp. 455–63.

P. 351 (fn)   Macdonald denounces conventions as "immoral and democratic": letter to Henry Becher, Mar. 15, 1862, LAC, Macdonald Fonds, vol. 587.

P. 352   Macdonald, "a strong and lasting government": letter to S. Amsden, Dec. 1, 1864, ibid., vol. 397.

P. 353   Macdonald, "the best, the cheapest": Ajzenstat, *Founding Debates*, p. 279.

P. 353   Macdonald, "lose their individuality": Reid, *Source-book*, p. 208.

P. 353   Macdonald, "it is an advance towards independence": ibid., p. 209.

P. 354   Dunkin, "What are we doing?": Ajzenstat, *Founding Debates*, p. 236.

P. 354   Cartier, "When we were united together": *Parliamentary Debates on Confederation*, p. 60.

P. 355   Mackenzie, "I do not think the federal system is necessarily a weak one": ibid., speech of Feb. 23.

P. 355   *Stratford Beacon*, "an unmistakably seedy condition": Waite, *Life and Times*, p. 156.

P. 356   Macdonald, "full of fight": Martin, *Britain and Confederation*, p. 244.

CHAPTER 20: THE ADMINISTRATION OF STRANGERS

P. 357   Macdonald, "declaration against the policy of Confederation": Creighton, *Politician*, p. 406.

P. 358   Macdonald, "any signs of weakness": Martin, *Foundations*, p. 365.

P. 358   Macdonald, "stick with the ship": Lockhart, "Macdonald Conservatism," p. 129.

P. 358   Macdonald on Tilley, "unstatesmanlike": Moore, *1867*, p. 169.

P. 358   Tupper, "under existing circumstances": Creighton, *Politician*, p. 409.

P. 359   Dorion, "This scheme is killed": Martin, *Foundations*, p. 365.

P. 360   Macdonald, "the most seminal mind": Waite, "Sir John A. Macdonald: The Man," p. 147.

P. 361   Howe, "live and die in insignificance": Waite, *Life and Times*, p. 71.

P. 361   Howe, "play second-fiddle to that damn'd Tupper": *Dictionary of Canadian Biography*, vol. X.

P. 361   Howe, "I am a dear lover of old England": Beck, *Howe*, p. 210.

P. 361   Howe, "You go down to the sea in ships": ibid., p. 202.

P. 361–62   Howe, "London [was] large enough": ibid.

P. 362   Howe, "with an Indian name": ibid., p. 201.

P. 362   Howe, "away from tidewater": Martin, *Causes of Confederation*, p. 44.

P. 362   Howe, "The builders of Babel"; Beck, *Howe*, p. 205.

P. 363   Tupper, "a great body of the trading men": Reid, *Source-book*, p. 277.

P. 363 (fn) Howe, "deadly weapons, so common": to George Moffat, May 8, 1849.

P. 364   Howe, "this crazy Confederacy": Slattery, *McGee*, p. 425.

P. 364   Brown, "we hear much talkee-talkee": Careless, *Brown*, vol. 2, p. 165.

P. 366   Ryerson, "a man does not love the King": Berger, *Sense of Power*, p. 103.

P. 366   Rev. Gray, "spirit of *submission*": ibid.

P. 367   "nationalistic history": ibid., p. 90.

P. 367   "the primacy of the community over individual selfishness": ibid., p. 103.

P. 367   Wood, "The bond of union between Canada and the other provinces": Ajzenstat, *Founding Debates*, pp. 215–17.

P. 368   Taché, "the last cannon which is shot": *Dictionary of Canadian Biography*, vol. IX.

P. 368   Collins, "more than any other Canadian statesman": Griffith, Speech to Kingston Historical Society.

P. 368   Davin, "the type of politician": Willison, *Reminiscences*, pp. 34–37.

P. 369   *British American*, "They are more American": Waite, *Life and Times*, p. 230.

CHAPTER 21: THE TURN OF THE SCREW

P. 371   Cardwell, "Our official dispatch": memorandum, Dec. 10, 1864, Colonial Office., *British North American Provinces Correspondence Respecting the Proposed Union* (London, 1867).

P. 371   Cardwell (to Monck), "to turn the screw": Batt, *Monck*, p. 109.

P. 372   Brown, "Dukes and Duchesses had to give way": Careless, *Brown*, vol. 2, p. 196.

P. 372   Galt, "down on the right knee": Skelton, *Galt*, pp. 379–80.

P. 373   Brown, "whether Darwin believed": Martin, *Britain and Confederation*, p. 264.

P. 373–74   Derby Day description: ibid., pp. 383–86.

P. 374   Brown, "are a different race from us": Careless, *Brown*, vol. 2, p. 197.

P. 374   Galt, "We were treated as if we were ambassadors": Martin, *Britain and Confederation*, p. 261.

P. 374   Macdonald, "This is the greatest honour": letter to Louisa, June 17, 1865, Johnson, *Affectionately*, pp. 98–99.

P. 375   *Telegraph*'s calculation of election result: Waite, *Life and Times*, p. 246.

P. 375   Tilley, "an expenditure of 8 or ten thousand dollars": Martin, *Foundations*, p. 372.

P. 375   Gordon, "I am convinced I can make (or buy)": ibid., vol. 2., p. 209.

P. 376   Brown, no "personal aspirations whatever": ibid., vol. 2, p. 201.

P. 377   Macdonald, "The union of all the Provinces is a fixed fact": *Ottawa Citizen*, Sept. 29, 1865.

P. 378   Brown, "Thank Providence—I am a free man": Careless, *Brown*, vol. 2, p. 207.

P. 378   Brown, "is a very serious matter for the Maritime provinces": ibid., p. 189.

P. 378   Brown, "a most inconvenient and inexpedient device": *Globe*, Aug. 8, 1866.

P. 379   Brown, "I want to be free to write": Waite, *Life and Times*, p. 43.

P. 379   Macdonald on Brown, "gave me assistance"; Moore, *Fathers*, p. 246.

P. 380   Memorial services for Lincoln in black churches: Winks, *Civil War*, p. 166.

P. 381   Monck, "helplessness, inertness and dependence": Stacey, "Fenianism," p. 248.

P. 381   McMicken detective, "one thousand dollars is offered in gold": Slattery, *McGee*, p. 303.

P. 382   Tilley to Macdonald, "Telegraph me in cipher" and "To be frank with you," and Galt to Macdonald, "That *means* had better be used": Martin, *Foundations*, pp. 373–74; and Wilson, "New Brunswick and Confederation," pp. 23–24.

P. 383   McMicken detective, "1,500 Fenians landed at Fort Erie": Senior, *Last Invasion*, p. 83, and following description of Fenian battles.

P. 383   *Globe*, "The autonomy of British America": Stacey, "Fenianism," p. 252.

P. 385   Monck to Macdonald, "valuable time is being lost": Reid, *Source-book*, pp. 280–81.

P. 386   Macdonald, "The proceedings have arrived at the stage that success is certain": ibid.

P. 386   Monck, "your right as a leader of the Government": ibid.

P. 387   Macdonald vomits on Government House chair: Batt, *Monck*, p. 34.

P. 387   Macdonald, "Look here McGee": Slattery, *McGee*, p. 337.

P. 387   Brown, "John A was drunk on Friday": Careless, *Brown*, vol. 2, p. 234.

P. 388–89   Macdonald, "The Bill should not be finally settled": Reid, *Source-book*, pp. 282–83.

P. 388   *Globe* scoop on BNA Act: Careless, *Brown*, vol. 2, pp. 240–41.

P. 389   Macdonald, "the Act once passed": letter to Tilley, Oct. 8, 1866, ibid.

CHAPTER 22: THE MAN OF THE CONFERENCE

P. 390   Langevin, "Macdonald is a sharp fox": Moore, *1867*, p. 212.

Pp. 390–91   Macdonald, "no minutes of the various discussions should be taken": Martin, *Foundations*, p. 385.

P. 391   Macdonald, "avoid any publicity": ibid., p. 386.

P. 391   *Morning Chronicle*, "vanity struck": Waite, *Life and Times*, p. 295.

P. 391   Howe, "lonely, weary and vexed": *Dictionary of Canadian Biography*, vol. X.

P. 392   Carnarvon, "occasionally so drunk as to be incapable": Martin, *Britain and Confederation*, p. 280.

P. 392   Macdonald, "for fear that an alarming story may reach you": letter to Louisa, Dec. 27, 1866, Johnson, *Affectionately*, pp. 102–103.

P. 393   Macdonald, "We are quite free to discuss points": Reid, *Source-book*, p. 243.

P. 394   Reilly, "I can't make bricks": Martin, *Britain and Confederation*, p. 282.

P. 395   Thring's draft legislation on independence: ibid., p. 190.

P. 395   Bury's proposal for agreement on independence: ibid.

P. 395   Howe, "the almost universal feeling": ibid., p. 171.

P. 396   Macdonald, "one of her own family, a Royal prince": *Parliamentary Debates on Confederation*, Feb. 6, 1865.

P. 396   Queen Victoria, "dearest Albert had often thought": Martin, "Queen Victoria and Canada," p. 227.

P. 396 (fn) "in some speeches he had said": Monck, *My Canadian Leaves*, p. 82.

P. 397   Disraeli, "It is so like Derby": letter to Lord Knutsford, July 18, 1889, LAC, Macdonald Fonds, vol. 529.

P. 397 (fn) Monck, "the natural yearning": Batt, *Monck*, p. 143.

P. 397 (fn) Tilley's letter on "Dominion": LAC, F/5002, T-54.

P. 398   Carnarvon, "derives its political existence": Scott, "Political Nationalism," p. 407.

P. 398   "One might almost say": P.B. Waite, "Ideas and Politics in British North America, 1864–66," PhD thesis, University of Toronto, 1953, p. 443.

P. 399   Smith, "the sentiment of provincial independence": *Macmillan's Magazine*, London, p. 408.

P. 402   Anderson, "imagined communities": Gwyn, *Nationalism Without Walls*, p. 20.

P. 403   "Not life, liberty and the pursuit of happiness": Morton, *Canadian Identity*, p. 111 (1961 ed.).

CHAPTER 23: TWO UNIONS

P. 406   Lady Macdonald, "My diaries as Miss Bernard": Reynolds, *Agnes*, p. 45.

P. 407   Lady Macdonald, "I also know that my love of Power is strong": ibid., p. 50.

P. 407   Macdonald, "I don't care for office for the sake of money": Thompson, *Reminiscences*, p. 231.

P. 408   Lady Macdonald, "I have found something worth living for" and "I often look in astonishment": Newman, *Album*, p. 86.

P. 408   Bernard, "everything to dissuade": *Dictionary of Canadian Biography*, vol. XII, Macdonald, p. 605.

P. 408   "tall, tawny, and . . . rather 'raw-boned'": Biggar. *Anecdotal Life*, p. 99.

P. 409   Lady Macdonald, "The French seem always wanting everything": Gwyn, *Private Capital*, p. 95.

P. 409   Lady Macdonald, "tearing down a steep forest roadway": Phenix, *Private Demons*, p. 164.

P. 410   Lady Macdonald, "A forcible yet changeful face": Macpherson, *Macdonald*, p. 315.

P. 410   Macdonald, "very fine eyes": ibid., p. 315.

Pp. 410–11 Lady Macdonald, "a delicious country for the rich": Reynolds, *Agnes*, p. 55.

P. 412   *Ottawa Citizen*, "a bunch of violets": ibid., p. 39.

P. 413   Macdonald, "My wife likes it from its novelty to her": letter to Louisa, March 21, 1867, Johnson, *Affectionately*, pp. 103–104.

P. 413   Carnarvon, "We are laying the foundation of a great State": Bliss, *Canadian History*, pp. 109–110.

P. 414   Macdonald, "H.M. said—'It is a very important measure'": letter to Louisa, March 21, 1867, Johnson, *Affectionately*, p. 104.

P. 415   Nova Scotian, "The great body of the house was utterly indifferent": Farr, *Colonial Office*, p. 16.

Pp. 415–16 Macdonald, "This remarkable event": letter to Lord Knutsford, July 18, 1884, LAC, Macdonald Fonds, vol. 529.

P. 416   McGee, "Everyone knew the result was a foregone conclusion": Martin, *Britain and Confederation*, p. 289.

P. 416   Royal Proclamation, 1763, Indians, "not be molested or disturbed": Russell, *Constitutional Odyssey*, p. 32.

P. 416 (fn) Lack of debate at Westminster on colonial subjects: Porter, *Absent-Minded Imperialists*, p. 107.

P. 418   Bennett "leaving their bones to bleach in a foreign land": Martin, *Britain and Confederation*, p. 62.

P. 418   BNA Act a blueprint for South Africa and Ireland: Hyam, *British Imperial Century*, p. 201.

P. 419   Macdonald, "We must, therefore, become important": Browne, *Documents on Confederation*, pp. 95–96.

CHAPTER 24: IDEA IN THE WILDERNESS

P. 421   Meredith, "John A. carried out of the lunchroom, hopelessly drunk": Gwyn, *Private Capital*, p. 97.

P. 421   Feo Monck, Ottawa "beastly": *Monck Letters*, p. 214.

P. 421   Meredith, "The more I see of Ottawa": Gwyn, *Private Capital*, pp. 36–37.

P. 422   Smith, "the tempering and restraining influences": *Macmillan's*, May 1865.

P. 422 (fn)   "A Canadian settler *hates* a tree": Jameson, *Winter Studies*, p. 49.

P. 423   Trollope, "The noblest architecture": Gwyn, *Private Capital*, p. 38.

P. 423   Macdonald, tower of West Block "like a cow bell": Slattery, *McGee*, p. 338.

P. 424   "a visionary, if slightly uncertain, idea in the wilderness": Gwyn, *Private Capital*, p. 38.

P. 425   McGee, "give way neither to Galt": Slattery, *McGee*, p. 392.

P. 428   Macdonald, "if the list were settled now": Pope, *Memoirs*, Appendix XV, pp. 727–28.

P. 429   Galt, "It is an ingracious and most unusual thing": Slattery, *McGee*, p. 392.

P. 430   Bourget, "l'obeissance à l'autorité constituée" and statement by Quebec bishops: Waite, *Life and Times*, pp. 300–301.

P. 430   Cartier, "The question is reduced to this": Ajzenstat, *Founding Debates*, p. 183.

P. 431   *Tribune*, "When the experiment of the 'dominion'": Shippee, *Canadian-American Relations*, pp. 198–99.

P. 431   Sumner, "a visible step": Callahan, *American Foreign Policy*, p. 308.

P. 431   Seward, "I know that Nature designs": Shippee, *Canadian-American Relations*, p. 200.

P. 432   Taylor, "events have presented to the people": Callahan, *American Foreign Policy*, p. 304.

P. 432   *Nor'Wester*, "Americanism has become rampant": Waite, *Pre-Confederation*, p. 147.

P. 432   Stanley, "Many people would dislike the long boundary line" and "if they choose to separate": Stacey, "Britain's Withdrawal," p. 15.

P. 433   Adderley, "It seems to me impossible": Waite, *Life and Times*, p. 317.

P. 433   *Times*, "We look to Confederation as the means of relieving this country": Stacey, "Britain's Withdrawal," p. 14.

P. 434   Galt, "I am more than ever disappointed": Skelton, *Galt*, pp. 410–11.

P. 435   Macdonald, "British North America is now merely a geographical description": letter to Monck, April 5, 1867, Pope, *Memoirs*, p. 730.

Pp. 435–36 Lady Macdonald, "This new Dominion of ours": Gwyn, *Private Capital*, p. 191.

P. 436   *Vindicator*, "some of them rush[ed] so closely": Louella Creighton, *Elegant Canadians*, pp. 170–71.

P. 436   *Morning Chronicle*, "Died! Last night at twelve o'clock," refusal to allow Queen's Proclamation, and Yarmouth with no gun salute: Granatstein and Hillmer, *First Drafts*, pp. 83–84.

P. 437   Brown, "With the first dawn of this gladsome midsummer morn": Careless, *Brown*, vol. 2, p. 252.

P. 438   *Reporter*, "From Halifax to Sarnia": Waite, "Ideas and Politics in British North America, 1864–66," thesis, p. 442.

P. 438   *Times,* "It supposes a nationality": Waite, *Pre-Confederation,*
         p. 251.

P. 439   Smith, "to hold together a set of elements": *The Week,*
         April 10, 1884.

P. 439   Gowan, "artificer in chief": Pope, *Correspondence,* p. 43.

Bibliography

BIBLIOGRAPHICAL NOTE

The motherlode of Macdonaldiana is located in the Library and Archives Canada (LAC), in Ottawa. His fonds comprise 805 rectangular cardboard boxes that, if stacked side by side, would stretch 37 metres. By contrast, the collection of Pierre Trudeau extends to 851 metres, or more than twenty times as long, and that of Brian Mulroney to 722 metres. The volume of paperwork generated by and for Canadian prime ministers thus expands to fill the capacity of the technology available to generate it, as well as the number of officials assisting in its production, and also, perhaps, to meet an ever-growing prime ministerial conviction of accomplishment.

Macdonald was well served, nevertheless. He claimed to have kept a copy of every letter he sent (largely true, his personal letters excepted) and to be able to put his hand on every letter he received (substantially untrue, according to his confidential secretary and biographer, Joseph Pope). After Macdonald's death, Pope, besides writing three books about him, devoted his retirement to sorting out what he called Macdonald's "appalling mass of correspondence." Between 1914 and 1917, Pope handed over 714 "bundles" of letters to the then Public Archives. Later rearranged professionally, these letters form the foundation of LAC's collection of Macdonaldiana. There are gaps: during his stints in opposition, 1862 to 1864 and 1873 to 1879, Macdonald wrote and kept little.

Additional material has been added over the years—the most recent, quoted in this book, being Macdonald's letter to a British lawyer on April 9, 1867, expressing his concern about possible American military action against the putative new nation. Gaps have been filled and the collection enriched, but the basic record is pretty much as it was a century ago.

Suggestions have been made that Pope was unduly protective of his former master, particularly because, after handing over his "bundles," he burned the rest. Pope insisted there was nothing in the residue that "could not stand the light of day." This is probably true. Pope, although a fierce defender of Macdonald, included in his books letters and papers that showed him in an adverse light; Queen's University principal George Munro Grant carped in his review of Pope's 1894 biography that it contained information about public figures that "contribute[d] nothing of the slightest consequence to our knowledge of the man or of the times."

All this material about Macdonald resides in the LAC cardboard boxes bearing the descriptor MG26-A. Besides Macdonald's outgoing letters (preserved in the form of copies of the originals, then stored in "letter-boxes"), the collection includes incoming letters from close to one hundred individuals with whom Macdonald corresponded regularly, and also his memoranda to the governor general and to the cabinet, state papers and ephemera such as railway tickets and programs for state occasions.

One invaluable aid to researchers exists now, as wasn't the case for Donald Creighton, who had to work entirely from the original handwritten letters and before the invention of the photocopier. In the early 1960s, the then National Library committed itself to publishing all of Macdonald's annotated correspondence. Two volumes were completed, covering the years 1836 to 1861. In the mid-1970s the project was halted for lack of funds. In fact a third volume, extending to mid-1867, was all but completed by this time; its contents are in the archives—Vol. 589, Macdonald Fonds. In addition, Pope published a selection of Macdonald's correspondence containing some 750 letters, as well as those in his Memoirs. The historian Keith Johnson (editor of the National Library

volumes) has published in the book *Affectionately Yours* the 205 extant letters exchanged between members of Macdonald's family.

To any researcher these materials are all an immense boon. But they
are incomplete. For Macdonald's entire post-Confederation term, nothing
has changed since Creighton's day (laptop computers and photocopiers
notwithstanding). Macdonald's later letters are available on microfilm, but
often these are almost unreadable due to the passage of time and the poor
quality of the original technology.

Here, Macdonald has been served less well than have two contemporaries of lesser consequence to Canadians. As a result of a federal grant,
the writings of Louis Riel have been published. As the result of another
federal grant, Queen's University in Kingston, which owes its existence in
part to Macdonald, is engaged in publishing the writings of British prime
minister Benjamin Disraeli (the seventh volume came out in 2006, with
about as many still to go). Yes to Riel, of course. Yes likewise to Disraeli,
Queen's having acquired a valuable collection of his writings. But why not
Macdonald's life record? (The author must declare an "interest," since the
research for Volume Two of this work will be a good deal slower.)

A last observation in this bibliographical note. Primary sources, such
as original letters, are of course the vein of gold for which every historian
searches. In fact a great many of the secondary sources listed in the succeeding pages contain primary material that their authors have panned,
either from Macdonald's original "appalling mass" of material or from
other contemporary sources. The great majority of the books and articles
and theses by professional historians listed below postdate Creighton's
research of the 1950s. This author thus has been able to peer both ahead
and backwards by standing on the shoulders of a great many first-rate
post-Creighton researchers. Whenever it seemed appropriate, a particular
author has been mentioned in the text or in a footnote. The purpose of
this note is to thank all the others who have helped do the work from
which this book has emerged.

PRIMARY SOURCES

Almost all of Macdonald's outgoing letters up to Confederation Day have been published in LAC's (then the National Library) two volumes for the period 1834 to 1861 or can be easily accessed in the intended third volume for the period 1862 to May 1867.

An additional important source of pre-Confederation material is contained in LAC's volumes of correspondence between Macdonald and particular individuals. Among these collections, the most important are Narcisse-Fortunat Belleau, E.W. Biggar, William Hume Blake and George Brown, all packed into Vol. 188 of the MG26-A Macdonald Fonds; Alexander Campbell, Vol. 194; George-Étienne Cartier, Vol. 202; Richard Cartwright, Vol. 204; Alexander Galt, Vol. 216; Archbishop Lynch, Vol. 228; D'Arcy McGee, Vol. 231; Gilbert McMicken and Allan MacNab, jointly, Vol. 246; Étienne Taché, Vol. 273; Leonard Tilley, Vol. 276; Charles Tupper, Vol. 282.

Other pre-Confederation volumes in the Macdonald Fonds are grouped under the heading of "Subject Files." Among these are Quebec Conference, Vol. 46; London Conference, Vol. 47; B.N.A Act drafts, Vols. 48, 49; Fenians, Vol. 56–58; Governors General Head, Vol. 74, and Monck, Vol. 75; Minutes of Council, Militia and Defence, Vol. 103; Intercolonial Railway, Vol. 120; Reciprocity, 1865–66 (Vol. 145); Visits to England, Vol. 161.

Other relevant private papers, mostly in the LAC collection, are George Brown, LAC (MG24-B40); Isaac Buchanan, Hamilton Public Library; Edward Cardwell, Public Records Office, London (30/48); Alexander Campbell, Ontario Archives (F-23); Mercy Coles, Diary, LAC (MG24 B66); Alexander T. Galt, LAC (MG27-ID8); James Gowan, LAC (MG27–1E17); John Rose (Macdonald Papers, Vol. 258–59); and Charles Tupper, LAC (MG26-F).

PARLIAMENTARY DEBATES/SPEECHES

Debates of the Legislative Assembly of United Canada, 1842–1856. (Transcripts of subsequent legislature debates to 1867 are in the process of being published by the Parliamentary Library.)

Parliamentary Debates on the Subject of the Confederation of the British North America Provinces, 3rd Session, 8th Provincial Parliament of Canada. Quebec: Hunter, Rose & Co., 1865.

Address of the Hon. John A. Macdonald to the Electors of the City of Kingston, with Extracts from Mr. Macdonald's Speeches Delivered on Different Occasions in the Years 1860 and 1861. No Publisher, 1861.

An invaluable selection of material on both the Confederation Debates and the equivalent debates in the provinces (Nova Scotia, New Brunswick, Prince Edward Island, Newfoundland, Manitoba, British Columbia) is contained in Janet Ajzenstat, ed., *Canada's Founding Debates* (Toronto: Stoddart, 1999).

OFFICIAL SOURCES

Specific relevant official sources are quoted in the notes for each chapter, such as, in Chapter 13, Governor General Head's memorandum on what it takes to govern Canada. In fact a great many documents and official communications of the period are in readily available books and articles. Among these:

Bliss, Michael. *Canadian History in Documents, 1763–1966.* Toronto: Ryerson Press, 1966.

Browne, G.P. *Documents on the Confederation of British North America.* Toronto: McClelland & Stewart, 1969.

Doughty, Arthur G., ed. "Notes on the Quebec Conference, 1864" *Canadian Historical Review* 1, no. 1 (1920).

Elgin, James Bruce, Earl of. *The Elgin-Grey papers, 1846–1852.* Edited by Arthur G. Doughty. Ottawa: Printer to the King, 1937.

Forbes, H.D., ed. *Canadian Political Thought.* Toronto: Oxford University Press Canada, 1985.

Granatstein, J.L., and Norman Hillmer. *First Drafts: Eyewitness Accounts from Canada's Past.* Toronto: Thomas Allen, 2002.

George Brown to his wife, 13 Sept. 1864, (George Brown Papers, pp. 1029–36), *Canadian Historical Review* 48, no. 1 (1967): 110.

Morton, W.L. *Monck Letters and Journals, 1863–1868: Canada from Government House at Confederation.* Toronto: McClelland & Stewart, 1970.

Ormsby, W.G. "Letters to Galt Concerning the Maritime Provinces and Confederation" *Canadian Historical Review* 34, no. 2 (1953).

Pope, Joseph, ed. *Confederation: Being a Series of Hitherto Unpublished Documents Bearing on the British North America Act.* Toronto: Carswell, 1895.

Reid, J.H. Stewart, Kenneth McNaught, and Harry S. Crowe. *A Source-book of Canadian History.* Toronto: Longmans, Green, 1959.

"Sir Edmund Walker Head's Memorandum on the Choice of Ottawa as the Seat of Government of Canada" Notes and Documents, *Canadian Historical Review* 16 (1935).

Smith, Wilfrid. Introduction to "Charles Tupper's Minutes of the Charlottetown Conference" *Canadian Historical Review* 48, no. 1 (1967).

Waite, Peter B. "Ed Whelan's Reports from the Quebec Conference" *Canadian Historical Review* 42, no. 1 (1961).

———. *Pre-Confederation.* Canadian Historical Documents Series, vol. 2. Scarborough, Ont.: Prentice-Hall of Canada, 1965.

Whelan, Edward. *The Union of the British Provinces, a Brief Account of the Several Conferences Held in the Maritime Provinces and in Canada, in September and October, 1864,* on the Proposed Confederation of the Provinces. Charlottetown, 1865.

NEWSPAPERS

The complete reports of the Toronto *Globe* for the period 1844 to 1867 are available on-line at the Toronto Public Library website, www.tpl.toronto.on.ca.

Extensive extracts from newspaper reports of the period are contained in: Silver, Arthur I. "Quebec and the French-Speaking Minorities, 1864–1917." Ph.D. thesis, University of Toronto, 1973.

————. *The French-Canadian Idea of Confederation, 1864–1900.* Toronto: University of Toronto Press, 1982.

Waite, Peter B. *The Life and Times of Confederation, 1864–1867: Politics, Newspapers, and the Union of British North America.* Toronto: University of Toronto Press, 1962. (Included is an extensive list of all relevant newspapers for the period, pp. 334–38.)

SECONDARY SOURCES

BOOKS ABOUT MACDONALD AND FAMILY
CONSULTED DURING THE RESEARCH

(A prime source of biographical and related material about all of the major figures of the time is the authoritative *Dictionary of Canadian Biography*, vols. 7 to 14.)

Adam, G. Mercer. *Canada's Patriot Statesman: The Life and Career of the Right Honourable Sir John A. Macdonald.* Based on the work of Edmund Collins, revised. Toronto: Rose, 1891.

Angus, Margaret. *John A. Lived Here.* Kingston: Frontenac Historic Foundation, 1984.

Biggar, E.B. *Anecdotal Life of Sir John Macdonald.* Montreal: Lovell, 1891.

Bliss, Michael. *Right Honorable Men: The Descent of Canadian Politics from*

Macdonald to Chrétien. Toronto: HarperPerennial Canada, 2004.

Collins, Joseph Edmund. *Life and Times of the Rt. Hon. Sir John A. Macdonald, Premier of the Dominion of Canada.* Toronto: Rose, 1883.

Creighton, Donald Grant. *John A. Macdonald.* Vol. 1, *The Young Politician,* and vol. 2, *The Old Chieftain.* Toronto: Macmillan of Canada, 1952.

———. *John A. Macdonald, Confederation and the West.* Winnipeg: Manitoba Historical Society, 1967.

Johnson, J.K. *Affectionately Yours: The Letters of Sir John A. Macdonald and His Family.* Toronto: Macmillan of Canada, 1969.

———. "John A. Macdonald." In *The Pre-Confederation Premiers: Ontario Government Leaders, 1841–1867,* edited by J.M.S. Careless. Toronto: University of Toronto Press, 1980.

———. *John A. Macdonald: The Young Non-Politician.* Ottawa: CHA Papers, 1976.

———, ed. *The Letters of Sir John A. Macdonald, 1836–1857.* Ottawa: Public Archives of Canada, 1968.

Johnson, J.K., and Carole B. Stelmack, eds. *The Letters of Sir John A. Macdonald, 1858–1861.* Ottawa: Public Archives of Canada, 1969.

Maclean, W.F. "The Canadian Themistocles." *Canadian Magazine* 4 (1894): 253–60.

Macpherson, J. Pennington. *Life of the Right Hon. Sir John A. Macdonald.* Saint John, N.B.: Earle Pub. House, 1891.

Newman, Lena. *The John A. Macdonald Album.* Montreal: Tundra Books, 1974.

Parkin, George R. *Sir John A. Macdonald.* T.C. & E.C. Jack, 1909.

Phenix, Patricia. *Private Demons: The Tragic Personal Life of John A. Macdonald.* Toronto: McClelland & Stewart, 2006.

Pope, Joseph. *Correspondence of Sir John Macdonald.* Toronto: Doubleday, Page, 1921.

———. *The Day of Sir John Macdonald: A Chronicle of the First Prime Minister of the Dominion.* Toronto: Brook, 1915.

———. *Memoirs of the Right Honourable Sir John Alexander Macdonald, First Prime Minister of the Dominion of Canada.* Toronto: Musson, 1894.

Reynolds, Louise. *Agnes: A Biography of Lady Macdonald*. Toronto: Samuel Stevens, 1979.

Smith, Cynthia M., with Jack McLeod, eds. *Sir John A.: An Anecdotal Life of John A. Macdonald*. Toronto: Oxford University Press, 1989.

Swainson, Donald. *Macdonald of Kingston: First Prime Minister*. Toronto: A Personal Library Publication, produced exclusively for Nelson, 1979.

————. *Sir John A. Macdonald: The Man and the Politician*. 2nd ed. Kingston: Quarry Press, 1989.

Waite, Peter B. *Macdonald: His Life and World*. Toronto: McGraw-Hill Ryerson, 1975.

————. Introduction to Donald Grant Creighton, *John A. Macdonald: The Young Politician, the Old Chieftain*. Toronto: University of Toronto Press, 1998.

Wallace, W. Stewart. *Sir John Macdonald*. Toronto: Macmillan of Canada, 1924.

Wilson, Keith. *Hugh John Macdonald*. Winnipeg: Peguis Publishers, 1980.

GENERAL WORKS CONSULTED

(Abbreviations: Canadian Historical Association—CHA; Macmillan of Canada—Mac-C; McClelland & Stewart—M&S; McGill-Queen's University Press—M-Q UP; Oxford University Press—OUP; University of Toronto Press—UTP)

Abrahamson, Una. *God Bless Our Home: Domestic Life in Nineteenth Century Canada*. Toronto: Burns & MacEachern, 1966.

Ajzenstat, Janet. *The Once and Future Canadian Democracy: An Essay in Political Thought*. Montreal: M-Q UP, 2003.

————, ed. *Canada's Founding Debates*. Toronto: Stoddart, 1999.

Ajzenstat, Janet, and Peter J. Smith. *Canada's Origins: Liberal, Tory, or Republican?* Ottawa: Carleton University Press, 1995.

Akenson, Donald H. *The Orangeman: The Life and Times of Ogle Gowan*. Toronto: Lorimer, 1986.

Aldous, Richard. *The Lion and the Unicorn: Gladstone vs Disraeli*. London: Hutchinson, 2006.

Batt, Elizabeth. *Monck: Governor General, 1861–1868*. Toronto: M&S, 1976.

Beck, J. Murray. *Joseph Howe*. Vol. 2, *The Briton Becomes Canadian, 1848–1873*. Kingston: M-Q UP, 1982.

———. *Joseph Howe, Anti-Confederate*. Ottawa: CHA booklets, no.17, 1968.

Berger, Carl. *The Sense of Power: Studies in the Ideas of Canadian Imperialism, 1867–1914*. Toronto: UTP, 1970.

———, ed. *Approaches to Canadian History*. Toronto: UTP, 1967.

Bissell, Claude T., ed. *Our Living Tradition: Seven Canadians*. Toronto: Published in association with Carleton University by UTP, 1957.

Black, Edwin R. *Divided Loyalties: Canadian Concepts of Federalism*. Montreal: M-Q UP, 1975.

Bliss, Michael. *Northern Enterprise: Five Centuries of Canadian Business*. Toronto: M&S, 1987.

———, ed. *Canadian History in Documents, 1763–1966*. Toronto: Ryerson Press, 1966.

Bodelsen, C.A. *Studies in Mid-Victorian Imperialism*. New York: H. Fertig, 1968.

Bonenfant, Jean-Charles. *The French Canadians and the Birth of Confederation*. Ottawa: CHA booklets, no. 21, 1966.

Bourne, Kenneth. *Britain and the Balance of Power in North America, 1815–1908*. London: Longmans, 1967.

Brown, Craig. *Upper Canadian Politics in the 1850s*. Toronto: UTP, 1967.

Buckner, Phillip. *Atlantic Canada before Confederation*. 3rd ed. Fredericton: Acadiensis Press, 1998.

———. *The Transition to Responsible Government:* British Policy in British North America, 1815–1850. Westport, Conn.: Greenwood Press, 1985.

Bumsted, J.M., ed. *Interpreting Canada's Past*. Vol. 1, *Pre-Confederation*. 2nd ed. Toronto: OUP, 1993.

———. *The Scots in Canada*. Ottawa: CHA, *Ethnic Groups in Canada*, 1982.

Calder, Jenni. *Scots in Canada*. Luath, 2003.

Callahan, James Morton. *American Foreign Policy in Canadian Relations.* Toronto: Mac-C, 1937.

Careless, J.M.S. *Brown of the Globe.* Vol. 1, *The Voice of Upper Canada 1815–1859,* and vol. 2, *Statesman of Confederation 1860–1880.* Toronto: Mac-C, 1959, 1963.

————. *Careless at Work: Selected Canadian Historical Studies.* Toronto: Dundurn Press, 1990.

————. *Colonists & Canadiens, 1760–1867.* Toronto: Mac-C, 1971.

————, ed. *The Pre-Confederation Premiers: Ontario Government Leaders, 1841–1867.* Toronto: UTP, 1980.

————. *The Union of the Canadas: The Growth of Canadian Institutions, 1841–1857.* Toronto: M&S, 1967.

Carty, R. Kenneth, and W. Peter Ward, eds. *National Politics and Community in Canada.* Vancouver: UBC Press, 1986.

Cartwright, Richard, Sir. *Reminiscences.* Toronto: Briggs, 1912.

Collard, Edgar Andrew. *Canadian Yesterdays.* Toronto: Longmans, Green, 1955.

Colquhoun, A.H.U. *The Fathers of Confederation: A Chroncile of the Birth of the Dominion.* Toronto: Brook, 1916.

Conrad, Margaret, and Alvin Finkel. *Canada: A National History.* Toronto: Longman, 2003.

Cook, Ramsay. *The Maple Leaf Forever: Essays on Nationalism and Politics in Canada.* Toronto: Mac-C, 1971.

Cornell, Paul G. *The Alignment of Political Groups in Canada, 1841–1867.* Toronto: UTP, 1962.

————. *The Great Coalition.* Ottawa: CHA booklets, no. 19, 1971.

Creighton, Donald Grant. *John A. Macdonald, Confederation and the West.* Winnipeg: Manitoba Historical Society, 1967.

————. *The Road to Confederation: The Emergence of Canada, 1863–1867.* Toronto: Mac-C, 1964.

Creighton, Donald Grant, et al. *Confederation: Essays.* Introduction by Ramsay Cook. Toronto: UTP, 1967.

Creighton, Luella. *The Elegant Canadians.* Toronto: M&S, 1967.

Dent, John Charles. *The Last Forty Years: Canada Since the Union of 1841.* 2 vols. Toronto: G. Virtue, 1881.

Dickason, Olive Patricia. *Canada's First Nations: A History of Founding Peoples from Earliest Times.* Toronto: M&S, 1992.

Dickinson, John A., and Brian Young. *A Short History of Quebec.* Montreal: M-Q UP, 2000.

Dyck, Harvey L., and H. Peter Krosby, eds. *Empire and Nations:* Essays in Honour of Frederick H. Soward. Toronto: UTP, 1969.

Dyer, Gwynne, and Tina Viljoen. *The Defence of Canada: In the Arms of Empire, 1760–1939.* Toronto: M&S, 1990.

Easterbrook, W.T., and Mel Watkins, eds. *Approaches to Canadian Economic History: A Selection of Essays.* Ottawa: Carleton University, 1991.

Errington, Jane. *The Lion, the Eagle, and Upper Canada: A Developing Colonial Ideology.* Kingston: M-Q UP, 1994.

Farr, David M.L. *The Colonial Office and Canada, 1867–1887.* Toronto: UTP, 1955.

Finlay, J.L. *The Structure of Canadian History.* Toronto: Prentice-Hall, 1997.

Forbes, H.D., ed. *Canadian Political Thought.* Toronto: OUP, 1985.

Francis, Daniel. *National Dreams: Myth, Memory and Canadian History.* Vancouver: Arsenal Pulp Press, 1997.

Francis, R. Douglas, Richard Jones, and Donald B. Smith. *Origins: Canadian History to Confederation.* Toronto: Harcourt Brace Canada, 2000.

Frankfurter, Glen. *Baneful Domination: The Idea of Canada in the Atlantic World, 1581–1971.* Don Mills, Ont.: Longman Canada, 1971.

Garner, John. *The Franchise and Politics in British North America, 1755–1867.* Ottawa: UTP, 1969.

Glazebrook, G.P. de T. *A History of Canada's External Relations.* Toronto: OUP, 1950.

———. *A History of Canadian Political Thought.* Toronto: M&S, 1966.

———. *A History of Transportation in Canada.* 2nd ed. Toronto: M&S, 1967.

Goodwin, Doris Kearns. *Team of Rivals: The Political Genius of Abraham Lincoln.* New York: Simon & Schuster, 2005.

Granatstein, J.L., and Norman Hillmer. *First Drafts: Eyewitness Accounts from Canada's Past.* Toronto: Thomas Allen, 2002.

Greer, Allan, and Ian Radforth, eds. *Colonial Leviathan: State Formation in Mid-Nineteenth Century Canada.* Toronto: UTP, 1992.

Guillet, Edwin. *Early Life in Upper Canada.* Toronto: Ontario Publishing Co., 1933.

Gwyn, Sandra. *The Private Capital: Ambition and Love in the Age of Macdonald and Laurier.* Toronto: M&S, 1986.

Hamelin, Marcel, ed. *The Political Ideas of the Prime Ministers of Canada.* Ottawa: Les Éditions de l'Université d'Ottawa, 1969.

Hammond, M.O. *Confederation and Its Leaders.* Toronto: McClelland, Goodchild & Stewart, 1917.

Harris, R. Cole, and John Warkentin. *Canada Before Confederation: A Study in Historical Geography.* New York: OUP, 1974.

Herman, Arthur. *How the Scots Invented the Modern World: The True Story of How Western Europe's Poorest Nation Created Our World and Everything in It.* New York: Three Rivers Press, 2001.

Hitsman, J. Mackay. *Safeguarding Canada: 1763–1871.* Toronto: UTP, 1968.

Hodgetts, J.E. *Pioneer Public Service: An Administrative History of the United Canadas, 1841–1867.* Toronto: UTP, 1955.

Hodgins, Bruce W., Don Wright, and W.H. Heick, eds. *Federalism in Canada and Australia: The Early Years.* Waterloo, Ont.: Wilfrid Laurier University Press, 1978.

Horn, Michiel, and Ronald Sabourin, eds. *Studies in Canadian Social History.* Toronto: M&S, 1974.

Hyam, Ronald. *Britain's Imperial Century, 1815–1914: A Study of Empire and Expansion.* London: Batsford, 1976.

Hyam, Ronald, and Ged Martin. *Reappraisals in British Imperial History.* Toronto: Mac-C, 1975.

Jameson, Anna. *Winter Studies and Summer Rambles in Canada.* Toronto: M&S, 1923.

Keefer, T.C. *Philosophy of Railroads and Other Essays.* Edited by H.V. Nelles. Toronto: UTP, 1972.

Knaplund, Paul. *The British Empire, 1815–1939*. London: H. Hamilton, 1942.

Langton, Anne. *A Gentlewoman in Upper Canada: The Journals of Anne Langton*. Toronto: Clarke, Irwin, 1950.

Langton, John. *Early Days in Upper Canada:* Letters of John Langton from the Backwoods of Upper Canada and the Audit Office of the Province of Canada. Edited by W.A. Langton. Toronto: Mac-C, 1926.

Lower, Arthur. *Canadians in the Making: A Social History of Canada*. Toronto: Longmans, Green, 1958.

———. *Colony to Nation: A History of Canada*. Toronto: Longmans, Green, 1946.

MacNutt, W. Stewart. *New Brunswick: A History, 1784–1867*. Toronto: Mac-C, 1963.

Martin, Chester. *Foundations of Canadian Nationhood*. Toronto: UTP, 1955.

Martin, Ged. *Britain and the Origins of Canadian Confederation, 1837–67*. Vancouver: UBC Press, 1995.

———, ed. *The Causes of Canadian Confederation*. Fredericton: Acadiensis Press, 1990.

McGrath, William Thomas. *Crime and Its Treatment in Canada*. Toronto: Mac-C, 1976.

McInnis, Edgar. *Canada, a Political and Social History*. Toronto: Holt Rinehart, 1982.

McKendry, Jennifer. *With Our Past Before Us: Nineteenth-Century Architecture in the Kingston Area*. Toronto: UTP, 1995.

McKillop, A.B. *Contours of Canadian Thought*. Toronto: UTP, 1987.

———. *A Disciplined Intelligence: Critical Inquiry and Canadian Thought in the Victorian Era*. Montreal: M-Q UP, 1979.

Mills, David. *The Idea of Loyalty in Upper Canada, 1784–1850*. Kingston: M-Q UP, 1988.

Minhinnick, Jeanne. *At Home in Upper Canada*. Toronto: Clarke, Irwin, 1970.

Moir, John S., ed. *Character and Circumstance: Essays in Honour of Donald Grant Creighton*. Toronto: Mac-C, 1970.

————. *The Church in the British Era, From the British Conquest to Confederation.* Toronto: McGraw-Hill Ryerson, 1972.

Monck, Frances E.O. *My Canadian Leaves: An Account of a Visit to Canada in 1864–1865.* London: Bentley, 1891.

Monet, Jacques. *The Last Cannon-shot: A Study of French-Canadian Nationalism, 1837–1850.* Toronto: UTP, 1969.

Moodie, Susanna. *Six Years in the Bush: Or, Extracts from the Journal of a Settler in Upper Canada, 1832–1838.* London: Simpkin, Marshall, 1838.

Moore, Christopher. *1867: How the Fathers Made a Deal.* Toronto: M&S, 1998.

Morris, James. *Heaven's Command: An Imperial Progress.* London: Faber & Faber, 1973.

Morton, W.L. *The Canadian Identity.* 2nd ed. Toronto: UTP, 1973.

————. *Contexts of Canada's Past: Selected Essays of W.L. Morton.* Edited by A.B. McKillop. Toronto: Mac-C, 1980.

————. *The Critical Years: The Union of British North America, 1857–1873.* Toronto: M&S, 1964.

————. *Manitoba: The Birth of a Province.* Winnipeg: Manitoba Record Society, 1965.

————. *The West and Confederation.* Ottawa: CHA booklet, 1968.

————, ed. *Monck Letters and Journals, 1863–1868: Canada from Government House at Confederation.* Toronto: M&S, 1970.

————, ed. *The Shield of Achilles: Aspects of Canada in the Victorian Age.* Toronto: M&S, 1968.

Muise, D.A., ed. *A Reader's Guide to Canadian History.* Vol. 1, *Beginnings to Confederation.* Toronto: UTP, 1982.

Munro, William Bennett. *American Influences on Canadian Government.* Toronto: Mac-C, 1929.

Newman, Peter Charles. *Company of Adventurers: How the Hudson's Bay Empire Determined the Destiny of a Continent.* Toronto: Penguin Canada, 2005.

Nicholas, H.G. *Britain and the U.S.A.* Baltimore: Johns Hopkins Press, 1963.

Noel, S.J.R. *Patrons, Clients, Brokers: Ontario Society and Politics, 1791–1896.* Toronto: UTP, 1990.

Osborne, Brian S. *Kingston: Building on the Past*. Westport, Ont.: Butternut Press, 1988.

Owram, Doug. *Promise of Eden: The Canadian Expansionist Movement and the Idea of the West, 1856–1900*. Toronto: UTP, 1980.

Pentland, H. Clare. *Labour and Capital in Canada, 1650–1860*. Toronto: J. Lorimer, 1981.

Pope, Maurice. *Public Servants: The Memoirs of Sir Joseph Pope*. Toronto: OUP, 1960.

Porter, Bernard. *Absent-Minded Imperialists: Empire, Society, and Culture in Britain*. New York: OUP, 2004.

Prentice, Alison. *Canadian Women: A History*. Toronto: Harcourt Brace, 1996.

Preston, Richard A. *The Defence of the Undefended Border: Planning for War in North America, 1867–1939*. Montreal: M-Q UP, 1977.

————. *Canadian Defence Policy and the Development of the Canadian Nation, 1867–1917*. Ottawa: CHA booklets, no. 25, 1970.

Pryke, Kenneth G. *Nova Scotia and Confederation, 1864–74*. Toronto: UTP, 1979.

Radforth, Ian Walter. *Royal Spectacle: The 1860 Visit of the Prince of Wales to Canada and the United States*. Toronto: UTP, 2004.

Reid, W. Stanford, ed. *The Scottish Tradition in Canada*. Toronto: M&S, 1976.

Roberston, J. Ross. *Old Toronto: A Selection of Excerpts from Landmarks of Toronto*. Edited by E.C. Kyte. Toronto: Mac-C, 1954.

Ross, George W. *Getting into Parliament and After*. Toronto: W. Briggs, 1913.

Roy, James. *Kingston: The King's Town*. Toronto: M&S, 1952.

Russell, Peter A. *Attitudes to Social Mobility in Upper Canada, 1815 to 1849*. E. Mellen Press, 1990.

Russell, Peter H. *Constitutional Odyssey: Can Canadians Become a Sovereign People?* Toronto: UTP, 1992.

Russell, William Howard, Sir. *Canada: Its Defences, Condition, and Resources, Being a Second and Concluding Volume of "My Diary, North and South."* Boston: Burnham, 1865.

Ryerson, Stanley B. *Unequal Union: Confederation and the Roots of Conflict in the Canadas, 1815–1873.* Toronto: Progress Books, 1968.

Schull, Joseph. *Laurier: The First Canadian.* Toronto: Mac-C, 1965.

Senior, Hereward. *The Fenians and Canada.* Toronto: Mac-C, 1978.

———. *The Last Invasion of Canada: The Fenian Raids, 1866–1870.* Toronto: Dundurn Press, 1991.

———. *Orangeism: The Canadian Phase.* Toronto: McGraw-Hill Ryerson, 1972.

Shaw, A.G.L. *Great Britain and the Colonies, 1815–1865.* London: Methuen, 1970.

Shaw, Matthew, *Great Scots!: How the Scots Created Canada.* Winnipeg: Heartland Associates, 2003.

Shippee, Lester Burrell. *Canadian-American Relations, 1849–1874.* New Haven, Conn.: Yale University Press, 1939.

Silver, A.I. *The French-Canadian Idea of Confederation, 1864–1900.* Toronto: UTP, 1982.

Simpson, Jeffrey. *Spoils of Power: The Politics of Patronage.* Toronto: W. Collins, 1988.

Skelton, O.D. *The Life and Times of Sir Alexander Tilloch Galt.* Toronto: OUP, 1920.

Slattery, T.P. *The Assassination of D'Arcy McGee.* Toronto: Doubleday Canada, 1968.

Stewart, Gordon T. *The American Response to Canada since 1776.* East Lansing: Michigan State University Press, 1992.

———. *The Origins of Canadian Politics: A Comparative Approach.* Vancouver: UBC Press, 1986.

Swainson, Donald, ed. *Oliver Mowat's Ontario.* Toronto: Mac-C, 1972.

Sweeny, Alastair. *George-Etienne Cartier: A Biography.* Toronto: M&S, 1976.

Tansill, Charles Callan. *Canadian-American Relations, 1875–1911.* New Haven, Conn.: Yale University Press, 1943.

Taylor, Charles. *Radical Tories: The Conservative Tradition in Canada.* Toronto: House of Anansi Press, 1982.

Thompson, Samuel. *Reminiscences of a Canadian Pioneer, 1853–1883.* Toronto: M&S, 1968.

Trofimenkoff, Susan Mann. *The Dream of Nation: A Social and Intellectual History of Quebec.* Toronto: Mac-C, 1982.

Tucker, Gilbert. *The Canadian Commercial Revolution, 1845–1851.* New Haven, Conn.: Yale University Press, 1936.

Tulchinsky, Gerald, ed. *To Preserve and Defend: Essays on Kingston in the Nineteenth Century.* Montreal: M-Q UP, 1976.

Underhill, Frank H. *The Image of Confederation.* Massey Lectures, 3rd series. Toronto: Canadian Broadcasting Corp, 1964.

———. *Upper Canadian Politics in the 1850's: Essays by F.H. Underhill [and others].* Introduction by Craig Brown. Toronto: UTP, 1967.

Wade, Mason. *The French-Canadians: 1760–1967.* Vol. 1, 1760–1911. Toronto: Mac-C, 1968.

Waite, Peter B. *The Charlottetown Conference.* Ottawa: CHA booklets, no. 15, 1970.

———, ed. *The Confederation Debates in the Province of Canada, 1865: A Selection.* Toronto: M&S, 1963.

———. *The Life and Times of Confederation, 1864–1867: Politics, Newspapers, and the Union of British North America.* Toronto: UTP, 1963.

Wallace, C.M., and R.M. Bray. *Reappraisals in Canadian History, Pre-Confederation.* 2nd ed. Scarborough, Ont.: Prentice-Hall Canada, 1996.

Wallace, Elisabeth. *Goldwin Smith, Victorian Liberal.* Toronto: UTP, 1957.

Warner, Donald. *Idea of Continental Union: Agitation for the Annexation of Canada to the United States.* Lexington: Kentucky UP, 1960.

Whelan, Edward. *Confederation of the Provinces.* Pioneer Publishing, 1865.

Whitelaw, William Menzies. *The Maritimes and Canada before Confederation.* Toronto: OUP, 1966.

———. *The Quebec Conference.* Ottawa: CHA booklets, no. 20, 1966.

Wilentz, Sean. *The Rise of American Democracy: Jefferson to Lincoln.* New York: W.W. Norton, 2005.

Willison, John, Sir. *Reminiscences, Political and Personal.* Toronto: M&S, 1919.

Wilson, A.N. *The Victorians.* New York: W.W. Norton, 2003.

Winks, Robin W. *The Civil War Years: Canada and the United States.* 4th ed. Montreal; Kingston: M-Q UP, 1998.

————. *The Relevance of Canadian History: U.S. and Imperial Perspectives.* Lanham: University Press of America, 1988.

Wise, S.F. *God's Peculiar Peoples: Essays on Political Culture in Nineteenth Century Canada.* Ottawa: Carleton University Press, 1993.

Wise, S.F., and Robert Craig Brown. *Canada Views the United States: Nineteenth-Century Political Attitudes.* Seattle: University of Washington Press, 1967.

Young, Brian. *George-Etienne Cartier: Montreal Bourgeois.* Montreal: M-Q UP, 1981.

Zazlow, Morris. *The Opening of the Canadian North, 1870–1914.* Toronto: M&S, 1971.

ARTICLES CONSULTED

(Abbreviations: CHA—Canadian Historical Association; CHR—*Canadian Historical Review*; *CJEPS*—*Canadian Journal of Economics and Political Science*; *CJPS*—*Canadian Journal of Political Science*; *JCS*—*Journal of Canadian Studies*; OH—*Ontario History*)

Abella, Irving M. "The 'Sydenham Election' of 1841" *CHR* 47, no. 4 (1966).

Angus, Margaret. "Health Emigration and Welfare in Kingston, 1820–1840." In *Oliver Mowat's Ontario*, edited by Donald Swainson. Toronto: Macmillan of Canada, 1972.

Atchison, J.H. "Sir John A. Macdonald: Nation-Builder" (review of Donald Grant Creighton, *John A. Macdonald*) *CJEPS*, 1956, no. 4.

Bailey, A.G. "The Basis and Persistence of Opposition to Confederation in New Brunswick" *CHR* 23 (1942).

Barber, William. "The Anti-American Ingredient in Canadian History" *The Dalhousie Review*, 1973–74.

Bellomo, J. Jerald. "Upper Canada Attitudes Towards Crime and Punishment (1832–1851)" *OH* 64 (1977).

Brown, George. "The Grit Party and the Great Reform Convention of 1859" *CHR* 16, no. 3 (1935).

Buckner, Philip A. "The Maritimes and Confederation: A Reassessment" *CHR* Dialogues, March 1990.

Burnet, J.R. "The Urban Community and Changing Naval Standards." In *Studies in Canadian Social History*, edited by Michael Horn and Ronald Sabourin. Toronto: M&S, 1974.

Burns, Robin. "D'Arcy McGee and the Economic Aspects of New Nationality" CHA *Historical Papers* 2 (1967).

Careless, J.M.S. "George Brown and the Mother of Confederation" CHA *Annual Report and Historical Papers* 39 (1960).

———. "Limited Identities in Canada" *JCS*, 1968, no. 1.

Cameron, David. "Lord Durham Then and Now" *JCS* 25, no. 1 (1990).

Chapman, J. K. "Arthur Gordon and Confederation" *CHR* 37, no. 2 (1956).

Cohoe, Margaret. "John A. Macdonald" *Historic Kingston* 38 (1990).

———. "John A. Macdonald—The Family Man" *Historic Kingston* 37 (1989).

Conway, John. "Politics, Culture and the Writing of Constitutions." In *Empire and Nations*, edited by Harvey L. Dyck and H. Peter Krosby. Toronto: University of Toronto Press, 1969.

Cook, Ramsey. "Quebec and Confederation" *Queen's Quarterly*, 1964–65.

Creighton, Donald Grant. "John A. Macdonald and the Canadian West" Historical Society of Manitoba, 1966–67, no. 23.

———. "Sir John Macdonald and Canadian Historians" *CHR* 29, no. 1 (1948).

———. "Sir John Macdonald and Kingston" CHA *Annual Report and Historical Papers* 29, no. 1 (1950).

———. "The United States and Confederation" *CHR* 39, no. 3 (1958).

Cross, Michael S, and Robert L. Fraser. "'The Waste that Lies Before Me': The Public and the Private Worlds of Robert Baldwin" CHA *Historical Papers* 18 (1983).

Duncan, Kenneth. "Irish Famine Immigration and the Social Structure of Canada West." In *Studies in Canadian Social History*, edited by Michiel Horn and Ronald Sabourin. Toronto: McClelland & Stewart, 1974.

Eggleston, Stephen. "The Myth and Mystery of PogG" *JCS* 31, no. 4 (1995–97).

Fallis, Laurence S. "The Idea of Progress in the Province of Canada: A Study in the History of Ideas." In *The Shield of Achilles*, edited by W.L. Morton. Toronto: M&S, 1968.

Feaver, George. "The Webbs in Canada: Fabian Pilgrims on the Canadian Frontier" *CHR* 58, no. 3 (1977).

Fingard, Judith. "The Winter's Tale: The Seasonal Contours of Pre-Industrial Towns in British North America" CHA *Historical Papers* 9 (1974).

Forsey, Eugene. "The B.N.A. Act" *Queen's Quarterly*, 1964–65.

Flynn, Louis J. "Canada's Greatest Scot: Sir John Alexander Macdonald, a Centennial Tribute" *Historic Kingston* 16 (1968).

Gibson, James A. "The Colonial Office View of Canadian Federation, 1858–1868" *CHR* 35, no. 4 (1954).

Gibson, Sarah, and Karyn Patterson. "A Tribute to Sir John A. Macdonald" *Historic Kingston* 33 (1985).

Greer, Allan. "The Birth of the Police in Canada." In *Colonial Leviathan: State Formation in Mid-Nineteenth Century Canada*, edited by Allan Greer and Ian Radforth. Toronto: University of Toronto Press, 1992.

———. "Historical Roots of Canadian Democracy" *JCS* 34 (1999).

Griffith, Rudyard. Speech to Kingston Historical Society, Jan. 11, 2005.

Hall, D.J. "'The Spirit of Confederation': Ralph Heintzman, Professor Creighton, and the Bicultural Compact Theory" *JCS* 9, no. 4 (1974).

Harper, Marjory. "Image and Reality in Early Emigrant Literature" *British Journal of Canadian Studies*, 1992, special edition.

Heintzman, Ralph. "The Political Culture of Quebec, 1840–1960" *CJPS* 16, no. 1 (1983).

———. "The Spirit of Confederation: Professor Creighton, Biculturalism and the Use of History" *CHR* 52, no. 1 (1971).

Hockin, Thomas A. "Flexible and Structured Parliamentarianism: From 1848 to Contemporary Party Government" *JCS* 14 (1979).

Johnson, Keith. "John A. Macdonald and the Kingston Business Community." In *To Preserve and Defend: Essays on Kingston in the Nineteenth Century*, edited by Gerald Tulchinsky. Montreal: McGill-Queen's University Press, 1976.

———. "Sir James Gowan, Sir John A. Macdonald and the Rebellion of 1837" *OH* 60, no. 2 (1968).

Jones, Ellwood H. "Ephemeral Compromise: The Great Reform Convention Revisted" *JCS* 3, no. 1 (1968).

Lockhart, A.D. "The Contribution of Macdonald Conservatism to National Unity, 1854–78" CHA *Annual Report and Historical Papers* 18 (1939).

Lower, Arthur. "The Character of Kingston." In *To Preserve and Defend: Essays on Kingston in the Nineteenth Century*, edited by Gerald Tulchinsky. Montreal: McGill-Queen's University Press, 1976.

———. "Political 'Partyism' in Canada" CHA *Annual Report and Historical Papers* 34 (1955).

MacDermot, T.W.L. "John A. Macdonald—His Biographies and Biographers" CHA *Annual Report and Historical Papers* 10 (1931).

———. "The Political Ideas of John A. Macdonald" *CHR* 14 (1933).

Malcolmson, Patricia E. "The Poor in Kingston, 1805–1850." In *To Preserve and Defend: Essays on Kingston in the Nineteenth Century*, edited by Gerald Tulchinsky. Montreal: McGill-Queen's University Press, 1976.

Martin, Chester. "Sir Edmund Head and Canadian Confederation, 1851–1858" CHA *Annual Report and Historical Papers* 9 (1929).

———. "The United States and Canadian Nationality" *CHR* 18 (1937).

Martin, Ged. "Archival Evidence and John A. Macdonald Biographers" *Journal of Historical Biography* 1 (2007) (on-line: http://www.ucfv.ca/history/JHB.htm).

———. "John A. Macdonald and the Bottle" *JCS* 40 (2006).

———. "John A. Macdonald: Scotsman or Canadian" Standard Life Lecture in Canadian Studies, Edinburgh, 2004.

————. "Painting the Other Picture: The Case Against Confederation." In *From Rebellion to Patriation: Canada and Britain in the Nineteenth and Twentieth Centuries*, edited by C.C. Eldridge. Aberystwyth: Canadian Studies Group in Wales, 1989.

————. "Queen Victoria and Canada" *American Review of Canadian Studies* 13 (1983).

————. "Sir John Eh? Macdonald: Recovering a Voice from History" *British Journal of Canadian Studies* 17 (2004).

Mathews, Robin. "Susanna Moodie, Pink Toryism and Nineteenth-Century Ideas of Canadian Identity" *JCS* 10, no. 3 (1975).

McRoberts, Kenneth. "Canada and the Multinational State" *CJPS*, 2001.

McSherry, James. "The Illness of the First Mrs. John A. Macdonald" *Historic Kingston* 34 (1986).

————. "The Invisible Lady: Sir John A. Macdonald's First Wife" *Canadian Bulletin of Medical History* 1, no. 1 (1984).

Monet, Jacques. "The Political Ideas of Baldwin and LaFontaine." In *The Political Ideas of the Prime Ministers of Canada*, edited by M. Hamelin. Ottawa: Éditions Ottawa: 1969.

————. "French-Nationalism and the Challenge of Ultramontanism." In *An Introduction to Canadian History*, edited by A.I. Silver. Toronto: Canadian Scholars' Press, 1991.

Morton, W. L. "The Conservative Principle in Confederation" *Queen's Quarterly* 80, no. 4 (1965).

————. "The Formation of the First Federal Cabinet" *CHR* 36, no. 2 (1955).

————. "The International Context of Confederation." In *Interpreting Canada's Past*, edited by J.M. Bumsted. 2nd ed. Toronto: Oxford University Press, 1993.

Ontario Historical Society. "Confederation: The Atmosphere of Crisis and the Ontario Fathers of Confederation." In *Profiles of a Province: Studies in the History of Ontario*, edited by Edith G. Firth. Toronto: Ontario Historical Society, 1967.

Otten, A.A. Van den. "Alexander Galt: The 1859 Tariff and Canadian Economic Nationalism" *CHR* 63, no. 2 (1982).

Paquin, Stéphane. "The Myth of the Compact Theory of Canadian Federation" www.canadahistory.com/sections/paperspaquin.htm

Patterson, Graeme. "An Enduring Canadian Myth: Responsible Government and the Family Compact" *JCS* 12, no. 2 (1977).

Preece, Rod. "The Political Philosophy of Sir John A Macdonald," Nicholas Nyiri and Toivo Miljan, Interdisciplinary Research Seminar, Wilfrid Laurier University Press, 1980.

————. "The Political Wisdom of Sir John A. Macdonald" *CJPS* 17, no. 3 (1984).

Radforth, Ian. "Sydenham and Utilitarian Reform." In *Colonial Leviathan: State Formation in Mid-Nineteenth Century Canada*, edited by Allan Greer and Ian Radforth. Toronto: University of Toronto Press, 1992.

Romney, Paul. "From the Rule of Law to Responsible Government: Ontario Political Culture and the Origins of Canadian Statism" CHA *Historical Papers* 23, no. 1 (1988).

————. "Provincial Equality, Special Status and the Compact Theory of Canadian Confederation" *CJPS* 22, no. 1 (1999).

Scott, Frank. "Political Nationalism and Confederation" *CJEPS*, 1945.

Smith, David. "National Political Parties and the Growth of a National Political Community." In *National Politics and Community in Canada*, edited by R. Kenneth Carty and W. Peter Ward. Vancouver: UBC Press, 1986.

Smith, David E. "Patronage in Britain and Canada: An Historical Perspective" *Journal of Canadian Studies* 22, no. 2 (1987).

Smith, Donald B. "John A. Macdonald and Aboriginal Canada" *Historic Kingston* 50 (2002).

Smith, Goldwin. "The Proposed Constitution for British North America" *Macmillan's Magazine*, 1865, London.

Smith, Jennifer. "Canadian Confederation and the Influence of American Federalism" *CJPS* 21, no. 3 (1988).

Smith, Peter J. "Ideological Origins of Canadian Confederation." In *Interpreting Canada's Past*, vol. 1, *Pre-Confederation*, edited by J.M. Bumsted. Toronto: Oxford University Press, 1993.

———. "The Dream of Political Union: Localism, Toryism and the Federal Idea in Pre-Confederation Canada." In *The Causes of Canadian Confederation*, edited by Ged Martin. Fredericton: Acadiensis Press, 1990.

Stacey, C.P. "Britain's Withdrawal from North America, 1864–1871" *CHR* 36, no. 2 (1955).

———. "British Military Policy in the Era of Confederation" CHA *Annual Report and Historical Papers* 13 (1934).

———. "Confederation: The Atmosphere of Crisis." In *Profiles of a Province: Studies in the History of Ontario*, edited by Edith G. Firth. Toronto: Ontario Historical Society, 1967.

———. "Fenianism and the Rise of National Feeling at the Time of Confederation" *CHR* 12, no. 3 (1931).

Stanley, George. "The Man Who Made Canada, 1865–1867," address to the Public Relations Society of America, Foundation for Public Relations Research and Education, 1963.

Stanley, George F.G. "Act or Pact: Another Look at Confederation" CHA *Annual Report and Historical Papers* 38 (1956).

———. "The Macpherson-Shaw-Macdonald Connection." In *Historic Kingston* 13 (1965).

Stewart, Gordon. "Macdonald's Greatest Triumph" *CHR 63 (1982)*.

———. "The Origins of Canadian Politics and John A. Macdonald." In *National Politics and Community in Canada*, edited by R. Kenneth Carty and W. Peter Ward. Vancouver: UBC Press, 1986.

Stewart, Gordon T. "Political Patronage Under Macdonald and Laurier, 1875–1911" *The American Review of Canadian Studies* 10, no. 1 (1980).

Stewart, Wallace. "The Growth of Canadian National Feeling" *CHR*, June 1920.

Swainson, Donald. "Alexander Campbell, General Manager of the Conservative Party (Eastern Ontario section)" *Historic Kingston* 17 (1969).

————. "Sir Henry Smith and the Politics of the Union" *OH* 66 (1974).

Talman, J.J. "The Impact of the Railway on a Pioneer Community" CHA *Annual Report and Historical Papers* 34 (1955).

Trotter, R.G. "British Finance and Confederation" CHA *Annual Report and Historical Papers* 6 (1927).

Turner, Allan R. "Mystery of the Confederation Table" *Saskatchewan History* 10, no.1 (1957).

Turner, Isabel. "Sir John A. Macdonald: The Person" *Historic Kingston* 46 (1998).

Ullmann, Walter. "The Quebec Bishops and Confederation" *CHR* 44, no. 3 (1963).

Underhill, Frank H. "The Development of National Political Parties in Canada" *CHR* 16, no. 4 (1935).

————. "Some Aspects of Upper Canada Radical Opinion in the Decade before Confederation" CHA *Annual Report and Historical Papers* 7 (1927).

Upton, L.F.S. "The Idea of Confederation, 1754–1858." In *The Shield of Achilles*, edited by W.L. Morton. Toronto: McClelland & Stewart, 1968.

Vipond, Robert. "Federal Principle and Canadian Confederation" *CJPS*, 1983.

Waite, Peter B. "Chartered Libertine? A Case Against Sir John A. Macdonald and Some Answers" Manitoba Historical Society, Transactions, 1975–6, Series 3, No. 32.

————. "Edward Cardwell and Confederation" *CHR* 43 (1962).

————. "The Political Ideas of John A. Macdonald." In *The Political Ideas of the Prime Ministers of Canada*, edited by Marcel Hamelin. Ottawa: Les Éditions de l'Université d'Ottawa, 1969.

————. "Sir John A. Macdonald: The Man" *Dalhousie Review*, 1967–68.

Wallace, Elizabeth. "The Origins of the Social Welfare State in Canada, 1867–1900" *CJEPS*, 1950.

Wallace, Carl. "Albert Smith, Confederation and Reaction in New Brunswick, 1852–1882" *CHR* 44 (1963).

Wearing, Joseph. "Pressure Group Politics in Canada West Pre-Confederation" CHA *Historical Papers* 2 (1967).

Williams, Alan F. "Trunk and Branch: A Celebration of Railways in Canada, 1836–1944" *British Journal of Canadian Studies* 15, no. 1 (1990).

Wilson, George. "New Brunswick's Entrance into Confederation" *CHR* 9 (1928).

Wilson, Ian. "Sir John A. Macdonald in History" *Historic Kingston* 41 (1993).

Wise, S.F. "God's Peculiar People." In *The Shield of Achilles*, edited by W.L. Morton. Toronto: McClelland & Stewart, 1968.

———. "John A. Macdonald, House of Commons Man" *Historic Kingston* 42 (1984).

Wright, Donald. "Reflections on Donald Creighton and the Appeal of Biography" University College of Fraser Valley, *Journal of Historical Biography* 1 (2007).

THESES

Best, Henry. "George-Etienne Cartier." Ph.D. thesis, Université Laval, 1969.

Burns, Robin B. "D'Arcy McGee and the New Nationality." Master's thesis, Carleton University, 1966.

Fraser, George Max. "Egerton Ryerson and His Political Relations with Sir John A. Macdonald, 1854–1872." Master's thesis, University of Toronto, 1922.

Gatner, Joseph. "The Defence Factor in Confederation of the British North American Provinces." Master's thesis, University of Ottawa, 1961.

Guest, Henry J. "Reluctant Politician: A Biography of Sir Hugh John Macdonald." Master's thesis, University of Manitoba, 1973.

Hodgins, Bruce W. "Attitudes Towards Democracy During the Pre-Confederation Debates." Master's thesis, University of Toronto, 1955.

Leighton, James. "The Development of Federal Indian Policy in Canada, 1840–1890." Ph.D. thesis, University of Western Ontario, 1975.

Lewis, J.P. "'The Lion and Lamb Ministry': John A. Macdonald and the Politics of the First Canadian Federal Cabinet." Master's thesis, University of Guelph, 2005.

Lockhardt, A.D. "The Early Life of John A. Macdonald, 1815–1844." Master's thesis, Queen's University, 1931.

Owram, Doug. "White Savagery: Some Canadian Reactions to American Indian Policy, 1867–1885." Ph.D. thesis, Queen's University.

Silver, Arthur I. "Quebec and the French Minorities, 1864–1917." Ph.D. thesis, University of Toronto, 1973.

Smith, Francis J. "Newfoundland and Confederation." Master's thesis, University of Ottawa, 1970.

Smith, Peter J. "The Ideological Genesis of Canadian Confederation." Ph.D. thesis, Carleton University, 1984.

Sowby, Joyce. "Macdonald the Administrator: Department of the Interior and Indian Affairs, 1878–1887." Master's thesis, Queen's University, 1986.

Stewart, Alice. "The Imperial Policy of Sir John A. Macdonald." Radcliffe College, 1946.

Teatero, William R. "A Dead and Alive Way Never Does: The Pre-Political Professional World of John A. Macdonald." Master's theis, Queen's University, 1978.

Waite, P.B., "Ideas and Politics in British North America, 1864–1866." Ph.D. thesis, University of Toronto, 1953.

Picture Credits

Agnes Etherington Art Centre, Kingston

Portrait of a young John A. Macdonald by W. Sawyer (p. ii)

Margaret Greene (originally thought to be Isabella Macdonald) (p. 75)

Archives of Ontario

Advertisement in Kingston Chronicle, July 3, 1821, microfilm N17-R1 (p. 27)

Robert Baldwin S2071 (p. 98)

Alexander Campbell S93 (p. 109)

City of Toronto Archives

Isabella Macdonald's bedroom PA121569 (p. 80)

Toronto, 1856 (p. 143)

City of Westminster Archives Centre

Marriage certificate for Agnes Bernard and John A. Macdonald (p. 411)

Library and Archives Canada

Helen Macdonald 68632297 (p. 12)

Oliver Mowatt C008361 (p. 49)

Isabella Macdonald C004815 (p. 60)

The young John A. Macdonald C003813 (p. 62)

Princess Street, Kingston PA062177 (p. 65)

Isabella Macdonald miniature PA121569 (p. 85)

Lord Durham, Edward Hall collection, C00618 (p. 91)

Louis-Hippolyte LaFontaine C005961 (p. 99)

Lord Elgin and family C006728 (p. 100)

Helen Macdonald in old age e007140959 (p. 107)

John Rose PA025959 (p. 114)

Ogle R. Gowan C023504 (p. 115)

Hugh John Macdonald as a baby C004814 (p. 118)

Margaret Macdonald e007140957 (C022818) (p. 134)

James Williamson e007140958 (p. 134)

Louisa Macdonald e007140956 (C022817) (p. 135)

John A. Macdonald C002831 (p. 147)

The Reverend Peter Jones PA215156 (p. 155)

Sir Allan McNab C005317 (p. 162)

George-Étienne Cartier C006166 (p. 178)

Huge John as a young boy C033956 (p. 187)

Grand Trunk Railway PA149747 (p. 194)

D'Arcy McGee CC21541 (p. 217)

Alexander Galt PA013008 (p. 220)

The Prince of Wales PA051553 (p. 232)

Delegates arriving at Charlottetown by Rex Woods PA164727 (p. 303)

Charlottetown Conference room C021421 (p. 305)

Prelude to Confederation by Jarvis Studios, Ottawa C002780 (p. 310)

Étienne-Paschal Taché PA074100 (p. 316)

John A. Macdonald 014918 (p. 342)

Charles Tupper PA026318 (p. 358)

Samuel Leonard Tilley PA026347 (p. 359)

Joseph Howe PA025486 (p. 360)

Queen Victoria CC001590 (p. 373)

Westminster Palace Hotel C010377 (p. 391)

The London Conference by John David Kelly, 1935, reproduced with permission of Rogers Communications Inc. C006799 (p. 395)

Agnes Bernard Macdonald PA118099 (p. 407)

Map of the Confederate Provinces by Chewett (p. 417)

Parliament Buildings, military review, May 24, 1867 PA022399 (p. 424)

John A. Macdonald, 1868 PA025336 (p. 440)

Library of Congress Prints and Photographs Division

Fort Sumter DRWG/US Key, no. 3 (B) [P&P] (p. 240)

William Seward LC-B813-1431 A[P&P] (p. 243)

McCord Museum

Place d'Armes, Montreal M993X.5.107 (p. 94)

Parliament Buildings under construction I-16295.0 (p. 202)

St. Louis Hotel I-21099.1 (p. 206)

Wilfrid Laurier MP-0000.1093.8 (p. 284)

Lord Monck I-4437.1 (p. 386)

McGill University Library, Rare Books and Special Collections

Eliza Grimason (p. 209)

Queen's University Archives

Orange Order arch, Kingston V23-Str-Princess-37 (p. 234)

Kingston, reading proclamation V23-His-Con-2 (p. 437)

Toronto Public Library

View of Quebec City, from William H. Bartlett, *Canadian Scenery Illustrated* (1854)
    (p. 18)

View of Kingston, from William H. Bartlett, *Canadian Scenery Illustrated* (1854)
    (p. 21)

View of Hallowell, from William H. Bartlett, *Canadian Scenery Illustrated* (1854)
    (p. 47)

George Brown T30668 (p. 139)

"Double shuffle" cartoon, 1858 (p. 176)

Grand Trunk Railway poster (p. 193)

Anne Brown (p. 271)

Fenian raid, Port Colborne, June 1, 1866 (p. 383)

Index

Notes: A page number in italic indicates a photograph or other illustration. The lowercase letter "n" following a page number indicates a footnote.

RICHARD GWYN is an award-winning author and political columnist, well known to readers of the *Toronto Star* and to TV and radio audiences. He is the author of two highly praised biographies, *The Unlikely Revolutionary* on Newfoundland premier Joey Smallwood and *The Northern Magus* on Pierre Elliot Trudeau. His most recent book, *Nationalism Without Walls: The Unbearable Lightness of Being Canadian*, was selected by *The Literary Review of Canada* as one of the 100 most important books published in Canada.